"A practical, straight-to-the-point guide for biotech leaders. It covers everything from valuation to partnerships-
a lab".

Se

"Congratulations on this book—a rare and insightful work that demystifies business development / mergers & acquisitions in biopharma".

Loïc Gonnet, *Global Head of Mergers & Acquisitions at Sanofi*

"A well-rounded and insightful book that covers key aspects of the biopharma industry. A great resource for both experienced professionals and those just starting out".

Naji Gehchan, *MD, MBA, Chief Medical & Development Officer, former Head of Global Development at Eli Lilly*

The Thriving Biopharma Business

In today's fiercely innovative and complex biopharmaceutical industry, successfully managing a pharmaceutical or biotech company from concept to patients requires exceptional strategic, leadership, and managerial abilities. This book is a definitive reference that uniquely integrates critical business, strategy, finance, Merger and Acquisition (M&A), regulatory, and intellectual property concepts.

Bringing new therapies to market is both a sought-after experience and a distinguished accomplishment. A biopharma leadership team that is able to master the critical levers covered in this book will drive unparalleled value creation through tremendous competitive advantage in the industry. Chapter by chapter, you'll delve into innovation, valuation, intellectual property, strategy, financing, pitching, transactions, contracts, and regulatory affairs. Through numerous case examples and concepts, you'll learn practical avenues to avoid pitfalls, drive value creation, and navigate the intricate world of the biopharma industry.

This book equips decision-makers, founders, investors, and industry professionals with frameworks, illustrations, and actionable ideas, enabling them to tackle the strategic and managerial challenges inherent in the evolution of a biopharma company. Elevate your strategic decisions, unlock new opportunities, and lead your company to success with this indispensable resource.

Alain Eudaric brings over 30 years of global expertise in biopharma, life sciences, and consulting, specializing in strategy, M&A, alliances, and innovation-led growth. He has held leadership roles at Kearney, Thermo Fisher Scientific, and Parexel International, driving transformative programs and business success. As President of Idea Pathways, Alain focuses on driving operational excellence and fostering innovative growth strategies for the biopharma industry. He is an alum from Harvard Medical School, Johns Hopkins University, MIT, Purdue University, and Ecole Centrale de Lille with advanced degrees in biotech, business, science, and engineering.

Jean-Noël Pellegrin has over 15 years of expertise in M&A and business development, with a proven track record of contributing to several hundred transactions. He began his career at EY before most recently joining Sanofi, where he has spent the last 20 years in France and the United States. His 30 years of combined experience across global public company finance, audit, accounting, and strategic transactions make him a trusted expert in valuing life sciences assets and structuring complex deals. He is an alum of Babson College and Sciences Po, with advanced degrees in business and finance.

The Thriving Biopharma Business

How to Unlock Value and Drive Success in Biotech and Pharma

Alain Eudaric and
Jean-Noël Pellegrin

Routledge
Taylor & Francis Group
NEW YORK AND LONDON

Designed cover image: © Getty Images

First published 2026
by Routledge
605 Third Avenue, New York, NY 10158

and by Routledge
4 Park Square, Milton Park, Abingdon, Oxon, OX14 4RN

Routledge is an imprint of the Taylor & Francis Group, an informa business

ISBN: 9781032983127 (hbk)
ISBN: 9781032976211 (pbk)
ISBN: 9781003598046 (ebk)

DOI: 10.4324/9781003598046

Typeset in Galliard
by codeMantra

Contents

Preface

Intended Audiences and Book Organization

This book is aimed at helping pharmaceutical, biotechnology, and associated professionals reflect upon and think through how to best create value as they usher their company and ventures through growth and development. While a background in science and business is desirable, this book should provide sufficient background to the drug development and business concepts to leaders with diverse backgrounds. In addition, this book provides practical perspectives on the biopharma industry for various concepts covered with numerous case examples throughout this book.

The authors have had the opportunity to jointly benefit from over 40 years of leadership and "hands-on" experience in business development, finance, strategy, and drug development that gave them insights into the core concepts underlying this book. The biopharma sector is often looked at as a collection of vertical silos with professionals who have deep professional expertise in one specific area of the biopharma industry. The approach used in this book is an opportunity to cover such grounds through a cross-functional lens necessary to thoughtfully plan for and assess overall asset or company valuation in this industry as well as help entrepreneurs make well-informed strategic decisions. This book offers a unique combination of strategy, business development, growth management, and M&A expertise alongside real-world biopharma industry perspectives on financing, pitching, intellectual property, and regulatory pathways. Readers looking to start with only a couple of chapters might start with Chapters 1 and 4, although this book has a clear thematic organization, as described below.

Chapter 1, "Setting the Stage for Biopharma Innovation", depicts the importance of storytelling as a fundamental skill required to develop a biotech or pharmaceutical business and provides a number of frameworks to support it. This chapter also serves as a general introduction covering basic concepts like the discovery, development, and commercialization process and the biopharma innovation landscape.

Chapter 2, "The Basic Valuation Toolkit", introduces the main underlying financial notions behind value creation. It presents essential concepts and approaches that will help pharmaceutical and biotechnology professionals and other related audiences better understand and use financial concepts to enhance the value of their programs and company. It covers the valuation of companies, the analytical support of business decisions, as well as valuation techniques at various stages of progression (early stage R&D, development stage, and commercialization stage).

Chapter 3, "The Rigors and Importance of Intellectual Property", provides an overview of this vast and complex field, to enable a strategic reflection for the pharmaceutical or biotech firm rather than provide a self-sufficient foundation. Indeed, intellectual property is a fundamental pillar of strategy and value creation for biopharma firms. This chapter covers in particular the concepts tied to technology transfer and major intellectual property approaches relevant to business development.

Chapter 4, "Strategy for Biopharma Companies", discusses strategy for biopharmaceutical companies with numerous frameworks, examples, and illustrations. This chapter addresses first general strategy concepts, frameworks, and processes. It then continues with strategic notions specific to the biopharma industry.

Chapter 5, "Company Financing", covers the main financing elements used in the industry, starting with core financing concepts, such as financing needs, investor types, and impact of financing. This chapter also covers specific financing approaches: industry partnerships and licensing, equity financing, debt financing, and grants.

Chapter 6, "Pitching Your Company", covers how a biopharma company leadership might need to pitch their ideas and business, be it to venture capital, institutional investors, banks, grant organizations, or simply to a potential partner. It specifically covers two types of pitches: elevator pitches and longer business pitches.

Chapter 7, "Understanding the Art of the Deal in Biopharma", covers the various aspects of biopharmaceutical deal-making. It starts with general deal concepts such as deal team, lifecycle, due diligence, negotiation, and value sharing. This chapter then covers the perspective of a seller first on a variety of deals (company, assets, licensing, equity, and options) followed by corresponding perspectives for a buyer. Lastly, this chapter touches upon collaborations that can serve as critical vehicles for biopharma value creation.

Chapter 8, "Contractual Considerations for Biopharma Deals", provides a view on the documentation that will secure the negotiated deal. This chapter provides considerations to apply to mainstream documents and transaction types.

Chapter 9, "Essential Regulatory Notions", provides an overview of essential regulatory concepts to consider at the strategic level, as regulatory approaches can represent fundamental value levers for the industry. This chapter also addresses prominent regulatory guideposts in the lifecycle of a biotech or pharmaceutical entrepreneurial journey.

Based on the authors' personal experience, this book should be particularly useful to biopharma entrepreneurs, founders, executives, and decision-makers. It is also designed as a much-needed reference for biopharma industry professionals and audiences including students in finance, biotech or entrepreneurship, biopharma finance professionals and investors, business support professionals in accounting and legal firms, technology transfer professionals from universities and hospitals, industry business development, and alliance professionals.

Semantics, Notations, and Important Caveat

The term "biopharma" is used throughout this book as a convenient shorthand to designate both pharma (small molecules or chemical-based drugs) and biotech (large molecules or drug derived from living organisms). The biopharma industry denotes both the pharmaceutical and biotech industries.

Notations designating millions of US dollars may be used interchangeably throughout this book between $m, $M, and $ million. Likewise, $b, $B, and $ billion all designate billions of US dollars.

This book is illustrative in nature and intended for educational and informational purposes. It is provided on an "as is" basis and does not substitute for, nor constitutes, professional advice. It does not constitute legal or financial advice, nor a source thereof, nor is it a solicitation to offer legal or financial advice; and no attorney – client relationship is formed. This book should not be used as a substitute for the advice of a competent attorney authorized to practice in your jurisdiction nor as a substitute for the advice of a competent financial advisor. The authors make no warranties, no guarantee, nor other promises, as to any results, financial, legal, or otherwise, that may be obtained from using this book. We disclaim any and all liability in the event that any of this book's content proves to be inaccurate, incomplete, or unreliable, or result in any investment or other losses.

The views expressed in this book are solely those of the authors and do not reflect the opinions or positions of any corporation or organization they may be affiliated with nor that of any corporation or organization that may have been mentioned. Product or corporate names mentioned in this book may be trademarked or registered and have been used only for identification purposes or to discuss educational concepts without intent to infringe.

Acknowledgments

We are grateful to our awesome families for the invaluable support they provided. From reading early drafts to giving advice on possible topics to allowing the "heads down" time required to write, too often at the expense of family time, they made this book possible. Thank you so much Rebecca, Xavier, and Kiara Eudaric. Thank you so much Estelle, Héloïse, Gabrielle, Raphaël, Mathilde, and Arthur Pellegrin.

This book would not exist without the contributions of all the biopharma industry leaders and professionals who collectively contribute to making the world a healthier place. We wanted to take this opportunity to acknowledge all the industry executives, mentors, and contributors who help develop the industry's much-needed future leadership while participating in their own rights.

Turning our initial idea into a book would not have been conceivable without the patient guidance and insights of the Taylor & Francis team, including Meredith Norwich and Bethany Nelson.

Lastly, we wanted to express our deep gratitude to all the friends, colleagues, contacts, and organizations that provided encouragement, support, insights, ideas, suggestions, guidance, input, or reviews, contributing each in their own special way. Particular thanks go to Karthik Balasubramaniam, Laure Berliner, Steven Eichel, Nona Ghazanfari, Jean-Baptiste De Labarthe, Erica Norey, Tara Ruggeri, Vincent Schmitt, Jim Shanahan, and Sumit Singh.

Alain Eudaric and Jean-Noël Pellegrin
March 17, 2025

Chapter 1

Setting the Stage for Biopharma Innovation

As an entrepreneur or leader in biopharma, you not only have all the opportunities and challenges of building a business but you also face one of the most complex, fast-evolving, and highly scrutinized industry environments. This chapter is designed to introduce all the aspects of building a thriving biopharma business.

We will cover the art of storytelling applied to this scientifically driven industry, but before that, here are some of the key characteristics that frame all facets of value creation in biopharma:

- Overall discovery, research, development, and commercialization process.
  Research and science-driven progress in regulatory-compliant and stepwise fashion is an essential element of value creation. The regulatory framework and regulatory authorities are discussed further in Chapter 9 devoted to this topic while related financial considerations are covered in Chapter 2.
- Risks that characterize the industry.
  As we will see, given the low probability of program success, risk is crucial to understand and incorporate in building iterative sequences of value improvement for any biopharma company. This affects strategic options as discussed in Chapter 4 for corporate strategy evaluation and selection. Risk is so central to the industry that it is literally considered in every single chapter.
- Leadership as a fundamental determinant of value.
  While generally true of any industry, leaders play a critical role in biopharma given the deal-intensive nature of the industry and significant capital requirements. Leadership skills particularly come into play in aligning strategy, financing, pitches, and deals – topics respectively covered in Chapters 4–7.
- Innovation landscape and alternate innovation approaches.
  Managing intellectual property is indeed another foundational characteristic of the biopharma industry – this is extensively discussed in Chapter 3, which is devoted to this topic.

DOI: 10.4324/9781003598046-1

- Additional considerations from strategic and business standpoints. Building value in biopharma hinges on successfully combining multiple angles, including scientific, legal, regulatory, financial, and strategic perspectives. Ultimately, all these aspects are combined in contractual considerations as illustrated by Chapter 8.

1.1 The Importance of Stories over Data

Starting a biopharma business book with storytelling might be unexpected but here it is! Having listened to many pitches and presentations, we will attest to the value of a biopharma leadership prepared and able to tell the story of their company in a crisp and convincing way. In a research-based industry, it is easy to rely heavily on science or scientific results – unfortunately, solid science might not be enough to create value even though it is arguably a particularly good start! Storytelling ability is an essential leadership skill, and if you remember only one point from this book, please remember this one.

Consider the saying about having "lots of data but no information"! What do your findings say about your company's product or technology beyond the data and fancy visual representations? How did you get there? Why is it valuable? Are there key insights you learned along the way that make your story memorable and inspiring? What makes your company or program a compelling investment story? What is it that you would like your audience to do after hearing your story? What have you done to facilitate such a call to action?

Biopharma companies often need to present complex scientific or financial notions in a convincing and compliant way. Certain results and events might be considered material to the company and require disclosure. In other situations, certain milestones might be critical to communicate during a pitch to venture capitalists as they represent a major de-risking step for the company. At other times, it might simply be a matter of keeping stakeholders (e.g., a patient association that supports the biopharma company's strategy) and shareholders appraised. Lastly, incomplete or potentially misleading communications may have serious legal ramifications both for the biopharma company and its leadership. Beyond compliance or regulatory aspects, the company might be unable to secure suitable funding if potential investors are not convinced by their story.

While there is an apparently endless supply of references on storytelling, the following sections provide concepts and considerations that might be particularly helpful for the biopharma industry. In addition to storytelling, biopharma firms, faced with complex science, significant investment needs, and varying levels of audience understanding and skepticism, may want to have a sound strategy that can inform and guide its various communications, be it public relations, investor relations presentations, or other forms of outreach.

1.1.1 Trust, Logic, and Emotions

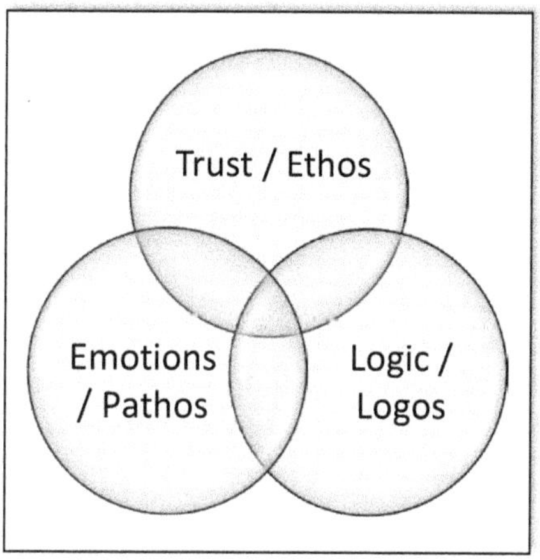

Figure 1.1 Aristotle's pillars of persuasion.

In his *Treatise on Rhetoric*, Aristotle explains the three dimensions of persuasion that give the speaker credibility: ethos or trust, pathos or emotions, and logos or logic (Figure 1.1).

Logos corresponds to logical persuasion and tends to be the default mode for many scientists and biopharma professionals who rely on science and facts to logically tell a story. The basic thread used with logos to build credibility is indeed that of reporting logic and facts, with limited attention to how messages are delivered or conveyed. One notable challenge with that preferred scientific approach is the complexity of the science for non-expert audiences who may not realize the logic, or the significance of the facts presented. Such communications are thus designed for expert audiences only. Essential techniques used for a logos approach include a well-structured and well-organized presentation, featuring precise points, quantified results according to study plan, specific references to previous studies, industry or diseases statistics, and comparisons with standards or publications. It is paramount for the communication to highlight logical reasoning with appropriate substantiation.

Ethos corresponds to credibility or trust and is frequently used in the biopharma industry, more specifically using Key Opinion Leaders, recognized prestigious institutions, and prominent industry venues or events. With ethos, the emphasis is given to endorsements by recognized and credible sources. While the technical complexity of the message remains, a less technical audience might get a sense that what the company has achieved is important in light of the prestigious speaker with impressive titles or the notorious venue. The main techniques used for an ethos approach include the use of authoritative references and similar "positioning" features like a prestigious scientific venue. It is paramount for the communication to inspire confidence based on specific authority figures.

While pathos tends to be often neglected in favor of the two previous modes, it is sometimes used in the industry as well, especially through positive and inspirational patient stories. Indeed, pathos corresponds to emotions and values. In a pathos approach, emphasis is given to patient perspectives rather than to scientific results: what benefits they receive from the treatment, how they suffer without any good treatment option, what dire consequences they face, etc. And while some therapeutic aspects may remain technical, most audiences would relate to disease implications for a parent, a friend, or someone they might be close to. They intuitively get a feel for the value of the therapy. Patient stories can have a lasting impact on a message, as they convey the value of biopharmaceutical therapies through the eyes of a patient. This can be especially important for businesses with compelling patient-centric considerations. Techniques for a pathos approach include the empathic articulation of compelling and moving stories, displaying personal passion, playing off positive or negative emotions, the inclusion of inspirational quotes, and the use of situational language to depict a specific patient's condition. It is paramount for the communication to trigger emotions or values for the audience.

Case Example: Press Releases Using Logos, Ethos, and Pathos Alternatively

Figure 1.2 provides illustrative and fictitious press releases for an imaginary XYZ BioTherapeutics company and a fictitious condition denoted Chronic Idiopathy (idiopathy is defined as a spontaneous disease or a disease of unknown cause), using respectively, from left to right, logos, ethos, and pathos orientations. Note the use of facts versus authority figures versus patient stories. On a related note, it is important to ensure press releases are professionally written as they reflect the credibility of the company.

Now, you might ask which of the three modes (logos, pathos, ethos) is more appropriate to use in your specific situation? The good news is that using all three typically makes you more persuasive. And while most industry professionals will have a sense for the dominant mode to use, the key is really to validate that you have accessed all three modes in your communication (or that you had a solid reason to exclude a given mode).

1.1.2 *Minto's Pyramid Principle*

This Pyramid Principle is named after Barbara Minto – it refers to a publication, authored by Barbara Minto, on using logic in writing and thinking that helps consultants organize and present their thoughts and recommendations. Her books have literally been used to train thousands of management consultants at several major consulting firms, including McKinsey, Kearney, Accenture, and Bain.

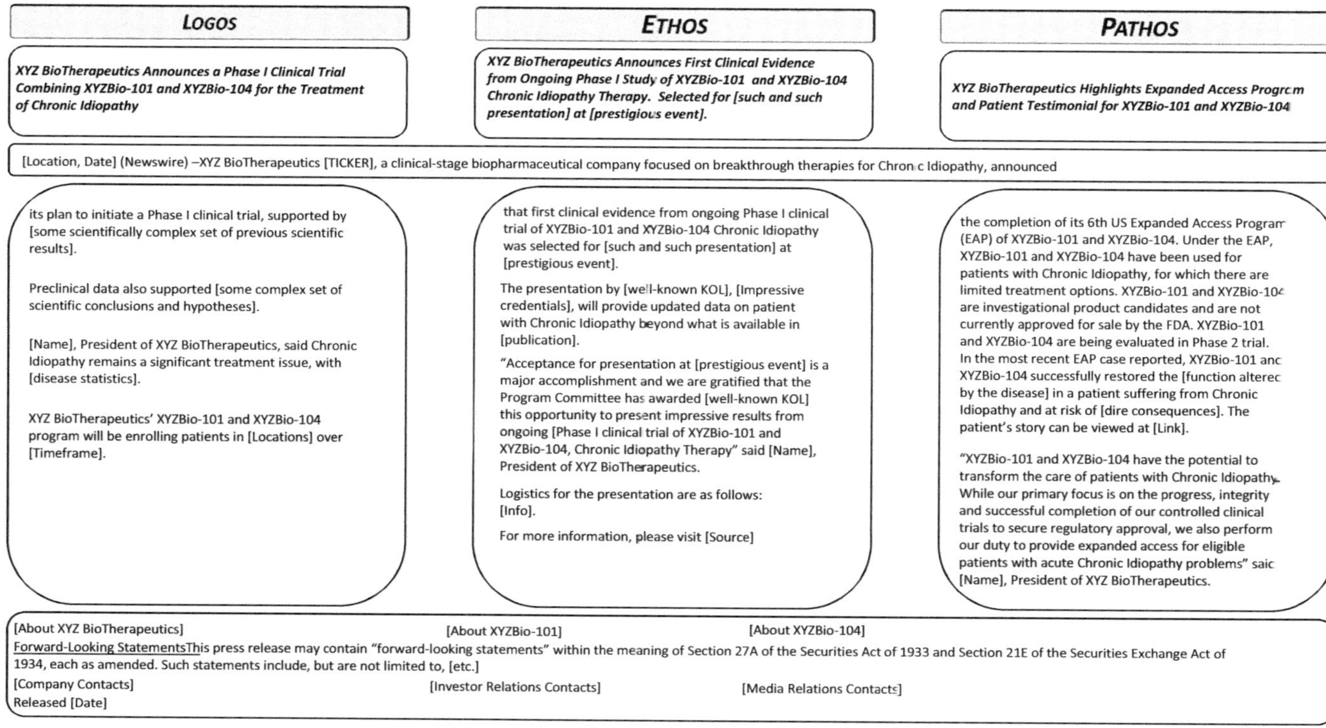

Figure 1.2 Fictitious press release illustrations.

The Minto Pyramid Principle (Minto, 1996) is a fantastic reference to have – it emphasizes clarity, logic, and rigorous thinking when you write, be it a presentation or an email.

One of the many very useful approaches that are derived from her book is the discipline to ensure everyone in your audience has access to the same understanding of the situation (e.g., the environment your biopharma company plays in, such as a therapeutic area and specific market) before discussing complications or disease challenges (e.g., unmet medical needs or competitive pressures) and then explaining your proposed resolution or how you address that challenge (e.g., the cure or treatment you provide along with supporting evidence and why it constitutes a better option). While such a presentation framework (situation – complication – resolution) might be considered straightforward, initial pitches from biopharma startups frequently fail to address its simple precepts. They are indeed part of traditional children's stories, those that start with "once upon a time" (the situation), continue with a challenge to be overcome or a quest to undertake (the complication), and close with a happy conclusion forever after (the resolution). As fond storytelling memories from childhood are common, there should be something valuable about the approach.

So, remember this "situation, complication, resolution" framework applicable to any good narratives!

1.1.3 Pick and Choose

In a high-stake environment like biopharma, it can be very tempting to include every single detail around a communication topic such as a regulatory event or clinical results. Once the company has met its transparency and reporting requirements, the leadership team should be savvy about how to communicate content that might feature numerous complex data, tables, analyses, and graphics, as is almost always the case with biopharma.

It is often most effective to keep the story concise (e.g., what are we saying in three simple sentences?) and then "pick and choose" a limited subset of data, images, and graphics that will easily and clearly support that simple main story. It is always surprising to see how extremely smart individuals will instead attempt to drown their audience with cryptic scientific data and strive to use the entire data set and results. For compliance purposes, a company might provide additional and detailed information in appendix or post it on their website. For added clarity, the images, tables, analyses, and graphics should ideally be understandable by an audience with minimal scientific training but without expertise in the field.

Most "pick and choose" communications, even done to the best company's ability, will likely leave gaps that, ideally, should also be addressed. A press release and a convention poster to highlight scientific results might convince general audiences but might leave scientific audiences wanting – which might be addressed through publication in a recognized peer-reviewed scientific journal. Conversely, a specialized scientific journal publication might not be accessible to all intended audiences and might require simplified additional communications.

1.1.4 The Power of Clear Visual Support

There seems to be evidence that a well-chosen picture is worth 18–30 words (quite different from the saying that "a picture is worth a thousand words" but still impressive). Indeed, image processing speeds can be between 13 and 80 milliseconds (Trafton, 2014). In comparison, in the United States, typical average reading and speaking speeds are often quoted in words per minute around 250 and 150, respectively. These represent processing speeds of 240 and 400 milliseconds per word for reading and speaking, respectively, compared with 13 milliseconds for an optimal image processing. Depending on whether an audience is reading or listening, these speed differences might imply that an image that clearly supports the story is worth 18 or 30 words. In addition, images might provide for stronger recall than the spoken word, notwithstanding the combination of the two. So do not miss an opportunity to use images or graphics that clearly support your message but do not force it!

1.1.5 Memorability

In addition to being well-structured (see Minto's Pyramid Principle above), convincing (see Trust, Logic, and Emotions above) and aligned to the right communication priorities (see Pick and Choose above), your story should ideally be one that your audience remembers. Beyond ensuring that the content is compliant, accurate, and not misleading, using the Clarity, Objectivity, and Gravitas towards Storytelling framework (or COGS) might be useful to make biopharma communication or presentation appropriately memorable (Figure 1.3).

Clarity is the basic foundation, enabling most audiences to easily understand the information or results presented, what they might mean for patients or for the company. For common business communications, being easily accessible by most audiences means an 8th grade level for the United States, which means, among other things, avoiding overtechnical content.

Objectivity is a balanced way to help your audience navigate through complex data and sometimes conflicting context from competitive industry communications that might cloud or otherwise cast doubts on your own communications. Consistent communication that is fair and balanced can reinforce the credibility and therefore the memorability of the message.

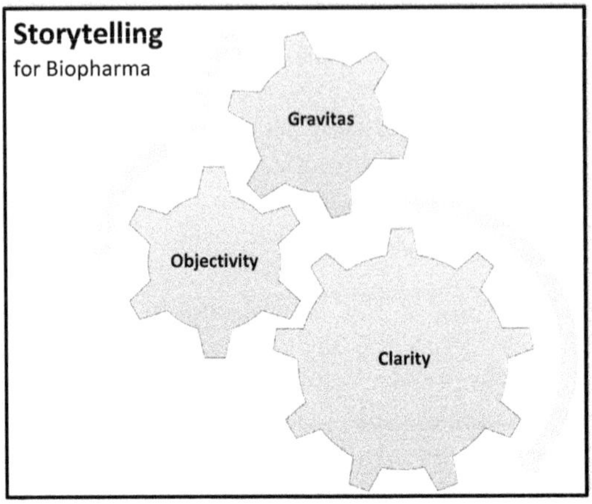

Figure 1.3 COGS framework: clarity, objectivity, and gravitas toward storytelling.

Crafting a fair and balanced communication for complex information might occasionally be a challenging exercise when done individually and typically benefits from advanced planning and independent review.

Gravitas or seriousness of purpose, displayed in the communication, should consider the potential impact this would have on patients afflicted with the indication or disease the drug is targeting. As biopharma communications relate to conditions that can seriously affect quality of life or even be life-threatening, it is important to convey a seriousness of purpose and reserve.

The storytelling part of the COGS framework refers to how you package clarity, objectivity, and gravitas into a structured cohesive message with a well-defined purpose. Whether you use Minto's Pyramid Principle or another approach, the communication should follow a specific organization structure, incorporating complex data into a thread that is easily followed and understood, fitting within the context of previous and ongoing communications, and achieve its purpose (e.g., call to action, clear and memorable take-away).

The way the storyline develops toward that purpose should be compelling for the broad variety of audiences biopharma firms usually cater to, such as patients, physicians, investors, and industry analysts. The combination of ethos, pathos, and logos might help make the communication compelling to all. As importantly, such communication should be made by spokespersons best able to establish a meaningful connection with the intended audience. Lastly, keep in mind that your communications can also be helpful to extended audiences, e.g., external communication might also inspire employees and reinforce the strategic direction of the company.

1.1.6 *Additional Storytelling Considerations*

Being effective at storytelling is a journey and not a destination. There are countless suggestions and references you can read to develop a custom itinerary that works best for you. In all cases, it takes ongoing practice. And you can exchange viewpoints with, or observe, millions of other fellow travelers.

You might want to ask yourself how you will stand out from the crowd. Are there aspects about your biopharma firm that can help you systematically stand out in your communications? A differentiating brand, a pioneering mechanism of action, etc.?

Perhaps there might also be a favorable venue or timing. What do you know about the current environment and ecosystem in which your biopharma company operates? Is there a week, day, or time when multiple similar communications from other biopharma firms might hinder or compete with your communication?

As for any communication, building an infrastructure and relationships helps. What can you do in advance to build media or influencers/Key Opinion Leader relationships, to establish communication channels such as social media and other avenues that will facilitate and energize your communications?

Lastly, as the saying goes, if you do not measure it, you cannot be serious about it. Despite your best efforts, there will always be room for improvement; what metrics will you have in place to detect such improvement opportunities and continue to improve your biopharma communications?

1.2 Drug Discovery, Development, and Commercialization Process

There are many steps required to successfully develop a drug in the biopharma industry (Figure 1.4). Even when reaching clinical stages, past early discovery and preclinical studies, the hurdles faced by a biopharma firm remain high with a complex development and commercialization execution.

The process, as captured in 28 FR 179 (January 8, 1963) 130.3 (a)(10), follows phases for drug testing explicitly laid out by the FDA in 1963 as part of regulations to strengthen control over investigational drugs in the United States (White Junod, 2017). Those phases offer a structured and systematic process to evaluate new investigational treatments, to ensure safety and effectiveness prior to seeking regulatory approval for commercialization. Phase 1 focuses primarily on safety before proceeding with further testing with larger populations. Phase 2 seeks further safety data and preliminary evidence of effect or efficacy. An efficacious therapy might be defined as more beneficial with treatment than without in the study population. Phase 3 is then a confirmatory study showing benefits and safety in

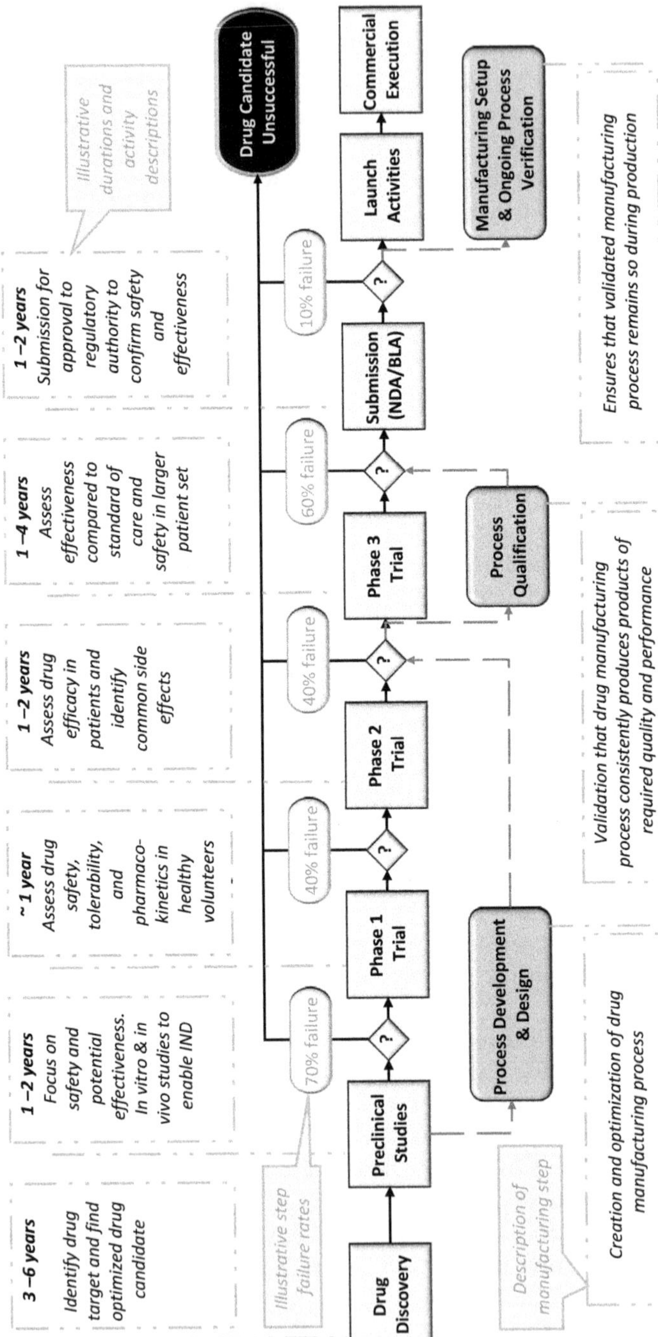

Figure 1.4 Traditional drug discovery, development, and commercialization process.

large patient populations: Phase 3 aims to determine whether the treatment is effective meaning that it provides improvements in health and underlying conditions for the overall population. In summary, Phases 1 through 3 focus on safety, efficacy, and effectiveness.

Given these focus points, the process depicted in Figure 1.4 provides a framework for program progression, regulatory pathways, and value creation as the probability of revenues and profits (from licensing or downstream commercial activities) increases. Regulatory pathways are discussed further in Chapter 9.

While the regulatory framework of Figure 1.4 remains valid, numerous transformative factors have come into play to accelerate and improve the process (Figure 1.5), e.g.:

- Real-world evidence: clinical evidence obtained from analyzing real-world data (i.e., electronic health records, patient claims, patient registries) to assess various aspects such as safety, effectiveness, and usage of medical interventions in everyday practice.
- Virtual studies (including in-silico studies): studies that utilize computational tools, simulations, and real-world data to generate insights and findings without relying on physical experiments, and possibly in conjunction with artificial intelligence.
- Artificial intelligence: use of algorithms and computer techniques to analyze data, optimize designs, and streamline the drug discovery and development process.

Such transformations have been supplemented by incremental industry and process innovations such as:

- Adaptive trial designs: studies with a protocol that allows for pre-planned modifications to trial procedures based on interim analyses. Intended to improve efficiency and relevance, such modifications might typically include sample size, dose, or treatment group changes.
- Decentralized clinical trials: having gained acceptance during the COVID pandemic, decentralized approaches are increasingly used, at least in part, in clinical study protocols. "Decentralized" refers to the use of remote methods, such as digital tools and virtual communication, allowing participants to engage remotely rather than from centralized clinical sites.
- Blockchain applications: blockchain might be defined as a secure, transparent, tamper-proof, decentralized, and verifiable ledger that records transactions across computer networks. Drug development uses have included improved drug traceability, tamper-proof records, and patient informed consent.

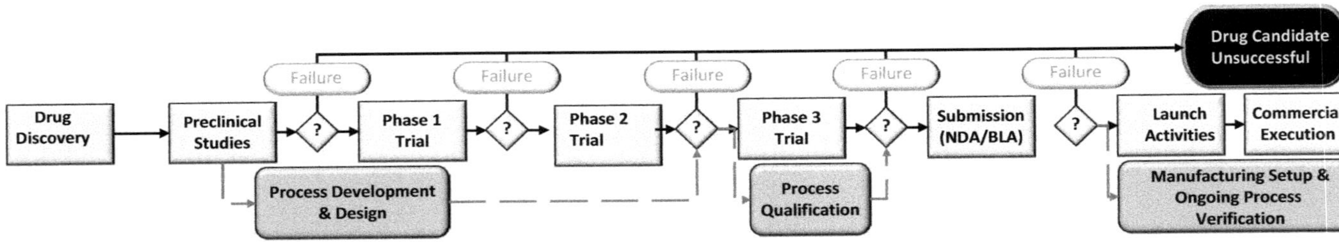

Evolving Drug and Biologics Discovery and Development Process – Illustrative Innovation Examples					
Factors	**Discovery**	**Preclinical**	**Phase 1**	**Phase 2**	**Phase 3**
Real- world evidence (RWE)	▪ Identification of unmet medical needs (e.g., health record and claims analysis)	▪ Genetic profiles, disease sub-types, modeling and hypothesis generation	▪ Patient selection an recruitment ▪ Baseline data and inclusion data (diversity) ▪ Support for dose determination / safety	▪ Dose selection (using previous treatments) ▪ Efficacy endpoints selection ▪ Standard of care comparisons	▪ Comparator, endpoint, and patient selection ▪ RWE subgroup analyses ▪ Recruitment strategies: centers, geographies ▪ Safety benchmarks
Virtual studies	▪ Target identification and validation (e.g., large-scale omics data analysis)	▪ Drug candidate optimization (molecular models, PK/PD models) ▪ Replace /optimize animal studies	▪ First-in-human simulation ▪ Adverse event predictions ▪ Patient stratification ▪ Predictive models using real-time study data	▪ Trial design and dose selection (simulation) ▪ Scenario simulation ▪ Refining endpoints and patient groups	▪ Study simulation and optimization ▪ Adaptive monitoring
Artificial intelligence (AI)	▪ Predictive drug candidate screening ▪ Polypharmacology and toxicity predictions ▪ De novo drug Design	▪ Identification of safety risks and biomarkers ▪ Prediction of suitable animal models, doses, and other study parameters	▪ First-in-human dose prediction and selection ▪ Simulation of ADME properties	▪ Patient stratification (identification of optimized subgroups) ▪ Dose-response models supplementing Phase 2	▪ Patient stratification and synthetic control arms ▪ Comparative effectiveness analysis (also using RWE)

Figure 1.5 Evolution of drug discovery and development process.

- Digital biomarkers: increasing in use sometimes in conjunction with artificial intelligence, they can be defined as physiological, behavioral, or clinical measures collected through digital devices, such as wearables, smartphones, or sensors.

1.3 A High-Risk Environment

As illustrated in Figure 1.4, significant clinical trial failure rates constitute a major source of uncertainty for the biopharma industry. Probability of success from Phase 1 to approval has been estimated to historically range from 3.4% in oncology to 33.4% in vaccines using data from 2000 to 2015 (Wong et al., 2019). In this environment where most products fail, there are many other risks to consider, as reflected by safe harbor statements made by public biopharma companies or in analyst reports:

- Early-stage trials may not reflect or fully predict results from later, larger-scale more expensive trials.
- Ability to secure the significant investments and capital required for drug development.
- Challenges with product coverage, pricing, and reimbursement.
- Collaboration (e.g., co-development, co-promotion) challenges.
- Competitive marketed products and pipeline.
- Risks to intellectual property, patent expiration, and generic competition.
- Adverse safety events and liability claims.
- Impact of unexpected external events (e.g., COVID-19 pandemic, tax changes).
- Supply chain disruptions and manufacturing challenges.
- Ability to build or leverage a suitable commercial infrastructure.
- Evolving industry regulations and jurisdictional differences despite harmonization efforts.
- Ability to attract and retain critical talent in an expertise-based industry.

De-risking the business is thus a major imperative in the biopharma industry to be able to create value for shareholders. As can be seen from the illustrative "S" shape in Figure 1.6 portraying the percentage of post approval value achieved at each clinical trial stage, a successful end of Phase 2 typically represents a key value inflection point in a development program. This is one of the reasons why a number of shareholders of biopharma companies consider an exit (i.e., selling the company or program) after the so-called "proof of concept" once efficacy has been demonstrated in a Phase 2 clinical trial.

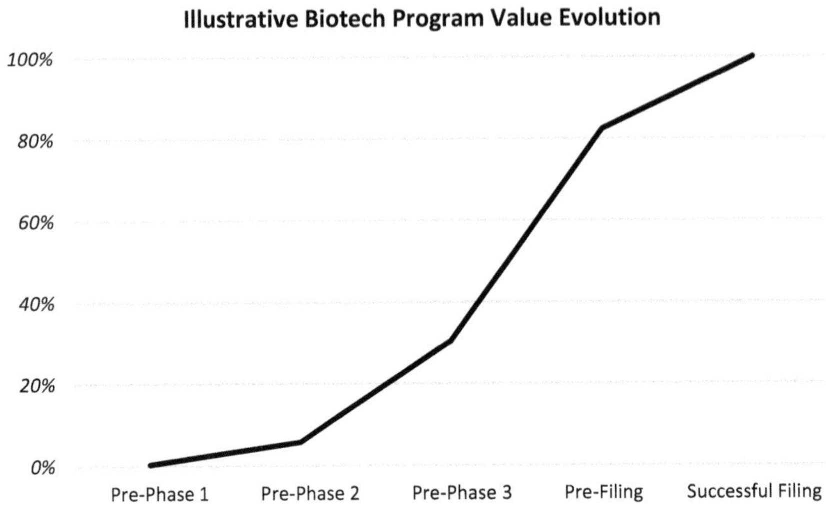

Figure 1.6 Illustrative biopharma program "S" curve.

Understanding how the risk profile of their biopharma firm evolves is an important consideration for the company's leadership to secure funding and conduct business development activities.

1.4 Leadership Team as Make or Break Factor

As we just saw, the biopharma industry involves high risks as well as complex scientific and regulatory paths to success. Having the right team to undertake such a journey is critical. For very early-stage companies, in light of the very low probabilities of success, the executive team represents an important consideration for investors to place a bet on the company. Early investors will try and assess whether the executive team has collectively all the skills and capabilities required to take the company to the next stage of evolution, usually preclinical. They might typically scrutinize scientific and medical expertise in a relatively narrowly defined area in addition to successful past experience and a solid business plan. As the company matures, expectations of the leadership team will likewise evolve to different or broader competences such as manufacturing process design experience, safety, and regulatory expertise as the firm enters preclinical. As the company nears proof of concept, clinical experience, external communication capabilities, and business development experience will ramp up in importance. As the company matures, the leadership team will need to clearly exhibit all the skills, capabilities, and experience required to quickly and effectively take the company to the next step of evolution (Figure 1.4), resulting in increased company value along the way.

The specifics of the biopharma industry tend to require adaptable, scientifically savvy leadership teams able to manage high-risk, capital-intensive, complex, and compliant long-term research and development activities, sometimes in collaboration with other organizations, in a global competitive environment. Thus, irrespective of the company stage, an effective biopharma leadership team, the CEO in particular will need to possess a relentless global innovation focus, a deep scientific and medical acumen, strong pragmatic financial capabilities (e.g., financing, planning, forecasting, analysis, deal-making), shrewd biopharma market know-how and patient awareness, an ability to collaborate or compete according to the context, and a demonstrated understanding of both regulatory and intellectual property environments.

1.5 The Biopharma Innovation Landscape

Innovation might be defined as the structure, process, and outcome of bringing about meaningful change. Biopharma companies might be defined as companies with biopharma R&D activity, intent on deriving their value creation from biopharma R&D, and that have one or more drugs in their pipeline.

The biopharma innovation ecosystem is extremely diverse between academia, incubators, small biopharma companies versus medium-sized and larger ones, platform companies, artificial intelligence (AI) and machine-learning companies focused on drug discovery and development, private research organizations, public institutions, nonprofits, and service companies (e.g., analytical services, contract research organizations, contract manufacturing organizations, regulatory services, bioinformatics, drug delivery, screening services, genomics or proteomics services). The United States alone counts a large number of biopharma companies (estimated between 5,000 and 10,000, depending on definitions and sources).

Overall, biopharma funding is significant given global annual funding levels (including initial public offerings, follow-on funding, and venture capital) ranging between US$58B and US$134B from 2019 to 2023 (IQVIA Institute for Human Data Science, 2024). Correspondingly, the total number of clinical trials started annually over the same time frame has ranged from 4,873 to 6,250 with a majority performed by emerging biopharma companies, defined as companies with less than US$200M in R&D spend and less than US$500M in revenue (Ibid).

In addition to being strongly influenced by R&D investments and underlying financing (see Chapter 5), biopharma innovation hinges on strong intellectual property (IP) protection (see Chapter 3) to secure the downstream revenues that make these investments possible as well as on effective regulatory pathways (see Chapter 9) that authorize said revenues. This remains true as companies, investments, IP, and regulatory environments all adapt to the latest industry evolutions and technological advancements (e.g., new modalities, decentralized clinical trials, use of AI in target identification, in drug discovery, or in pharmacovigilance) in the context of global health, macroeconomic environments, and various jurisdictions' sociopolitical mandates.

1.5.1 Internal vs. External Innovation

Internal innovation refers to innovative products or therapies derived within the confines of a company, i.e., invented and developed internally, whereas external innovation designates innovative products or therapies obtained by the company from other organizations. While internal innovation remains essential for most companies, it is clear that external innovation plays a critical role. A significant majority of FDA-approved drugs for the top 20 biopharma companies have been based on external innovation in recent years (Schuhmacher et al., 2023).

Irrespective of the source, biopharma innovations need to meet three concurrent requirements, namely desirability, feasibility, and viability. Desirability stands for the level of unmet needs for a specific condition or disease that the innovation will alleviate. Feasibility is characterized by the financial, operational, and scientific ability to identify, develop, and commercialize a compound with the desired safety and efficacy characteristics required in order to provide the therapeutic effect expected for a specific condition or disease, as normally reflected by the target product profile. Viability corresponds to the ability to generate sufficient commercial revenues or public funding to justify the risks and significant upfront R&D costs. Successful biopharma innovation requires significant unmet needs or potential improvements over the standard of care, technical ability, financial means, and large-enough economic potential given established regulatory and IP environments.

Case Example: Different Models of Biopharma Innovation

Biopharma companies can use different approaches to innovation as a function of their business model and their competences (Pisano, 2015), as illustrated in Figure 1.7. In terms of value, while technical innovation can often be

		Technical and Scientific Biopharma Competences	
		Current	New
Biopharma Business Model	New	**Disruptive Innovation** • Value-based contracts (e.g., health-outcome-based) • Drug subscription models • Indication-based pricing for drugs used in multiple indications with different observed performance • Drug-device combination of existing diagnostic with existing therapy	**Game-Changing Innovation** • Innovative autologous cell therapies or allogenic cell therapies requiring treatment centers and value chain approaches different from traditional biopharma
	Current	**Traditional Innovation** • Development of new compound with established mechanism of action using classic development program and planning on using existing therapeutic area salesforce, targeting physicians currently prescribing an existing drug	**Technical Innovation** • Development of new compounds using a new biologics platform (e.g., mRNA) or new advanced modalities (e.g., protein degradation)

Figure 1.7 Biopharma innovation as a function of business model and competences.

modeled the same way as traditional innovation, disruptive or game-changing innovations can be more challenging to model financially as they represent a different business model, typically with different financial cash flows.

As shown in the example above, biopharma innovation can be multidimensional – which is also reflected in the ecosystem leveraged by the biopharma company. We have just discussed the option of using different business models. A company might alternatively elect to offer "innovation as a service" as a number of platform companies do, developing compounds up to a certain stage and then selling or licensing them to biopharma companies that take on development and commercialization. Yet another approach consists in combining the company's innovative offering with other products and services (e.g., combination therapies, drug device approaches, treatment centers). Additional aspects that might provide an extended innovation landscape may include free patient or clinical support lines, patient access services, smart drug packaging, patient adherence and monitoring apps, payment credit to payers for insufficient health outcomes, and branding aspects (e.g., multi-indication drugs, private label). In summary, innovation should capture at least three dimensions: business model, therapeutic approach inclusive of the biopharma product, and patient experience.

Case Example: DIY Innovation, Strategy, Business, or Landscape Framework

CUSTOM 2X2 FRAMEWORK CREATION

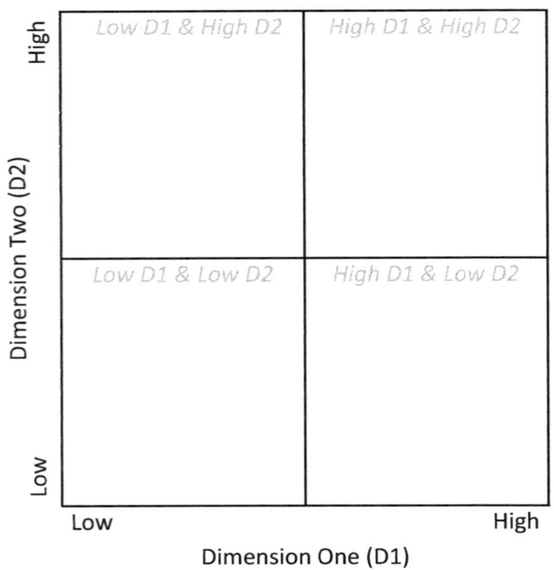

Figure 1.8 Do It Yourself (DIY) 2X2 framework.

- Brainstorm aspects (i.e., dimensions) relevant to portray your innovation, strategy, business, or landscape.
- Pick two relatively independent dimensions you believe are most important.
  - Represent one dimension on a horizontal axis with “high” vs. “low” (or equivalent range) at each end of the axis
  - Represent the other dimension on a vertical axis with “high” vs. “low” (or equivalent range) at each end of the axis
- You now have four quadrants between the two dimensions.
- Evaluate what each of the four quadrants or boxes above might mean for an innovation, strategy, business, or landscape. Find examples, illustrations or options for each box. You can even rename each quadrant by using a descriptive name instead of generic names like “Low D1 & High D2”
- If this attempt does not provide any insight, start over with new independent dimensions!

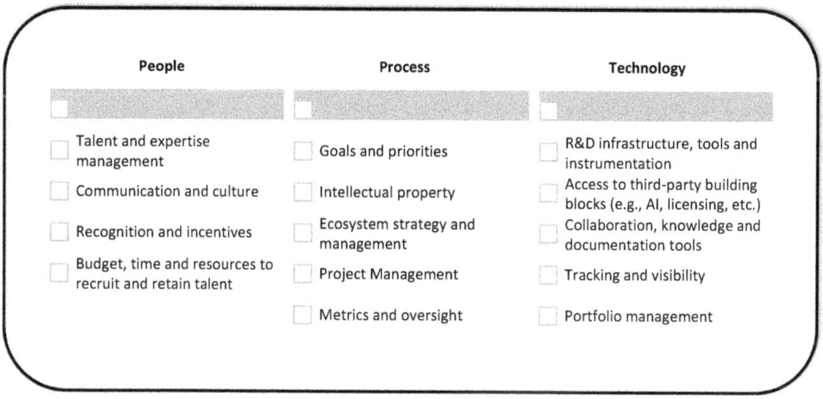

Figure 1.9 Illustrative internal innovation environment.

Analyzing and planning for biopharma innovation can be challenging and might require new thought models or frameworks. Since we are talking about innovation, inventing a new framework for a specific situation might occasionally be achieved by using the generic 2-by-2 framework creation approach depicted in Figure 1.8 (hint: this is an old management consulting trick that can also be used for strategy, business, or landscape analysis in addition to innovation!). Notice how this generic approach might have been used to derive the framework provided in Figure 1.7 by using "business model" and "competences" as dimensions and using "existing" versus "new" as axis ends on both dimensions.

Establishing the right internal environment is particularly important for biopharma where innovation tends to be more holistic and the result of scientific research. Within a given biopharma company, although specifics vary, such environment is usually a combination of people, process, and technology aspects (Figure 1.9).

For early-stage companies, the ecosystem in which they reside can play a critical role in facilitating a suitable innovative environment. Indeed, there are ecosystems that encourage entrepreneurial ventures in the United States by providing three different types of support (Bettanti et al., 2021):

- Support for entrepreneurial aspirations by providing local pockets or clusters of entrepreneurs, exposure and easier access to investments, technology transfers, and global opportunities.
- Support of entrepreneurial attitudes by instilling a culture of risk failure acceptance, making cultural allowance, and facilitating networking opportunities.

- Provision of the underlying infrastructure required for entrepreneurial ventures, such as availability of talent and expertise, business support options, incubator or startup space, and adoption openness for new therapies and biopharma products.

Such ecosystems, like the Greater Boston Area or the Greater Paris Area (inclusive of Paris-Saclay), tend to include a plethora of different stakeholders. They might include innovation centers, patient advocacy groups, lobby groups, outsourcing suppliers, such as CROs or CDMOs, professional support (Legal, IP, Banking, Accounting, etc.), dynamic financial markets (Angel Investors, VCs, Equity firms, etc.), universities, university hospitals, research organizations, government organizations (Ibid).

1.6 Alternate Innovation Avenues

While most biopharma innovation references deal with new molecules, they are by no means the only pathway to innovation. Other noteworthy innovation models might include:

- Therapeutic area expansion.
  Novel therapeutic approaches can be designed using therapies already marketed for other indications. And since the drug has already been approved, the biopharma firm already knows a lot about it, its safety profile and so on. As a result, the probability of success in early trials tends to be higher. An example of such therapeutic area expansion is Exenatide, a drug approved by the FDA in 2015 to treat Type 2 Diabetes that was later investigated for Parkinson's Disease (Scavone et al., 2019).
- Generics and biosimilars.
  As an alternate and equivalent option to an already approved therapy that has gone off patent, generics, and biosimilars might represent incremental innovation, with the first one benefiting from advantageous regulatory incentives in certain jurisdictions. Depending on the strategy of the generic/biosimilar firms, they might attempt to deliver incremental innovations, such as new and improved formulations, different dosage, and different delivery methods.
- Repositioning of failed assets.
  Drugs that have failed or been shelved for distinct reasons can sometimes be leveraged toward new medical uses. The company already has

extensive knowledge of the drug and its performance at least in preclinical studies and typically in early clinical studies. Such an approach might be constrained by reduced IP protection since the remaining patent life might be limited or nonexistent (Talevi & Bellera, 2020).

- Value chain adjustments.
  With the COVID-19 pandemic that dominated 2020, biopharma companies faced numerous supply chain challenges and clinical trial disruptions, putting much of the industry innovation potential in jeopardy. This gave rise to unprecedented cooperations, several companies adjusting their value chain. Sanofi started providing commercial scale manufacturing for COVID-19 vaccines to BioNTech and Johnson & Johnson in 2021 – clearly an innovative business model.

1.7 Strategic and Business Considerations

Financial transactions are a core part of biopharma innovation. As most firms do not have the financial means to independently make the required R&D investments given the risks involved, they have to enter into transactions aimed at enabling further developments or generating the appropriate returns for the results achieved.

Whether the intent of a transaction is to secure investments to enable future developments, to share risks with another company, or simply to enact an exit strategy after hitting certain development milestones, the choice of the specific transaction should be consistent with the company's strategic and financial objectives.

The transaction approach should also reflect market conditions and shareholders' expectations for risk returns, ownership, and control. The macroeconomic environment can play a very influential role on the types of deals predominantly observed in the biopharma industry. An environment unfavorable to public offerings and venture capital funding might encourage debt financing by larger companies or out-licensing by smaller companies to secure the cash flows necessary to support ongoing drug development.

The biopharma company's executive leadership needs to develop and cultivate industry relationships in anticipation of future potential deals as well as in the context of collaborations and partnerships.

Overall, the various strategic and operational situations may result in very different transactional approaches (Figure 1.10) that will be clarified in Chapter 7.

WIDE SPECTRUM OF POSSIBLE BIOPHARMA TRANSACTIONS

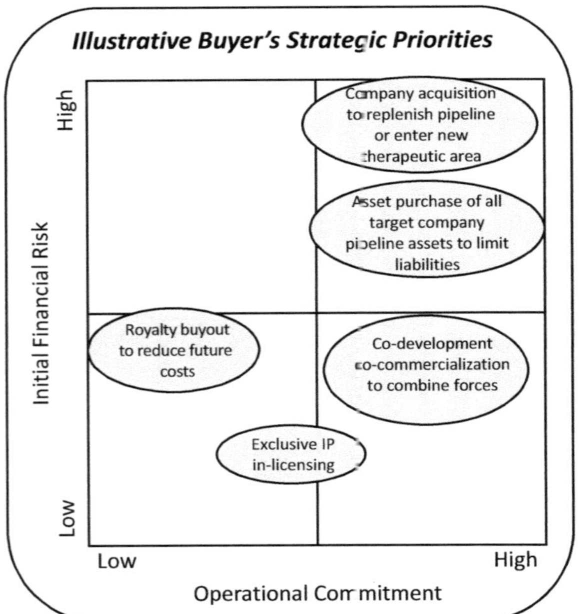

Illustrative Transaction Types

Transaction objectives	Possible transaction type(s)
Acquire ownership of specific tangible and intangible assets	Asset purchase
Acquire full control of intangible assets	In-licensing
Share program risks and rewards	Partnership or collaboration agreement
Commercialization with partial commercial presence	Licensing agreement with co-promotion, co-commercialization
Share R&D costs while maintaining strategic flexibility	Research collaboration with options to select candidates
Sale in exchange for short-term financial gains	Asset sale, out-licensing
Eliminate future burden on gross margins	Royalties buy-out

Figure 1.10 Illustrative diversity of transactions.

References

Bettanti, A., Lanati, A., & Missoni, A. (2021). Biopharmaceutical innovation ecosystems: a stakeholder model and the case of Lombardy. *The Journal of Technology Transfer, 47*(6), 1948–1973. https://doi.org/10.1007/s10961-021-09890-1

IQVIA Institute for Human Data Science. (2024). *Global Trends in R&D 2024.* https://www.iqvia.com/insights/the-iqvia-institute/reports-and-publications/reports/global-trends-in-r-and-d-2024-activity-productivity-and-enablers

Minto, B. (1996). *The Minto Pyramid Principle* (New and exp. ed. ed.). Minto Internat.

Pisano, G. P. (2015, June 1). You need an innovation strategy. *Harvard Business Review, 93,* 44. https://search.proquest.com/docview/1683591374

Scavone, C., di Mauro, G., Mascolo, A., Berrino, L., Rossi, F., & Capuano, A. (2019). The new paradigms in clinical research: from early access programs to the novel therapeutic approaches for unmet medical needs. *Frontiers in Pharmacology, 10,* 111. https://doi.org/10.3389/fphar.2019.00111

Schuhmacher, A., Hartl, D., Hinder, M., Gassmann, O., & Dodel, A. (2023). Investigating the origins of recent pharmaceutical innovation. *Nature Reviews Drug Discovery, 22,* 781–782. https://doi.org/10.1038/d41573-023-00102-z

Talevi, A., & Bellera, C. L. (2020). Challenges and opportunities with drug repurposing: finding strategies to find alternative uses of therapeutics. *Null, 15*(4), 397–401. https://doi.org/10.1080/17460441.2020.1704729

Trafton, A. (2014, January 16). *In the Blink of an Eye. MIT Neuroscientists Find the Brain Can Identify Images Seen for as Little as 13 Milliseconds.* MIT.edu. Retrieved 6/13/2022, from https://news.mit.edu/2014/in-the-blink-of-an-eye-0116

White Junod, S. (2017, October 27). *FDA and Clinical Drug Trials - A Short History.* Retrieved 12/4/2024, from https://www.fda.gov/media/110437/download#:~:text=Ancient%20civilizations%20relied%20on%20medical,their%20clinical%20and%20experimental%20grasp.

Wong, C. H., Siah, K. W., & Lo, A. W. (2019). Estimation of clinical trial success rates and related parameters. *Biostatistics, 20*(2), 273–286. https://doi.org/10.1093/biostatistics/kxx069

Chapter 2

The Basic Valuation Toolkit

This chapter introduces the main financial notions behind value creation, described in the context of biopharmaceutical companies.

There are numerous situations in which it is important for a biopharma firm to assess a value using tools from this chapter, e.g.:

- Identify and prioritize highest value assets taking into account probability of successful development.
- Substantiate appropriate company valuation to financial investors.
- Negotiate strategic equity investments in the firm with a major biopharma partner.
- Support business development negotiations regarding licensing rights to a given program.

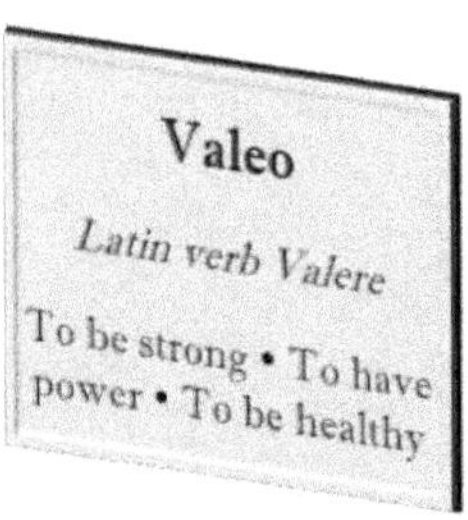

Figure 2.1 Valere.

As valuation is a fundamental notion for the chapter, let us start with a definition of value. Value can be used as a gauge along a company's evolution.

The etymology of value comes from the Latin verb valere (Figure 2.1) and helps us understand that value measures the capacity of a biopharma firm to prevail, perform strongly, and remain financially healthy.

A simple gauge for a biopharma company's value is the monetary measure of company equity:

$$\text{Equity} = \text{Assets} - \text{Liabilities}$$

The value of the biopharma company is what it manages to create (referred to as Assets) over what it has committed to (referred to as Liabilities). In a biopharma firm, the leadership team will guide the team through research, development of programs, and commercialization to gradually increase the value of the company, thanks to the contributions made by such programs.

DOI: 10.4324/9781003598046-2

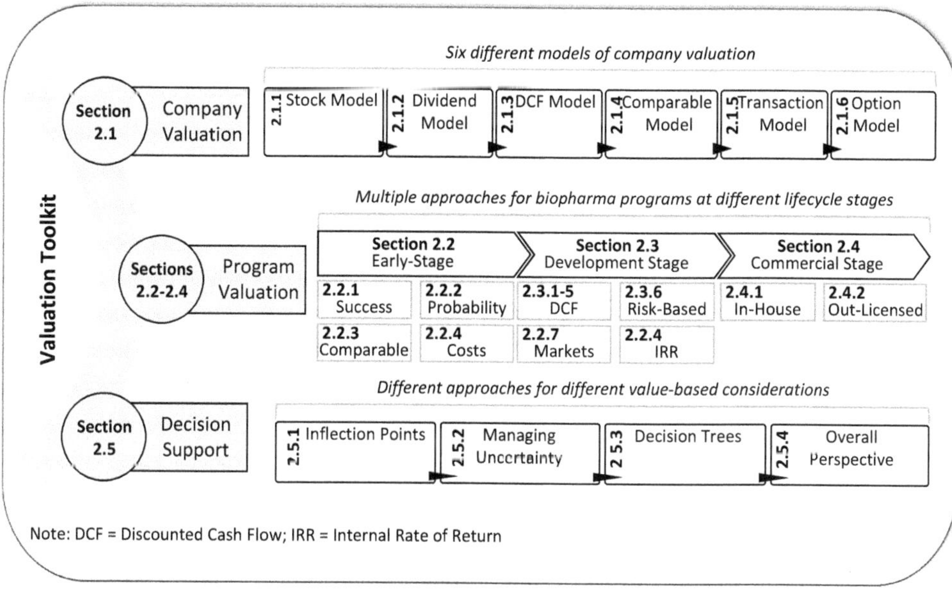

Figure 2.2 Biopharma valuation toolkit.

This chapter presents concepts and approaches that will help pharmaceutical, biotechnology, and associated professionals better understand and use financial models to enhance the value of their programs and the company. We start with various company valuation approaches in Section 2.1. Then Sections 2.2–2.4 cover program valuation approaches for early stage, development stage, and commercial stage, respectively. Lastly, Section 2.5 focuses on the use of valuation tools for program decision-making (Figure 2.2).

Caution should be used not to derive improper expectations from valuations. First, valuations, even when done well, do not necessarily provide a suitable view of the value they model – hence the importance of using different approaches and trying to triangulate or validate findings. Like any model, valuation models include assumptions that may or may not be totally accurate. In addition, such assumptions might evolve over time so that the model created months prior may no longer be valid. Ultimately, the true measure of value is what the company secures in the marketplace. The valuation approach is simply a discussion tool to help get there!

2.1 Company Valuation

Section 2.1 provides company valuation approaches taking a shareholder's perspective.

2.1.1 Stock Valuation

Stock or common stock represents ownership in the underlying company. They are also referred to as equity or equity securities. The collective shareholders own what is left of the company after the company has met its various obligations (e.g., debts and other liabilities).

The main characteristics of such stock are the *residual claim* (the shareholders get what is left after the company has met its obligations) and the *limited liability* (the most shareholders stand to lose is what they have invested if the company is unable or marginally unable to meet its obligations).

Voting rights – note that normally, each stock also gives a unit of rights regarding the decisions made by shareholders, such as electing board members. For a simple company with 200 voting shares issued, owning 30 shares gives the owner the right to vote for 15% of the company shareholders (30 votes out of 200 votes).

Access to stock valuation is straightforward when the company is publicly listed on a stock exchange: one can simply check the latest price online as transactions are frequent and published by the stock exchange in question.

For private companies, stock valuation is less accessible: the stock is typically much less liquid in that it changes hands less frequently and its value is less often updated – typically only with material events, significant company disclosures (e.g., clinical trial results, new licensing agreement), or financing rounds (e.g., series B financing).

Stock valuation can be established using different methods, which is of particular interest for private companies:

- Intrinsic value approaches (e.g., discounted cash flow method or dividend discount model).
- Relative value approaches (e.g., comparing the stock to similar companies that are publicly listed or for which transactions have been published).

Note that intrinsic value approaches can also be applied to publicly listed companies, which can then be compared with the stock price available from the stock exchange on which the company stock is traded. A significant difference between the stock price and the intrinsic value might point to potential investment opportunities if the stock is currently undervalued by the market compared with its intrinsic value.

2.1.2 Dividend Discount Model

This valuation approach, based on company's stock, only makes sense for companies that pay dividends (fixed payment per share to each shareholder) on a regular basis in a predictable way. This valuation assumes that the dividends received over time represent the relevant source of value of the stock to shareholders. It thus takes the payments expected to be received over time and discount them to represent today's value of all those future payments.

A typical valuation would look as follows.

$$\text{Intrinsic value of the stock} = \sum_{n=1}^{\infty} \frac{D_n}{(1+d)^n}$$

Equation 2.1 Dividend model stock price intrinsic value.

where

- d is the discount rate suitable for an investment with a risk similar to the biopharma firm for the shareholder.
- D_n is the dividend given to each stockholder in year n.
- The symbol Σ designates, as always, the sum of the series (here $\frac{D_n}{(1+d)^n}$) when the index n goes from the lower value listed to the higher value listed (here from 1 to infinity).

The formula above can be greatly simplified, and estimated as follows, in the case of fixed dividends $D_n = D$:

$$\text{Intrinsic value of the stock} = \frac{D}{d}$$

Equation 2.2 Fixed dividend stock price intrinsic value.

Note:
The simplified formula can provide a reasonable approximation of the intrinsic value, by neglecting $\epsilon(N)$ in the following exact formula, for a sufficiently large number of years N with a fixed dividend D, a discount rate d, and no dividend paid after year N:

$$\text{Intrinsic value of the stock} = \frac{D}{d} + \epsilon(N)$$

Equation 2.3 Fixed dividend model stock price intrinsic value.

where the omission error $\epsilon(N)$ is provided by: $\epsilon(N) = -\frac{D}{d}\left[\frac{1}{1+d}\right]^{N+1}$.

Case Example

Biopharma firm XZYBio is expected to give dividends of US$20M for the first 50 years and represents a risk that would warrant a 15% discount rate for shareholders. What would be the intrinsic value of the stock using a dividend discount model, assuming the stock has no significant value after 50 years of dividends?

Intrinsic value of XYZBio: US$20M / 0.15 ~ US$133M.

To validate the intrinsic value approximation, one can compute the error $\epsilon(50)$ using the omission error formula above and find $\epsilon(50) \sim (\$0.1M)$.

This dividend discount model valuation approach is unusual for earlier-stage biopharma firms since they tend to have heavy R&D investment and no revenues early in the company lifecycle, making predictable dividends impractical.

2.1.3 Discounted Cash Flow to Equity

This method is used to directly assess the equity value of a company. The approach designation is derived from taking a shareholder's investor perspective. As we saw earlier, stockholders get what is left after the company has met its various liabilities as part of the firm's cash inflows might belong to debtholders.

When using this approach to value a stock price, we model the cash flows that are free to equity holders to withdraw from the firm; hence the designations Free Cash Flow to Equity (FCFE) and Discounted Cash Flow (DCF) valuation.

This approach uses the firm's fundamentals to assess the intrinsic value of its assets and liabilities. It is applicable when one can reasonably model what the products and services will generate as revenues and what will need to be spent to conduct R&D and operations over a relevant time frame (5–20 years). Revenues might include those from non-marketed products (e.g., licensing revenues).

This valuation approach requires estimates over the forecast time frame:

- Company's net income.
  - Obtained by estimating its underlying components: net sales, revenue from collaborations or grants, cost of goods sold (cost directly related to the items sold), distribution costs, operating expenses (R&D, sales, general, and administrative costs), non-operating expenses (items not linked to the day-to-day operations, including interest expenses the firms pays for its debt financing). If the company owes contractual payments (e.g., royalties impacting gross margin) to third parties in the context of a license agreement, these payments will also be considered in the forecast.
  - Tax on profits are included in the forecast (e.g., for a US entity, federal and state income tax).

- Various adjustments.
  - Costs that do not represent real cash flows, i.e., accruals for stock-based compensation, depreciation, and amortization.
  - Capital expenditures: any new capital the firm needs to spend on major investment (equipment, facilities).
  - Changes in working capital due to the company's growth – calculated as current assets minus current liabilities, this can be expressed as a percentage of net sales. Current assets are assets expected to convert to cash within a year whereas current liabilities are those liabilities expected to be paid to creditors within a year. Working capital thus represents the capital required to enable day-to-day operations within the year.
  - Any principal payment the company needs to make on existing debt.
  - Any additional debt the company takes on.

These various estimates will provide an estimate of the free cash flows to equity (FCFE) over the time frame in question.

Entries and calculations are typically provided in a table, such as Table 2.1. For simplicity, only five years are shown in that specific table.

Since debt has been factored in, the cash flows obtained represent what is left to equity holders.

Two further elements are required for this FCFE valuation approach:

- Terminal value defined as the residual value of the company at the end of the forecast time frame.
- Equity discount rate defined as the required rate of return for shareholders.

The terminal value (TV) is often estimated using a stable growth model:

$$TV = \frac{FCFE_{n+1}}{d - g}$$

Equation 2.4 FCFE TV.

where

- n is the number of years in your previous forecast time frame, so that $FCFE_{n+1}$ is the FCFE the year following the last year of the forecast time frame,
- d is the equity discount rate,
- g is the growth rate in FCFE past the forecast time frame. Note that, for this to make sense, $g<d$.

Table 2.1 Free cash flow to equity template

	Year 1	*Year 2*	*Year 3*	*Year 4*	*Year 5*
Revenues					
Cost of Goods Sold (COGS)					
Distribution Cost (Distr)					
Gross Profit (GP = Rev – COGS – Distr)	*Calculated*	*Calculated*	*Calculated*	*Calculated*	*Calculated*
Operating Expenses (OE)					
Operating Income (OI = GP – OE)	*Calculated*	*Calculated*	*Calculated*	*Calculated*	*Calculated*
Non-Operating Expenses (NOE)					
Income before Tax (IBT = OI – NOE)	*Calculated*	*Calculated*	*Calculated*	*Calculated*	*Calculated*
Tax (T = –IBT * effective tax rate)	*Calculated*	*Calculated*	*Calculated*	*Calculated*	*Calculated*
Net Income (NI = IBT – T)	*Calculated*	*Calculated*	*Calculated*	*Calculated*	*Calculated*
Depreciation & Amortization (DA)					
New Capital Spending (NCS)					
Change in working capital (ΔWC) with increase >0					
Operating Cash Flow (OCF = NI + DA – NCS – ΔWC)	*Calculated*	*Calculated*	*Calculated*	*Calculated*	*Calculated*
Principal debt repayment (DR)					
New debt issue (ND)					
Free Cash Flow to Equity (FCFE =OCF – DR + ND)	*Calculated*	*Calculated*	*Calculated*	*Calculated*	*Calculated*

The equity discount rate is the minimum return (hurdle rate) that an investor is expecting to receive for their investment in equity, which is a function of the level of risk assumed by the investor when investing. An appropriate discount rate must be applied to the FCFE. The equity discount rate ***d*** is often estimated using what is called a Capital Asset Pricing Model (CAPM):

$$d = r_f + \beta\left(r_m - r_f\right)$$

Equation 2.5 CAPM.

where

- r_f is the expected rate of return for risk-free investments. Long-term government bond rates are often used as proxy: analysts may use the Yield on 20-Year US Treasury Rate as risk-free rate, which is considered risk-free since backed by the US government.
- β is a measure of the non-diversifiable risk corresponding to the company (β is also a measure of the stock volatility compared to the market, which means if $\beta > 1$, the value of the stock will tend to increase or decrease more than the market average does).
- r_m is the expected market return, making $\left(r_m - r_f\right)$ the equity risk premium for the market risk involved – i.e., how much of an additional reward (compared to a no-risk investment), the investors will want to receive in order to take the additional risk inherent to the specific market.

Note that for a private company, obtaining a value for β is not straightforward. In practice, industry professionals will use an industry average β that best mimics the company's characteristics or, alternatively, the β of a comparable publicly listed company.

Case Example: Cost of Equity Calculation for Sarepta Therapeutics Inc (NASDAQ: SRPT, December 30, 2022)

Table 2.2 Illustrative CAPM calculation

r_f	4.14% (U.S. Department of the Treasury)
β	1.04 (Morningstar, 2022)
$\left(r_m - r_f\right)$	6.0% (Nunes et al.)
Cost of Equity	10.38% = 4.14% + 1.04* 6.0%

Complementary risk factors may be relevant: a size risk premium might be added if the company is in the bottom deciles of market capitalization (Ibbotson & Harrington, 2021), as CAPM might not fully account for higher returns expected of smaller companies.

When an investment is illiquid given contractual limitations on selling the stock (e.g., restricted stock) or when a specific investment might be difficult to market to third parties in order to sell it, it is customary to discount the final valuation to reflect the illiquidity. Such considerations can be empirical in nature however, and the use of a discount will always need to be justified. There are diverse approaches available to support the estimation of discount for lack of marketability. An option-based method is commonly used by analysts as the protective put method first described by Chaffe (2013) or the modified put analysis model developed by Finnerty (2012).

Now, we are finally able to provide the valuation for the stock price:

$$\text{Intrinsic value of the stock} = \frac{1}{S}\left[\left(\sum_{k=1}^{n}\frac{\text{FCFE}_k}{(1+d)^k}\right)+\frac{TV}{(1+d)^n}\right]$$

Equation 2.6 FCFE stock price intrinsic value.

where

- FCFE_k is the FCFE for the year k.
- d is the equity discount rate.
- TV is the terminal value, as provided above.
- S is the number of outstanding common stock for the company.
- The discount factor used in any year k is given by the formula: $1/(1+d)^k$.

Optional Mid-Year Convention Adjustment

Financial analysts may apply a mid-year convention assuming that in any given year, cash flows are generated at the midpoint of the period instead of the end-of-year discount approach above, to provide for a more realistic scenario. Using the same notations as above:

$$\text{Intrinsic value of the stock} = \frac{1}{S}\left[\left(\sum_{k=1}^{n}\frac{\text{FCFE}_k}{(1+d)^{k-0.5}}\right)+\frac{\text{TV}}{(1+d)^{n-0.5}}\right]$$

Equation 2.7 Stock price intrinsic value using mid-year convention.

Case Example: Fictional Stock Valuation Using FCFE

Table 2.3 FCFE of fictional company with yearly revenue growth of 4%

(US$M)	*Year 1*	*Year 2*	*Year 3*	*Year 4*	*Year 5*
Revenues	$182	$189	$197	$205	$213
Yearly Growth, %	-	4%	4%	4%	4%
Cost of Goods Sold (COGS)	$33	$34	$35	$37	$38
Distribution Cost	$18	$5	$5	$5	$5
Gross Profit (GP = Rev – COGS – Dist. Cost)	*$131*	*$150*	*$156*	*$163*	*$169*
% of Revenues	*72%*	*80%*	*80%*	*80%*	*80%*
Operating Expenses (OE)	$7	$10	$35	$37	$38
% of Revenues	*4%*	*5%*	*18%*	*18%*	*18%*
Operating Income (OI = GP – OE)	*$124*	*$140*	*$121*	*$126*	*$131*
Non-Operating Expenses (NOE)	$3	$4	$5	$6	$7
Income before Tax	*$121*	*$137*	*$116*	*$120*	*$124*
Tax *(assuming illustrative tax rate of 23%)*	$28	$31	$27	$28	$28
Net Income (NI = OI – NOE - Tax)	*$93*	*$105*	*$90*	*$92*	*$95*
Depreciation & Amortization (DA)	$8	$10	$11	$11	$11
New Capital Spending (NCS)	$8	$10	$6	$7	$8
Change in working capital (rWC)	(1)	(1)	(2)	(2)	(2)
Operating Cash Flow (=NI + DA – NCS - rWC)	*$92*	*$104*	*$93*	*$95*	*$97*
Principal debt repayment (DR)	-	-	$4	$4	$4
New debt issue (ND)	$40	$20	-	-	-
FCFEk (=NI + DA – NCS – rWC – DR + ND)	*$132*	*$124*	*$89*	*$91*	*$93*
Discounting parameter *k*	0.5	1.5	2.5	3.5	4.5
DF = Discount factor 1/(1+*d*)^*k*, assuming *d* = 7.0%	0.97	0.90	0.84	0.79	0.74
Discounted value of FCFEk (= FCFE * DF)	*$128*	*$112*	*$75*	*$72*	*$69*

Sum of Discounted value of FCFEk	*$455*	*21%*
Discounted Terminal Value (assuming g = 4%)	*$1,754*	*79%*
Total Intrinsic Value of Equity	***$2,209***	***100%***
S = number of outstanding common stock	*50,000,000*	
Intrinsic Value of the Stock	***$44.19***	

This example provided in Table 2.3 used a short forecast horizon of 5 years for presentation purposes, resulting in a large terminal value worth 79% of the total value of equity. With a 15-year horizon and identical assumptions, the terminal value's weight would be reduced to 39%.

This TV-based model, best used for a biopharma company with commercial revenues and a diversified portfolio of marketed products or stable income from services, would be less appropriate for smaller biopharma companies:

a Only biopharma companies that are at a very advanced stage own marketed products, and their portfolio is generally concentrated on a few products.
b Smaller biopharma companies must support heavy R&D expenses as well as general and administrative (G&A) expenses and generate yearly losses during the mid-term forecast horizon.

For the valuation of such biopharma companies, practitioners use a forecast over a longer horizon (typically 20 years in line with the duration of a patent protection), and they model the commercial revenues and costs *over the lifecycle of the main company's products*, based on assumed commercial launch, ramp-up until patent expiry, then sales erosion. R&D costs forecast is established for the main products. Services revenues and unallocated costs (other R&D and G&A) are then added to complete the financial projection. The TV is used only when justified by commercially established products (for example, when a product is switched from prescription to over-the-counter).

2.1.4 Comparable Company Analysis

Doing a stock valuation using a comparable company analysis consists in using company ratios and stock prices from comparable companies. As opposed to the FCFE approach, this method, also named "Guideline Public Company Method", does not use company fundamental/internal performance forecasts to evaluate a stock intrinsic value but rather uses the price of known companies. The usual challenge with this approach is the identification of comparable companies and suitable ratios. Ratios often used in other industries to establish an intrinsic stock value include the price to earnings ratio and the enterprise value to EBITDA (Earnings before Interest, Tax, Depreciation, and Amortization) ratio. For early biopharma companies without revenue, those ratios cannot be used as the companies do not have positive earnings.

What is often done is to try and find equivalent publicly traded companies. Equivalent companies are defined as similar along all the following dimensions:

- Technology/therapeutic area (e.g., cell therapy for oncology).
- Stage of development for lead product (e.g., Phase I or Phase II) and pipeline.
- Market segments and commercial potential.
- Size of the company (employees, international presence, pipeline depth).

When starting a valuation approach based on comparable companies, one should:

- Select comparable companies based on the specificities of each selected company and their relative position within the same sector.
- Attempt and delineate causes that might positively or negatively explain their relative performance in multiples (and how business drivers might have influenced such multiples over time).
- Check the accounting consistency behind the financial aggregates used to measure the financial performance of each selected company.

Traditional sources of information for such analyses include analyst reports, industry reports, and specialized subscription databases. Private company data may also be used for such comparable analyses when available.

Comparable Stock Valuation Using P/E Ratio

The Price Earnings Ratio (P/E ratio) is often used to compare the relative price of a company's stock to similar companies within a given industry segment. This is because for the most part, firms competing in a given industry will tend to have similar business and earnings patterns, making such ratio an insightful lens into a company's relative value.

The P/E ratio is typically calculated in one of two ways:

P/E ratio = Market Capitalization/Total Net Earnings, or
P/E ratio = Stock Price Per Share/Earnings Per Share.

The two calculations above are equivalent since:

Market Capitalization = Number of Outstanding Common Shares × Stock Price Per Share, and
Total Net Earnings = Number of Outstanding Common Shares × Earnings Per Share.

As earnings multiple, the P/E ratio is intended to measure a company's viability and its potential to earn profits compared with peers. Earnings multiple ratios are meaningful for firms with positive earnings since the goal is to evaluate the profitable stage.

The inverse of P/E ratio, called Earnings Yield (= Earnings Per Share/ Stock Price Per Share), likewise provides a representation of a company's potential to earn profits compared with peers.

P/E ratios are used either based on trailing or forward earnings. The trailing P/E is based on the last 12 months earnings divided by the weighted-average shares outstanding over that period, whereas the forward P/E ratio is based on future earnings estimates (i.e., next 12 months).

The last 12 months or future periods are typically adjusted to align with financial quarters: in February, looking at a company with a fiscal year ending in December, the trailing P/E will be based on January through December of the previous year and the forward P/E will be based on January through December of the current year.

Such comparisons have limitations: significant depreciation or other non-cash expenses can distort the analysis. Using other metrics like the EV/ EBITDA ratio described below might alleviate these limitations.

A high Price Earnings Ratio is often representative of "growth stocks" as it implies favorable future trending. It indicates that investors have high expectations, justified or not, of future earnings, accepting a higher price point per unit of past (or projected) earnings.

The P/E ratio can also be used to value a private company – or business unit – by utilizing the average P/E of a group of equivalent publicly traded companies. Ranges between high and low measuring points should be used to expose the level of uncertainty based on the valuation of other companies, as well as the value creation that might result from higher growth expectations (since growth stocks are associated with higher P/E ratios).

Case Example: Comparable Valuation Using P/E Ratio

If a group of equivalent listed companies shows an average trailing P/E ratio of 23 and a forward P/E ratio of 24, we can multiply these indicators by the earnings of the private company to obtain its valuation range:

The example (Table 2.4) assumes comparable expectations to the competition or the sector for Private Company A. Note the discount used for lack of marketability as private companies are harder to trade, and thus bear more risk than public counterparts traded in an active stock exchange. Often, investors and equity analysts apply a discount factor to private companies due to this lack of marketability. The discount may be company-specific but consensus ranges from 30% to 50%.

Table 2.4 Equity value using P/E ratio

US$ millions	*Valuation using trailing P/E*	*Valuation using forward P/E*
P/E Ratio (Sector Average or Median)	23	24
Private Company A's Earnings: (= E)		
Earnings 12 previous months (year N)	$22.4	
Expected Earnings for year N+1		$32.5
Implied Market Value of Equity (MVE =P/E Ratio * E)	$515	$780
Discount Factor for Lack of Marketability (=D)	30%	30%
Implied Equity Value of Private Company A (=MVE * (1 – D))	$361	$546

Comparable Stock Valuation Using EV/EBITDA Ratio

The EV/EBITDA ratio measures the relation between a company's Enterprise Value (EV) and its Earnings Before Interest, Taxes, Depreciation & Amortization (EBITDA). The EV/EBITDA ratio is widely used to compare the relative value of different companies, in complement to other methods.

The EV can be calculated as follows: EV = Equity + Debt – Cash

where the equity value is measured by the market capitalization = stock price * total number of outstanding stocks.

The EBITDA represents a company's profits or earnings without non-cash elements such as depreciation and amortization and is viewed as an approximation of the cash flow generated by the business on an annual basis (before interest and taxes).

The EV/EBITDA ratio thus shows how many times investors would have to pay its EBITDA value to acquire the entire business (e.g., 10 times, written as "10x").

Note that EV is derived from market capitalization, influenced by the market perception of different firms. A higher multiple can be caused by a higher expected growth rate or lower risk factors.

As with the P/E ratio, the EV/EBITDA multiple can be used, in complement to other valuation approaches, to value a private company by utilizing the average multiple of equivalent publicly listed companies. Unlike the P/E ratio, the EV/EBITDA ratio is not affected by the capital structure of companies (earnings are affected by interest payments whereas EBITDA is not), so many analysts consider EV/EBITDA to more reliably measure the ability of companies to generate long-term profits.

EV/EBITDA multiple valuation should be used with caution as it does not factor in the differences in capital expenditures between companies, and it can be difficult to compare companies with different growth rates, different market positioning, product mix, etc.

Other multiples like the Enterprise Value/Revenue ratio would raise fewer comparability issues than the previous two ratios. It is common to look at median values for the EV/Revenue ratio in a specific segment of the biopharma industry (median being less sensitive than average to outliers/extreme cases), often as a consistency check on earnings-based multiples.

EV/EBITDA and EV/Revenue multiple methods are frequent valuation approaches used to guide investment decisions, when relevant, and should be complemented by other methods.

Case Example: Company A Stock Comparable Valuation

Private company designated "Company A" developed a cell therapy technology platform that allowed them to build a pipeline of drug programs. The lead compound expects readout of Phase 1 in 3 months and the other programs are either at preclinical or research stages. After reviewing public companies, the group portrayed in Table 2.5 appeared reasonably close to Company A in terms of pipeline, development stage, and technology, thereby constituting a set of comparable companies.

Table 2.5 lists the market capitalization 200-Day equal to the 200-Day stock price moving average times the number of shares outstanding as of the evaluation date, in order to limit the effect of short-term trends. The term "moving average" indicates that every day, the average is updated by replacing the oldest number by the most recent. The market cap 50-Day is also provided.

Net cash is obtained by subtracting the cash position from the debt as of December 31, 2021, according to the company's annual report balance sheet statement.

Lastly, the enterprise value is obtained by subtracting that net cash position from the market capitalization.

This small group of similar listed company valuations provides for an average enterprise value of US$140m with a US$127m median and a US$65m–$242m range.

Assuming Company A has 10 million shares outstanding and a net cash position of US$100 million, this comparable analysis implies a share valuation in the US$10–US$23 range (Table 2.6).

In addition to providing rough estimates of stock prices using comparable companies, such a method is useful as a consistency check for other valuation methods. It is best to use the following practices:

Table 2.5 Comparable companies selected as of May 2022

Company	*Technology/TA*	*Main assets – stage*	*Employees*	*Market cap 50-Day (US$m)*	*Market cap 200-Day (US$m)*	*Net cash (US$m)*	*Enterprise value 200-Day (US$m)*
Magenta Therapeutics, Inc. (MGTA)	Hematopoietic stem cells (HSCs) transplants	• MGTA-117 – Phase I/II • MGTA-145 GTx SCD – Ph. II • CD45- ADC – IND enabling	75	$138m	$284m	$177m	$107m
Actinium Pharmaceuticals, Inc. (ATNM)	Bone marrow transplant (BMT), and other adoptive cell therapies	• CD45 BMT I-131 – Phase III • CD45 GTx, Cell Th. – Phase I • CD33 AML - Phase I	32	$124m	$143m	$78m	$65m
Molecular Templates, Inc. (MTEM)	Engineered toxin body (ETB) drug platform	• MT-5111 – Phase I • MT-0169 – Phase I • MT-6402 – Phase I	261	*$133m*	$242m	$95m	$147m
Adaptimmune Therapeutics plc (ADAP)	Peptide enhanced affinity receptor (SPEAR) T-cell therapies platform	• MAGE-A4 afami-cel – Filing • ADP-A2M4CD8– Ph. II/ • AFP-ADP-A2AFP– Phase I	494	*$311m*	$586m	$344m	$242m

Table 2.6 Company A comparable valuation

Enterprise value range	Less: net debt, or plus: net cash of Company A	Implied equity value of Company A	Total shares out standing of Company A	Implied value per share	Discount for lack of marketability	**Implied value per share for Company A**
$65M - $242M	$100M	$165M – $342M	10M	$16.50 – $34.20	35%	**$10.73 – $22.23**

- The starting sample, used to find equivalent companies, should avoid selection bias. The selection should include the public companies that operate in the same or comparable line of business, at a similar stage of development. Ideally, the selected companies should present undisputable similarities in terms of technology, stage of development, market segments, pipeline, and partnerships.
- When applied to a private company, the analysis should include the use of a discount for lack of marketability to reflect its illiquidity.

2.1.5 *Precedent Transactions Analysis*

Precedent transaction analysis or establishing a stock valuation using Merger and Acquisition ("M&A") transactions consists in using the prices at which companies (or operating units of companies) have been sold to derive indications of company value.

Similar to the "Comparable Company Analysis", the "Precedent Transactions Analysis" (also called "Guideline Company Transactions Method", or "Guideline Merged and Acquired Company Method") uses a multiple-based approach to derive an implied range of company valuation.

The approach encompasses the following six steps:

Step 1: Selection of M&A transactions using disclosure filings or online databases. The main challenge of this approach is the identification of comparable acquired companies along with suitable ratios. The companies selected for comparison should be part of the same sector and have known performance indicators.

Step 2: Collection of aggregate purchase price for each selected transaction ("comps"). Such price is either expressed as *equity value* (transaction price strictly limited to the acquisition target's equity) or as *enterprise value* (transaction price encompassing the target's equity and its net debt).

Step 3: Collection of performance indicators for each comparable transaction. Revenues, EBIT ("Earnings Before Interest, Tax"), EBITDA

("Earnings Before Interest, Tax, Depreciation, and Amortization"), Earnings (or "Net Income") are most typical. Adjustments for material non recurring items may be made to these indicators

Step 4: Calculation of the relevant transaction multiple *for each selected transaction*. Table 2.7 provides the most common multiples.
The Enterprise value/EBITDA multiple is most common as it is not distorted by differences in non-cash expenses like depreciation and amortization. EBIT is used in situations where depreciation and amortization are unavailable.

Step 5: Calculation of multiple mean, median, and range for the selected transactions.

Step 6: Value calculation. The implied company value is calculated by multiplying the multiple (calculated in Step 5 as mean, median, or range) by that company's underlying performance indicator (i.e., company's actual performance indicator for the multiple's denominator).

Table 2.7 Transaction multiples

Multiple	*Formula*
Equity value	$\frac{\text{Equity value of transaction}}{\text{Net Income}}$
EV/EBITDA	$\frac{\text{Enterprise value of transaction}}{\text{EBITDA}}$
EV/EBIT	$\frac{\text{Enterprise value of transaction}}{\text{EBIT}}$
EV/Revenue	$\frac{\text{Enterprise value of transaction}}{\text{Revenue}}$

Case Example: Precedent Transactions Valuation

Fictitious company NewLabs owns a large, diversified portfolio of OTC and branded generic products in several countries. Last fiscal year, it recorded US$2,100M in revenue, 21% EBITDA margin, US$350M net debt, and no material non-recurring items. EV/EBITDA and EV/Revenue are both suitable metrics for NewLabs's sector valuation.

Precedent transactions for diversified pharmaceutical companies shows average EV/EBITDA ranging from 8.4× to 10.5× and average EV/Revenue from 1.8× to 2.1×.

Using a precedent transactions valuation approach provides an equity value range from US$3.4B to US$4.3B (Table 2.8).

Table 2.8 Precedent transaction equity value calculations

	Low	*High*
EV/EBITDA (comps) (=Multiple)	**8.4×**	**10.5×**
NewLabs EBITDA: (= E)	$440	$440
Implied NewLabs Enterprise Value (EV = Multiple * E)	$3,696	$4,620
NewLabs Net Debt	$300	$300
Implied NewLabs Equity Value	$3,396	$4,320
	Low	*High*
EV/Revenue (comps) (=Multiple)	**1.8x**	**2.1x**
NewLabs Revenue: (= R)	$2,100	$2,100
Implied NewLabs Enterprise Value (EV = Multiple * R)	$3,780	$4,410
NewLabs Net Debt	$300	$300
Implied NewLabs Equity Value	$3,480	$4,110

2.1.6 *Options*

Although common, options represent a sophisticated concept for biopharma and other industries.

An option can be defined as a contract giving its owner the right but not the obligation to buy (those are called a call option) or to sell (those are called a put option) an underlying asset or interest at a specific price on or before a certain date.

Options are used to value future uncertain opportunities, like the opportunity for a large pharma to license or acquire a biotech development program in the future depending on their Phase 2 results whereas Phase 2 has not started yet. This approach can be used to assess the value for a biotech firm to benefit from future yet uncertain opportunities.

Other common option instances include stock options granted to key biopharma employees as part of their compensation package. Such options allow the employees to purchase stock at a predefined price (called strike price) over a certain period of time and typically vest over time (meaning they acquire the rights to effectively exercise such options over time, like over 3 or 4 years, as employees remain with the company).

There are several valuation methods that can be used for options, including the following:

- Binomial option model.
- Black-Scholes option model.
- Monte Carlo approach.

The binomial option model is based on a binary approach that defines up or down incremental movements for the asset value (hence the name binomial) whereas Black-Scholes uses a normal distribution approach for the outcomes. In contrast, the Monte Carlo approach uses random variations to simulate realistic input. While we will not get into the technical comparisons of these methods, we will illustrate the use of options for biopharma with Black-Scholes.

Black-Scholes Valuation Model

$$\text{Value of call option} = S\ N(d_1) - Ke^{-rt}\ N(d_2)$$

Equation 2.8 Call option value.

where $d_1 = \dfrac{ln\left(\dfrac{S}{K}\right)+\left(r+\dfrac{\sigma^2}{2}\right)t}{\sigma\sqrt{t}}$, $d_2 = d_1 - \sigma\sqrt{t}$ and N() designates the cumulative standardized normal distribution values, with the following five input variables:

- S is the current value of the underlying asset (e.g., the current stock price for stock options).
- K is the strike price of the option.
- t is the life of the option (also called "time to maturity" or "time to expiration").
- r is the risk-free interest rate for the life of the option t.
- σ^2 is the variance in the ln logarithm value of the underlying asset. σ represents the volatility of the asset (it is technically the standard deviation of the log returns for the asset).

This model is meant for options on non-dividend-paying marketable common stocks when the options can only be exercised on the expiration date. If the company is expected to pay constant dividends until the option term, the present value of the dividends expected to be paid during the remaining term of the option has to be deducted from the stock price.

Note that, using the same notations as above, the value of the corresponding put option can be calculated as

$$Ke^{-rt}\ N(-d_2) - S\ N(-d_1).$$

Equation 2.9 Put option value.

Case Example: Vertex Pharmaceuticals Incorporated (VRTX) Stock Option Valuation Using Black-Scholes

Under US GAAP and IFRS, the notes to the financial statements show the total value of all employee stock options outstanding, using estimated market value from option valuation models.

Vertex 2021 annual report (Form 10-K) provides the information summarized in Table 2.9.

Using Black-Scholes Equation 2.8 and Microsoft Excel, one might arrive at that same average stock option value (within a rounding error margin), as illustrated in Figures 2.3 and 2.4.

Closely held early-stage companies might present additional valuation difficulties for stock options. Yet, such valuations might be required by regulations (e.g., IRC 409A in the United States). The AICPA Audit and

Table 2.9 Vertex 2021 annual report option stated value

Company (ticker)	Expected volatility	Expected term in years	Risk-free interest rate	Expected dividend yield	Weighted-average exercise price	Market price of common stock (on the grant date)	Weighted-average grant-date fair value per share
VRTX	35.03%	4.5	0.86%	—	US$217.20	US$217.20	US$65.94

	A	B	C	D	E	F	G	H	I
1	S = 217.2	in USD $		ln (S/K)	= LN(B1/B2)			exp(-r*t)	=EXP(-B4*B3)
2	K = 217.2	in USD $		r + σ^2 / 2 =	B4+B5^2/2				
3	t = 4.5	in years		σ * sqrt(t)=	B5*SQRT(B3)				
4	r = 0.0086	percentage							
5	σ = 0.3503	percentage		d1 =	= ((LN((B1/B2)))+(B4+(B5^2)/2)*B3)/(B5*SQRT(B3))			N(d1) =	= GAUSS(F5)+0.5
6				d2=	= F5-(B5*SQRT(B3))			N(d2) =	= GAUSS(F6)+0.5
7									
8				**Value =**	**= B1*I5-(B2*(EXP(-B4*B3))*I6)**		**in USD $**		
9									

Figure 2.3 Vertex 2021 annual report option value formulas in Excel.

S =	$ 217.20	in USD $	ln (S/K)	0.00000	exp(-r*t)	0.962039
K =	$ 217.20	in USD $	r + σ^2 / 2	7.00%		
t =	4.50	in years	σ * sqrt(t)	0.74310		
r =	0.86%	percentage				
σ =	35.03%	percentage	d1 =	0.42363	N(d1) =	0.66408
			d2=	-0.31947	N(d2) =	0.37469
Value =	**$65.94**	***in USD $***				

Figure 2.4 Vertex 2021 annual report option calculated value using Excel.

Accounting Practice Aid, entitled Valuation of Privately Held Company Equity Securities Issued as Compensation (AICPA, 2016) contains guidance for the allocation of value between preferred equity and common equity. The option pricing method ("OPM") is one of the methodologies suggested by this Practice Aid for allocating this value.

2.2 Discovery-Stage Valuation

This section explores how to value a company, research library, platform, or discovery activity. Firms operating mostly or even solely in the discovery space may take very different approaches, including building lead libraries, reference libraries, delivery or discovery platforms, and biosimulation. Valuing a discovery portfolio can be challenging and require significant due diligence and judgment considering the very early-stage nature of the underlying activities. Given the ongoing evolution of the space and the wide variety of approaches, a systematic approach is not always practical. This said, below are some of the most common approaches in the authors' experience along with illustrative examples.

Valuation professionals exercise judgment to determine which valuation approaches are the most appropriate for the specific characteristics of the company at the valuation date. Ideally, professionals will try and use several approaches to triangulate a finer valuation with a higher degree of confidence.

2.2.1 Valuation Based on Success of Resulting Drug Candidates

One of the easiest ways around the valuation issue is to fall back to tying the valuation to future development success. When a discovery solution seems promising, a later stage biopharmaceutical company might enter into a research agreement and offer an "opt-in" payment on lead selection plus milestone-based payments tied to development. Such an approach essentially avoids the issue of valuation for early-stage discovery programs.

Indeed, the approach is built on a logical construct with relation between achievement and value, enabling the biopharmaceutical company to get more valuable assets for its money:

- The biopharmaceutical company pays only for success and cannot be forced to pay as the milestone attainment must be acknowledged.
- Milestone payments escalate in value as successive results are met.

With this construct, the value of the discovery solution is the probability to meet the predefined technical criteria that will trigger future contractual milestones in the context of one or several collaboration agreements, less the amount of research costs required to reach these triggering points.

Case Example: Discovery Research Collaboration

In 2020, AbCellera and Eli Lilly entered into an agreement to co-develop antibody products for the treatment and prevention of COVID-19. The collaboration leverages AbCellera's rapid pandemic response platform, developed under DARPA Pandemic Prevention Platform Program, and Lilly's global capabilities for rapid development, manufacturing, and distribution of therapeutic antibodies (Lilly, 2020).

Under the terms of the agreement, AbCellera and Lilly equally share initial development costs toward a product, after which Lilly is responsible for all further development, manufacturing, and distribution.

AbCellera received a US$15-million milestone payment from Lilly, plus US$198.3 million in royalties for the sale of doses in 2020 (Silcoff, 2021). Deal terms resulting from such transactions may constitute a notable portion of the valuation of biopharma companies such as AbCellera.

2.2.2 *Probability-Based or Model-Based Valuation*

A more sophisticated approach would be based on the scientific merits of the technology in terms of successful outcome probabilities, using benchmarks or known valuation estimates of such outcomes. When two or more outcomes (e.g., different compounds) are enabled by the technology, the various valuation estimates are simply added to one another.

This approach is often used to assess the potential value of a technology platform. The platform should be considered sufficiently mature, protected against the competition (by its innovative differentiation and IP protection), and productive to justify a value over a forecast horizon of at least 10 years. The approach assumes that enough R&D expenses and capital expenditures will be projected to maintain the technology over time.

Case Example: Technology Platform Valuation Approach

Let us take the case of an innovative biopharma company with a technology platform that generates an average of two drug candidates per year. These drug candidates can be either out-licensed to biopharmaceutical partners or developed in-house.

Based on the company's strategy, the valuation approach assumes that each year, one drug candidate is out-licensed while the other is developed in-house, applying the following model:

- Value from out-licensing: the valuation of out-licensed drug candidates is based on today's risk-adjusted value of future income (calculated using a measure defined later in Section 2.3.6: the risk-adjusted net present value or rNPV) for each new licensing agreement (upfront, milestones, royalties to be perceived upon achievement of future outcomes). Over the forecast horizon (which should be at least over 20 years to be able to forecast sales-based financial terms like royalties and sales milestones), future incomes will be staggered with an assumption of one new out-licensing agreement per year.

- Value from in-house programs: the valuation of the internal drug candidates is based on today's risk-adjusted value of future free cash flows per program (calculated using rNPV), with the assumption they will obtain IND and start the development. Each program will be modeled based on benchmarks:
  - Time per phase up to regulatory approval, probability, and R&D expenses per phase, based on industry averages.
  - Commercial forecast per product based on industry standards (typical commercial curve, peak of sales assumption per therapeutic indication, typical COGS, and commercial expenses as percentage of sales).
  - Applicable discount rate and tax rates used by the company.

As mentioned, the various valuation estimates are simply added to one another. Thus, the overall value of the technology platform is the sum of the risk-adjusted net present value of out-licensed programs and the risk-adjusted net present value of in-house programs. Note that to value the entire biopharma company, other non-program-related elements should be added to the valuation approach, such as grants that the company might receive, tax credits carried forward, non-allocated expenses, and capital expenditures over the forecast horizon.

Case Example: Partner-Only Technology Platform Valuation

Now let us take a similar example for a private platform company that never develops programs in-house but exclusively partners with biopharma companies that then take on development and commercialization. We defined the following simplified financial elements as of January 2022:

- Forecast horizon over 20 years from 2023 to 2042.
- Past activities: partnerships with 95 biopharma companies representing 425 therapeutic programs, out of which 55 have entered clinical stage, and one product had been approved.
- Future activities: range of 15–25 programs per year (assuming a yearly progression of 3%) and an average of two successful programs per deal.
- Standardized partner program and probabilities model (Table 2.10).
- "Reference net sales curve" with US$800M peak sales per successful program.
- Operating expenses represent an average benchmark rate of 15% of revenue, decreasing from 32% to 10% over the forecast horizon.
- Fixed corporate income tax of 23%.
- Capital expenditures of US$20M per year.
- Corporate discount rate of 10% plus 3% incremental discount for lack of marketability.

Table 2.10 Standardized partner program model

	Deal terms (US$M)	*Probability to reach next phase*	*Market authorization probability*
Upfront	1.8	100%	5%
Milestone Research1	0.6	50%	5%
Milestone Research2	0.6	100%	9%
Milestone at IND	1.5	60%	9%
Ph1 result Milestone	2.5	80%	16%
Ph2 result Milestone	5.0	31%	19%
Ph3 result Milestone	15.0	66%	63%
Milestone upon Approval	40.0	95%	95%
Sales Milestone1 (sales ≥ US$250M)	25.0	100%	100%
Sales Milestone2 (sales ≥ US$500M)	50.0	100%	100%
Sales Milestone3 (sales ≥ US$1B)	75.0	100%	100%
Royalties	5.0%	100%	100%

Under these assumptions, a risk-adjusted Net Present Value of future cash flows (explained later in Section 2.3.6) provides a financial valuation of US$2.2B for the company (US$2.8B for out-licensing operations minus US$0.6B for operating expenses and capital expenditures).

Adimab, headquartered in Lebanon, NH might be considered as an example of company using such technology platform approach as of 2022.

2.2.3 *Valuation Based on Comparable Deals*

A way to value early-stage activities is to look at what the market paid for them in the past. Such an approach, while not really assessing the underlying value of the discovery activities and assets, has the merit of being pragmatic in terms of what it would take to acquire them from a supply and demand market perspective. The comparison with relevant precedent transactions helps assess market prices for similar R&D programs in similar geographies/markets.

Case Example: Comparable Discovery Valuation

The research and collaboration transactions in Table 2.11 were deemed relevant as they met the required characteristics of antibody-conjugated technology in oncology at the preclinical stage.

Excluding one low-value outlier, this example indicates that the transaction might on average fetch US$20m upfront with milestones in the low US$400m range. Such an approach provides useful insights but requires a sample of recent similar situations.

Table 2.11 Comparable transactions

Licensor/Licensee	*Deal year*	*Description of transaction*	*Upfront*	*Milestones*	*Royalties (max rate)*
CytomX Therapeutics/ AbbVie	04-2016	Co-development/ co-promotion	US$30 m	US$470 m	US profit share Ex-US tiered double-digit
LegoChem Biosciences/Pyxis	01-2021	Exclusive license	US$9.5 m	US$285 m	Royalties (unspecified)
LegoChem Biosciences/CStone	10-2020	Exclusive license	US$10 m	US$353 m	Tiered royalties (unspecified)
CytomX/Pfizer	06-2013	Collaboration & Exclusive license	US$25 m	US$610 m	Tiered double-digit royalties
MultiCell/Oxis Biotech	*03-2015*	*Collaboration & Exclusive license*	*US$0.5 m*	*US$13 m*	*3%*

2.2.4 *Valuation Based on Costs*

Another approach consists in evaluating the cost savings resulting from avoiding corresponding drug discovery activities. It involves costing out what it would take to achieve the same discovery outcomes without the benefits of the technology considered for acquisition, licensing, or partnership. This approach can be used at a very early stage of a spin-off company for example.

Case Example: Cost-Based Discovery Valuation of Intellectual Property Rights Licensed by a Company

Due diligence provided an assessment that a team of 5 researchers would be necessary during a period of 36 months, to build an equivalent intellectual property with sufficient freedom to operate, for a total estimated cost of US$2,350,000, including full salary cost and laboratory supplies costs, equipment, which represents the fair value of these rights.

2.3 Development-Stage Valuation

In this section, we adopt the perspective of a company, seeking to measure the value of its individual programs on behalf of its shareholders. We use the term "program" to designate the development and commercialization of an asset toward a specific indication. Such an asset could be a combination therapy, a single drug, a biological product, or digital therapeutics. A program typically consists of several clinical studies and other key development activities that may or may not run concurrently. Larger biopharma firms or technology platform biopharma companies will have a portfolio of programs whereas smaller biopharma firms might have a single program.

Past the discovery phase, successfully managing programs represents the "bread and butter" operational activities of biopharmaceutical companies and one of the main avenues through which they create value. Such operational execution is regulatory-compliant, scientifically based, cross-functional, and strongly process-driven while serving as an important model input for valuation and deal considerations.

2.3.1 *Objectives and Principles of the Net Present Value*

Net Present Value (NPV) is another term commonly employed to designate a Discounted Cash Flow (DCF) approach.

An essential characteristic of NPV is its additive property, which allows financial analysts to add up the intrinsic value of various programs into an overall company model: the NPV for combined programs A and B is equal to the sum of program A's NPV and program B's NPV. This also allows to compare A and B within the company's portfolio. Prior to considering the

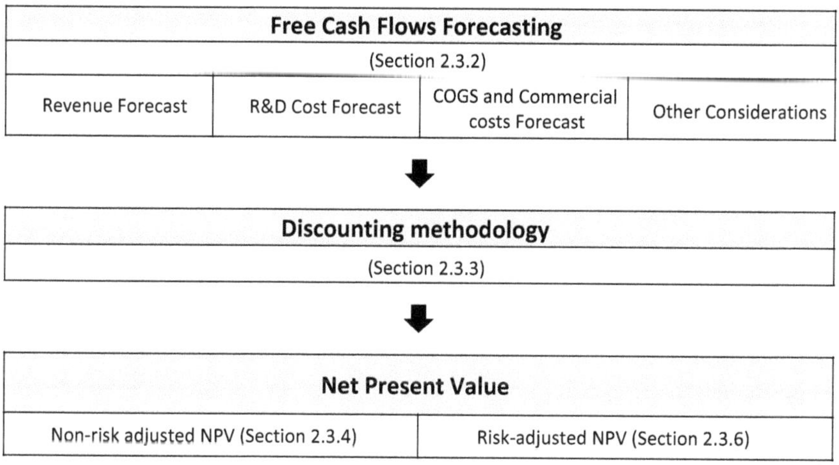

Figure 2.5 NPV calculation process.

aggregation of various programs, we will focus the remainder of this section on the biopharma asset program level (i.e., a specific compound that the company intends to develop and bring to market for a specific indication only).

Relation between NPV and value creation: if a program's NPV is strictly positive, the investment opportunity creates value. If it is negative, it destroys value unless nonquantifiable benefits have been excluded from the calculation.

The following sections explain how to calculate such an NPV as portrayed in Figure 2.5.

2.3.2 *Forecasting Free Cash Flows*

Revenue Forecast

There are two types of revenues to consider in the biopharma environment:

- Projected revenues from marketed products.
- Other revenues such as income from collaborations, licenses, and grants.

The former might require building a predictive revenue model based on projects' expectations while the latter would typically be linked to specific contractual agreements.

As illustrated in Figure 2.6, when estimating and forecasting commercial revenues, biopharma companies typically build a market-based revenue forecast leveraging three types of sources:

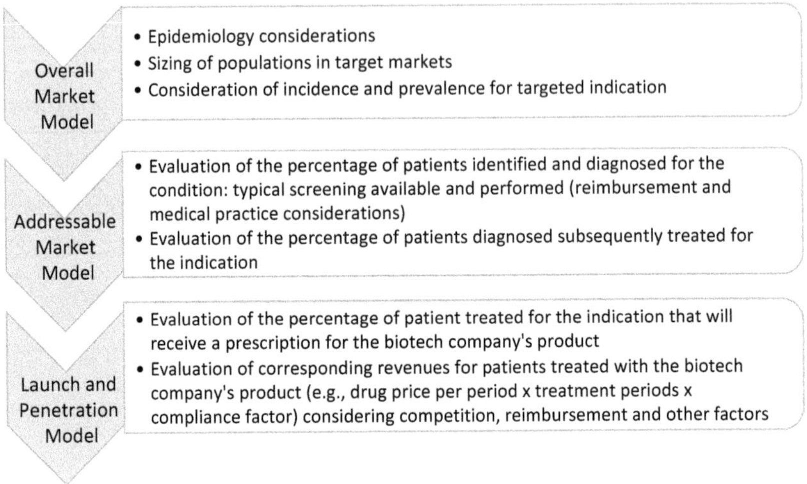

Figure 2.6 Conceptual market-based revenue forecasting model.

- In-house assumptions based on the company's scientific and market research.
- Secondary research from analysts, market research firms, or industry reports.
- Performance analogies to similar products over time.

Modeling the overall market demand consists of using epidemiology data to define the relevant target patients' population segment. This patient-based model will use key country statistics regarding prevalence, incidence by age group, and gender. Prevalence is defined as the proportion of a population with specific target characteristics in a given time period, whereas incidence designates the number of new occurrences for the disease, injury, or other medical conditions over a specified period.

The total market demand estimates should factor underdiagnosis (e.g., symptoms may not be apparent in children below 5), treatment relevance (e.g., disease might only affect certain age groups or gender), country-specific aspects (e.g., access to diagnosis and treatment), and population growth by segment.

The smaller addressable market takes into account patients for whom the therapeutic approach would be relevant, especially to justify deeper penetration or increased efficacy.

Assessing the expected market share within the target patient population or addressable market consists in evaluating the different classes of current and prospective treatments that represent competitive alternative therapeutic approaches. The proportion of patients receiving each product treatment within each class needs to be estimated. The positioning of the new product versus current and future alternative is evaluated based on relative product profiles. Major considerations include:

- Targeted label versus standard of care and relevant comparators.
- Prescriber segmentation, actual physician prescribing factors.
- Market entry order.
- Competitive differentiation versus other products in class, in terms of efficacy, safety profile, or convenience.
- Other factors such as system enablers and barriers to adoption.

Getting from expected market share to units sold estimates requires ancillary considerations, such as patient compliance, treatment frequency, and underlying causes. Treatment compliance is usually a factor in the revenue model, especially for medication that require consistent and reliable use (e.g., auto-injectables).

The last step in the revenue model is product price, often determined by analogy to other products. When applicable, a distinction is made between gross price and net price, the difference being an assumption on rebates and discounts generally negotiated with healthcare providers.

Case Example: Patient-Based Revenue Forecast

Let us consider a forecast for a fictitious Exon-Link product in the United States (a similar approach is usually done for additional relevant territories). Exon-Link is a potential orphan drug targeted at Duchenne Muscular Dystrophy in patients amenable to exon "N" skipping.

The revenue forecast is established in four steps:

1. Determination of the prevalent population for Exon-Link (Table 2.12).
2. Determination of the number of patients (Table 2.13).
3. Estimation of units sales (Table 2.14).
4. Revenues estimation (Table 2.15).

Such forecast, built for each year by relevant market territory, is based on complex assumptions, making the identification of major uncertainties critical to understanding the business case sensitivities. Here, the exceedingly high revenues per patient on a small number of patients would point to the need for strong due diligence regarding reimbursements and payments to validate the forecast.

Table 2.12 Estimated prevalent population

		Current year (2023)	*Launch year (2032)*	*Peak market share (2038)*	*End of forecast (2045)*
Total population – United States		The starting point of our patient-based model is the country-specific population forecast for each year covered in the forecast.			
	A	339,996,564	355,412,200	364,161,174	371,715,154
Population Males 5–24 years		Most individuals affected by the disease are male, between the ages of 5 and 24 years			
	B	16%	16%	16%	16%
	C = A * B	54,399,450	56,865,952	58,265,788	59,474,425
Prevalent population (D= Prevalence rate)		In North America, DMD prevalence is 6 per 100,000 individuals.			
	D	0.006%	0.006%	0.006%	0.006%
	E=C*D	3,264	3,412	3,496	3,568

R&D Costs Forecast

R&D costs include all operational costs related to internal tasks as well as sub-contracting costs and project management costs for the program. Payments related to licensed rights (i.e., upfront and milestone payments due before regulatory approval) may be expensed as R&D costs (acquired in-process R&D) or capitalized, depending on the accounting treatment (see Section 3.1.9). Non-allocated R&D costs may include leasing of equipment used by several programs, or costs associated with non-program-specific laboratory activities. G&A expenses (costs not related to direct operations) would not be recorded as R&D costs.

R&D costs and duration depend on key drivers:

- The size of clinical studies (size, costs, and timeline), the number of patients enrolled, the exclusion and inclusion criteria, the number of arms, the dose selection. Another important factor to consider is the use of solutions (AI-enabled or not) that might significantly reduce study costs and timelines.
- The Chemistry, Manufacturing, and Controls ("CMC"), including the production cost of clinical samples, which could represent more than 20% of overall clinical costs, depending on the type of compound and technology.

Table 2.13 Number of patients using the product

		Current year (2023)	*Launch year (2032)*	*Peak market share (2038)*	*End of forecast (2045)*
		Symptoms start ages 2–6. We assume patients to be diagnosed above age 5 (78% of prevalent population).			
Diagnosis rate (%)	F	78%	78%	78%	78%
Patients diagnosed with disease	G=E*F	2,545	2,660	2,726	2,782
Patients amenable to exon "N" skipping (%)		Exon 51 used as benchmark.			
	H	13%	13%	13%	13%
Patients eligible to treatment	I=G*H	331	346	354	362
		Assumption regarding patients with access to healthcare.			
Access rate (%)	J	85%	85%	85%	85%
Potential drug-treated patients	K=I*J	281	294	301	307
Market share assumptions		Market share evolution assumes a medium-to-rapid uptake curve based on expected product's differentiation: 1. Product has potential to be more efficient than standard of care, with a positive safety profile. 2. Monthly dosing (vs. weekly today) and intravenous (like competition). 3. Assumed market share curve is an uptake curve reaching the peak of market shares (75% in current scenario) in 2038 (6 years post-launch). 4. Peak market share in 2038 (patent expiry) assumed to be maintained during 4 years until loss of market share is expected due to new entry.			
Market share (%)	L	-	16%	75%	6%
Patients using Product Exon-Link	M=K*L	-	46	226	18

- The cost of other clinical supplies (comparators).
- Potential studies that might be requested by regulatory authorities in parallel or subsequently to regular studies, especially for innovative therapies with uncertain regulatory pathways.

Table 2.14 Number of product units sold

		Current year (2023)	*Launch year (2032)*	*Peak market share (2038)*	*End of forecast (2045)*
		Illustrative assumed values for future Product's prescribing information			
Dose in mg/kg of body weight	N	30			
Average weight of patients (kg)	O	20			
Frequency	P	once weekly			
Ratio mg/mL	Q	50			
Dosage mL /week/ patient	R=O*P/Q	12			
Total mL /year/ patient	S=R*52	624			
Total units administered per year (in mL), Product Exon-Link	T=N*S	0	28,892	140,966	11,511

Table 2.15 Product pricing and net revenues

		Current year (2023)	*Launch year (2032)*	*Peak market share (2038)*	*End of forecast (2045)*
Gross Selling Price in USD per mL		U= Price before any rebate, discount, based on analysis of current cost per patient, assuming an annual price increase of 2.0%.			
	U	—	1,200	1,351	1,552
Gross sales per year in USD	V=T*U	—	34,669,973	190,500,688	17,869,169
Average rebates, discounts	W	30%			
Net Revenue of Product Exon-Link in USD (US)	Σ = V*W	—	24,268,981	133,350,482	12,508,419

The costs per period and timeline up to each significant next milestone should result from this analysis. For collaborative or partnership programs, it will be essential to delineate costs supported by each party.

The R&D costs forecast precision depends on the valuation purpose and the forecast owner (internal employees with access to more precise information versus external analysts).

Forecast and estimates for clinical development phases will initially be high level (e.g., average cost per study over typical study durations) and refined as further information becomes available (e.g., clinical study protocol, patient enrollment performance).

Case Example: R&D Costs Forecast of Phase 1-Ready Program

A biotech firm was able to provide the summary R&D costs forecast in Table 2.16 using preliminary assumptions on:

- Identification of the different clinical studies required under the development plan.
- Applicable toxicological studies and long-term studies.
- Number of patients and duration per phase.
- Average clinical study cost per patient (benchmark values).
- Ratio of supplies and manufacturing process development costs to clinical studies costs.
- Cost estimates for comparators.
- Project management and regulatory expenses.
- Program-specific capital expenditures.

The company expects a refined forecast from the project management teams around Phase 2, as more precise parameters become available:

- Expected enrollment and attrition rates, considering expected countries and centers.
- Refined clinical study duration estimates.
- Enhanced cost projections for CDMO (Contract Development and Manufacturing Organization) and CRO (Clinical Research Organization) costs.

Cost of Goods Sold (COGS) Forecast

COGS, or cost of sales, include all costs used to create a commercialized product or service: materials, manufacturing, storage and shipment costs, and costs related to inventory losses. Applicable royalties due to third parties are typically included in COGS, as applicable (royalties are usually based on net sales).

Table 2.16 Summary R&D costs forecast of Phase 1-ready program as of 2023

Compound: XYZ-01 *Indication: MALS*	*Phase start (first patient in)*	*Phase com pletion*	*2023*	*2024*	*2025*	*2026*	*2027*	*2028*	*2029*	*2030*	*2031*	*2032*	*Total costs (US$M)*
Project management, regulatory, others			2	2	2	2	2	2	2	2	4	3	23
Phase 1 (80 patients)	3Q23	2Q24	8	12									20
Phase 2 (360 patients)	3Q24	4Q27			39	29	20						88
Phase 3 (1,500 patients)	3Q28	2Q31						119	119	119	48		405
Total R&D expenses (M$)			10	14	41	31	22	121	121	121	52	3	536

The difference between sales and COGS is the gross margin or gross profit.

When forecasting COGS, it is important to consider fixed versus variable components as a function of expected volumes over time. COGS are normally considered fully variable when:

- Production is fully outsourced. The forecast might be built using a cost per unit assumption, which can vary with contractual production volumes.
- COGS can be estimated as percentage of revenue based on comparable products. Such COGS ratios are based on sales in value and are adjusted per territory.

Biopharma COGS are typically influenced by volume, productivity, and manufacturing constraints. Forecasting COGS for innovative therapies leveraging early-stage technologies might prove challenging (e.g., stem cell therapy early days). In such situations, various scenarios might be required with sensitivity analyses to assess the impact of such uncertainty on the business case.

Case Example: Estimation of Syringe COGS

A fictitious biotech firm was able to estimate the cost of their injection device filled with sterile drug at US$5.8–US$7.7 per injection, using outsourcing, as shown in Table 2.17.

Table 2.17 Total COGS of API-filled device

Injection component for bottom-up calculation	*Estimated cost*	*Source for estimate*
Active Pharmaceutical Ingredient (API) 1 vial required per injection	US$ 3.0/vial	Quotes from suppliers assuming at least 0.5 M units and 2-month lead time.
Cost of bulk product excluding API 1 device required per injection	US$4.2 per device below 5 million; US$2.3 above 5 million	Long-term agreement negotiated with a medical devices manufacturer. Minimum volume of 1 million.
Cost of Fill and finish	US$0.5 per device	Comparison with previous devices.

Total:	US$7.7 per injection for annual volume between 1M and 5M units, US$5.8 per injection for annual volume above 5M units.

Table 2.18 Cost of sales ratio, Sarepta Therapeutics, Inc.

	For the three months ended		*For the six months ended*	
US$ (in thousands)	*June 30, 2022*	*June 30, 2021*	*June 30, 2022*	*June 30, 2021*
Products, net Revenues[a]	211,237	141,839	400,062	266,765
Cost of sales[b]	37,795	19,515	69,238	41,861
Cost of sales ratio	18%	14%	17%	16%

Sarepta Therapeutics (2022).

[a] All sales are only realized in the US market. Revenues from product sales are recorded at net sales price.

[b] Excluding amortization of in-licensed rights.

Case Example: Estimation of COGS as Percentage of Revenue

A company with a gene therapy program identified Sarepta Therapeutics commercial products in the United States as comparable, especially as the production of these comparable injectables is sourced from Contract Manufacturing Organizations. Based on the analysis provided by Table 2.18, the company is planning on a cost-of-sales ratio in the range of 14%–18% of net revenues for their gene therapy technology in the US market.

Sales, General, and Administrative (SG&A) Costs Forecast

In biopharma, SG&A Costs typically include the costs for the following activities and functions:

- Field sales force and representatives.
- Medical affairs.
- Medical advertising, brochures, and related materials.
- Patient education and assistance.
- Physician education.
- Brand investments.
- Market research and analytics.
- Marketing management.
- Advertising and promotional activities.
- Samples.
- Post-launch clinical studies and related activities (such as Risk Evaluation and Mitigation Strategy).
- G&A expenses.

The organization of activities and resources will heavily depend on the operating model relevant to the therapeutic area, the level of competition, the specific asset/brand strategy, market maturity, the innovative nature of the technology, and synergies with existing programs.

Case Example: SG&A Forecast for Program Nearing Phase 3 Completion

A biopharma firm with an innovative compound in a mature market is planning on a strong commercial investment at and following launch to maximize revenues for estimated US$800M peak sales as provided in Table 2.19.

Since the sales force has to be in place at least one quarter before launch for training and preparation, the 2 years before launch represent an increasing percentage of the first-year sales force costs.

For advertising and promotion, a percentage of launch year's expenses was used in the year before the launch. Expenses for conferences and market research were also added 2 years before launch.

At the program level, G&A expenses are minimal. Such expenses are generally not allocated to programs and are forecasted at the company level.

Program TV

In contexts where it is not practical nor necessary to use a long forecast time frame, DCF models use a terminal value as provided by Equation 2.4.

Calculating a TV after 5–10 years of forecast horizon is common for projects related to consumer healthcare, generic brands on mature markets, products with a strong brand, and low expected competition (niche specialty products).

For competitive patented products, it might be preferable to avoid using a TV and rather use a longer forecast horizon to the expiry date since minimal cash inflows are usually expected after patent expiry or loss of exclusivity.

Putting It Altogether – Program Free Cash Flows

Using the elements previously covered in this section, a company can forecast the free cash flows for each year within the forecast horizon: similarly to Table 2.1, the free cash flow FCF_k for a given year, k is given by Equation 2.10 where the various sub k designate the value for year k.

$$\begin{aligned}FCF_k &= \text{Revenue}_k - \text{COGS}_k - \text{R\&D}_k - \text{SG\&A}_k \\ &- \text{Non Operating Expense Allocation}_k + \text{Depreciation/Amortization}_k \\ &- \text{New Capital Expenditures}_k - \Delta\text{Working Capital}_k\end{aligned}$$

Equation 2.10 Program free cash flow for year k.

2.3.3 *Discounting Methodology*

The Weighted-Average Cost of Capital, or "WACC" as it is commonly called, is the minimum return (hurdle rate) expected by the company in conducting business.

As a general rule, a discount rate needs to align with the valuation's intent. When assessing stock prices in Section 2.1.3, we used a discount rate defined from a shareholder's viewpoint: the cost of equity.

Table 2.19 SG&A forecast

MUSD	*L − 4*	*L − 3*	*L − 2*	*L − 1*	*Launch year*	*L + 1*	*L + 2*	*L + 3*	*L + 4*	*L + 5*	*L + 6*	*L + 7*	*L + 8*	*L + 9*
Sales Forecast	**—**	**—**	**—**	**—**	**40**	**160**	**280**	**400**	**520**	**600**	**680**	**800**	**480**	**288**
Sales Force	—	—	2	8	30	45	47	49	51	53	55	57	34	20
Advertising & Promotion	—	—	2	9	15	81	102	100	90	47	26	18	11	6
Medical, marketing	—	—	4	6	6	10	11	11	11	11	11	12	7	4
Other SG&A expenses	—	—	1	5	8	8	9	9	9	9	10	10	6	4
Total SG&A expenses	**—**	**—**	**9**	**28**	**60**	**144**	**168**	**168**	**161**	**120**	**102**	**96**	**58**	**35**
SG&A ratio (%)	—	—	—	—	*150%*	*90%*	*60%*	*42%*	*31%*	*20%*	*15%*	*12%*	*12%*	*12%*

In contrast, when discounting free cash flows to obtain the NPV for a company project or program, we must use a discount rate that reflects the company's access to capital (debt, stock, and preferred stock), rather than only the expectations of a common stock shareholder. Specifically, for a company's project or program, we would use the WACC as a discount rate.

The non-simplified formula for the WACC is provided by Equation 2.11.

$$WACC = \frac{E}{E+D+PS} \cdot r_E + \frac{D}{E+D+PS} \cdot r_D + \frac{PS}{E+D+PS} \cdot r_{PS}$$

Equation 2.11 WACC formula.

where

- E, D, and PS represent the market value of the equity (common stockholders), debt and preferred shares reflecting the financing mix of the company.
- r_E represents the cost of equity as provided by Equation 2.5.
- r_D represents the after-tax cost of debt.
- r_{PS} represents the cost of preferred stock.

Typically risks associated with the ownership of preferred stocks are lower than that of equity but higher than risks associated with debt. In the formula above preferred stock is not always separated from common stock, depending on the preferred stock characteristics.

As preferred stock is almost always combined with equity for discount rate calculations, the WACC formula is used in its ubiquitous simplified form:

$$WACC = \frac{E}{E+D} \cdot r_E + \frac{D}{E+D} \cdot r_D$$

Equation 2.12 Simplified WACC formula.

The after-tax cost of debt r_D is calculated based on the current company borrowing costs to finance projects (pre-tax cost of interest-bearing debt) and the current tax rate of the company (since interests on debt are tax-deductible). If a biopharma firm can borrow at a rate of 7% and has a current tax rate of 25%, its after-tax cost of debt r_D would be $7\% \cdot (1 - 25\%) = 5.25\%$.

Case Example: Simplified WACC Calculation for Fictitious Large Pharma Company

The WACC can be calculated as illustrated in Table 2.20.

Table 2.20 WACC calculation for a large pharma company

r_f	4.14%	Yield of 20-Year US Treasury Rate
β	0.63	Based on financial press
$(r_m - r_f)$	6.0%	Based on standard financial information on cost of capital
Cost of Equity	**7.92%**	**= 4.14% + 0.63*6.0%**
Cost of Debt (pre-tax)	3.46%	Estimate based on company's most recent 10-Q
Marginal tax rate	21%	Estimate based on company's most recent 10-Q
Cost of Debt	**2.73%**	**= 3.46% *(1 − 21%)**
Equity value ($M)	129,180	Market capitalization as of end of period from financial press
Debt value ($M)	36,854	Total interest-bearing debt from most recent 10-Q
Equity weight	77.8%	
Debt weight	22.2%	
WACC	**6.77%**	**= 7.92% * 77.8% + 2.73% * 22.2%**

Note that this result is typical of a large biopharma company. For a small biopharma firm, the WACC would be significantly higher, e.g.:

- The non-diversifiable risk (i.e., β used in Equation 2.5) is typically higher for a small biopharma company.
- Early-stage companies use relatively less debt financing, giving more weight to the cost of equity, which is much higher than the cost of debt.

Overall, in developed countries, the WACC for a large biopharma company may be as low as 6%–8%, versus 10%–15% for smaller publicly listed biopharma firms, and 15%–20% for small private biopharma firms.

While the equity discount rate is a nominal rate and thus includes expected inflation, the WACC might not incorporate all the financial risks a firm might need to take into account. Additional factors might be considered, according to each company's financial policies:

- Geography.
  Doing business in some countries is perceived as riskier for countries experiencing macroeconomic instability or restrictive tax and monetary policy. Adjustments to the discount rate are made to capture the specific uncertainty of doing business in such territories.

- Uncertainty of Cash Flows.
  The level of uncertainty is higher for programs in development versus projects considered as more predictable. Certain corporate policies might require incorporating such risk profile differences by adding specific percentage points to the discount rate.

2.3.4 *Program NPV*

The NPV is the net cumulative sum of the future cash inflows and outflows for the program, adjusted for the cost of capital of the biopharma firm, as provided by Equation 2.13.

$$\text{NPV} = \left(\sum_{k=1}^{n} \frac{\text{FCF}_k}{(1+r)^k} \right) + \frac{\text{TV}}{(1+r)^n}$$

Equation 2.13 Program NPV.

where

- FCF_k is the free cash flow as defined above.
- r is the cost of capital (WACC).
- *TV* is the terminal value, if relevant for the valuation case.

2.3.5 *NPV as an Insightful Metric*

In a given program, the financial investment before launch is substantial considering R&D expenses, capital expenditures specific to the project, pre-approval payments to third parties for in-licensing rights, and pre-launch commercial expenses. The cumulative discounted cash flows typically reach a maximum negative value around the launch year and the breakeven point is often achieved only years after launch. This point corresponds to the discounted payback period of the program, during and after which the cumulative NPV becomes positive. This provides a measure of the high financial risks involved with the development of life sciences projects, even when the product is at an advanced stage.

To better understand the financial risk, it is possible to deconstruct the NPV between an Investment NPV, including pre-launch items and a Commercial NPV, including launch and post-launch items.

$$\text{NPV} = \text{Commercial NPV} - \text{Investment NPV}$$

Equation 2.14 NPV deconstruction between investment NPV and commercial NPV.

where

- Investment NPV = – NPV(R&D Expenses) – NPV(Pre-launch Capex) – NPV(other pre-launch items).
- Commercial NPV = NPV of applicable territories and applicable indications.

If the program creates value (NPV>0), the commercial NPV, denoted C, is greater than the investment NPV, denoted I, and the resulting C/I ratio is greater than one.

The C/I ratio provides a measure of "return on investment" and can be used to compare different programs, or to compare different scenarios for a given program.

When using NPV as a metric, one should note the following:

- NPV is strictly a going forward view based on future cash flows and does not take into account sunk costs (i.e., costs spent to date).
- The NPV approach described used a standalone basis with all allocations necessary to operate the program. The impact of other programs or activities also needs to be taken into account.
- The NPV model described so far is based on a successful deterministic approach (success is a given) that does not take into account critical risks of failure that are prominent in biopharma.

Comparing the NPV of a licensed program seen from the licensee, as calculated above, with the NPV of the program seen by the licensor, as illustrated in Section 2.4.2, will offer insights into the distribution of value.

2.3.6 *Risk-Adjusted Net Present Value*

Risk-adjusted Net Present Value (rNPV) adjusts the NPV approach by integrating probabilities of achieving intermediate milestones along the development plan up to final regulatory approval. This is paramount for the biopharma industry where a program will incur significant development costs that have a much higher probability compared with distant commercial profits that have a lower probability.

Specifically, the rNPV approach adjusts all discounted cash flows for each period with the probability that they occur based on the R&D probability of success (see Equation 2.15). The NPV represents the potential value assuming technical and regulatory success, whereas the rNPV represents the expected value given the technical and regulatory probabilities of success.

The rNPV approach thus uses an adjusted free cash flow value for each period k:

$$\text{rNPV}_k = P(k) \cdot \text{NPV}(\text{FCF}_k) = P(k) \cdot \frac{\text{FCF}_k}{(1+r)^k}$$

Equation 2.15 Risk-adjusted net present value contribution from period k.

Where

- FCF_k is the free cash flow used in the NPV approach (see Equations 2.10 and 2.13).
- $P(k)$ is the probability that the project will reach this period k. This "risk-adjustment factor" is the cumulative probability applied to each period of the forecast.

This probabilistic approach involves two important concepts:

- The probability of each development phase to be successful and reach the next one ("Probability of Success", or "POS"), highlighting that after each phase, it is possible that the project has to be stopped.
- The probability of obtaining regulatory approval, also called Probability of Technical and Regulatory Success (PTRS). PTRS encompasses the various phases and their POS.

At the program level, the following milestones are typically used:

- Preclinical stage success or failure.
- Phase I success or failure.
- Phase II success or failure.
- Phase III success or failure.
- New Drug Application submission success or failure.

A deep understanding of the clinical development plan and regulatory pathway is critical to determine the rNPV since Phase I and Phase II might be combined (then called "Phase I/II") or Phase II results might be sufficient for submission (then called "Phase II/III" or "pivotal"). Note that probabilities of success tend to vary significantly with the therapeutic area and modality.

Case Example: Illustrative POS by Phase

As can be seen from Table 2.21, regulatory approval and subsequent commercial launch will be possible if the program successfully completes all development phases, which represents a PTRS of 16.0%. In comparison, an event based on the successful completion of Phase 2 (like the initiation of

Table 2.21 Program POS and PTRS

Phase	*Phase probability of success*	*Phase probability to start*
Phase 1 (in progress)	60.0%	100.0%
Phase 2	45.0%	60.0%
Phase 3	66.0%	27.0%
Filing/submission	90.0%	17.8%
Approval	N/A	16.0%
	PTRS	**16.0%**

Phase 3 or the payment of a milestone upon Phase 2 favorable results for example) would have 27.0% probability to occur.

Overall, rNPV can be calculated with Equation 2.16.

$$r\text{NPV} = \left(\sum_{k=1}^{n} \frac{P(k) \cdot FCF_k}{(1+r)^k} \right) + \frac{P(n) \cdot TV}{(1+r)^n}$$

Equation 2.16 rNPV formula.

where

- FCF_k is the free cash flow for period k used in the NPV approach (see Equations 2.10 and 2.13).
- $P(k)$ is the probability that the project will reach this period k.
- r is WACC.
- TV is the terminal value, if relevant for the valuation case.

For simplicity, Equation 2.16 provides for a unique probability $P(k)$ for period k. Conceivably two successive development steps A and B might occur in the same period k. In such a scenario, it is important to note that the free cash flows associated with each ($\text{FCF}(A)_k$ and $\text{FCF}(B)_k$ respectively) would have different cumulative probabilities, instead of a single one, with the probability $P(k)_B$ for the second step B lower than the probability $P(k)_A$ of the first step A: $P(k)_B = P(k)_A \cdot \text{POS}(A)$ where $\text{POS}(A)$ denotes the probability of success of step A.

As done for NPV Equation 2.14, the rNPV can also be deconstructed in two parts:

$$\text{rNPV} = \text{Investment rNPV} + \text{Commercial rNPV}$$

Equation 2.17 rNPV deconstruction between investment rNPV and commercial rNPV.

And a risk-adjusted C/I ratio can likewise be computed as follows: Commercial rNPV/Investment rNPV. As for the standard C/I ratio, a value greater than 1 for the risk-adjusted C/I ratio would typically be expected of a sound investment.

The risk-adjusted C/I Ratio is occasionally utilized in the industry, often with the perspective of portfolio prioritization, along with other ratios like the Productivity of R&D (or R&D Productivity Index).

$$\text{Productivity of R\&D} = (\text{Program rNPV}) \;/\; (\text{Program rNPV of R\&D})$$

Equation 2.18 Productivity of R&D ratio for a development program.

Although rNPV reflects a probabilistic approach, it is important to also consider specific potential risks or uncertainties during the development of the program: ability to scale-up manufacturing, evolution of programs developed by competitors, changes in regulatory environment. Such factors will traditionally be addressed through scenarios and sensitivity analyses.

2.3.7 *Valuation for Multiple Markets/Multiple Indications*

The previous sections assumed a single commercial forecast for a given program for simplicity. When the commercial forecast of a program includes multiple indications or multiple geographies and jurisdictions, it is usually recommended to distinguish between them. This is particularly true when the specific assumptions have a significant influence on the commercial forecast, e.g.:

- Varying launch dates per country.
- Pricing, reimbursement conditions, and payor negotiations.
- Different exclusivity periods in different countries.
- Country-specific epidemiology.
- Country-specific factors that affect patient identification or diagnosis.

After building the free cash flows forecast for each significant market and applying the relevant discount rate per country, the commercial NPV of each targeted territory is calculated and the Total Commercial NPV is the sum of all individual NPVs. The NPV of R&D costs might be calculated separately (e.g., when WACC and tax might differ).

R&D costs specific to certain countries (e.g., country-specific clinical studies), may be included as part of that country's NPV.

We can write the formula, which can be applied at indication's level or program's level:

$$\text{Program (or indication) NPV} = \\ \text{Sum of Commercial NPV per market} + \text{R\&D NPV}$$

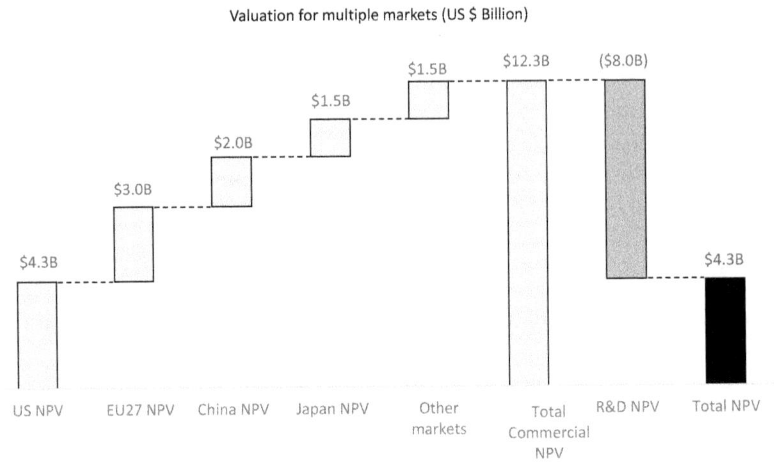

Figure 2.7 Program valuation for multiple markets.

A recapitulative waterfall summary like Figure 2.7 is customary to show which market contributes the most to the overall return on R&D investment.

This rNPV approach would be entirely similar to that of the NPV.

For a multi-indication compound, the company would follow a similar approach for each indication and then summarize the overall value across indications.

As we mentioned the additive properties of NPVs, the intrinsic value of all company programs could be calculated this way by evaluating each and every company program the same way. The overall intrinsic enterprise value of the company would then be obtained by adding company elements not covered by the R&D and commercial forecasts, e.g.:

- Non-allocated R&D expenses.
- G&A expenses.
- Other elements impacting cash flows like income from collaborations or capital expenditures not related to specific programs.
- Potential tax credit carried forward.
- Ancillary activities (e.g., royalties/milestones not captured in program forecasts).

2.3.8 *Internal Rate of Return*

The Internal Rate of Return (IRR) provides the program annual average return on its investment. The IRR is calculated on the non-discounted free cash flows used in the NPV approach: the IRR is the value of the discount rate that results in a zero NPV for these free cash flows.

An IRR can be compared with the normal company discount rate the same way an NPV is compared with zero:

- If IRR > WACC, the project will create value: NPV>0.
- If IRR = WACC, the project does not create nor destroy value: NPV=0.
- If IRR < WACC, the project will destroy value: NPV <0.

It is possible to define a risk-adjusted internal rate of return (rIRR) by using risk-adjusted free cash flows instead of the non-discounted free cash flows used in the NPV approach.

The notion of rIRR is to the rNPV what the IRR is to the NPV. The risk-adjusted internal rate of return (rIRR) is the discount rate that will provide a zero rNPV. To determine if an investment creates value, the rIRR would be compared with the cost of capital the same way an rNPV would be compared with zero.

The concept of internal rates of return can offer advantages over the concept of NPV (be they risk-adjusted or not). Whereas you know whether a project is worth pursuing based on a positive NPV, the IRR provides a sense for how robust the odds of value creation are. When a project with an IRR of 10% is compared with another project with an IRR of 16%, we know that the profitability of the latter is higher and gives a greater safety margin.

2.4 Commercial-Stage Valuation

2.4.1 *In-House Product Valuation*

Once a product has received marketing approval and the program has reached the commercial stage, valuations are typically refined:

- Development and regulatory authorizations hurdles have been cleared, although regulatory approval may be conditioned to post-marketing studies and risk-management approaches.
- Manufacturing is in place.
- Terms for pharmaceutical pricing and reimbursement are established.
- New data is generated around physician prescribing behavior, patient adherence, distributors' activity, etc. Such statistical time series can support more detailed product forecasts.

This rich data trove enables many analytical refinements, such as sales force performance, market response to disease awareness campaigns, commercial partnership benefits, impact of competitors activity, and "cannibalization" of existing marketed product with new formulation.

This said, at the commercial stage, the expected value is no longer adjusted for technical and regulatory development-stage risks. Rather, using the estimated probability of different commercial scenarios is meaningful to represent the value of an in-market product.

Case Example: Evaluation of Disease Awareness Campaign Proposal

A biopharma has a marketed drug where low diagnosis rates are significantly hurting financial performance. In order to evaluate the value of a proposed disease awareness campaign representing a US$20M incremental commercial expense, they evaluate two scenarios: scenario A representing a base case without the campaign and scenario B with the campaign. As shown in Table 2.22, scenario B increases the commercial-stage valuation by 13% from US$469M to US$528M, justifying the commercial investment in the campaign.

2.4.2 *Out-Licensed Program Valuation*

A noteworthy revenue source for biopharma companies comes from out-licensing activities. Such revenues are linked to specific contractual agreements the company is party to as licensor (e.g., payments over time for specific activities, out-licensing milestone payments, and royalties).

When reaching commercial stage, typically, the company will already have recognized pre-commercial revenues from such licensing agreements, e.g., milestone payment for positive Phase 3 results and regulatory approvals.

Under many agreements, the out-licensed program continues to generate revenues for the company in the form of royalties and sales milestones.

Case Example: Licensor's Valuation of Program in Launch Year

Having just received FDA approval, the program under review is in launch year "L" with a patent expiration in year L+10 (which terminates licensing payments).

The out-licensing agreement stipulates:

- Royalties of 8%, 10%, 12%, 14% respectively for sales ranges of 0–US$ 250M, US$250M–US$500M, US$500M–US$750M, above US$750M.
- 10% milestones payments for sales thresholds: US$250M, US$500M, US$750M, and US$1B.

Using the net sales forecast provided by the licensee, Table 2.23 indicates a total program value of US$275M at launch time.

Table 2.22 Scenario planning for disease awareness campaign

SCENARIO A	**2024**	**2025**	**2026**	**2027**	**2028**	**2029**	**2030**	**2031**	**2032**	**2033**
Prevalent population (thousands)	*224*	*215*	*206*	*197*	*189*	*181*	*173*	*166*	*159*	*152*
Diagnosis rate	**35%**	**36%**	**36%**	**37%**	**38%**	**39%**	**39%**	**40%**	**41%**	**42%**
Patients diagnosed (thousands)	78	77	75	73	71	70	68	67	65	64
Treated patient rate	90%	90%	90%	90%	90%	90%	90%	90%	90%	90%
Patients treated (thousands)	71	69	67	66	64	63	61	60	59	57
Product market share (%)	22%	22%	21%	21%	20%	20%	13%	8%	6%	5%
Sales Forecast (US$M)	**186**	**178**	**170**	**162**	**154**	**147**	**93**	**59**	**41**	**34**
Gross margin (US$M)	156	149	143	136	124	120	78	50	34	28
Commercial expenses (US$M)	28	27	25	24	23	22	14	9	6	5
Operating profit before tax (US$M)	129	123	117	112	100	98	64	41	28	23
Tax (US$M)	(32)	(31)	(29)	(28)	(25)	(25)	(16)	(10)	(7)	(6)
Change in working capital (US$M)	2	2	2	2	2	1	11	7	4	1
Free cash flow (US$M)	98	94	89	85	77	75	58	38	25	19
Yearly DCF (US$M)	93	81	71	61	50	44	31	18	11	8

NPV Scenario A	**$469M**

SCENARIO B

US$20M Incremental Commercial Expenses in 2024–2025.
Increased diagnosis rate reaching 60% by 2031 vs. 40% in scenario A.

[Scenario B forecast details intentionally omitted]

NPV Scenario B	**$528M**

Table 2.23 Valuation of out-licensed program at launch time

Year	*L*	*L + 1*	*L + 2*	*L + 3*	*L + 4*	*L + 5*	*L + 6*	*L + 7*	*L + 8*	*L + 9*	*L + 10*
Figures in US$M											
Licensee's Net Sales forecast	40	160	280	400	520	600	680	704	728	752	800
Income from sales milestones	**—**	**—**	**25**	**—**	**50**	**—**	**—**	**—**	**—**	**75**	**—**
8% Royalties 0–250M	3	13	20	20	20	20	20	20	20	20	20
10% Royalties 250–500M	—	—	3	15	25	25	25	25	25	25	25
12% Royalties 500–750M	—	—	—	—	2	12	22	24	27	30	30
14% Royalties >750M	—	—	—	—	—	—	—	—	—	0	7
Income from royalties	**3**	**13**	**23**	**35**	**47**	**57**	**67**	**69**	**72**	**75**	**82**
Total out-licensing income	**3**	**13**	**48**	**35**	**97**	**57**	**67**	**69**	**72**	**150**	**82**
Tax	(1)	(3)	(12)	(9)	(24)	(14)	(17)	(17)	(18)	(38)	(21)
Free cash flow	2	10	36	26	73	43	50	52	54	113	62
Mid-year discount convention	0.5	1.5	2.5	3.5	4.5	5.5	6.5	7.5	8.5	9.5	10.5
Discount factor	0.95	0.87	0.79	0.72	0.65	0.59	0.54	0.49	0.44	0.40	0.37
DCF	**2**	**8**	**28**	**19**	**48**	**25**	**27**	**25**	**24**	**46**	**23**

NPV (from Launch Year)	**$275M**

2.5 Value-Based Program Decisions

Biopharma companies face important decisions when managing their internal programs to optimize the value created by the company. The major themes in that respect tend to be as follows:

- Defining the major value inflection points in a program. Understanding the points at which the program value changes significantly, those program turning points, is critical to optimize value creation.
- Managing high stakes under uncertainty. Such effective management is at the core of the biopharma industry, and the use of valuation tools can help assess the potential impact of uncertainties.
- Making portfolio and indication selections. Making decisions between different program directions is another situation where valuation tools come in handy to evaluate the impact of the decisions made.
- Providing consistently sound strategic direction adapted to the latest context. The company and program leadership teams need to perform financial and strategic assessments at appropriate points in the process to proactively steer the company in the right direction throughout program lifecycles. This is often done by combining the different methodologies and toolkit provided in this chapter.

Each of these themes is further developed in the following sections.

2.5.1 Evaluating the Next Value Inflection Points of a Program

A value inflection point can be defined as a specific and meaningful change in information concerning a program's research and development plan, showing decisive progress milestone and accomplishments.

Such a milestone is generally a data-driven outcome or event, e.g., data readout, regulatory feedback, intermediate clinical assessment. It might capture the attention of investors and generally justifies the need for a business case update.

Case Example: Value Inflection Points for Discovery Program

Three inflection points have been defined for a discovery program: in vitro study results, in vivo study results, and obtention of the IND status, as shown in Figure 2.8. Favorable outcomes at each of these points represents value improvements and de-risking of the program, thereby making it an attractive time to look for further investments. This is an important consideration since program run rates increase along the way as depicted in the same figure.

One practical way to quantify the effect of a successful value inflection point on the program value is to use the rNPV approach seen in Section 2.3.6. If

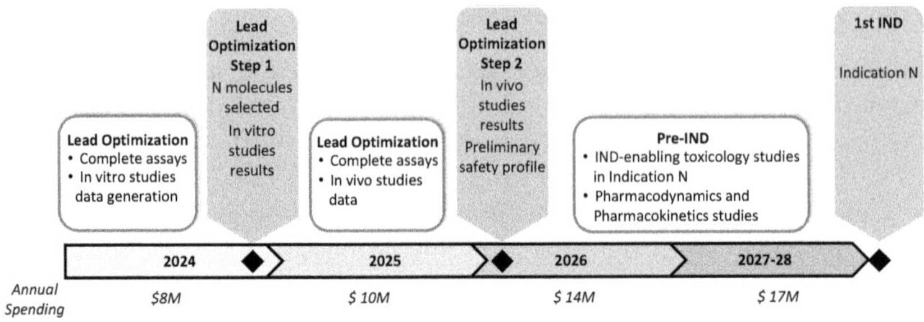

Figure 2.8 Discovery program value inflection points.

the inflection point is successful, the program continues and rNPV increases as sunk costs until the inflection point are no longer included and future cash flows are discounted over a shorter period of time. The program represents a higher value proposition when presented to new investors.

From a valuation perspective, critical milestones are those with the highest impact on the program's rNPV. For example, if the Phase 2 success rate for an immune-inflammatory program is estimated at 33%, achieving this inflection point will constitute a major increase in rNPV as there is a significant increase in PTRS (see Figure 2.9). Even if one were to calculate a revised rNPV from inception (i.e., with sunk costs from inception) with adjusted probabilities of 100% for known successes, there is a notable increase in such revised rNPV as illustrated by Figure 2.9.

It should be noted that rNPV might not always constitute a well-suited metric for the opportunity under investigation or its inflection points (e.g., early programs use different valuation approaches as seen in Section 2.2). In addition, factors not considered in the rNPV approach can increase the value of a program, e.g.:

- The IP (particularly the freedom to operate) will only be considered indisputable at a future point in time, when the patents landscape is clarified. Such a clarification usually represents a critical value inflection point.
- The management of a program by an experienced management team in the field or through a partnership between experienced firms can increase its chances of success. Establishing such management might provide for a critical value inflection point.

2.5.2 *Using Valuation Tools to Manage Uncertainties*

There are many potential challenges or sources of uncertainty that may need to be addressed or at least evaluated within a biopharma program such as lack of reliable biomarkers, challenging targets, new mode of action,

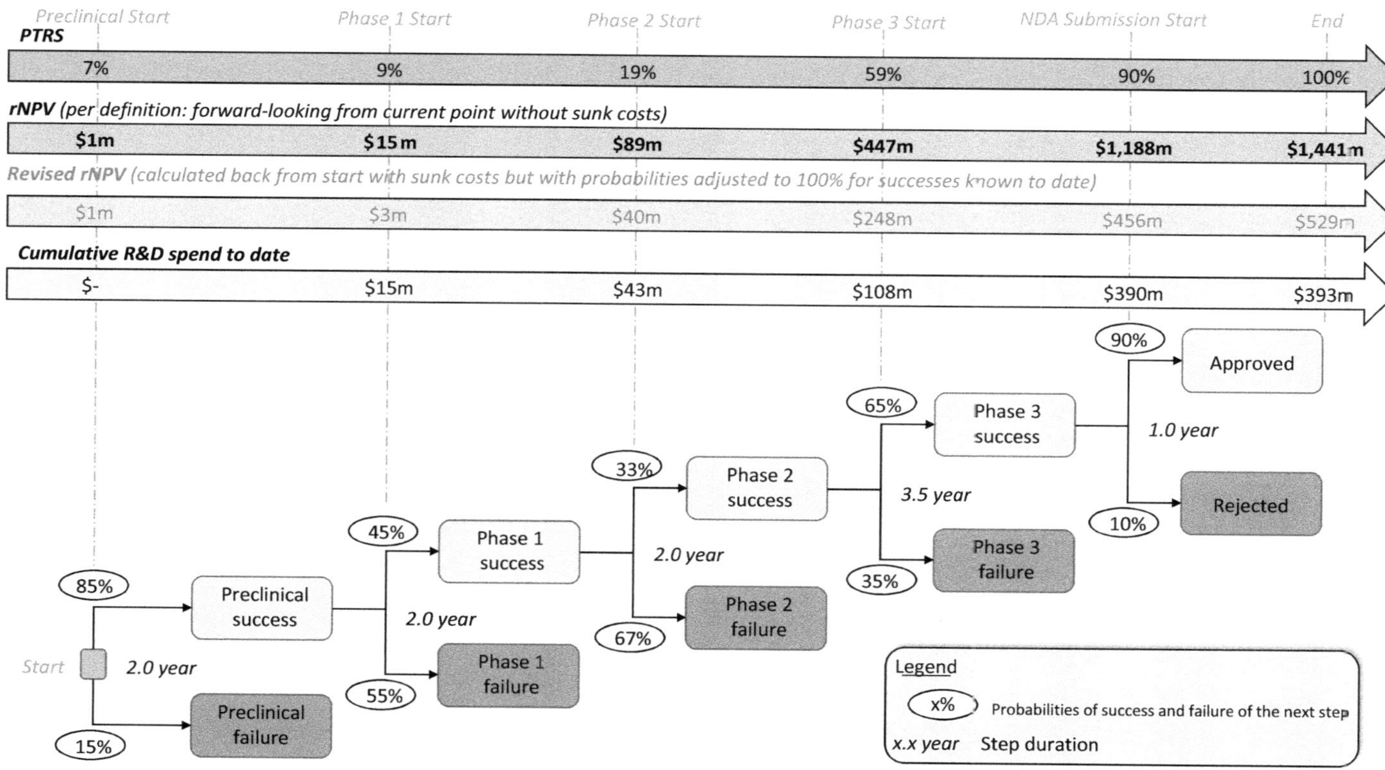

Figure 2.9 Illustrative scenario tree for an immune-inflammatory program.

limitations of animal studies for targeted indication, exacting inclusion/exclusion criteria, and expected study enrollment challenges.

Understanding the impact of such uncertainties on a business case or program can be made easier with the use of appropriate valuation tools. Below are three tools commonly used for that purpose.

rNPV Sensitivity Analysis

The rNPV sensitivity analysis is performed by selecting independent valuation variables (or assumptions) that might best represent a program's uncertainties, and basing calculations on the different values to test for the selected variables. This is typically done one variable at a time.

Case Example: rNPV Sensitivity Analysis for Phase 2 Program

The leadership team of a program about to enter Phase 2 needs to evaluate the impact of three major sources of uncertainty on commercial activities as well as different views on the probability of success of the current phase given specific R&D productivity improvements made:

- Significant net sales forecast range due to limited market study information.
- Potential commercial launch delay of 2 years (combined with longer and more expensive R&D phase).
- Range of drug pricing at US launch given limited pricing strategy views.
- Probability of success range for Phase 2.

Having looked at the football field graph (so named as it looks like one – see Figure 2.10), the team decides to emphasize epidemiology studies further given the significant potential upside and net sales sensitivity. They also

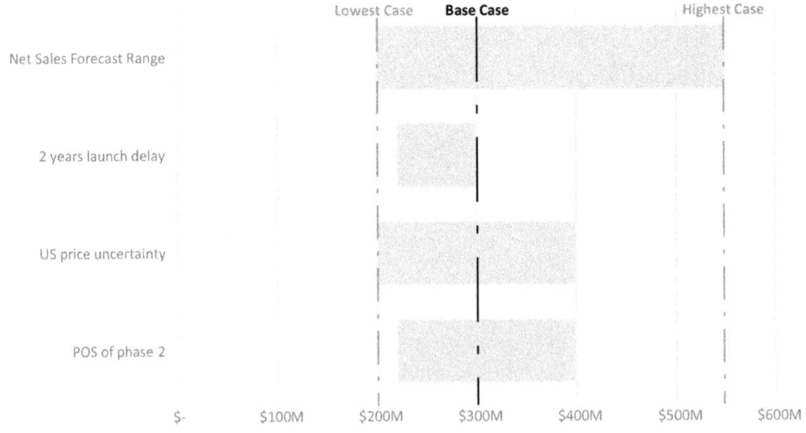

Figure 2.10 "Football field" view of phase 2 program rNPV.

conclude that the impact of the other uncertainties remain acceptable compared with the base case.

Scenario Planning

Whereas the previous tool looked primarily at the effect of a single independent variable, program team considerations might involve several interdependent factors that form sensible alternatives. In such situations, one will typically build alternative scenarios from a base case. It is common to have two scenarios, one favorable and one unfavorable (e.g., a favorable scenario might correspond to the obtention of Fast Track FDA designation whereas the unfavorable scenario being the standard route with one competitor having received Fast Track designation).

Case Example: Scenario Analysis for Program Entering Phase 2b

Given the multiple assumptions at their disposal, when reviewing the business plan, the program team considers two main scenarios:

- Favorable scenario: Phase 2b confirms the First-in-Class profile of the compound resulting in higher prices, preventing launch delay, and increased probability of success.
- Unfavorable scenario: Phase 2b does not confirm the First-in-Class profile of the compound, resulting in moderate prices, adding a 6-month launch delay, and using standard probability of success.

Monte Carlo Simulation

The two previous tools were based on a limited number of sensitivity evaluations. In comparison, there are computational methods and tools that allow for larger number of iterations, based on variations of several variables. Such an approach can predict development program NPV outcomes by simulating variations in price, COGS, and market share. A Monte Carlo simulation is one of the predominantly used computational methods. It uses repeated random sampling and specified input variables to predict or simulate the likelihood of results ranges related to uncertain outcomes or events.

A Monte Carlo simulation will usually provide a distribution curve of thousands of NPV and rNPV outcomes for a given program. Such an approach is still an intrinsic valuation method based on the program's underlying assumptions.

The "Monte Carlo" NPV or rNPV can be considered as more accurate as it considers all identified events and uncertainties with their estimated range of possible outcomes. It is a relevant tool for portfolio analysis (ranking all programs in descending order of value), or when a context requires to simulate a vast range of combinations, along with certain confidence intervals based on a large number of simulated scenarios. However, it can be hard to use as a management tool, as its processing is not easy to understand, and no Profit and Loss (or Cashflow) statement is derived from it.

2.5.3 *Valuation Tools and Decision Trees*

Decision trees are flowchart-like graphical representations representing the successive decisions that need to be made along with their potential outcomes, considerations, or probabilities. They can support complex decision-making, such as biopharma program decisions that drastically affect the program's value creation potential. Using financial implications in the form of NPV or rNPV as potential outcomes can be helpful to the program team in driving such decisions.

Case Example: Technology Options for Program Ready to Enter Phase 1

A biopharma leadership team has two major technology alternatives, denoted A and B, for their flagship program about to enter Phase 1. They feel that having Phase 1 results would allow them to make a much more informed decision than having to choose at this stage as the program is about to enter Phase 1. As illustrated by Figure 2.11, choosing to pursue one route versus another will have implications on key program metrics. Given the importance of time to market considerations for this specific program, they would want to avoid doing two Phase 1 studies sequentially if the first technology failed. From a financial perspective, they can support the additional Phase 1 if deemed necessary.

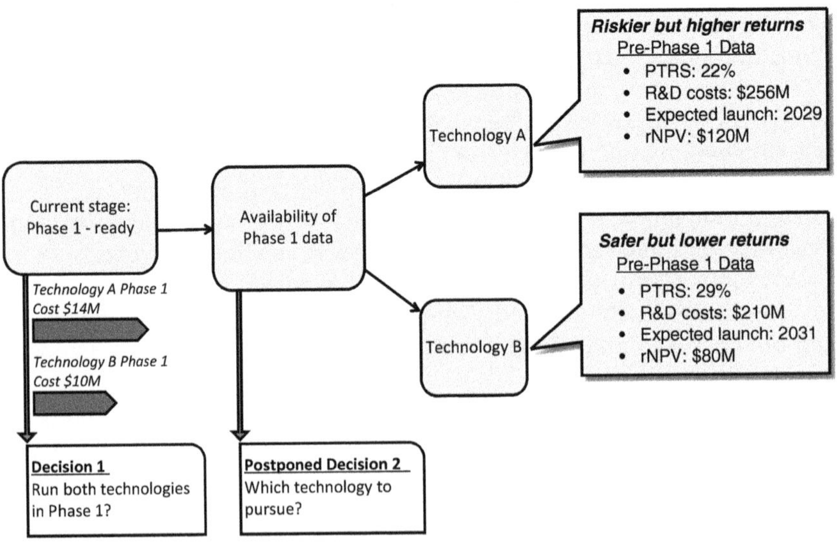

Figure 2.11 Program decision tree.

So, the company has two decisions to make:

1. Whether to run both technologies in parallel for Phase 1.
2. Which technology to select.

If the decision is taken to run both technologies, it will cost an additional amount of US$10M–US$14M depending on the additional study considered, and the company might still have the option to develop the alternate technology if Phase 1 results are unfavorable for their default technology choice.

Given technology A's POS in Phase 1 is 60%, there is a 40% likelihood that the company would choose to pursue Technology B. The converse figures are 70%/30% for technology B's POS in Phase 1 and choice of technology A.

Using the pre-Phase 1 information available today, the team decides that running both technologies in parallel for Phase 1 makes sense since the probability-weighted rNPV for each alternate technology is higher than the incremental cost of running both technologies:

- Probability of pursuing Technology B * pre-Phase 1 Technology B rNPV > Added Phase 1 costs.
  40% × US$80M = US$32M > US$10M
- Probability of pursuing Technology A * pre-Phase 1 Technology A rNPV > Added Phase 1 costs.
  30% × US$120M = US$36M > US$14M

Decision trees are helpful tools to support decision-making and measure the financial implications of alternative choices: effect on the R&D cost forecast and cash burn rate, effect on the program's technical metrics (e.g., time to launch, probability of success) and financial performance (rNPV, IRR).

2.5.4 Overall Perspective

The various valuation tools and approaches provided in this chapter should be used at appropriate and regular points during the program lifecycle. At the preclinical and Phase 1 stages, valuations tend to be high level and preliminary, as focus is typically centered on therapeutic indication priorities and program safety profile derisking. At more advanced stages starting around Phase 2, more detailed assumptions become necessary for sound valuations using multiple R&D and commercial considerations.

The various valuation approaches have the following recommended practices in common.

- Acknowledge the applicability and limitations of the valuation model.
- Triangulate findings, not to rely on a single valuation model since there is no perfect one. It is helpful to combine intrinsic approaches (e.g., NPV,

rNPV, IRR, rIRR) with relative methods (e.g., comparable products, transactions with comparable assets).

- Emphasize essential value levers highlighted by the model, for the leadership team to use and further enhance value.
- Position the asset, program, license, or acquisition under analysis within the wider strategic context (e.g., company level) to be able to effectively discuss its implications.

References

AICPA. (2016). *Accounting and Valuation Guide: Valuation of Privately-Held-Company Equity Securities Issued as Compensation*. Wiley.

Chaffe, D. B. H., III. (2013). Option pricing as a proxy for discount for lack of marketability in private company valuations: A working paper. *Business Valuation Review, 12*(4), 182–188. https://doi.org/10.5791/0882-2875-12.4.182

Finnerty, J. D. (2012). An average-strike put option model of the marketability discount. *Journal of Derivatives, 19*(4), 53–69. https://doi.org/10.3905/jod.2012.19.4.053

Ibbotson, R. G., & Harrington, J. P. (2021). *STOCKS, BONDS, BILLS, AND INFLATION® (SBBI®)*.

Lilly. (2020, March 12). *AbCellera and Lilly to Co-develop Antibody Therapies for the Treatment of COVID-19*. Retrieved 2/2/2023, from https://investor.lilly.com/news-releases/news-release-details/abcellera-and-lilly-co-developantibody-therapiestreatment#:~:text=VANCOUVER%2C%20British%20Columbia%20and%20INDIANAPOLIS,%2DCoV%2D2%20novel%20coronavirus

Morningstar. (2022, December 20). Sarepta Therapeutics Inc SRPT. Retrieved 12/20/2022, from https://www.morningstar.com/stocks/xnas/srpt/quote

Nunes, C., Harrington, J. P., Aboulamer, A., & Grabowski, R. J. *Recommended U.S. Equity Risk Premium and Corresponding Risk-Free Rates*. https://www.kroll.com/en/insights/publications/cost-of-capital/recommended-us-equity-risk-premium-and-corresponding-risk-free-rates

Sarepta Therapeutics, I. (2022). *Form 10-Q – Quarterly Period Ended* June 30, 2022. U.S. Securities and Exchange Commission. https://www.sec.gov/edgar.shtml

Silcoff, S. (2021, May 13). *Vancouver Biotech Firm AbCellera Made Nearly $200-Million in Royalties in 2020 from Its COVID-19 Treatment*. The Globe and Mail. Retrieved 2/2/2023, from https://www.theglobeandmail.com/business/article-abcellera-made-200-million-in-royalties-from-its-covid-19-treatment/

U.S. Department of the Treasury. (n.d.). *Daily Treasury Par Yield Curve Rates*. Retrieved 10/13/2024, from https://home.treasury.gov/resource-center/data-chart-center/interest-rates/TextView?type=daily_treasury_yield_curve&field_tdr_date_value_month=202212

Chapter 3

The Rigors and Importance of Intellectual Property

Intellectual Property, commonly referred to as IP, is a fundamental concept in biopharma given the need to safeguard future revenues after sizable upfront investments and R&D costs. It is essential to strategy and value creation. IP laws are complex, requiring professional expertise, differing across geographies despite harmonization efforts, and evolving frequently over time. This chapter should not be used to derive legal opinions nor should it be considered as legal advice but rather to illustrate IP concepts and approaches and IP system differences.

3.1 General Orientation on IP

3.1.1 IP 101

IP laws and regulations typically try and achieve a challenging balance in the biopharma industry: encouraging innovation while making therapies accessible to patients and thus appropriate for payer structures within each jurisdiction.

Biopharma companies must regularly assess the uncertainties or risks their IP might face, be it under special circumstances (e.g., humanitarian considerations made to waive patent protections for COVID-19 medicines in 2021 during the COVID-19 pandemic) or under normal circumstances.

IP refers to products of the mind, protected by law from unauthorized usage by others. Now there are many interesting aspects around this simple IP definition:

- "Property" and "product" indicate that IP can be *owned*, like a car or a chair, and it can be assigned, licensed, or transferred through a will or otherwise.
- "Intellectual" and "product of the mind" emphasize the intangible nature of IP. They also highlight the *necessity for the mind to have created* something, such as an idea, a process, or an invention. Defining

DOI: 10.4324/9781003598046-3

and interpreting what may or may not constitute such a product can, however, be challenging, as demonstrated by the many legal proceedings around IP.

- "Protected by law" has strong implications as it ties the IP definition to a specific *legal system*. As a result, IP is linked to a jurisdiction, often a geography where the IP applies. Different types of IP may have different legal contexts. In the United States, there are different types of IPs defined by law: copyrights, patents, trademarks, designs, and trade secrets.
- "Unauthorized usage" raises a fundamental consideration for IP in that it gives the owner of the IP the *right to exclude others* from using the specific IP, rather than necessarily conferring the owner an affirmative right to produce something based on that IP. From an economic perspective, IP rights could be interpreted as a time-bound monopoly grant to the owner.

Case Example: IP Legal Basis in the United States

The US Constitution (Figure 3.1) provides the legal basis for IP in the United States.

Figure 3.1 The Constitution of the United States (Credit: National Archives).

Section 8, clause 3 of Article 1 provides the basis for trademarks: "Congress shall have Power [...] to regulate commerce with Foreign Nations, and among the several States, and with the Indian Tribes".

Section 8, clause 8 of Article 1 authorizes Congress to enact patent and copyright law: "Congress shall have Power [...] to promote the Progress of Science and useful Arts, by securing for limited Times to Authors and Inventors the exclusive Right to their respective Writings and Discoveries".

Another important consideration is that in the United States, States retain concurrent jurisdiction to regulate IP under the 10th Amendment to the Constitution: "The powers not delegated to the United States by the Constitution, nor prohibited by it to the States, are reserved to the States respectively, or to the people".

As very well put by BIO (2016), "Intellectual property is the lifeblood of the biotechnology industry". In biopharma, common intellectual properties include specific molecules/products, processes (e.g., production), or methods and uses (e.g., transgenic approach).

Below are a few arbitrarily selected illustrative IP assets:

- US11079393B2 – US patent assigned to Biogen MA Inc, regarding a method of monitoring the change of the alpha-4 integrin activities in an individual. Application granted on 08/03/2021 and adjusted expiration anticipated for 03/03/2032. Title: "Methods for determining differences in alpha-4 integrin activity by correlating differences in sVCAM and/or sMAdCAM levels".
- US8580841B2 – US patent assigned to Arena Pharmaceuticals Inc., regarding chemical compounds for the treatment of autoimmune and inflammatory disorders. Application granted on 07/22/2009 and adjusted expiration anticipated for 03/05/2030. Title: "Substituted 1,2,3,4-tetrahydrocyclopenta[b]indol-3-yl)acetic acid derivatives useful in the treatment of autoimmune and inflammatory disorders".
- US11179367B2 – US patent assigned to Vertex Pharmaceuticals Inc., regarding a pharmaceutical composition comprising a specific compound to treat cystic fibrosis. Application granted on 11/23/2021 and expiration anticipated for 02/04/2039. Title: "Pharmaceutical compositions for treating cystic fibrosis".

In biopharma, internal rates of returns can be in the low single-digit percentages, with a cost to bring an asset to market around US$2 billion accounting for the cost of failure (Mathieu, 2018). One should note, however, the significant range of R&D cost estimates to bring a new therapy to market – see discussion by Wouters et al. (2020), estimating a mean investment of US$1.3 billion while noting the range of estimates from US$0.3 billion to US$2.8 billion in recent publications. The higher end of the range belongs to DiMasi et al. (2016), a source often quoted in biopharma conferences. Regardless of where an asset ends up being within such a wide R&D cost range, it still represents a significant investment that can only be justified by expectations of correspondingly significant downstream profits for the private institutions undertaking such risky investments. IP ownership is a way to help safeguard downstream profits, making IP a critical enabler for the biopharma industry to prosper. As a direct consequence of its enabling nature for value creation, IP is a critical due diligence area in biopharma corporate development activities.

As illustrated in Figure 3.2, IP uses different forms of protection covered under different regulations.

Patents – Generally for 20 years from filing	Temporary right to exclude others from making, using, offering to sell or selling invention for the jurisdiction or geographical territory considered.
Copyrights – 70 years past author death; or for work for hire: up to 120 years	Temporary exclusive rights to original works of authorship as soon as an author fixes the work in a tangible form of expression.
Trademarks – As long as use is continuous	Exclusive rights to word, phrase, symbol, design, or a combination thereof, established from ongoing usage for specific goods and services and in specific geography where provided (registration provides increased protection).
Trade Secrets – As long as secrecy and value are maintained	Exclusive rights for as long as all three requirements are maintained: information has economic value by not being generally known, has value to others who cannot obtain it, AND is subject to reasonable efforts to maintain secrecy.

Figure 3.2 Main forms and duration of IP protections in the United States.

Patents

Patents are geared toward inventions. Patents are a temporary right to exclude others from making, using, offering to sell, or selling the invention for the jurisdiction considered. It is important to note that a patent does not provide affirmative rights to make something – it is a right to exclude. Securing a patent requires a proactive approach, filing in the jurisdiction in question, following the required process, and paying the corresponding fees. As for any IP, the owner will need to take steps they deem appropriate to protect it against infringement.

Copyrights

Copyrights are geared toward creative works and protect original works of authorship, e.g., books, novels, paintings, movies, and photographs (U.S. Copyright Office, 2021). In contrast to patents that involve an application process, in the United States, copyrights are automatically granted as soon as the author fixes original work in a tangible form of expression, meaning the work is realized onto a sufficiently permanent medium; copyrights last until 70 years after the author's death in the case of a single author, 70 years after the last author's death for joint work, and in the case of work for hire, 95 years post publication or 120 years post creation, whichever is sooner.

Trademarks

Trademarks are geared toward brands. A trademark identifies the source of biopharma goods or services, confers legal protection of the biopharma brand(s) and helps guard against counterfeiting and fraud (United States

Patent and Trademark Office, 2021). The trademark can be "any word, phrase, symbol, design, or a combination of these things that identifies your goods or services". In the United States, trademarks are owned by your biopharma firm as soon as you start, and as long as you continue, using them for your goods or services. Note that the protection afforded is only for those specific goods and services. Registration is not a requirement for trademarks although such federal registration does provide increased protection.

Trade Secrets

Trade secrets are geared toward confidential business information. Trade secrets correspond to valuable information your company has elected to keep secret. While there is no time limit for trade secret protection in the United States, the underlying information needs to satisfy and continue to satisfy all three important requirements to qualify and continue to qualify as trade secrets (United States Patent and Trademark Office, 2019):

1. Be economically valuable because of not being known by others.
2. Represent value to others who cannot obtain it.
3. Be subject to reasonable efforts by the company to maintain secrecy.

As soon as one of the above three requirements is no longer met, the information in question no longer qualifies as a trade secret.

Note also that there are other forms of IP beyond patents, copyrights, trademarks, and trade secrets although typically not used in biopharma in the United States. Mask works (series of related images encoding three-dimensional patterns) come under a different type of IP protection in the United States. Other jurisdictions might have different forms of IP protection, like utility models discussed later in the chapter.

Lastly, IP represents a significant value driver in the biopharma industry: looking at startup funding from VC companies, Zhou et al. (2016) provided insightful evidence:

- Startups with trademark applications received significantly higher funding.
- Startups with patent applications received even higher funding.
- Startups with both patent and trademark applications received higher funding than companies with just one of the two.

Similarly, it might be worth noting that half of mature biotech firms (defined as those biotech companies with a market capitalization north of US$5 billion) have no approved product but rely on income generated from licensing deals (Deloitte, 2021). This really puts in perspective the value of IP when the financial performance of many large firms rests entirely on it!

3.1.2 *Patents*

United States

In the United States, patents are covered under Title 35 of the United States Code of Laws, e.g.:

- *Scope/definition*: §101 – "Whoever invents or discovers any new and useful process, machine, manufacture, or composition of matter, or any new and useful improvement thereof, may obtain a patent therefor".
  Limitation: "no patent may issue on a claim directed to or encompassing a human organism".
- Novelty requirement: §102.
- Non-obvious subject matter: §103.
- *Patent rights*: §154 – "right to exclude others from making, using, offering for sale, or selling the invention throughout the United States or importing the invention into the United States, and, if the invention is a process, of the right to exclude others from using, offering for sale or selling throughout the United States, or importing into the United States, products made by that process".
  Term: "beginning on the date on which the patent issues and ending 20 years from the date on which the application for the patent was filed".

There are three types of patents in the United States: utility patents (most common for biopharma), design patents (to protect the appearance of an item rather than its structure or function), and plant patents (as the name indicates, to protect new varieties of plants).

Deciphering a US Utility Patent Number: US N,NNN,NNN XY

- The prefix US denotes a US publication.
- The number N,NNN,NNN corresponds to the number of a utility patent without letters (the inclusion of a letter prefix would indicate other documents, e.g., D for a design patent or PP for a plant patent).
- When present, the XY at the end typically corresponds to a status, e.g.: A1 for published application, B1 for utility patent not previously published, B2 for utility patent previously published, etc.

In 2013, the United States moved from a "first to file" approach, away from a "first to invent" approach when there are competing inventors or inventions. This made the United States more closely aligned with the rest of the world.

As we saw, not everything is patentable in the United States – the invention needs to be useful, novel, and non-obvious. Unchanged biological materials are not patentable as illustrated by the historic Myriad Genetics patent case (Association for Molecular Pathology v. Myriad Genetics, Inc. 2013). Some of the lessons learned in that Supreme Court case included:

- "A naturally occurring DNA segment is a product of nature and not patent eligible merely because it has been isolated".
- "Complementary DNA is patent eligible because it is not naturally occurring".
- "Uncovering the precise location and genetic sequence [...] [of genes for genes existing in nature is] not patent eligible".

Patent US11268070B2, granted in 2022 to Cellular Engineering Technologies, provides an interesting contrast to the Myriad Genetics case. The patent relates to a method to produce a safer (virus-free and oncogene-free), induced pluripotent stem cells whereas stem cells occur naturally (Cellular Engineering Technologies, 2022).

Separately, immoral subject matter is not patentable as it would not meet the utility requirements of Section §101 of US Code Title 35 since, given the harm to society, the invention would not be deemed to offer any benefit. Likewise, mathematical formulas or mental processes, as abstract intellectual concepts, are not patentable under Section §101. Natural laws or phenomena would not be patentable either.

Given the immoral subject matter exclusion from patentability, ethical considerations and societal benefit can be critically important for biopharma IP. Morality issues might be raised for patents relating to human cloning, human – animal hybrids, or embryonic stem cells depending on the jurisdiction.

IP5

While it is much beyond the scope of this book to cover all IP systems, we will occasionally touch upon the IP systems for Europe, Japan, China, and South Korea in addition to the United States. This specific group of countries (Table 3.1) was selected because they constitute the so-called IP5, the five largest IP offices in the world (IP5, 2019). As shown in Figure 3.3, they represented over 80% of biotech-related patents worldwide in 2018.

Table 3.1 Overview of patents within IP5

Patents	*United States*	*Europe*	*Japan*	*China*	*South Korea*
Main Legal Reference(s)	US Code Title 35 CFR Title 37	European Patent Convention (EPC)	Patent Act and Utility Model Act	China Patent Law	Korean Patent Act and Korean Utility Model Act
Regulator	Congress	European Parliament	National Diet	National People's Congress	National Assembly
Patent Office	United States Patent and Trademark Office (USPTO)	European Patent Office (EPO)	Japan Patent Office (JPO)	China National Intellectual Property Administration (CNIPA)	Korean Intellectual Property Office (KIPO)
Country code	US	EP	JP	CN	KR
Initial patent term	20 years from filing (for utility patent)	20 years from filing	20 years from filing (for patent vs 10 years for utility model)	20 years from filing (for invention vs 10 years for utility model)	20 years from filing (for patent vs 10 years for utility model)
Timeline performance: first action pendency & total pendency averages (2020)	Using target compliance rates[a] 95.7% < 14 month 98.1% < 36 month	4.3 months 23.7 months	10.1 months 14.8 months	14.4 months 20.0 months	11.1 months 15.8 months

Source: EPO et al. (2021).

a The USPTO changed to measuring target compliance rate in 2020 rather than measuring pendency averages. For reference, 2020 pendency averages for USPTO were as follows: 14.8 months for first action pendency and 23.3 months for total pendency.

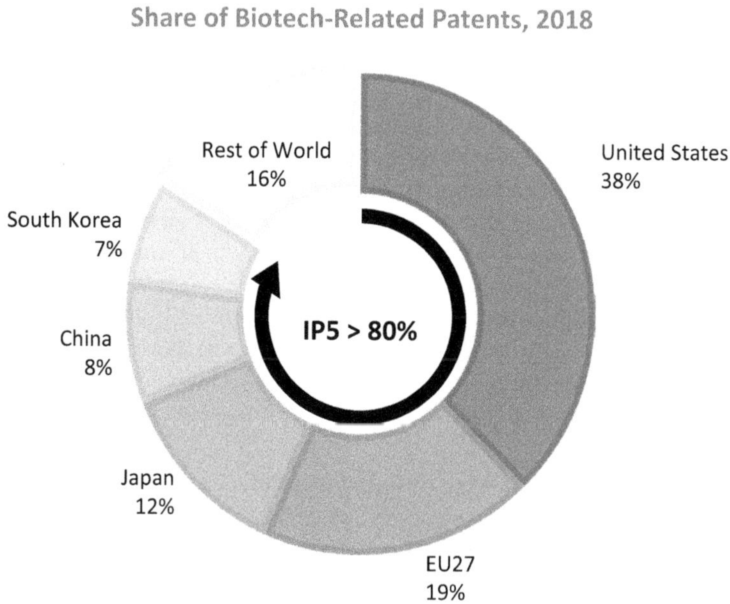

Figure 3.3 Global distribution of biotech-related patents.

Europe

The European Patent Office (EPO) has 38 member states (all members of the European Union plus 11 other states). See European Patent Office (2021). Similarly to the United States, the European Patent Convention (EPC) stipulates a patent term of 20 years from filing in all the applicable jurisdictions. The EPC was established as an international instrument or special treaty.

EPC (2020 version) patentability criteria are as follows:

- Scope/definition including both novelty and inventive step/non-obvious requirements, plus use/function: "European patents shall be granted for any inventions, in all fields of technology, provided that they are new, involve an inventive step and are susceptible of industrial application".
- Explicit exclusions from definition: "following in particular shall not be regarded as inventions:
    - Discoveries, scientific theories and mathematical methods.
    - Aesthetic creations.
    - Schemes, rules and methods for performing mental acts, playing games or doing business, and programs for computers.
    - Presentations of information".

- Additional exclusions: "European patents shall not be granted in respect of:
  - Inventions, the commercial exploitation of which would be contrary to 'ordre public' or morality; such exploitation shall not be deemed to be so contrary merely because it is prohibited by law or regulation in some or all of the Contracting States.
  - Plant or animal varieties or essentially biological processes for the production of plants or animals; this provision shall not apply to microbiological processes or the products thereof.
  - Methods for treatment of the human or animal body by surgery or therapy and diagnostic methods practiced on the human or animal body; this provision shall not apply to products, in particular substances or compositions, for use in any of these methods".

Additional considerations were included in EPC Chapter V (Biotechnological inventions: Rules 26 through 34), as well as in the 1998 EU Directive 98/44/EC (directive on the legal protection of biotechnological inventions).

The following distinction within EPC Rule 27 is particularly notable:

- "Biotechnological inventions shall also be patentable if they concern:
  - biological material which is isolated from its natural environment or produced by means of a technical process even if it previously occurred in nature.
  - [...] plants or animals if the technical feasibility of the invention is not confined to a particular plant or animal variety.
  - a microbiological or other technical process, or a product obtained by means of such a process other than a plant or animal variety".

Japan

The Japan Patent Office (JPO) has an additional category compared with the US and EU patent approaches. That additional category is called utility models and might sometimes be referred to as minor patents. They are designed for inventions with a shorter lifecycle, characterized by the potential for an early implementation and a creative idea relating to the shape of products, their structure, and other technological aspects. Compared with patents, the technological incremental innovation of a utility model would typically be of less significance. Accordingly, the protection period for utility models is 10 years, half of the patent protection period.

The Japanese Patent Act (2019 version) defines inventions in Article 2, as "highly advanced creation of technical ideas utilizing the laws of nature". As a corollary, arbitrary methods not based on laws of nature (e.g., finance or taxation methods, certain encryption approaches) are typically not patentable.

Article 29 provides further guidance on patentability: requirement of "industrial applicability", invention must not be in the public domain, non-obvious for a "person of ordinary skill in the art of the invention".

The patent term is established by Article 67: "The term of a patent right expires after a period of 20 years from the filing date of the patent application". Japan has a first-to-file approach (rather than first to invent).

According to Article 32, "an invention that is likely to disrupt public order, corrupt public morals or harm public health may not be patented".

Additionally, it is important to note that the Japanese Patent Act Article 35 requires fair compensation of employees who create patentable inventions in Japan.

One notable contrast in the Japan system compared to the United States is the absence of data exclusivity. This is relevant for follow-on regulatory submissions that might use the data submitted for the regulatory approval of the branded drug.

Worldwide

Managing patents and IP is a complicated matter and can also be expensive, especially for a small biopharma company with limited budgets. While there are broad common themes between patent jurisdictions (e.g., first-to-file rule, societal interest, novelty, and non-obvious nature), there are also differences (e.g., patentable subject matter/explicit exclusions, notion of utility model, grace periods for disclosures).

It is thus important for a biopharma firm to think about its invention in the context of its different markets and the resulting IP strategy implications.

On that note, biopharma geographies considered might typically include, in addition to the IP5:

- Larger economies like India, Brazil, Russia, Taiwan, and Mexico.
- Easier countries (no translation required) like Canada, Australia, New Zealand, and South Africa.
- Other specific countries according to specific situation and opportunities.

Biotech and pharmaceutical firms should thus identify early on the jurisdictions, geographies, and markets that will be important and relevant to their innovations. These should closely align with the financial and market models the biopharma firm is using. This said, due to lengthy biopharma development times and high upfront costs, deferring patent filing is desirable only to the extent that the biopharma firm does not risk losing the IP rights for the compounds it develops (a challenging proposition in a competitive environment with a first-to-file rule). Often times for new drug products, this approach results in a relatively early filing occurring toward the end of the discovery stage, before the compound enters pre-clinical stage.

Additional considerations that might inform country selection and guide a global patent strategy also include various national and regional aspects:

- Regulatory requirements for local clinical trials.
- Market exclusivity and potential extensions (e.g., pediatric, orphan drug).
- Data exclusivity (regulator not using data previously submitted to approve generics).
- Marketing approval/patent term extension linkage.

Taking into account clinical trial and commercial priorities, linkages between patent offices, patent office processing speed, or pendency performance should not only point the biopharma firm in the right direction for a global patent strategy (e.g., one might look at the Pareto curve for global market coverage versus cumulative patent costs as you add countries) but also inform the company on aspects to watch for such as publications, disclosure risks, and invention positioning.

This global patent approach brings up the Patent Cooperation Treaty (PCT). PCT makes it possible to seek patent protection for an invention in each of a large number of countries by filing an international patent application in a PCT contracting state, typically with the patent office of that state. A PCT application automatically sets the PCT application date as filing date with each of the contracting states selected, thus generating the equivalent of a national filing in each of these states. The process is then optimized, thanks to an international search by a competent International Searching Authority (ISA) and an international publication.

With over 150 countries eligible for PCT, the international PCT approach is highly likely to cover most if not all geographies of interest to a biopharma firm.

A typical biopharma global patent approach uses the following approach (USPTO, 2019; World Health Organization et al., 2020, p. 67) with further details illustrated in Figure 3.4:

- Pursue a first filing (provisional application) in one primary geography.
- File a PCT application in a timely fashion.
- Use Patent Prosecution Highway (PPH) Program when notified of allowable claims – PPH is a fast-track examination approach that speeds up the process for corresponding applications for the applicable jurisdictions and patent offices (USPTO, 2024b).
    - For biopharma firms considering patents in other Asia countries, it might be interesting to note that the JPO has a PPH agreement with other ASEAN countries: Indonesia, Malaysia, Philippines, Singapore, Thailand, and Vietnam.
- Undergo PCT national phase.

- At this stage, patent prosecution happens in the relevant individual jurisdictions.

- Assuming a patent is issued, the biopharma firm then needs to maintain and defend the patent, as required and desired.
  - At this stage, the biopharma firm will also pursue downstream opportunities: continue development in-house, license, co-develop, etc.

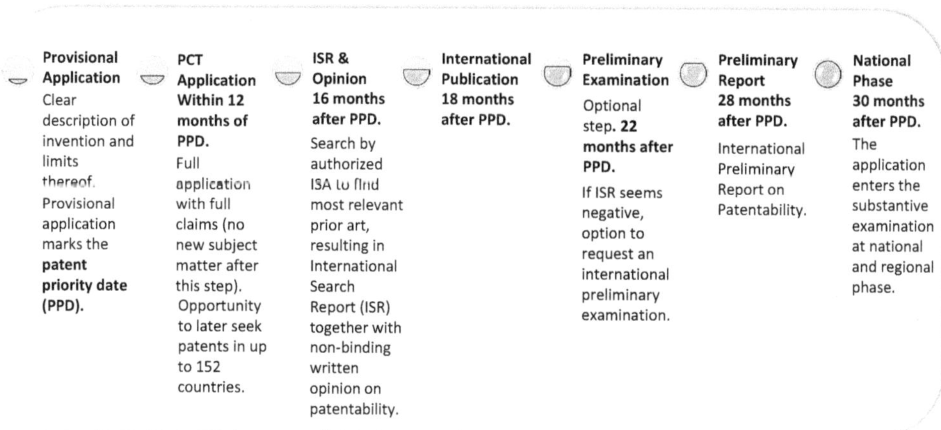

Figure 3.4 Typical global patent approach.

3.1.3 *Copyrights*

Copyright is intended to protect creative work. Similarly to patents, there can be important differences between jurisdictions; the United States uses the concept or original work fixed in a tangible medium, whereas China focuses on the original creation that can be reproduced in a tangible form. Copyright aspects that may vary with the jurisdiction include work for hire copyright duration, ownership of work made for hire, "fair use", registration, and use of copyright symbol. "Fair use" refers to the use of copyrighted work without permission under specific conditions (e.g., limited use) and in certain specified circumstances (e.g., for education, research, analysis, and news reporting). International sources of copyright law include the 1886 Berne Convention (that establishes a basis for automatic obtention of copyright protection), the 1952 Universal Copyright Convention, the 1994 Agreement on Trade-Related Aspects of Intellectual Property Rights (TRIPS), and the 1996 WIPO Copyright Treaty. Table 3.2 provides a high-level copyrights comparison for IP5.

Copyrights typically provide the owner with two different types of rights: moral rights and economic rights. As the names indicate, economic rights

Table 3.2 Overview of copyrights within IP5

Copyrights	*United States*	*Europe*	*Japan*	*China*	*South Korea*
Main Local Reference(s)	1976 Copyright Act. 17 U.S.C. §102a	Charter of Fundamental Rights of the EU. EU Directives 96/9/EC, 2001/29/EC, 2006/116/EC, 2009/24/EC, 2012/28/EU, 2019/790/EU	1970 Copyright Act (amended June 12, 2020)	2010 Copyright Law (amended October 17, 2020)	1957 Copyright Act (amended December 8, 2020)
Copyright Authority	US Copyright Office	EU Commission	Agency for Cultural Affairs	Copyright Protection Center of China	Korean Copyright Commission
Standard copyright duration	70 years after the death of the (last surviving) author	70 years after the death of the (last surviving) author	70 years after the death of the (last surviving) author	50 years after the death of the (last surviving) author or 50 years from publication	70 years after the death of the (last surviving) author
Selected "Work for Hire" considerations	Different duration: shorter between 120 years post creation & 95 years post publication	Not harmonized	Needs to be made public under employer's name (except computer programs that do not have publishing requirements)	Author(s) might retain copyright subject to right of use by employer	Needs to be made public under employer's name (except computer programs that do not have publishing requirements)
Registration required before filing a lawsuit	Yes	No	No but possible	No but possible	No but possible

protect the economic value of the copyrighted work whereas moral rights protect the moral values of the author.

Moral rights typically correspond to the owner's reputation, honor, and persona; they might include the right to decide whether or not to make the work public, to use a pseudonym versus a real name, to select the medium in which the work is made available or to maintain the integrity of the content. Moral rights have been defined in Article 6 of the Berne Convention as the "right to claim authorship of the work and to object to any distortion, mutilation or other modification of, or other derogatory action in relation to, the said work, which would be prejudicial to his honor or reputation".

Economic rights are those typically associated with copyright, i.e., control rights over copyrighted work in a way that allows them to derive financial rewards from said work. Economic rights may include rights of reproduction, right of performance, right of presentation/adaptation, right of transmission/distribution, rights of lending/subscription.

Depending on the jurisdiction, moral rights may not necessarily be transferable or assigned in the same way as economic rights. They might not have the same duration either.

Typically, copyright does not protect work with expired copyright protection, single words, mathematics, works created by nature, ideas, themes, and facts.

Case Examples: Selected Illustrative Copyright Uses in the Biopharma Industry

- Company logo with special design or work of art.
- Drawing/illustration of a mechanism of action made by a biopharma firm.
- Biopharma company employees commonly distribute and share, internally or externally, copyrighted materials in the form of journal articles, images, publications, technical literature, research papers, and so on. Whether or not they do so in a fashion compliant with copyright law is a separate question.
- Replicating art rendering and packaging of medications could be construed as copyright infringement – see Sun Pharmaceuticals Industries Ltd versus Cipla Ltd and the corresponding judgment by the Madras High Court 2021 case # 1980 (C. SARAVANAN, 2021).

Generic companies may not generally be liable for copyright infringement for replicating medication labels in the United States since the Hatch-Waxman Act requires them to reproduce the branded medication label: "information to show that the labeling proposed for the new drug is the same as the labeling approved for the listed drug". As a result of this Food and Drug Administration (FDA) requirement, copying the drug label does not typically constitute copyright infringement.

For product packaging, work that might otherwise fall under copyright protection might need to comply with regulatory guidance, thereby constraining the author's freedom to create. In the United States, the Food & Drug Administration provides safety considerations that will affect container labels and carton design (FDA, 2022b).

3.1.4 Trademarks

Biopharma firms prominently use trademarks for the company name and drug products. Beyond these, firms have numerous additional naming opportunities, such as for clinical trials, accompanying devices, drug classes, terms used for compounds/pharmacopeia, and of course the various digital assets the company might use.

Establishing a company name, which will then constitute the company's trademark, can represent a simple emotional investment at the outset of a brainstorming session conducted by the company founders or go all the way to an expensive name selection using an outside marketing agency. It is commonly the former and might or might not be a very comprehensive exercise.

Selecting proprietary names for drug products is usually a more involved multi-year exercise, representing an optimized outcome between ideal commercialization decisions, the need to follow regulatory authority review decisions, and, in particular, patient safety considerations.

In the United States, the proprietary name falls under the dual jurisdiction of the US Patent and Trademark Office (USPTO) and the FDA. While the USPTO focuses on traditional trademark law for registration requests (like use/intent to use, distinctive nature of the mark for the product and geographies, and so on), the FDA's optic is a patient safety one to "help minimize proprietary name-related medication errors and otherwise avoid adoption of proprietary names that contribute to violations of the Federal Food, Drug, and Cosmetic Act and its implementing regulations" (FDA, 2020). In such a context, safety testing may represent a critical component in seeking approval for a proprietary name. The organization within the FDA that reviews names is the Division of Medication Error Prevention and Analysis, within the Office of Surveillance and Epidemiology of CDER (Center for Drug Evaluation and Research). The European Medicines Agency (EMA) has a corresponding name review process, made more complicated by the multitude of languages used in the EMA jurisdiction. EMA has a specific form for "proposed invented names" along with naming guidelines (EMA, 2021).

Although in the United States, a biopharma company does not need to register a trade name with the USPTO (ongoing use might be sufficient), for proprietary drug names, it must follow the FDA process before using the name. In fact, in a post-marketing pharmacovigilance setting, the FDA might even "consider a change to the proprietary name to address safety issues resulting from name confusion errors" (FDA, 2022a). On a related

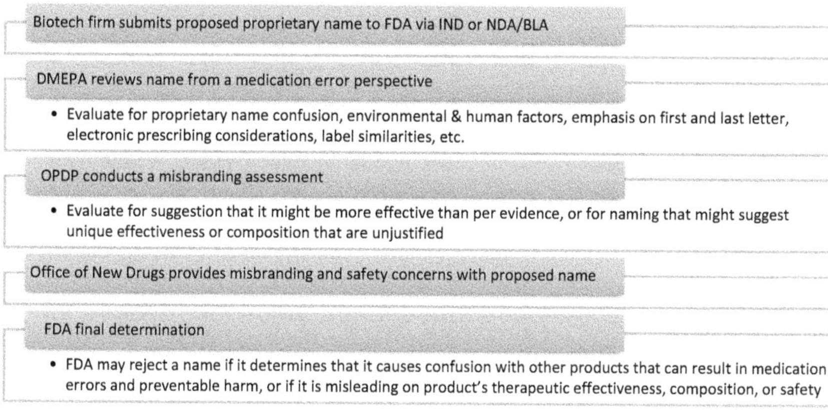

Figure 3.5 Illustrative FDA proprietary name approval process.

note, trademark offices might require ongoing use for a trade name to remain valid – and, until the drug is approved for marketing by regulatory authorities, the biopharma firm might be able to meet such ongoing usage requirements via clinical trials. In recent years, the FDA has rejected one in four names versus one in two for the EMA (Cohen et al., 2021).

Establishing a global proprietary drug name can be a lengthy process and might conservatively be started 2 or 3 years prior to NDA/BLA/Marketing Approval (Figure 3.5).

Drugs and biologics might also be the object of specific regulations for non-proprietary names (FDA, 2019). Such generic names are considered public domain names and International Nonproprietary Names (INN are requested from the World Health Organization and serve to make it easier to identify pharmaceutical substances or active ingredients; they are almost always identical to their US adopted name counterparts) are provided on the World Health Organization website (WHO, 2002). In the United States, the assignment of non-proprietary names is done by the US Adopted Names Council.

Case Examples: Selected Illustrative Trademark Uses in the Biopharma Industry

- Any proprietary drug name.
- A trademark could be used for a generic drug to signal manufacturing quality, link it to a humanitarian cause, or highlight another differentiating characteristic.
- Counterfeit drugs might be construed as trademark infringement.

Table 3.3 provides a summary overview of trademarks within the IP5 countries, highlighting a similarity of practice between them.

Table 3.3 Overview of trademarks within IP5

Trademarks	*United States*	*Europe*	*Japan*	*China*	*South Korea*
Main Local Reference(s)	Trademark Act of 1946, 15 § U.S.C. 1051, Lanham Act, Prescription Drug User Fee Act, Generic Drug User Fee Amendment	EU Directive 2015/2436 EU Regulations 2017/1001, 2018/625, 2018/626	Trademark Act (Act No. 127 of April 13, 1959) PMD Act	Trademark Law of the People's Republic of China (amended April 23, 2019)	Trademark Act No. 71 of November 28, 1949 (amended December 22, 2020)
Trademark Authority	United States Patent and Trademark Office (USPTO)	European Union Intellectual Property Office (EUIPO)	Japan Patent Office (JPO)	China National Intellectual Property Administration (CNIPA)	Korean Intellectual Property Office (KIPO)
Trademark Basis, Registration & Duration	First-to-use basis. Registration optional. Continued use required to maintain trademark. Registration to be renewed every 10 years, indefinitely	First-to-file basis. Registration required. Valid for 10 years; can be renewed indefinitely 10 years at a time	First-to-file basis. Registration required. Valid for 10 years; can be renewed indefinitely 10 years at a time	First-to-file basis. Registration required. Continued use required to maintain trademark. Valid for 10 years; can be renewed indefinitely 10 years at a time	First-to-file basis. Registration required. Valid for 10 years; can be renewed indefinitely 10 years at a time
Use of Proprietary Drug Name – Linkage to Drug Development	FDA review of proposed proprietary name at IND and NDA/BLA stages. Final FDA approval with NDA/BLA	Centralized review of proposed proprietary name by Name Review Group (NRG) as part of EMA marketing authorization	Proposed proprietary name review is part of review for PDMA marketing approval	Proprietary Name Review can be requested with new drug submission	MFDS marketing approval: approval granted to a brand name, not to pharmaceutical substances

3.1.5 Trade Secrets

Trade secrets do not require registration and are commonly used in the biopharma industry to protect practices that provide the company with a competitive advantage or economic benefit. As discussed, they need to have economic value, be of value to others since known to a few, and be the object of protection efforts.

The case example on the right provides an illustration of what a large pharmaceutical firm like GSK might consider a trade secret and how it might go about protecting it.

Further case details are available from Judge Paul W. Grimm (2022).

Additional trade secret considerations and examples can be found in Nealey et al. (2014).

The 1994 TRIPS Agreement, with 2005 Geneva amendment, establishes minimum standards for trade secrets for all World Trade Organization members. Table 3.4 provides a brief overview of the trade secret frameworks within IP5.

Depending on the jurisdiction, additional considerations may include right to information, freedom of expression, and whistleblowing regulations. One should note that the

Trade Secret Case Example: GSK versus Denise Brooks

US District Court for the District of Maryland.
Case No. 8:22-cv-00364-PWG

Denise Brooks was a GSK employee from November 2006 until January 13, 2022. As Quality Systems Lead, Ms. Brooks had access to and possession of what GSK considers trade secrets, specifically including GSK's manufacturing procedures and regulatory compliance. As GSK was investing payments charged to Ms. Brooks' GSK-issued credit card, she resigned before the investigation was complete.

GSK alleged that after her January 13, 2022 resignation, she exchanged her old GSK laptop for a new GSK one she left GSK with and that contained all her previous files and emails. GSK sued.

On February 15, 2022, GSK's motion for a temporary restraining order (TRO) was granted. TRO ordered Ms. Brooks to refrain from accessing, using, or disclosing GSK confidential information or data, to immediately return all GSK property, to refrain from deleting any GSK-owned media, documents, or data, to provide proof she did not retain copies via third-party inspection, and to preserve documents relevant to the TRO.

On May 5, 2022, after absences and non-compliance, a new GSK motion for civil contempt and sanctions (fine of US$200 per day until she has complied with TRO) was granted. (…)

Table 3.4 Overview of trade secret frameworks within IP5

	Trade secret framework
United States	Uniform Trade Secrets Act of 1985. Basis for State laws. Economic Espionage Act (EEA) of 1996, federal law. Defend Trade Secrets Act of 2016, amendment to EEA.
Europe	Minimum standards set by 2016 Directive (EU) 2016/943 on the protection of undisclosed know-how and business information (trade secrets) against unlawful acquisition, use and disclosure. Member States can set higher standards.
Japan	Unfair Competition Prevention Act of 1993 followed by 1994 TRIPS ratification.
China	Legal context separated into different laws, with Anti-Unfair Competition Law (amended in 2019) as primary reference.
South Korea	Unfair Competition Prevention and Trade Secret Protection Act of 1961, amended in 2009. Additional acts may apply depending on circumstances.

acquisition of trade secrets is generally legal if obtained either through independent discovery, through reverse engineering, or by using any alternate legal commercial practice.

Finally, collaboration has become more prominent in the biopharma industry, especially after the COVID-19 pandemic. Firms need to keep in mind the requirements for trade secrets in such an operational context and take reasonable steps to protect trade secrets. This might mean ensuring labels or stamps on corresponding documents indicating their confidential or secret nature; it might mean ensuring a confidentiality agreement or non-disclosure agreement is signed before sharing information; it might mean restricting physical and virtual accesses and so on. While enabling collaborations is critical, it should not be at the expense of the company's IP assets.

3.1.6 Freedom to Operate (FTO) Concept

What Is FTO? The Rocking Chair Story

Imagine you just invented and patented in the United States the curved pieces that go under a rocking chair – one could argue that for all intents and purposes you invented the rocking chair (Figure 3.6).

FTO would mean that you can make and sell in the United States a rocking chair without infringing on any third-party's IP.

But if, after checking, you find out that there is a third-party US patent on the seat of the chair – a shaped surface people seat on – you might not be able to make or sell the rocking chair you had envisioned and thus would not have FTO.

Figure 3.6 Rocking chair by Hudson and Brooks (MET, 1971.161).

To assess the freedom to operate for their products, biopharma companies will often hire an IP lawyer to conduct what is called an FTO search or FTO analysis. For the designated jurisdictions and geographies (anywhere the company intends to manufacture, distribute, sell, or import products), the IP lawyer will search for, investigate, and assess any intellectual properties the company might be infringing upon (patents, utility models, designs, trademarks, or copyrights). Based on that research and analysis, the IP lawyer will provide an "FTO opinion". If favorable, it would be an indication that the biopharma company should be able to proceed with R&D and commercialization with minimal risk of infringing on third-party IP at this specific point in time. If unfavorable, the opinion would highlight specific infringement risks. It might be worth noting in this respect that there are typically many patentable aspects to an invention (e.g., for a biopharma compound, the compound itself, the formulation, the indications, the claims based on clinical trial results, and manufacturing aspects). The company might then consider licensing agreements or partnerships to avoid infringement lawsuits. Other options might include making inventions that circumvent high-risks patents, modifying the product to avoid infringements, abandoning the product in favor of another one, waiting until the third-party patent expires, challenging the validity of the third-party patent, or simply taking the risk and betting that the third party will not take legal action. As a side note, licensing might not necessarily be expensive, especially for academic or nonprofit organizations as some large corporations might be inclined to offer more generous terms to such organizations.

As opposed to a patent that does not suppose positive rights, a favorable FTO opinion indicates the company should likely be able to make, distribute, and sell their product with minimal IP infringement risks. There are two important aspects to note for an FTO opinion: first, it is an opinion after careful analysis but not a guarantee; second, it is only valid at the time of the analysis as patent, legal systems, and IP landscapes change over time. In addition, given the many patentable aspects, ongoing evaluation of new aspects is required as development progresses. FTO represents a key due diligence area for biopharma transactions and investments.

One IP strategy exercise sometimes used in connection with FTO is that of patent mapping or patent landscape analysis: the biopharma firm together with their IP counsel will analyze and evaluate the patents relevant to the company's competition and establish a suitable patent and IP strategy.

3.1.7 *IP Management*

Many building blocks are used to effectively manage IP: strategy, management plan, software, organization, processes, and policies.

Innovation Strategy

IP strategy constitutes the basis of the biopharma company's innovation strategy within the ecosystem in which the firm operates. That IP strategy should be designed with the longer-term perspective of its innovation strategy as illustrated by Figure 3.7, a figure derived from Heiden and Peters (2020).

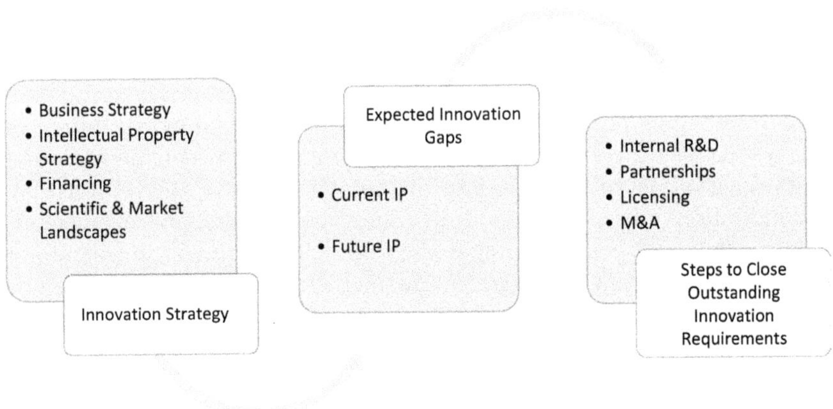

Figure 3.7 How a biopharma firm's innovation strategy guides IP-related initiatives.

Like most strategic initiatives, IP-related initiatives will typically include risks and thus a risk-management component. This is especially important for the biopharma industry given its capital-intensive nature. Such considerations might give rise to licensing options or purchase options common in biopharma transactions.

IP Management Plan

An IP management plan guides how IP is managed and is usually captured in a controlled document or IP management software. While there are varying structures and formats, the plan typically covers the topics in the following textbox.

IP Management Plan

- Revision date and applicability
- Basic definitions and scope
- IP priorities and directions.
- Procedures for General IP Management.
    - Organization.
    - Information repositories.
    - IP Portfolio management.
    - Disclosures.
    - Responsibilities and workflows.
    - Ownership.
    - Incentive programs.
    - Conflicts of interest.
- Sections for different types of IP: patents, copyright, trademarks, and trade secrets.
- Procedures for IP search (internal and external).
- Procedures for collaborations regarding IP: CDA, licensing, claiming inventions, etc
- IP Infringement, opposition, enforcement, etc
- Various forms with process and applicability.

Use of IP Management Software

Such software is used by groups that manage IP on an ongoing basis such as IP law firms or in-house IP offices. IP management software can cover many functions and its adoption, like any digitalization, requires transformation and process adjustments. It can help manage the numerous deadlines related to trademarks, copyrights, and patents (a process called "IP docketing"). It also provides centralization, automation, and tools for IP management (e.g., legal updates for various geographies, references, automated communications and tasks, improved file management and communications accessibility on a subject matter, reporting, service integration for patent, and trademark maintenance).

IP Organization

The team responsible for IP provides a consistent source of information and helps minimize IP risks. Two major factors are usually considered in its organization:

1. Effective business alignment (e.g., common approach, integration and joint decision-making, strategic contributions).
2. Optimized work efficiency (e.g., allocation of expert resources to high-value added tasks, finding routine/automation solutions for lower value activities like docketing).

IP Processes and Policies

Policies and procedures should be well-articulated to be easily accessible and understandable by all company employees. Policies and procedures:

- Consider key contributors (internal team, scientific advisers, collaborators, suppliers).
- Facilitate business operations.
- Take into account company culture (biopharma industry R&D process, traditional biopharma marketing approaches, including publication and conferences, company growth stage, communication style, operational practices, etc.).
- Facilitate (or at least not detract) innovation talent recruiting and retention.

Having a formal approach (e.g., lab notebooks) rather than depending on a few key employees can help secure buy-in and facilitate implementation. Including IP in employee training and professional development (including rewards and recognition) can contribute to effective IP management.

Now that we have seen the building blocks of IP management, let us look at IP in the context of clinical development and clinical trials.

3.1.8 *IP and Clinical Development*

As discussed, drug candidates are usually patented at the discovery stage. Such patents typically cover active ingredients or chemical compounds with additional patents to cover a number of variations around structure, delivery, formulations, composition of matter, etc. These patents can protect the commercial potential of the biopharma firm by excluding competitors from producing equivalent compounds.

However, the clock started ticking against the typical 20-year protection from the filing date (excluding provisional applications). By the time the biopharma firm has completed the multi-year pre-clinical and clinical trial stages and secured regulatory marketing approval, only part of the 20-year protection remains. There are, however, additional IP protections tied to clinical trials and regulatory approvals.

Let us take the case of the United States. FDA approval provides for a regulatory marketing exclusivity of at least 5 years for new chemical entities, regardless of patent status, commencing on FDA approval, as codified in 21 CFR 314 & 316. Marketing exclusivity refers to the period during which the branded drug is protected from generic drug competition.

In addition, the United States passed in 1984 the Hatch-Waxman Act, also known as "Drug Price Competition and Patent Term Restoration Act of 1984". Balancing innovation with affordability, the Act established the basis for the generics industry while preserving incentives for biopharma innovation.

More specifically, the Act provides for the following:

- Safe Harbor.
    - The Act exempts generic manufacturers from patent infringement (research exemption) during development work toward FDA approval, before patent has expired. This allows for faster generic introduction as it allows generic manufacturers to have completed development while the branded drug patent is still in force, and apply for generic approval as the patent expires.
- Abbreviated New Drug Application (ANDA) approval process.
    - Allowing generic manufacturers to reference the branded drug manufacturer's safety and efficacy data rather than undergoing similar independent studies.
- Patent listing/Orange Book.
    - The Orange Book is an FDA database of patents covering approved pharmaceuticals and includes the first approved generic (see exclusivity below) in addition to other US-approved generics.
- Patent Term Restoration.
    - Restoring for one patent, up to 5 years of the patent term lost to the lengthy development process required for FDA approval, as codified in 21 CFR 60.
- Exclusivity.
    - 3-year exclusivity for (only the) improved version of a branded chemical drug that required additional clinical studies for approval (e.g., new indication or new dosage form).
    - 180-day exclusivity for first marketed generic, following launch, under specific conditions (ANDA application plus paragraph IV certification that a branded product patent is unenforceable, invalid, or will not be infringed upon by the generic product).

The Hatch-Waxman Act has enabled a stronger generic presence in the United States:

- As of 2021, 90% of all prescriptions dispensed in the United States are for generic drugs (U.S. Food and Drug Administration, 2022).
- In contrast, prior to the Act, only 19% of all prescriptions dispensed in the United States were for generic drugs (PhRMA, 2018).

As noted, the Act provides for one patent up to 5 years of patent restoration, in addition to the 3-year exclusivity for an improved version of the branded drug. The IP owner, who might typically have several patents on a drug product, must select the one patent that will benefit from the patent term extension (PTE).

The mechanics used to calculate the PTE can be complex: the PTE is half the IND or testing phase (starting after patent grant) plus the NDA phase minus delays due to the manufacturer, not to exceed 5 years post patent cliff and for the extended patent not to exceed 14 years from NDA. The PTE request also needs to be timely (within 60 days of NDA), filed with USPTO prior to patent expiration, and is applicable only for the first extension of an active ingredient (in cases where a patent might cover several products). The PTE is normally in addition to (and independent from) any patent term adjustment that may otherwise be obtained from the USPTO.

Case Example: Simple PTE Calculation

Assume patent grant prior to IND, 5 years between IND and NDA filings as well as 1 year between NDA filing and approval, and 6 months of delays due to the manufacturer. PTE = $5/2 + 1 - 0.5 = 3$-year extension.

In 1992, the United States passed the Prescription Drug User Fee Act, commonly designated as PDUFA. The intent of the Act was to increase the market exclusivity available to the branded drug by reducing the FDA review time. PDUFA is reauthorized by the US Congress every 5 years. To help make the review process more predictable, biopharma companies pay two user fees under PDUFA (unless exempt): an application fee when submitting an NDA or BLA, and an annual program fee for approved prescription products without an approved generic product.

For biotech firms, more importantly, the US Congress established in 1997 the BLA (Biologics License Application) under section 351 of the Public Health Service Act. This was followed in 2009 by the Biologics Price Competition and Innovation Act or BPCIA. Under the BPCIA, biotech manufacturers have 12 years of exclusivity for a new branded biologics following the BLA approval. In contrast to the Orange Book used for NDAs, biologics approved with a BLA are listed on the FDA Purple Book. Note that Title 37 (Patents, Trademarks and Copyrights) of the Code of Federal

Regulations treats NDA and BLA similarly for the application of PTE and the calculations above.

Independently from the PTE, a biopharmaceutical company may obtain different exclusivity periods (from the standard 5-year exclusivity) in certain cases:

- Pediatric studies offer an extra 6 months of marketing exclusivity, as codified in section 505(A) of the FDA Modernization Act of 1997.
    - Note that such extension, when granted, attaches to all dosage forms and all indications (as opposed to only the product studied in the pediatric population).
- Orphan Drug designation provides for a 7-year exclusivity post NDA/BLA for the indication.
    - Based on the Orphan Drug Act of 1983 (with final rule of June 12, 2013), the FDA has authority to grant orphan drug designation to a drug or biological product. Such designation qualifies the sponsors for specific incentives: tax credits for qualified clinical trials, exemption from user fees, potential 7-year market exclusivity post approval.
    - Orphan drug designation typically corresponds to a disease or condition that affects fewer than 200,000 people in the United States (orphan drug designation might be granted for a disease or condition with higher prevalence when the drug will not be profitable within 7 years following FDA approval).
    - The FDA website provides a searchable database of orphan drug designations and approvals.
- Certain antibiotic drugs in the case of certain diseases may be eligible for a 5-year exclusivity added to any other exclusivities granted for the drug.
    - This is based on the GAIN Act (Generating Antibiotic Incentives Now) passed in 2012, as part of FDA Safety and Innovation Act (FDASIA).
    - Qualifying products are designated as QIDPs (qualified infectious disease products).
    - Biologics are not qualified for QDIP designation (Food and Drug Administration, 2021).
    - QDIPs are given priority review by the FDA.

Case Example: QDIP

A drug has received both QIDP and orphan drug designations, in addition, a pediatric exclusivity: it thus qualifies for a 10.5-year market exclusivity (7 year from orphan drug + 5 year from QIDP + 0.5 year from pediatric studies). Note that in this example the various exclusivities are all added but that may not be the case for all exclusivities listed in Table 3.5.

Table 3.5 Summary of US IP protection from clinical development and regulatory approval

Category	*Drug (Filing under Section 505 of the Food, Drug, & Cosmetics Act)*	*Biological product (Filing under Section 351 of Public Health Service Act)*
Initial Patent Protection	20 years from filing	20 years from filing
Patent Term Extension	Up to 5 years for one patent	Up to 5 years for one patent
New Product Exclusivity	5 years from NDA approval	12 years from BLA approval
Pediatric Extension	6 months incremental exclusivity for all dosage and all indications	6 months incremental exclusivity for all dosage and all indications
Orphan Drug Designation	7-year exclusivity from NDA for product and indication + additional incentives	7-year exclusivity from BLA for product and indication + additional incentives
Qualified Infectious Disease Product Designation	5-year incremental branded product exclusivity	Not applicable
New Clinical Investigation Exclusivity	3-year at time of approval based on new clinical investigations by NDA applicant to demonstrate substantial evidence of effectiveness	Not applicable

In addition, as we will see in Chapter 9, there are faster FDA programs available to manufacturers to facilitate and expedite the development and review of new drugs that address unmet medical needs for serious diseases. Such programs might result in longer market IP protection given their faster approval.

Other geographies governed by other regulatory agencies typically have regulations that affect and extend the IP of biopharma companies as part of their regulatory approval process, as illustrated below with Europe and Japan.

Europe

Directive 2001/83 and Regulation 726/2004: **Global Marketing Authorization**

- **8-year of data protection** (see note below).

  - Data exclusivity period during which another applicant cannot rely on the data for another marketing authorization submission.
  - Generic applications can start after that time frame.

- **10 years of marketing protection** (concurrent with data protection).
  - Market exclusivity period can be extended to a maximum of 11 years in case of additional indications with significant clinical benefits within the first 8 years.
  - Market protection is the period during which a generic, hybrid, or biosimilar cannot be marketed.

Regulation 141/2000: **EU Orphan Drug Regulation**

- Conceived for conditions affecting 5 in 10,000 or less in the community.
- 10-year market exclusivity (no generic applications allowed).
  - Can be reduced to 6 years post-authorization if criteria are no longer met.
- + 2 years of market exclusivity for completing a pediatric investigation plan.
- Fee reductions, access to centralized procedure, protocol assistance.

Regulation 1901/2006: **Pediatric Use**

- 6-month extension of SPC (supplementary protection certificate) with pediatric investigation completion or waiver. This applies to the product covered by the authorization in place.

Regulation 469/2009: **Supplementary Protection Certificate Regulation**

- Up to 5-year SPC granted on approval calculated as follows: duration from patent filing date to first marketing authorization date, minus 5 years, capped at 5 years (not counting pediatric use extension).
- Example: for a patent filed on 11/25/2006 and a first marketing authorization granted on 11/25/2014, the SPC will be 2014 – 2006 – 5 = 3 years.

Note: as of March 2025, the European Parliament approved reforms, including a shortened minimum period of data protection from 8 years to 7.5 although the legislative process had still to be finalized (Harte & Kaufman, 2024).

Japan

Japan has **no data exclusivity system per se** but uses instead the notion of a **reexamination period** that serves as post-marketing surveillance. During that reexamination time frame, any manufacturer that would seek product approval would need to provide the same level of documentation and data as for a de novo drug application, thereby preempting the entry of generic during that reexamination period. After the reexamination period is over, a generic manufacturer can use a more streamlined application format.

Typical reexamination periods in Japan:

- New drugs with new active ingredients: 8 years (minimum of 6 years).
- New drugs with new administration route: 6 years.
- Drugs for new indications, or new dosage or new administration: 4 years (maximum of 6 years).
- Orphan drugs: 10 years (range of 6–10 years).

No pediatric extension per se in Japan, however, pediatric studies might impact/extend the reexamination period to collect suitable corresponding data.

Exclusivity coming from patent term:

- During the term of the patent, manufacturing or using or selling an item covered by the patent would constitute infringement.
    - Does not apply to clinical trials per Article 69 of Japanese Patent Act allowing use for experimental or research purposes.
- **PTE of up to 5 years** possible per Article 67.2 of Japanese Patent Act.

National Health Insurance (NHI) Listing

- For a generic to effectively compete with a branded product, they typically need to figure on the NHI Price List, a list typically revised twice a year in June and December, thereby providing additional exclusivity to the branded drug as the generic manufacturer has to wait for the next list update.

There are many possible considerations in setting an optimal IP approach, from options to prolong exclusivity periods to options that might secure exclusivity through new dosages that improve adherence or efficacy, new formulations with better storage characteristics, new delivery routes, improved delivery device, etc. As a biopharma firm seeks to maintain its competitive advantage resulting from exclusivity, it is also important to consider public relations implications as some of the approaches can result in criticisms from the public or even bear litigation risks.

3.1.9 Accounting Considerations for IP

Because IP is intangible, its management may be linked to material accounting considerations that influence how the biopharma company values and reports IP in its financial statements.

The section provides, through various tables (Tables 3.6–3.12) and case examples, either under US Generally Accepted Accounting Principles (US GAAP) or under International Financing Reporting Standards (IFRS), illustrations of the types of IP accounting issues biopharma company leadership teams might need to consider in connection with the company's value creation potential.

Note that due to ongoing accounting standard evolution, these illustrations may or may not follow the latest accounting practices and guidelines.

Accounting Standards Discussed

- US GAAP (Generally Accepted Accounting Principles)
  - ⇨ Rules, standards, and procedures, issued by FASB (Financial Accounting Standards Board).
  - ⇨ Standards are referenced as Accounting Standards Codification or ASC.
  - ⇨ Typically followed by US public companies.
- IFRS (International Financing Reporting Standards)
  - ⇨ Rules, standards, and procedures, issued by IASB (International Accounting Standard Board).
  - ⇨ Standards are referenced either as IAS or as IFRS.
  - ⇨ Typically followed by companies outside the United States.

Table 3.6 Treatment of internal R&D to develop intangible assets

US GAAP	IFRS
Guidance from ASC 730 (Research and Development): By default, **R&D costs** such as personnel costs, indirect costs, and R&D activities performed by third parties **are expensed**. However, expenditures (acquired or constructed) that have an alternative future use and a separate economic value can be capitalized.	Guidance from IAS 38 (Intangible assets): **Research costs are expensed.** **Development costs are capitalized**, if the biopharma company can demonstrate all the following for the intangible asset: 1. Technical feasibility to complete it and make it available for use/sale. 2. Intent to complete and use/sell. 3. Ability to use/sell. 4. How it will generate probable future economic benefits. 5. Availability of resources to complete development. 6. Ability to reliably measure expenditures during development.

Why Capitalize IP Costs?

Doing so aligns costs with the lifespan of an intangible asset. Capitalizing biopharma development costs effectively reduces losses during development phases while correspondingly decreasing profits later as capitalized amounts are depreciated every year. However, due to the inherent risks of failure in the pharmaceutical development, the IFRS criteria above generally represent a tall order for the biopharma sector until regulatory approval has been obtained.

Table 3.7 IP infringement lawsuit

US GAAP	IFRS
Guidance from ASC 450 (Contingencies): 1. **If a lawsuit loss is probable** (i.e., >75%) and reasonably **estimable** (e.g., settlement offer made by the company), **accrual and disclosure are typically required**. Charge made to income for most probable loss (contingent liabilities shown as liabilities on balance sheet and as expenses on income statement). Legal fees can also be accrued depending on accounting policy. 2. If loss is not both probable and reasonably estimable, no accrual required but disclosure is required.[a] 3. If the party potentially infringed upon has not notified the biopharma firm: neither accrual nor disclosure required.	Guidance from IAS 37 (Provisions, Contingent Liabilities and Contingent Assets): Although there are technical differences on the specific amount to use where applicable, the **treatment is similar to US GAAP** depending on probability and estimate reliability (also, IFRS uses provisions versus US GAAP loss contingency). However, IFRS uses a lower threshold of 50% (versus US GAAP of 75%), resulting in higher provision levels.

[a] Under US GAAP, in case number 2 above, an example of improbable loss might be a situation where the biopharma firm believes that a patent infringement lawsuit is without merit and intends to vigorously defend itself. IFRS may yield the same answer as long as the probability is below its lower threshold.

Table 3.8 In-licensing (pre-approval)

US GAAP	**IFRS**
Guidance from ASC 730 (R&D): As **license** is acquired **before regulatory approval** and is not an ongoing business, payments are treated as acquired in-process R&D and **expensed as R&D costs**, provided there is no other alternative future use for the acquired in-process R&D. **Upon regulatory approval**, license **approval milestone payment** would be **capitalized** and depreciated over the asset life. Additional accrual vs expensing considerations exist for sales milestone payments.	Guidance from IAS 38 (Intangible assets): For a license acquired before regulatory approval, IFRS would differ from US GAAP the same way that IFRS R&D intangible asset treatment differs from US GAAP. **License before regulatory approval may correspondingly be expensed or capitalized.**[a] **Upon regulatory approval, approval milestone payment** would be **capitalized** and depreciated over the asset life.

[a] Under IFRS, there is an important distinction made depending on which party continues drug development.

- When the licensee takes over development, milestones and upfront payments for the IP are capitalized if they meet the criteria listed. This approach applies when R&D is internalized or when R&D is reimbursed to the licensor at cost.
- When the licensor continues development without R&D reimbursement by the licensee, the part of the upfront payment corresponding to the fair value of *future* licensor R&D work (not reimbursed) is expensed and not capitalized. The remainder of the upfront amount is capitalized as purchase price for the IP license, according to IAS 38.

Case Example: In-Licensing Agreement under US GAAP

In 2019, Vertex Pharmaceuticals entered into a strategic R&D collaboration agreement with Kymera Therapeutics. Kymera received an upfront payment of US$50M and Vertex received exclusive rights to license up to six protein targets, for which Kymera may receive up to US$170M per target plus royalties (Vertex Pharmaceuticals Incorporated, 2022, p. 106).

Vertex determined that substantially all fair value of the collaboration was attributable to in-process R&D and that no substantive process was acquired that would constitute a business. They concluded that they did not have any alternative future use for the acquired in-process R&D per ASC 730 and expensed the US$50M upfront payment to R&D (Vertex Pharmaceuticals Incorporated, 2022, p. 106).

Table 3.9 Out-licensing

US GAAP	IFRS
Guidance from ASC 606 (Revenue Recognition): Company **recognizes upfront payment** (non-refundable) **when license is granted**. Company should recognize **revenues for sales-based or usage-based royalties as the later of the two happens: sales or usage** (as applicable), after corresponding company's performance **obligations** under licensing agreement **have been met**. Licensing revenues may be reported under "other operating income" (policy election) since not part of ordinary activities for a biopharma firm.	Guidance from IFRS 15 (Revenue Recognition): **Treatment like US GAAP** for the most part.

Note that, for out-licensing, additional considerations and accounting treatments come into play with additional licensing components, such as milestones, additional lump-sum payments over time, options to additional IP, other performance obligations (e.g., sales force assistance), and termination penalties (ASC 606 includes more guidance than IFRS 15).

Table 3.10 IP treatment for company or asset acquisition

US GAAP	IFRS
Guidance from ASC 805 (Business combinations): Intellectual property is recognized at fair market value if (1) the IP arises from legal or contractual rights or (2) it can be readily separated from the business being sold. Such **identifiable intangibles need to be recognized as a separate asset** from goodwill. Typically, patents and trademarks meet the requirement of identifiable intangibles. Fair value assessment is covered under **ASC 820**.	Guidance from IFRS 3 (Business combinations): Like for US GAAP, generally all **identifiable intangibles** acquired in a business combination are **measured independently**. Patents, trademarks, and copyrights are typically valued **using an income framework** (other methods include market value and cost framework) – See **IFRS 13** (Fair Value Measurement).

The main difference between US GAAP and IFRS resides in the mandatory concentration test for US GAAP imposing an asset acquisition grouping of similar assets when the fair value is concentrated, versus the optional use of concentration test in the case of IFRS.

Table 3.11 Asset sale

US GAAP	IFRS
Guidance from ASC 820 (Valuations): As selling assets or intellectual properties such as patents, trademarks, and copyrights is not normally part of ordinary biopharma firm activities, the **net proceeds** (net of book value) are considered **gains** rather than revenues **on** the company's **income statement.** Barring ongoing obligations, the gain is recognized at the time of the transaction closing.	Guidance from IFRS 13 (Fair Value Measurement) and IFRS 5 (Non-current assets held for sale and discontinued operations): **Same treatment as US GAAP**. On a related note, the company acquiring the asset should measure it at fair market value plus transaction costs directly attributable to the acquisition (IAS 39).

Why Sell IP When It Is a Critical Biopharma Value Driver?

There might be many reasons for a biopharma firm to sell IP assets. The company might be trying to gain the full value from assets it does not utilize or under-utilizes. It could also be that the company does not have the strategic intent or necessary capabilities to develop and commercialize corresponding products. Or the company might simply need the financial proceeds from the sale to pursue other priorities.

Table 3.12 IP impairment

US GAAP	IFRS
Guidance from ASC 350 (Intangibles—Goodwill and Other): Impairment test for intangibles is similar to that of tangible assets: comparing the carrying value of intangible asset to the value of the asset in use (sum of undiscounted cash flows from the asset) and **recognizing any deficit in the carrying value as impairment loss.**	Guidance from IAS 36 (Impairment of assets): Impairment approach is slightly different from US GAAP: IFRS compares carrying value to the higher of the value in use and the fair value minus selling costs; any **deficit is** then **recognized as impairment**.

The main difference between US GAAP and IFRS is that impairments can be reversed under IFRS but not under US GAAP.

What Constitutes an IP Impairment?

IP can be impaired when its value is unexpectedly drastically diminished. This could happen if the IP is voided as the result of a lawsuit or in the case of a biopharma program when significant toxicity or side-effects are discovered that drastically diminish the value of the program.

3.2 Technology Transfer (T2) and Exclusivity

3.2.1 T2

A biopharma company may develop technology in-house or leverage external innovation, depending on many factors, such as speed to market, required expertise, technology gaps, and market opportunities. As the name indicates, T2 is about transferring technology from one organization to another. T2 may be opportunistic or result from the company's strategic implementation.

Case Example: US T2 Environment

Many legal acts have been passed in the United States to encourage T2, e.g.:

- Stevenson-Wydler Act of 1980.
  First major technology transfer law that required federal laboratories to actively participate in, and allocate a percentage of their budget to, T2 activities.
- Bayh-Dole Act of 1980.
  Also known as Patent and Trademark Law Amendments Act, it permitted the transfer of ownership from federal labs and government organizations to private contractors and exclusive licensing of federal inventions. The Act intended to address the fact that less than 5% of federal patents had been commercially licensed.
- Small Business Innovation Development Act of 1982.
  This Act required federal agencies to provide funding to small businesses for R&D activities related to the agencies' mission by establishing the SBIR (Small Business Innovation Research) program. Participating agencies identify R&D topics and receive proposals from small businesses; awards are then competitively granted to small US-owned businesses addressing the topics. In 2021, the SBIR program total award obligation was US$3.9 billion.
- Federal Technology Transfer Act of 1986.
  This Act made T2 an individual responsibility considered in performance evaluations for corresponding federal employees. The Act established

collaboration frameworks for federal labs to work with private companies (e.g., Cooperative Research and Development Agreements or CRADAs) and T2 incentives (e.g., federal inventors receiving a share of royalties).

- Facilitating Access to Science and Technology Executive Order 12591 of 1987.
  This Order required federal labs to transfer title of patents to private contractors, as permitted by law, while retaining a royalty-free license. It also enabled technical support from federal labs to contracting parties.
- Small Business Research and Development Enhancement Act of 1992 and Small Business Technology Transfer (STTR).
  This Act established the STTR program. Like SBIR, participating federal agencies select R&D topics for which small businesses make proposals and awards are then granted. The main difference is that with STTR small businesses are required to partner for a minimum of 30% of the effort with a US university, nonprofit or a federally funded R&D center.
- National Technology Transfer and Advancement Act of 1995.
  This Act amended the Stevenson-Wydler Act to make CRADAs more attractive to companies with increased incentives for federal inventors and permanent funding for the federal technology transfer consortium.
- America COMPETES Act of 2007.
  This Act provided support for increased focus and funding on basic research as well as Science Technology Engineering Mathematics education. The Act was reauthorized in 2010 and in 2022.

Without getting into further details on the numerous legislations relevant to T2 in the United States, below are takeaway points for small biopharma companies:

- Opportunities for small firms to receive federal funding on R&D topics that might be connected to the biopharma firm's research.
- Opportunities for T2, exclusive licenses or title transfer, and university collaborations.
- Strong incentives for federal laboratories to collaborate with small companies of less than 500 employees, as would be the case for most small biopharma firms.
- Existing mechanisms are in place for collaborations.

This illustrates the interest for a biopharma startup to investigate T2 opportunities as they could help generate significant increases in company value. Such opportunities may come with specific reporting obligations that need to be strictly adhered to.

T2 Process

As illustrated by Figure 3.8, T2 involves a proactive exploratory process with partners.

We use the term T2 mainly in the context of transactions and business development. Biopharma companies use such T2 when outsourcing drug and biologics manufacturing to a contract development and manufacturing company (CDMO) or to a contract manufacturing company (CMO). They likewise use T2 to support global health initiatives in low-income countries. Universities and nonprofit organizations have created T2 departments to manage the IP generated by their own researchers. And academic healthcare institutions have formed biopharma startups using T2 for the innovations they discovered. In all cases, it is important to establish clear goals as well as a suitable scope for T2, to have defined roles and responsibilities, established clear and documented processes, as well as practical oversight and committed leadership.

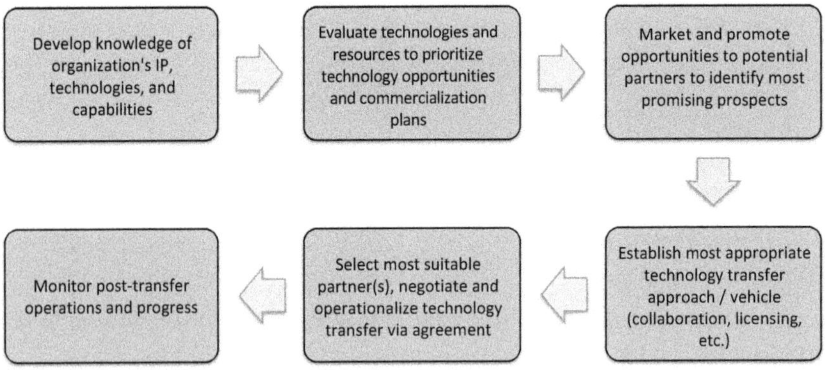

Figure 3.8 T2 process.

T2 Mechanisms

There are different mechanisms or dimensions possible for T2 (Figure 3.9). Some may be used implicitly whereas others might be explicit and correspond to legally binding documents.

The most common T2 approaches typically include one or several of the following: collaboration, workshop, market research, licensing, alliances, publications, marketing, consulting, mentoring, incubators, personnel exchange, employee mobility in absence of suitable employment contract

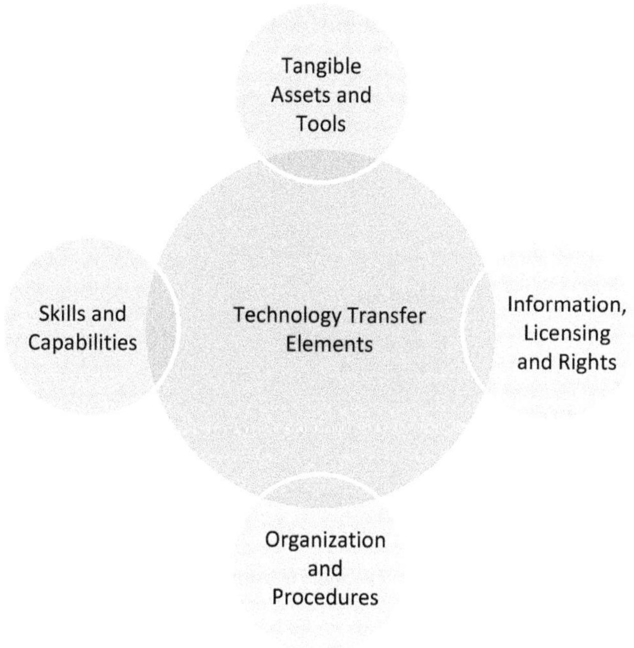

Figure 3.9 Dimensions of technology transfers.

clauses (e.g., non-compete, confidentiality, etc.), remote or on-person communication, technical assistance, use of company systems (internal or external), and use of facilities. As the firm matures, the company's positioning to bring in technology tends to rely initially on founders' credibility and evolves toward ultimately relying on the company's credibility – see Figure 3.10.

Finding T2 Partners

Networking and cultivating medium to long-term relationships relevant to the biopharma firm's industry segment is an integral role of their business development leadership. Finding T2 partners is thus an extension of such outreach. Below are typical sources of information for T2 opportunities in biopharma.

An important T2 source to consider is encompassed by government agencies. In the United States, most federal laboratories have a T2 office. They also have incentives to out-license technologies and work with smaller businesses. The National Institutes of Health has a T2 office and historically provides ways to search its technologies online with explicit objectives

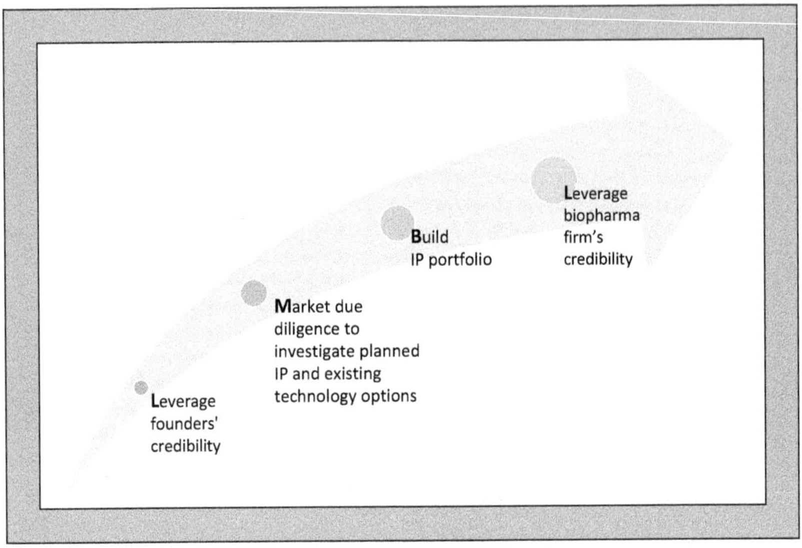

Figure 3.10 Approaches used to secure T2 evolve as a company matures.

for licensing and collaboration. Other relevant US federal agencies with a T2 office include the Centers for Disease Control and Prevention and the National Cancer Institute.

Many leading universities have a Technology Transfer Office (TTO) that gathers internal inventions, patents them, and seeks to commercialize them – see Johns Hopkins University, Harvard University, and MIT. Universities might have their TTO post specific T2 opportunities online (e.g., school-specific website). For a biopharma firm, it is therefore important to be aware of universities conducting research in their areas of interest since they should keep track of corresponding T2 opportunities.

In the United States, TTO professionals are commonly members of the Association of University Technology Managers or AUTM. The AUTM has a searchable innovation marketplace where biopharma firms can find innovations representing T2 opportunities. Findings will typically include the details of the technology, its advantages, its potential applications, and contact information for the IP owner's representative.

Hospital and various nonprofit TTO are also an important source to explore for biopharma firms in search of T2 opportunities.

Identifying holders of relevant patents constitutes another major source of T2 opportunities for a biopharma company. There are many ways and tools to look for patents of interest to, or synergistic with, a biopharma firm's IP portfolio. Below are a few free commonly used online tools that might be of interest.

- Google patents: https://patents.google.com/.
- US Patent Office: https://www.uspto.gov/patents/search/patent-public-search.
- Tools like the Lens: https://www.lens.org/.

Other avenues used by biopharma companies to proactively uncover T2 opportunities include:

- Scouting teams, typically used by larger biopharma corporations.
- Professional associations like MassBio or International Partnering in Lifescience Society.
- Incubator companies.
- Industry publications and events.

3.2.2 *Exclusive Rights Versus Non-exclusive Rights*

When dealing with T2, one very important aspect to consider from a competitive perspective is whether the recipient will have exclusive access to the technology. Take the case of a technology transferred from a university to a biopharma startup via an IP licensing agreement. That license could be:

- Exclusive: no other company or individual will receive a license to the IP in question.
- Exclusive for the biopharma industry (partial exclusivity): no other company or individual will receive a license to the IP in question in any biopharma field. Another company might be able to license the IP for the automotive industry. Note that such partial exclusivity could also be narrower and cover only a specific therapeutic area (oncology, diabetes) within the biopharma industry.
- Exclusive for the United States (partial exclusivity): no other company or individual will receive a license to use the IP in question in the United States. Another company might be able to license the IP for China (assuming the licensor also owns the IP for China).
- Non-exclusive: the university will be able to license the same IP to other companies in the same region(s) and in the same industry (on a non-exclusive basis).

3.3 IP Transactions

3.3.1 *Different Forms of Licensing*

Licensing is arguably the most common T2 method used by biopharma companies (e.g., a company licenses IP rights on a drug candidate from another organization). Let us start with some pertinent definitions.

Licensing is an agreement that allows the licensee (e.g., a biopharma startup or big pharma) to use the IP owned by the licensor (e.g., a university or hospital) in exchange for a form of consideration, often a financial payment.

Sub-licensing refers to the practice of licensing IP already licensed (e.g., Party B licenses IP from IP owner Party A and then Party C licenses that same IP from Party B. In that situation, Party B sub-licenses to Party C).

Straight licensing refers to regular licensing, whereas licensing option refers to the ability but not the obligation to license IP in the future over some defined time frame and sometimes upon achievement of specific conditions or milestones.

Transferability of a license is different from sub-licensing: when Party B licenses IP from Party A and then transfers that license to Party C, Party C becomes the license holder and Party B no longer has a license to Party A's IP.

When establishing a licensing agreement, each party needs to consider the following aspects:

- Nature of licensed IP. While patents are often the object of biopharma licensing, other IP might still be critical to the use of the underlying technology; technical knowledge might be required in addition.
    - In specific contexts such as a licensor owning an early-stage platform technology, licensing agreements will make specific provisions for both the following concepts:
        - Foreground IP (also called "New IP") means all IP that arises or is obtained or developed by either Party pursuant to the agreement.
        - Background IP means any IP controlled by a party prior to the effective date of the agreement.
- Commercially reasonable efforts refer to the carrying out of obligations or tasks by a Party in a sustained manner using commercially reasonable and diligent efforts in good faith.
- Co-development: will the licensor and licensee further develop the technology (e.g., drug candidate) jointly or will the licensee take over development?
- Co-marketing, co-promotion, or co-commercialization. Will the licensor and licensee jointly market the drug post approval or will the licensee do so independently?

- Exclusivity. Given the significant biopharma development and commercialization costs, exclusive licenses are common. Non-exclusive licenses could be negotiated with several generic manufacturers.
- Scope. It is important to understand both geography (e.g., USA-only versus worldwide) and field of use (e.g., oncology-only versus all therapeutic areas) for which licensing rights are conferred.
- License payment structure (e.g., equity, upfront payment, milestone payments, and royalties).
- Additional clauses and considerations.

See Reslinski and Wu (2016), among others, for further information on licensing agreement concepts.

Case Example: Co-promotion Agreement

In 2022, specialty pharma company Cumberland Pharmaceuticals (NASDAQ: CPIX) entered into a national co-promotion agreement with Verity Pharmaceuticals for Cumberland's new Sancuso oncology support product (PRNewswire, 2022).

With its established US presence, Verity will promote Sancuso through its national oncology sales organization, allowing Cumberland to offer Sancuso to physicians and oncology clinics they do not cover.

The two companies should benefit from commercial synergies by sharing in the incremental contribution margin resulting from Verity's efforts.

3.3.2 *In-Licensing*

In-licensing simply refers to licensing from a licensee's perspective: obtaining the rights to use the IP owned by the licensor.

From a strategic positioning perspective, licensees will tend to:

- Pursue strong programs.
    - Strategically aligned with internal objectives (e.g. primary therapeutic area, complementary asset that does not compete with existing portfolio).
    - Scientifically attractive (e.g., strong differentiation).
    - Robust evidence and reliable data.
- Pick large-scale deals (e.g., worldwide scope, multi-indications scope) with high rIRR.
- Focus on comparable deals and recent transactions to target a payment structure.

- Try and position payments post major risks when performance is demonstrated.
- Consider offering equity to strengthen the strategic partnership and maintain cash runway for further developments.

Case Example: Licensing Prior to Major Milestone

When a licensor still needs to complete a major milestone within a relatively short time frame, a licensee might prefer to negotiate a staggered approach, with limited front-loaded payment(s) and a right of first refusal (or right of first negotiation) to enter into a licensing agreement or an M&A discussion when the major milestone is met.

Case Example: In-Licensing Agreement

In 2022, Remix Therapeutics and Janssen Pharmaceuticals established a strategic collaboration and licensing deal. Remix will receive an upfront payment of US$45M with over US$950M in milestones payments contingent on Remix's therapies reaching a variety of clinical and commercial milestones (Bayer, 2022).

The licensing deal commits Remix to developing three targets applicable to immunology and oncology for Janssen. The cash flows from the licensing deal combined with an earlier 2020 seed round of US$81M provides sufficient capital to advance multiple programs into the clinic (Bayer, 2022).

3.3.3 Out-Licensing

Out-licensing simply refers to licensing from a licensor's perspective: granting the rights to use one's IP to one or several licensees.

From a strategic perspective, licensors will tend to:

- Consider in-house needs for, and strategic relevance of, the IP.
- Contrast with IP portfolio objectives, the stage of IP development, additional know-how, and capabilities required, applicable therapeutic indications, as well as market potential.
- Evaluate ideal licensees (size, resources, type of companies for which the license would be a strategic fit, ability to commercialize, incentives, needs and gaps, etc.) to ensure the licensee's interests align with the licensing objectives.
- Target an optimal licensing stage and evaluate the ROI of advancing an asset or program to the next stage prior to out-licensing (e.g., value of licensing post Phase II could be better than licensing post Phase III).

Case Example: Out-Licensing Agreement

In 2021, Sanofi entered into an exclusive worldwide license agreement with Corteria Pharmaceuticals, a new company backed by Kurma Partners, for two research-stage cardiovascular assets intended to treat heart failure in specific patient sub-populations. The license, which includes a CRF2 agonist peptide and an anti-vasopressin mAb, will allow Corteria to pursue Sanofi's endeavors in the cardiovascular space to develop interceptive therapies for heart failure, thereby targeting a major unmet medical need with high impact on the quality of life of patients (Sanofi, 2023).

3.3.4 *Collaboration without IP Exchange*

In such a collaboration, the biopharma companies do not exchange IP but still contribute to the collaboration, based on their respective expertise and strengths. Such situations may not technically qualify as IP transactions, although they may feature temporary grant of non-exclusive rights and future agreements options or cross-company investments to better align incentives. Let us look at what such collaborations might look like through two case examples.

Case Example: AstraZeneca and Silence Therapeutics Collaboration

In 2020, AstraZeneca and Silence Therapeutics established a collaboration to develop gene-silencing drugs in several therapeutic areas: metabolic, cardiovascular, respiratory, and renal (Staines, 2020).

Each company brings their respective expertise to the collaboration:

- AstraZeneca: expertise in selecting specific gene targets that would be of development and commercial interest.
- Silence Therapeutics: small interfering RNA (siRNA) technology that can selectively inhibit targeted genes, thereby silencing the production of disease-causing proteins.

The collaboration agreement sets the companies to work together on five targets in the first 3 years, with the option for AstraZeneca to extend it to five additional targets. Silence Therapeutics designs siRNA molecules targeting the genes identified by AstraZeneca and manufactures materials for toxicology and Phase 1 studies. Past discovery, AstraZeneca takes the lead for clinical trials and commercialization.

During the research collaboration period, Silence and AstraZeneca granted reciprocal non-exclusive licenses under their respective IP, with the sole purpose to conduct the activities assigned to each partner under the research plans (Silence Therapeutics & AstraZeneca, 2020).

Under this agreement, Silence Therapeutics has the option to negotiate for co-development of two drugs starting from Phase 2 and receives payment from AstraZeneca (upfront payment, target selection payment, development milestones, market milestones). AstraZeneca also made a US$20M equity investment into Silence Therapeutics.

Case Example: Gilead Sciences and Arcus Biosciences Collaboration

In 2020, Gilead and Arcus established a 10-year partnership to co-develop and co-commercialize next generation cancer immunotherapies (Gilead Sciences, 2020).

Gilead made upfront equity investments in Arcus securing two board seats. Gilead also provides ongoing R&D support to Arcus.

Beyond gaining immediate rights to Zimberelimab (this licensing constitutes an exception to the separate IP approach), Gilead has co-commercialization opt-in rights on any Arcus program over 10 years unless Arcus opts out.

In addition to benefiting from Gilead's R&D support, equity investments, and financial support, Arcus continues to conduct research on new targets independently.

3.3.5 Cross-Licensing Collaborations

As opposed to the previous section, in a cross-licensing collaboration, the biopharma companies share IP with one another in both directions. This type of collaboration between competitors can make sense when parties depend on each other's Platform IP to enable the development of their respective products. In the authors' experience, it is a less common model.

Case Example: Editas Medicine and BlueRock Therapeutics Collaboration

In 2019, Editas Medicine and BlueRock Therapeutics established a strategic research collaboration and cross-licensing agreement (BlueRock Therapeutics, 2019).

The collaboration provides BlueRock with access to engineered cell medicines in neurology, cardiology, and immunology while Editas gains access to engineered cell medicines in oncology, including solid tumors and blood cancers.

BlueRock Therapeutics brings its induced pluripotent stem cell (iPSC) platform to the table, whereas Editas Medicine brings its CRISPR genome editing technology, granting non-exclusive rights to each other's technology in order to create new engineered cell medicines.

Each party is eligible for milestone and royalty payments for medicines developed in the other party's field.

3.3.6 Non-Proprietary Assets

Biopharma strategic approaches typically rely on proprietary assets. There might still be situations, however, where a non-proprietary or open innovation approach might be advantageous. These are common situations where iterative unencumbered incremental innovations from several parties might be highly beneficial. Such non-proprietary tools, technologies, or libraries obtained in an open-source environment can also be coupled with internal proprietary assets to secure a viable competitive business model. Lastly, use of non-proprietary assets might increase the value of a specific transaction when network effects are a critical consideration.

3.3.7 Secondary Geographies

After a drug has been approved in primary regions, it might be helpful to consider licensing for secondary regions that are not as strategic to the manufacturer.

For strategic or financial reasons, some licensors opt for a strategy based on multiple regional licensing agreements, rather than a unique agreement on a global basis.

Local conditions (e.g., legal jurisprudence), tax implications can also have an effect on the territorial scope of the licensing agreements.

Case Example: Hikma and Sun Pharma Licensing Agreement

In 2020, Hikma and Sun Pharma established an exclusive licensing agreement for ILUMYA for the Middle East and North Africa region (Hikma Pharmaceuticals, 2020). The drug, a monoclonal antibody used for psoriasis treatment, was already approved by the FDA. Under the agreement, Hikma would be responsible for registration and commercialization of the product in all countries in the Middle East and North Africa.

3.3.8 Platform IP

A platform IP is a right (patent, trademarks, trade secrets) securing a novel and innovative technology underlying a portfolio of future therapeutic products. A platform patent requires indisputable scientific data on a technology that will not be specific to a therapeutic target or compound but will be used for a wide variety of therapeutic applications. The technology can encompass new modalities, improved routes of delivery, new development or production methods, and improvements can also be patented.

A platform IP can be a major asset allowing the company to deploy an out-licensing strategy. It can provide further protection in addition to a product-related IP.

Platform IP in the biopharma field tends to describe innovative materials that underlie, help create, or serve as the foundational basis for numerous products, and thus the licensing of such IP needs to be carefully considered in light of business strategy, including how the business intends to monetize their discoveries though licensing, collaboration, or otherwise.

For example, in some instances, platform IP does not need to be licensed as the partnering company will not be involved in the part of development that utilizes the Platform IP. But if the Platform IP is incorporated as a component of a drug substance that is intended for administration to patients, and that Platform IP can serve as a basis for numerous drug substances, it may make business sense to only offer non-exclusive licenses to potential partners.

Case Example: IP Platform

Regenxbio Inc. has developed a proprietary therapeutic platform based on adeno-associated virus (AAV) used as vectors in gene and cell therapy. All Regenxbio's internal product candidates utilize the AAV viral vectors from the company's technology platform, as well as programs partnered by the company with other biopharma companies (Regenxbio, 2025).

3.4 Impact of AI

The term artificial intelligence, or AI, commonly refers to computer systems able to perform complex tasks historically associated with human capacity such as making decisions, solving problems, or answering questions.

3.4.1 *Patents*

As the biopharma industry is making increasing use of AI through a growing number of tools, applications, and use cases, understanding the evolving AI regulatory framework and AI's implications on IP ownership and invention patentability is absolutely critical for biopharma companies (see illustrative example in Figure 3.11). While the benefits expected from using AI are significant (e.g., substantial improvements in discovery and clinical timelines combined with higher probability of success), the rapid AI adoption has come with complex and evolving legal and regulatory frameworks driven in part by individual legal precedents such as *Thaler v. Vidal*, No. 21-2347 (Fed. Cir. 2022) in the United States.

When an AI solution is used to accelerate and improve a drug design that might otherwise take a long time to do via traditional means, the human value-added component in the new drug is harder to demonstrate and easier to challenge (see Pannu factors listed in Figure 3.11). In particular, if the human contribution is insufficient, a patent might not be possible. In addition, while an AI cannot legally be the inventor since not a natural person,

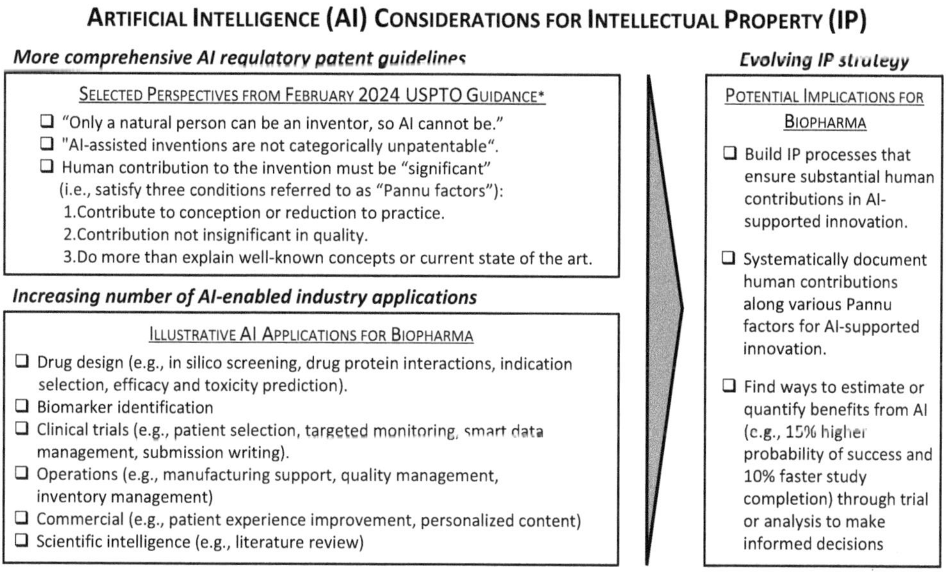

* USPTO (2024). *Inventorship Guidance for AI-Assisted Inventions.* Retrieved on 1/11/2025 from https://www.regulations.gov/document/PTO-P-2023-0043-0001.

Figure 3.11 AI considerations for IP.

the individual(s) that designed the AI solution might lay claim on making contributions to the new drug and being a sole or joint inventor, which would be a significant issue in the case of an external AI solution. So, the program acceleration and cost-savings enabled by AI might come at the expense of less robust IP. This might jeopardize in turn the exit strategy of a small biopharma company (that could have a less secure IP despite promising Phase 2 results) or the commercial potential of a large biopharma product (that could be subject to heavy royalties).

To help with the application of Pannu factors, the USPTO issued the five guiding principles for determining the inventorship of an AI-assisted invention (USPTO, 2024a):

1. A natural person's use of AI does not negate their contributions as inventor, but they need to contribute significantly.
2. Only recognizing or presenting a problem to an AI does not rise to the level of conception necessary to be an inventor but constructing the prompt to elicit a particular solution could.
3. Recognizing the output of an AI as invention is not sufficient to be an inventor without making a significant contribution to the output or in other ways like an experiment required to validate invention practice.

4. A natural person who develops an essential building block for the invention may be considered as having made a significant contribution – in some situations, the natural person that designed, built, or trained the AI supporting the invention may have made a significant contribution.
5. Simply owning or overseeing an AI used in the creation of an invention, without providing a significant contribution, does not make the natural person an inventor.

As these guiding principles illustrate, the use of AI by biopharma companies necessitates a preliminary determination of the source of innovation and the assurance of certain requirements in order to secure the resulting IP. The use of AI has significant operational implications, e.g., ensure that:

- Particular attention is given to IP ownership clauses in contractual agreements, when using external AI solutions and tools, to avoid sole or joint inventorship claims by the supplier.
- Internal patent processes take into account the threshold of significant human contributions.
- AI systems and input are the result of significant human contributions (e.g., specialized processes and systems) where feasible to show significant upstream contributions, while ensuring all these human contributions are sufficiently documented.
- AI outputs are combined with, or followed by, human contributions that materially change and complement these outputs where feasible, while ensuring all these human contributions are sufficiently documented.

3.4.2 *Copyrights*

Alongside patents, copyrights are the main IP tools affected by AI. As of January 2025, regulatory guidance on how AI affects copyrights is still evolving and significant parts of expected regulatory guidance have yet to be released on AI-enabled authorship. One could, however, envision an evolution similar to the one described above for the USPTO guidance, where a determination of the importance of what was provided by a natural person versus by AI in terms of output and what has been used in terms of inputs (with considerations given to the training data used by AI and their copyrighted nature).

3.4.3 *Trademarks and Trade Secrets*

Trademarks and trade secrets are arguably less affected by AI than patents and copyrights, as evidenced by their much lower coverage in AI-related published discussions of IP. In the case of trademarks, AI might actually contribute to trademark enforcement by offering an improved set of tools (e.g., trademark search, mark monitoring, or other enforcement tools); however, AI also comes with similar human contributions determination requirements as well as its own set of complications (e.g., who is liable for infringing AI-generated trademarks, increasing gray areas, resulting from the closer resemblance of AI-generated trademarks to existing ones). Trade secrets when effectively implemented would by definition not be as accessible to AI and effective AI-enabled trade secret approaches would likewise be protected.

References

Association for Molecular Pathology v. Myriad Genetics, Inc. 12-398 1 (Supreme Court of the United States 2013). https://www.supremecourt.gov/opinions/12pdf/12-398_1b7d.pdf

Bayer, M. (2022, February 17). Remix Therapeutics Signs Janssen Licensing Deal That Could Top $1B. *Fierce Biotech*. https://www.fiercebiotech.com/biotech/remix-therapeutics-signs-licensure-deal-janssen-could-exceed-1-billion

BIO. (2016, May 2). *Intellectual Property*. Biotechnology Innovation Organization. Retrieved 6/24/2022, from https://www.bio.org/policy/intellectual-property

BlueRock Therapeutics. (2019, April 3). *Editas Medicine and BlueRock Therapeutics Enter Strategic Research Collaboration and Cross-Licensing Agreement to Combine Genome Editing and Cell Therapy*. Retrieved 8/10/2022, from https://www.bluerocktx.com/editas-medicine-and-bluerock-therapeutics-enter-strategic-research-collaboration-and-cross-licensing-agreement-to-combine-genome-editing-and-cell-therapy/

Cellular Engineering Technologies. (2022, March 8). *The USPTO Issues a Patent to Cellular Engineering Technologies for Producing a Safer Induced Pluripotent Stem Cell*. Retrieved 6/24/2022, from https://cet.bio/march-8-2022-press-release/

Cohen, M., Zanoletty, A., Harris, D. & Linvill-Neal, D. (2021, July 20). *The Inside Track on Drug Naming Safety Standards*. ISMR. Retrieved 6/27/2022, from https://www.ismp.org/sites/default/files/attachments/2021-07/The%20Inside%20Track%20on%20Drug%20Naming%20Standards-%20Handouts.pdf

Deloitte. (2021). *Realising a Biotech's Potential – What Is Required to Scale Successfully?* Deloitte Development LLC.

DiMasi, J. A., Grabowski, H. G., & Hansen, R. W. (2016). Innovation in the pharmaceutical industry: New estimates of R&D costs. *Journal of Health Economics, 47*, 20–33. https://doi.org/10.1016/j.jhealeco.2016.01.012

EMA. (2021, December 6). *Guideline on the Acceptability of Names for Human Medicinal Products Processed Through the Centralised Procedure*. EMA. Retrieved 6/27/2022, from https://www.ema.europa.eu/en/guideline-acceptability-names-human-medicinal-products-processed-through-centralised-procedure

EPO, JPO, KIPO, CNIPA, & USPTO. (2021). *IP5 Statistics Report*. Online: IP5. https://link.epo.org/ip5/IP5%20Statistics%20Report%202020%20final_23122021.pdf

European Patent Office. (2021, October 1). *European Patent Guide.* Retrieved 6/24/2022, from https://www.epo.org/applying/european/Guide-for-applicants/html/e/index.html

FDA. (2019, March). *Nonproprietary Naming of Biological Products: Update Guidance for Industry.* Retrieved 6/27/2022, from https://www.fda.gov/regulatory-information/search-fdaguidance-documents/nonproprietary-naming-biological-products-update-guidance-industry

FDA. (2020, December). *Best Practices in Developing Proprietary Names for Human Prescription Drug Products – Guidance for Industry.* Retrieved 6/27/2022, from https://www.fda.gov/media/88496/download

FDA. (2022a, June 21). *Medication Errors Related to CDER-Regulated Drug Products.* Retrieved 6/27/2022, from https://www.fda.gov/drugs/drug-safety-andavailability/medication-errors-related-cder-regulated-drug-products

FDA. (2022b, May). *Safety Considerations for Container Labels and Carton Labeling Design to Minimize Medication Errors – Guidance for Industry.* Retrieved 6/27/2022, from https://www.fda.gov/media/158522/download

Food and Drug Administration. (2021, May). *Qualified Infectious Disease Product Designation — Questions and Answers, Guidance for Industry.* Retrieved 7/30/2022, from https://www.fda.gov/media/148480/download

Gilead Sciences. (2020, May 27). *Gilead Sciences and Arcus Biosciences Establish 10-Year Partnership to Co-develop and Co-commercialize Next-Generation Cancer Immunotherapies.* Retrieved 8/10/2022, from https://www.gilead.com/news-and-press/press-room/press-releases/2020/5/gilead-sciences-and-arcus-biosciences-establish-10-year-partnership-to-co-develop-and-co-commercialize-next-generation-cancer-immunotherapies

Harte, M., & Kaufman, P. (2024, June 25). *The European Parliament Approves Reforms to the EU's Rules for Medicines.* Carpmaels & Ransford. Retrieved 3/7/2025, from https://www.carpmaels.com/the-european-parliament-approves-reforms-to-the-eus-rules-for-medicines/

Heiden, B., & Peters, R. (2020). IP and Open Innovation—Managing Technology Push and Pull. *Les Nouvelles – Journal of the Licensing Executives Society, LV No. 2*(June 2020), 138–142. https://ssrn.com/abstract=3583024

Hikma Pharmaceuticals. (2020, June 15). *Hikma and Sun Pharma Enter into Exclusive Licensing Agreement for ILUMYA™ for the Middle East and North Africa Region.* Hikma. Retrieved 8/10/2022, from https://www.hikma.com/media/11cobm4a/sun-agreement-ilumya-final-hikma-version.pdf

IP5. (2019). *About IP5 Co-operation.* Retrieved 10/17/2024, from https://www.fiveipoffices.org/about

Mathieu, M. (2018). In Mathieu M. (Ed.), *PAREXEL Biopharmaceutical R&D Statistical Sourcebook 2018/2019* (2018/2019 ed.). PAREXEL International Corporation. https://www.amazon.com/PAREXEL-Biopharmaceutical-Statistical-Sourcebook-2018/dp/0996346260

Nealey, T., Daignault, R. M., & Cai, Y. (2014). Trade secrets in life science and pharmaceutical companies. *Cold Spring Harbor Perspectives in Medicine, 5*(4), a020982. https://doi.org/10.1101/cshperspect.a020982.

Paul W. Grimm (2022).MEMORANDUM OPINION. GlaxoSmithKline LLC v. Brooks, 22-364 1 (District Court for the District of Maryland 2022). https://www.govinfo.gov/content/pkg/USCOURTS-mdd-8_22-cv-00364/pdf/USCOURTS-mdd-8_22-cv-00364-0.pdf
PhRMA. (2018, June 30). *What Is Hatch-Waxman?* PhRMA.org. Retrieved 7/29/2022, from https://phrma.org/-/media/Project/PhRMA/PhRMA-Org/PhRMA-Org/PDF/D-F/Fact-Sheet_What-is-Hatch-Waxman_June-2018.pdf
PRNewswire. (2022, May 9). Cumberland Pharmaceuticals Announces Key Co-Promotion Agreement with Verity Pharmaceuticals to Expand Support for Sancuso. https://www.prnewswire.com/news-releases/cumberland-pharmaceuticals-announces-key-co-promotion-agreement-with-verity-pharmaceuticals-to-expand-support-for-sancuso-301542387.html
Regenxbio. (2025). *Therapeutic Pipeline.* Retrieved 3/7/2025, from https://www.regenxbio.com/therapeutic-programs/
Reslinski, M. A., & Wu, B. S. (2016). The value of royalty *Nature Biotechnology, 34*(7), 685–690. 10.1038/nbt.3624
Sanofi. (2023). *Out* – Licensing. Retrieved 10/19/2024, from https://www.sanofi.com/en/partnering/partnering-focus-areas/out-licensing
Silence Therapeutics, & AstraZeneca. (2020, March 24). *Research Collaboration, Option and License Agreement.* Retrieved 3/7/2025, from https://www.sec.gov/Archives/edgar/data/1479615/000095012320009257/cik0001479615-ex106_56.htm
Staines, R. (2020, March 25). *AZ Adds Gene Silencing Tech to Pipeline with Silence Therapeutics Deal.* pharmaphorum. Retrieved 8/10/2022, from https://pharmaphorum.com/news/az-adds-gene-silencing-tech-to-pipeline-with-silence-therapeutics-deal/
Sun Pharmaceuticals Industries Ltd vs Cipla Ltd, (Madras High Court 2021). https://www.mhc.tn.gov.in/judis/index.php/casestatus/viewpdf/586229
U.S. Copyright Office. (2021, January 21). *What Is Copyright?* Retrieved 6/24/2022, from https://www.copyright.gov/what-is-copyright/
U.S. Food and Drug Administration. (2022). *Office of Generic Drugs 2021 Annual Report – Ensuring High-Quality, Affordable Generic Drugs Are Available to the American Public.* Silver Spring, MD: https://www.fda.gov/media/156066/download United States Patent and Trademark Office. (2019, February 7). *Trade Secrets/Regulatory Data Protection.* Retrieved 6/24/2022, from https://www.uspto.gov/ip-policy/trade-secret-policy
United States Patent and Trademark Office. (2021, March 31). *What Is a Trademark?* Retrieved 6/24/2022, from https://www.uspto.gov/trademarks/basics/what-trademark
USPTO. (2019, October 16). *United States Patent and Trademark Office's Website.* Retrieved 6/25/2022, from https://www.uspto.gov/
USPTO. (2024a). Inventorship Guidance for AI-Assisted Inventions. *Federal Register, 89*(30), 10043–10051. https://www.govinfo.gov/content/pkg/FR-2024-02-13/pdf/2024-02623.pdf
USPTO. (2024b, July 6). *Patent Prosecution Highway (PPH) – Fast Track Examination of Applications.* Retrieved 10/20/2024, from https://www.uspto.gov/patents/basics/international-protection/patent-prosecution-highway-pph-fast-track

Vertex Pharmaceuticals Incorporated. (2022, February 9). *FORM 10-K (Annual Report)*. Retrieved 7/25/*2022, from https://www.annreports.com/vertex/vertex-ar-2021.pdf

WHO. (2002, January 31). *International Nonproprietary Names Programme and Classification of Medical Products*. WHO. Retrieved 6/27/2022, from https://www.who.int/teams/health-product-and-policy-standards/inn/

World Health Organization, World Intellectual Property Organization, & World Trade Organization. (2020). *Promoting Access to Medical Technologies and Innovation* (2nd ed.). Book Now Ltd.

Wouters, O. J., McKee, M., & Luyten, J. (2020). Estimated research and development investment needed to bring a new medicine to market, 2009–2018. *JAMA, 323*(9), 844–853. 10.1001/jama.2020.1166

Zhou, H., Sandner, P. G., Martinelli, S. L., & Block, J. H. (2016). Patents, trademarks, and their complementarity in venture capital funding. *Technovation, 47* (January 2016), 14–22. https://doi.org/10.1016/j.technovation.2015.11.005

Chapter 4

Strategy for Biopharma Companies

4.1 General Strategy Concepts

4.1.1 Strategy Introduction

Before diving into this chapter, it is essential to highlight that strategy demands a level of rigor comparable to the scientific methodology that defines the biopharma industry. Strategy requires a disciplined fact-based approach in order to be objective, rather than blindly following the latest idea that may or may not be suitable for the company. Facts are irrefutable statements that nobody can debate whereas assumptions are hypotheses to verify or monitor.

Case Example: Facts Versus Hypotheses for Program Strategy

A biopharma company has a chronic heart disease product in Phase 2. Given unmet needs, the team anticipates a launch in 4–5 years and believes it will not face major competition for 10 years, thus expecting to independently drive the market.

However, their conviction turned out to be overly optimistic:

- Hypotheses made:
  Forecasters analyzed clinicaltrials.gov data finding only one minor case for a small biotech with a single instance of relevant study outside the United States and extremely limited information. Hence, they assumed that there would not be any noteworthy competition.
- Facts discovered later:
  The "minor case" is a well-known biotech headquartered in Spain running a Phase 1b study in Australia. Their website indicates a new mechanism of action and strong chances for breakthrough medication status. According to the website, the company is considering a European VC round to finance an accelerated Phase 2–3, or alternatively an out-licensing approach. An accelerated Phase 2–3 combined with breakthrough status and successful

DOI: 10.4324/9781003598046-4

approval would likely result in a market entry closely following the launch time frame expected by the asset team.

The asset team should have gathered facts about the small program rather than assuming it was not meaningful. They would have built contingencies for a second player entry. Moving forward, the team established more proactive fact-based approaches with scenarios that incorporate market dynamics.

A strategy is normally specific to the company implementing it, as demonstrated by the following case examples.

Case Examples: Strategic Statements

- Therapeutic area leadership strategy:
  "Biogen is the leader in neuroscience with a robust and diversified portfolio across disease areas and therapeutic modalities". The company sees neuroscience as "Neuroscience is an area with significant unmet needs, representing a compelling value creation opportunity". Biogen counts on its "strong talent and specialized expertise in neuroscience" to "leverage the interconnectivity and shared biology across diseases" in this therapeutic area (Biogen, 2021).
- Global industry leadership strategy:
  Pfizer aims to be the global leader in multiple therapeutic areas with an extremely broad scope. With over 1 billion patients treated globally with its medicines and vaccines, the company describes itself as a "global biopharmaceuticals business focused on three broad therapeutic areas": primary care, specialty care, and oncology. To do so, the company combines a honed internal focus and the pursuit of external innovation, focusing on speed of execution (Pfizer, 2022, 2023).
- Discovery platform niche strategy:
  Adimab, founded in 2007, sees itself as "the premier antibody discovery and optimization" provider according to its website. With over 105 partners and over 475 programs, the company focuses on early-stage activities (e.g., in vitro and in vivo discovery, antibody engineering, and bispecific), leaving development and commercialization activities to partner companies like Biogen, GSK, Lilly, Merck, Novo Nordisk, and Takeda (Adimab, 2009).
- Low-cost strategy:
  Viatris is an exceptionally large generic manufacturer, intent on having a durable high-margin portfolio in global core therapeutic areas. Viatris focus on execution to ensure a strong capacity to compete in the lower price generic market, e.g.: comprehensive portfolio in targeted areas, speed to entry, enhanced commercial execution capabilities, and end-to-end operational capabilities (Viatris, 2022, 2023a, 2023b).

Strategy Definition and Importance

Strategies may differ widely that begs the question of strategy's definition and importance.

With origins in the military and war literature, the concept of strategy evolved into a distinct discipline in the business world, encompassing a plethora of definitions:

> **Importance of a Sensible Biopharma Strategy: Setting the Company on the Right Path**
>
> The strategy
>
> - Sets expectations for investors and potential funding sources ⇨ **Right Commitment**.
> - Implements the company's mission and vision for its various stakeholders ⇨ **Right Goals**.
> - Articulates how the company will compete effectively and differently in the marketplace ⇨ **Right Positioning**.
> - Recognizes as well as prioritizes R&D objectives and investments, inclusive of licensing opportunities ⇨ **Right Thinking**.
> - Clarifies how the company will achieve its goals, reinforcing internal alignment and enabling effective delegation ⇨ **Right Plan**.
> - Communicates how the company will go about allocating its resources effectively and efficiently, thereby elucidating its risk profile ⇨ **Right Activities**.

- "Developing a competitive strategy is developing a broad formula for how a business is going to compete, what its goals should be, and what policies will be needed to carry out those goals". (Porter, 1980).
- "Competitive strategy is the search for a favorable competitive position in an industry […] to establish a profitable and sustainable position against the forces that determine industry competition". (Porter, 1985).
- "Organizational strategy begins with the desire of an organization to outperform the market. A strategy is a set of concrete plans to help the organization accomplish this goal. […] Fundamentally, a strategy is a commitment to undertake one set of actions rather than another and this commitment necessarily describes an allocation of resources". (Oster, 1994).
- "Strategy determines […] the purpose […], selects the businesses […], attempts to achieve a long-term, sustainable advantage […], identifies the distinct managerial tasks […], is a coherent, unifying, and integrative pattern of decisions, […], is an expression of the strategic intent of the firm, […]". (Hax & Majluf, 1996)"Business strategy aims at obtaining

superior financial performance by seeking a competitive positioning that allows the business to have a sustainable advantage over the firm's competitors". (Hax & Majluf, 1996).
- "Competitive strategy is about being different. It means deliberately choosing a different set of activities to deliver a unique mix of value". (Porter, 1996).
- "Ultimately, strategy is a way of thinking, not a procedural exercise or a set of frameworks". (Bradley et al., 2011).

As these definitions suggest, developing a meaningful strategy for a biopharma company requires the following:

- Innovative thinking to define a distinct value proposition to patients, clinicians, and payer organizations.
- Operating differently from competitors by leveraging a unique combination of integrated activities.
- Making deliberate tradeoffs that strengthen this integration while affirmatively forgoing other activities.

The unique integration safeguards the company's unique value proposition since replicating integrated activities is harder for competitors than duplicating a standalone activity.

Typical Biopharma Routes to Create Value

For a given biopharma program, the mutually exclusive tradeoffs previously mentioned are frequently manifested through four value-creation paths, as biopharma companies execute their strategy:

- Commercialization: the company develops and commercializes drugs in-house.
- Licensing: the company out-licenses IP at defined value inflection points.
- Cooperation: the company collaborates with partners to develop and/or commercialize products.
- M&A exit: the company, or part thereof, gets sold to another biopharma company, usually after reaching a suitable milestone.

Industry-Driven Characteristics of Strategy

Independently of the paths selected, a biopharma company's strategy will typically integrate key industry characteristics:

- Capital-intensive.
  Mirroring stepwise R&D funding requirements, the strategy should enable staggered stages of value creation and risk reduction, each achieving

specific financial outcomes and milestones suited to targeted investors (e.g., return on capital for venture capitalists or rNPV improvements for biopharma partners), especially when external funding is required.

- Expertise-based.
  The strategy should facilitate the recruitment and retention of expert talent in critical functional domains, including science, discovery, bioinformatics, modeling and data, clinical development, regulatory, commercial launch, and leadership.
- IP-oriented.
  IP and freedom to operate are indispensable considerations for a biopharma strategy.
- Asset-focused.
  Strategy should guide the company's asset selection and prioritization: therapeutic areas or indications, geographies, R&D stages, product types, modalities, pathways, targets, platforms or technology, mechanism of action, market size and market access, unmet needs, setting of care, disease severity or patient impact, etc.
- Regulated.
  Strategy needs to steer the company effectively through regulatory pathways, e.g. at a program level, pursuing a suitable Target Product Profile, leveraging effective biomarkers and relevant endpoints, improving standard of care or healthcare outcomes, tackling unmet needs, decreasing or eliminating side-effects, increasing patient convenience factors (oral route, delivery mechanism, less frequent administration), or simply providing non-inferior medication with better economics (home care, generics).
- Intricate commercial activities.
  The strategy must accommodate complex promotion and pricing approaches, involving multiple parties with differing restrictions, incentives, and priorities. Pricing arrangements involve negotiation with payer organizations to ensure appropriate coverage and access for target patient populations. Additionally, prescription drug usage hinges on the influence of physician prescribers who are disconnected from pricing agreements but need to be convinced. The sales and distribution model is subject to stringent regulations and radically different from other industries emphasizing medical professional education rather than direct patient engagement. Lastly, marketing communications are strictly controlled and confined to the approved product label.

Delineation between Strategy and Operations

It is important to distinguish strategy from operations as some biopharma professionals might occasionally conflate the two or mistake operational execution for strategy. Strategy is characterized by a longer-term focus, typically spanning 3 years or more, whereas operations deal with more immediate activities within the year. Strategy is articulated through a strategic plan while operations are detailed in operating and management plans. Additionally, strategy incorporates a wide range of internal and external inputs whereas operations center primarily on driving internal activities, often guided by internal metrics, though external benchmarks might be a factor. Operational activities and decisions support and implement the broader strategic directions and decisions.

Strategy Levels

Companies with multiple businesses have three different strategy levels: corporate strategy, business strategy, and functional strategy (Hax & Majluf, 1996). For biopharma firms with a single business, there is no need to distinguish between corporate strategy and business strategy.

- Corporate strategy is the highest-level strategic perspective used in the biopharma company. It encompasses all businesses rather than focusing solely on individual divisions or programs. This strategy sets the overarching direction that subordinate strategies at the business and functional levels must align with and drives the allocation of resources to these lower tiers.
- Business strategy applies to companies with distinct businesses (e.g., specialty care, vaccines, general medicine, and consumer healthcare). It is crafted for an individual business unit, aiming to achieve optimal positioning and performance vis-à-vis competitors, while adhering to corporate strategy guidelines.
- Functional strategy addresses the expressed or implicit support needs stemming from corporate and business unit strategies. Set for a given company function (e.g., Finance, Business Development, Supply Chain, Procurement, or Clinical Operations), the functional strategy assesses the functional core competencies essential for enabling corporate and business strategies.

Strategic Management Model and Strategic Planning

Regardless of the strategy level, managing strategy within a biopharma company is an adaptive process, comprising distinct phases: strategy formulation, strategy selection, development of tactics for the chosen strategy, strategic control, and continuous improvement. This process is referred to as a strategic management model.

In the formulation phase, the leadership team defines or revisits the corporation's business mission and vision, followed by a business environment assessment using various tools, frameworks, and analyses. That assessment should identify external opportunities and threats (the "O" and "T" components of the SWOT analysis depicted in Figure 4.1). The team also

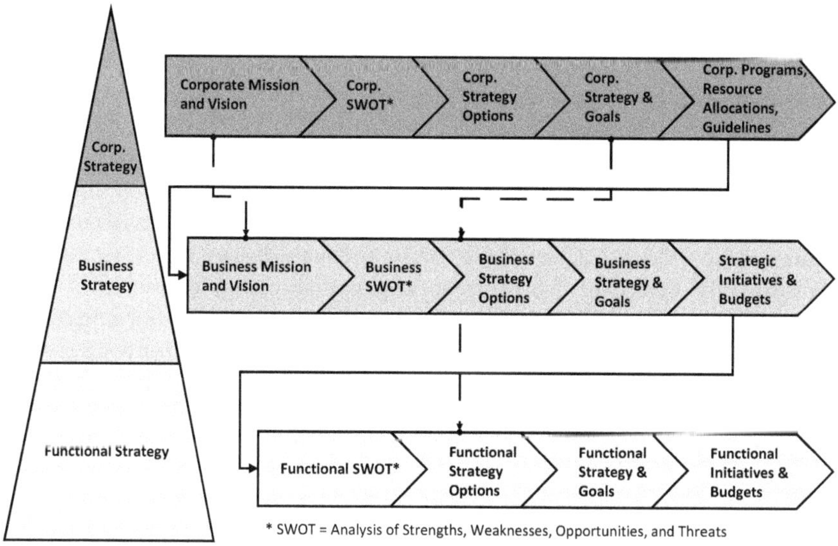

Figure 4.1 Strategic management model with different strategy levels.

examines the internal business characteristics, using additional frameworks and tools, highlighting the company's strengths and weaknesses (the "S" and "W" components of the SWOT analysis shown in Figure 4.1). Once the SWOT analysis is complete, the strategy team can brainstorm, evaluate multiple strategic alternatives, and derive further strategic options.

The subsequent step involves selecting a strategy to implement. Various selection methods and facilitation techniques can be utilized, from subjective team voting to quantitative forced ranking. For a more analytical approach, the Positioning – Sustainability – Valuation – Flexibility framework (Ghemawat, 1991) can be employed to evaluate the strategy's merit. This framework examines whether the strategy provides a unique competitive advantage, its sustainability, the value it creates, and its adaptability.

Once the strategy leadership team selects a strategy using their chosen methodology, the next phase involves developing plans in the form of corporate programs, business initiatives, and functional initiatives. This includes implementing appropriate controls to monitor internal and external factors and addressing key areas of strategic vulnerability. These plans are accompanied by a suitable budget, allowing the company to consolidate financial projections and confirm the overall strategic approach's financial feasibility.

Finally, multiple feedback loops are incorporated throughout the process to refine and enhance the selected strategies.

Navigating Strategic Frameworks

To foster critical thinking and to maintain objectivity, the field of strategy resorts to numerous concepts and frameworks. Given the extensive number of frameworks covered in this chapter (over 15), Figure 4.2 serves as a useful reference for navigating these tools. Note that many frameworks and concepts were used within specific contexts (e.g., general concepts versus biopharma concepts, internal assessment versus environmental scan), which does not preclude their applicability to other situations. Additionally, selecting the most appropriate framework involves a considerable degree of judgment (e.g., choosing among the four suggested frameworks for internal assessment, or exploring alternate options) – see Section 4.5 on this topic.

4.1.2 Vision and Mission

Vision

Having a clear and compelling vision is important for a company as it portrays the leadership's aspirations for the organization and serves as a foundation for effective communication with investors and stakeholders.

A company's vision consists of two elements: a core ideology and an envisioned future. The core ideology comprises aspirations, principles, and contextual statements that define the company's purpose and upholds its values and culture. The envisioned future outlines what the firm aims to become, achieve, create, or change.

A vision is designed to inspire and endure over time, though it may be revisited and refined after several years.

Crafting and articulating a powerful vision is critical, tying back to the importance of storytelling introduced in Chapter 1. The company's vision should be communicated in a way that is both practical and exciting: emotions and simplicity often resonate more than complex logic. The architect of Notre Dame de Paris was credited with engaging simple bricklayers, explaining they were not just building a wall, but constructing the wall of the world's most beautiful cathedral! Leaders should strive to convey their vision in terms that deeply resonate with their audience.

Mission

While the vision presents a future view of the company and its destination ("where to"), the mission covers "what" the company will do, "whom" it will serve, and addresses "why". Note that the "why" may be detailed in a separate "purpose statement", enabling the mission statement to focus exclusively on the "what".

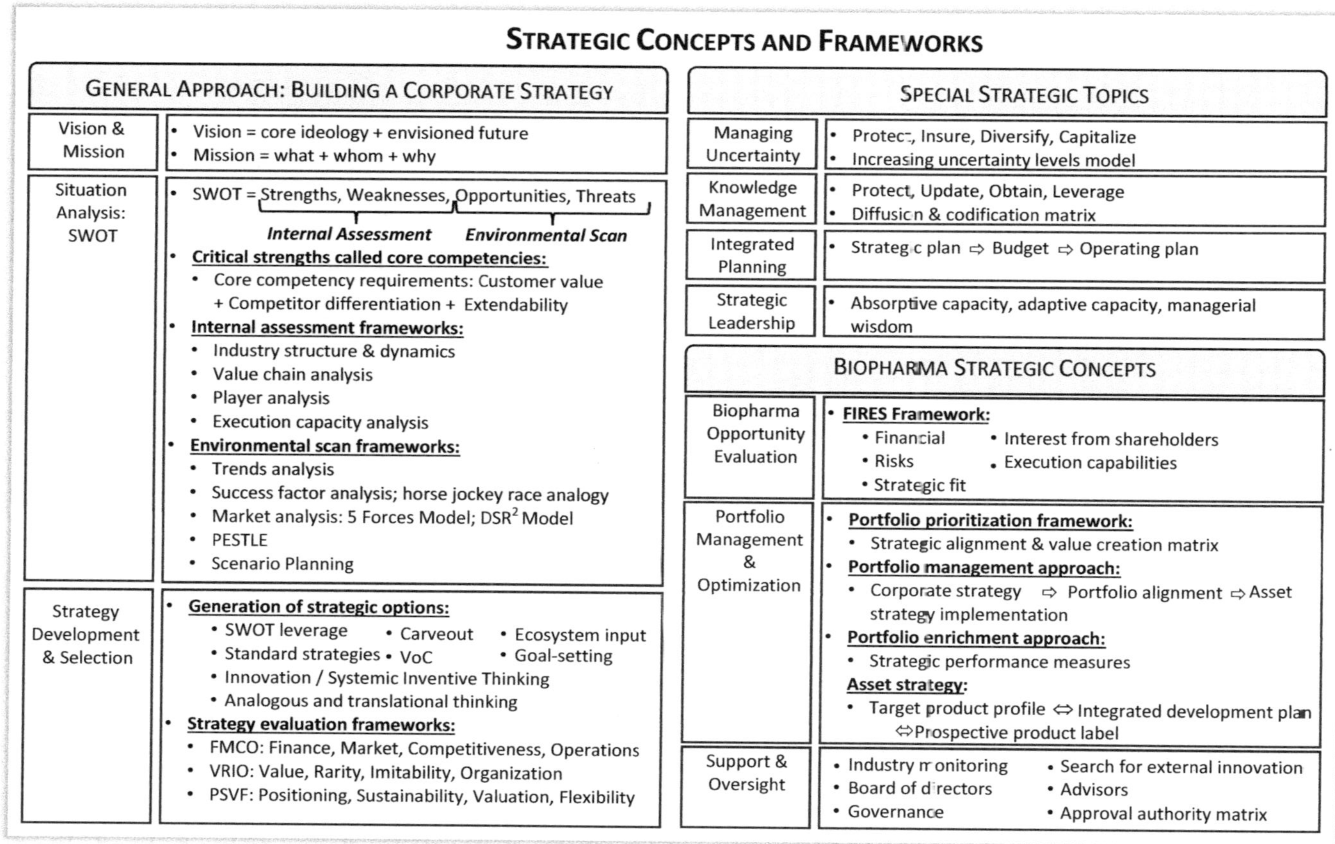

Figure 4.2 Navigating strategic tools and frameworks.

Simply put, the mission describes the actions the company will take to realize its vision. A mission statement typically establishes boundaries and priorities for the company's activities. To ensure practicality, mission statements should be concise and highlight the outcomes the company seeks to achieve (rather than prescribe methods to get there).

Mission for Nonprofit Organizations

While a mission is important for a for-profit organization, it is paramount for a nonprofit organization. In a for-profit setting, management has the fiduciary responsibility to maximize value and profits for shareholders within the broader context of stakeholder management. In contrast, in a nonprofit, management needs to ensure that resources are allocated exclusively to activities aligned with its mission. The nonprofit's mission both guides and constrains what activities the nonprofit should undertake.

Case Example: Vision and Mission

Cytokinetics is a late-stage biopharmaceutical company with the following vision and mission (Cytokinetics, 2023a, 2023b).

- Vision
  "Our vision is to be the leading muscle biology biopharma company that meaningfully improves the lives of patients with diseases of impaired muscle function through access to our pioneering medicines".
- Mission
  "We are committed to developing potential medicines that may improve the health span of people living with cardiovascular and neuromuscular diseases of impaired muscle function".

Mission and Vision are powerful tools for biopharma leadership teams. Internally, they drive strategic thinking, establish resource allocation boundaries, mobilize efforts or investments toward defining priorities, and guide decision-making. Externally, they are used to secure support (e.g., IRS tax exemption in the case of nonprofits, alignment with patient groups for certain diseases or therapeutic areas), communicate priorities to partner organizations, reinforce a clearly defined company positioning, and facilitate public relations.

4.1.3 SWOT Analysis

SWOT analysis is a widely recognized framework designating Strengths, Weaknesses, Opportunities, and Threats. The first two components focus on an internal assessment of the company: Strengths highlighting unique activities and capabilities that drive competitiveness and Weaknesses representing areas where competitors excel. The latter two components analyze the environment faced by the company: Opportunities representing value-creation options to be acted on swiftly and Threats representing risks to the company's value and its ability to generate it. Each SWOT dimension is evaluated in the context of the company's mission and vision, providing a robust foundation for strategy generation.

A preliminary SWOT analysis is commonly done through leadership brainstorming. It is, however, critical to validate the main SWOT entries with supporting facts or findings to enable the leadership team to establish an appropriate path forward. This validation can occur a priori by ensuring participants come prepared (e.g., collecting relevant information, reviewing provided reports), a posteriori by assigning participants to validate critical points, or through a combination of both approaches. During validation or preparation, employing a structured approach or specific framework is highly beneficial.

While countless frameworks and approaches can be used for an effective SWOT analysis, we will cover only a few in this section for instruction purposes. Regardless of the chosen framework, one essential requirement is objectivity and reliance on factual evidence. The discipline required is comparable to that used to substantiate or refute a clinical trial hypothesis. Ultimately, the finalized SWOT analysis should present a concise set of salient points that will guide the strategy, rather than an extensive list of vague or unsubstantiated assertions.

Case Example: Sources of Information

A key requirement for effective SWOT analyses is specificity and objectivity. Below are potential sources to access independent and factual biopharma information for strategic evaluations.

- Regulatory authority websites such as https://www.fda.gov/.
- Clinical trial information from ClinicalTrials.gov.
- OECD information on oecd.org such as key biotechnology indicators.
- Industry association information such as BIO (Biotechnology Innovation Organization) and PhRMA (Pharmaceutical Research Manufacturers of America).
- Fact-based analyses from leading consulting companies.
- Syndicated market research and independent databases.
- Unbiased internal company performance reports.
- Uncontroversial press releases.
- Public company presentations, especially investor-day presentations that might include further details on strategy, financials, and initiatives.

- Subscription-based pharmaceutical databases providing business development and financing information, data analytics, and related research reports.

Case Example: Illustrative SWOT Entries for Moderna, Inc. as of April 30, 2023.

Moderna is a US-based biopharma company with a growing mRNA platform. Moderna's mission is to "deliver the greatest possible impact to people through mRNA medicines"; their focus is to use their mRNA platform and infrastructure to address infectious and serious diseases (Moderna, 2014). As of December 2022, the company had 36 programs in active clinical trials, including three in Phase 3, and its COVID-19 vaccines had been approved in over 70 countries (Moderna, 2023).

An analyst performing a SWOT analysis of Moderna at the end of April 2023 starts with the following entries.

- Strength:
  Extensive clinical-stage development portfolio offering diversified industry exposure and options.
  - Justification provided by the analyst: the development pipeline of 48 programs covers 33 different infectious disease vaccine programs (27 in the clinic), 2 active development programs in systemic secreted and cell surface therapeutics modality, 3 active development programs in cancer vaccines modality, 2 active development programs in intra-tumoral immuno-oncology modality, one in regenerative therapeutics modality, 6 in systemic intracellular therapeutics modality, and one in inhaled pulmonary therapeutics modality.
- Weakness:
  Limited number of commercial stage products, product sales to date consisting of COVID-19 vaccines to governmental organizations.
  - Justification provided by the analyst: as of December 31, 2022, only two Omicron-targeting bivalent vaccines have been authorized.
- Opportunity:
  The mRNA approach opens the development of new modalities. As of early 2023, Respiratory Syncytial Virus (RSV) and flu vaccines represent potential launch opportunities in 2024.
  - Justification provided by the analyst: positive topline data from Phase 3 trial of mRNA-1345, a vaccine candidate targeting RSV in older adults; favorable interim results from Phase 3 trial of mRNA-1010, a vaccine candidate targeting seasonal influenza in adults.

- Threat:
  mRNA attractiveness increased competition that could limit freedom to operate and reduce commercial potential in a number of areas.
  - Justification provided by the analyst: increasing number of well-funded biotechnology competitors such as CureVac, BioNTech, Argos Therapeutics, Translate Bio, Ethris, and Arcturus.

Internal Assessment – Strengths and Weaknesses

The goal of the internal assessment is to objectively pinpoint strengths and weaknesses most relevant to the biopharma strategy. Maintaining an objective, fact-based, and outcome-oriented approach is essential. The objective is not to generate extensive, unsubstantiated, and unactionable lists of strengths and weaknesses but rather to produce a concise set of relevant, well-documented strengths and weaknesses that can effectively inform the company strategy definition and selection.

When thinking about a company's strengths, one central notion is that of a core competency. A core competency can be defined as a company's capability that meets three requirements (Hamel & Prahalad, 1996):

1. Customer value:
   It means that the capability, whether or not visible to the customer, must make a disproportionate contribution to the customer-perceived value.
2. Competitor differentiation:
   It means that few companies should have that capability.
3. Extendability:
   It means that the capability is not limited to one product or service but applies across different ones.

Identifying, understanding, developing, and applying core competencies is essential in strategy. A biopharma company acquisition usually results in acquiring its core competencies whereas a product licensing approach might not.

There are numerous approaches and frameworks that can be used toward internal assessments – below are four frameworks that might be used to establish a short, prioritized list of documented relevant strengths and weaknesses that can be acted upon (see Figure 4.3):

- Industry structure and dynamics.
- Value chain analysis.
- Player analysis.
- Execution capacity analysis.

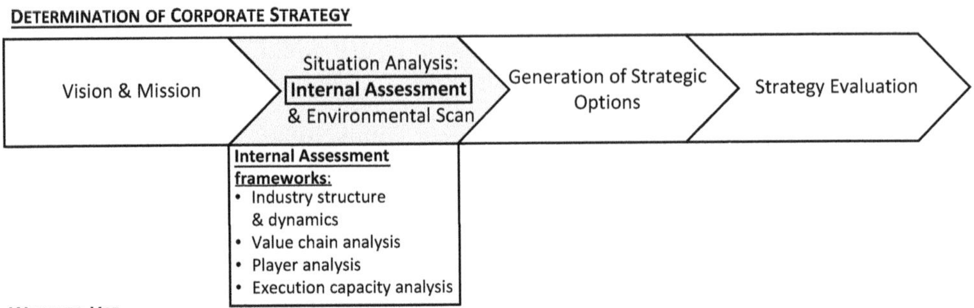

WHEN TO USE

Industry Structure & Dynamics	Value Chain Analysis	Player Analysis	Execution Capacity Analysis
• Considering entering a new therapeutic area or a new market • Assessing ability to compete and impact on profitability *Note that this framework, like others here, can also provide insights for "Environmental Scan"*	• Gauging competitive advantage that might result from differentiation • Assessing coordination and integration performance across different functional areas • Evaluating internal processes and assessing opportunities for cost or quality improvements	• Identifying strengths and weaknesses in the context of alliances and partnerships • Uncovering patient or clinician market segments or characteristics, and identifying product success factors • Identifying company core competencies	• Assessing operational capabilities that would help gain a competitive advantage • Identifying gaps in resources or skills that could exclude strategic options • Gauging organizational efficiency and effectiveness

Use of any of these frameworks provides different insights or perspectives and is at the discretion of the strategy team: custom frameworks or brainstorming might also be used instead.

Figure 4.3 Selection of internal assessment framework.

Industry Structure and Dynamics

An important prerequisite to assessing a company's situation is defining the industry in which it operates. Incorrectly setting industry boundaries can be detrimental. One useful approach is to carefully consider what, in the eye of the customer, could compete with or diminish the demand for the specific market need the company aims to address. Differentiating between small molecules and large molecules might not necessarily make sense. Additionally, in the biopharma industry, the notion of customer can be complex and multidimensional as it includes patients, clinicians, and payer organizations, among others.

Value Chain Analysis

A value chain analysis (Porter, 1985) consists in graphically representing the high-level business processes for the company's industry, analyzing interconnections within and outside of the various companies. It is helpful to understand for each step of the value chain (i.e., each high-level business process), who the players are and what that step's value contribution (inclusive of the profit margin made at that step) is to the overall

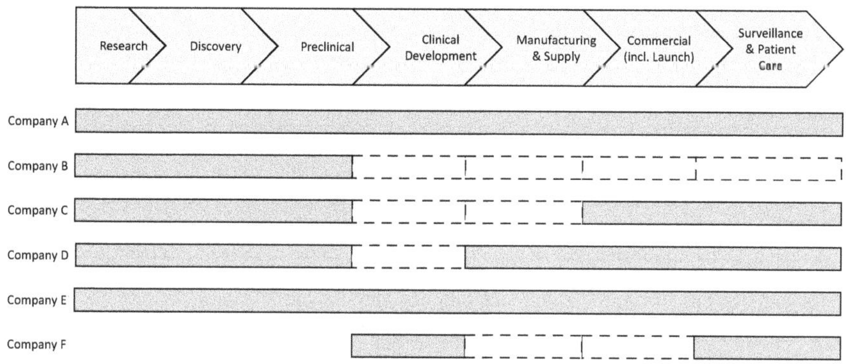

Figure 4.4 Illustrative biopharma value chain.

chain (Figure 4.4). Understanding a company's value chain might provide insights on a company's core competencies, optimal resource allocation, and cost-saving opportunities. It can also highlight dependencies on supply chain partners and potential vulnerabilities or strategic constraints for the company. Value chain considerations were brought to the forefront of the biopharma industry's attention during the 2020 COVID pandemic that severely disrupted company activities throughout the world.

When analyzing a value chain, one should analyze both real and virtual value chains (Rayport & Sviokla, 1995). Below are illustrative virtual capabilities that might be relevant in the biopharma value chain:

- Research: disease mechanism models.
- Discovery: data mining and artificial intelligence (AI) capabilities.
- Clinical development: digital biomarkers.
- Manufacturing/supply: clinical trial, supply depot, and commercial demand simulation or AI-based insights, considering various inputs and constraints.
- Commercial: decision support for clinicians.
- Surveillance and patient care: remote monitoring.

Keeping virtual or digital aspects in mind is an integral requirement given the important potential contributions that can be made by AI and data sciences at large.

Case Example: Purposeful Value Chain Positioning

AbCellera Biologics Inc. might be described as a platform discovery company. Specifically, the company built an end-to-end antibody discovery platform, as pictured in Figure 4.5, through internal development and vertical integration resulting from external acquisitions of complementary technologies (AbCellera, 2020):

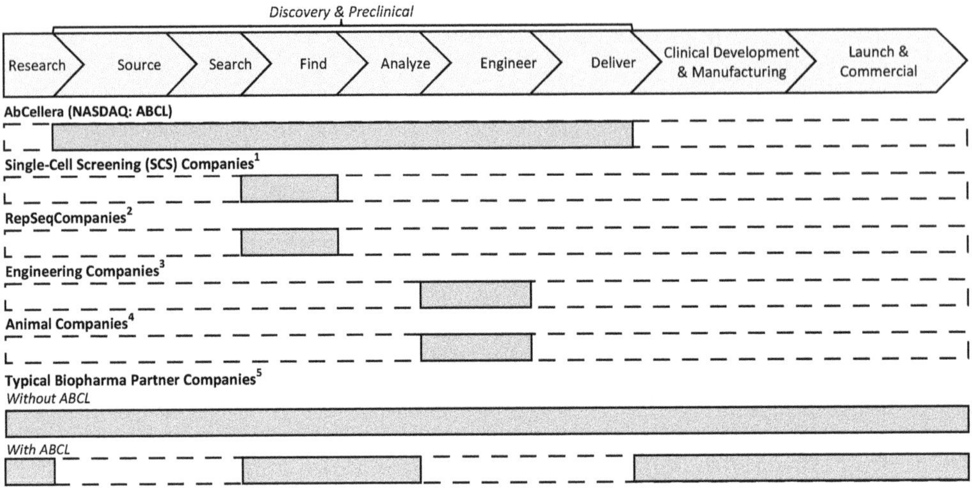

Notes: [1]Companies that provide access to similar technologies in the field of single-cell screening: Berkeley Lights, HiFiBio, Ligand, Sphere Fluidics.
[2]Companies that provide access to Immune repertoire sequencing (or RepSeq), such as 10X Genomics, Adaptive Biotechnologies, Atreca and Distributed Bio.
[3]Companies that provide access to bispecific antibody engineering technologies such as Abbvie, Genmab, Merus. and Zymeworks
[4]Companies that provide access to discovery technologies using genetically engineered rodents such as Ablexis, Crescendo Biologics., Harbour Antibodies, Kymab, Ligand and RenBio.
[5]AbCellera forges partnerships with its customers which are drug developers of all sizes, from large cap to small biopharma. The customer often participates in the identification and analysis of viable antibody drug candidates.

Figure 4.5 Illustrative value chain application for AbCellera.

- "Source".
  AbCellera combines proprietary immunization with genetically engineered mouse technologies, including the proprietary suite of humanized mice acquired in connection with the 2020 Trianni acquisition, to provide a diverse source of human antibodies.
- "Find".
  Following the 2017 Lineage acquisition, AbCellera integrated high-throughput RepSeq technology with its single-cell screening technology to provide comprehensive profiling and functional characterization of antibody diversity.
- "Engineer".
  AbCellera acquired rights to OrthoMab's bispecific technology in 2020 to design and produce bispecific antibodies.

On the digital side, AbCellera's AI-powered antibody discovery platform allows for faster, lower cost, and more accurate antibody discovery. Multidimensional data sets generated from AbCellera's partnerships (particularly in steps "Find" and "Analyze") are fed back into its AI engine to improve its accuracy, creating a feedback loop that can be leveraged for rapid response (Park et al., 2022).

Instead of focusing on one or a few steps within the discovery process as many emerging and established life sciences companies, AbCellera integrated technologies that address each step, offering a more complete solution for its biopharma partners who take on the resulting antibody drug candidates through drug development and commercialization.

Player Analysis

A player analysis broadly lists current and potential competitors, sometimes grouped in broader categories if the number of companies is extensive, referred to as "players". It then lists their strategic intent (what they claim they will do), their realized strategy (what they have actually done, which may diverge from their strategic intent), objectives, capabilities, and any other relevant dimensions.

Such analysis is often presented as a table with lines corresponding to the various players and columns representing the various dimensions. Insights on the industry can be drawn by comparing and contrasting two salient dimensions, often visualized through a 2×2 framework (see Chapter 1).

Such player analysis can offer substantiated insights into a company's strengths or weaknesses by facilitating objective comparisons to other players.

A noteworthy player analysis variation is the concept of benchmarking study, often conducted externally through an industry association or a consultant to protect confidential information specific to participating companies. Benchmarking provides specific information on how a company performs in particular areas relative to peers, making it easier to identify relative strengths and weaknesses.

Case Example: Pan-RAF Inhibitor Player Analysis as of May 2023

In oncology, a pan-RAF inhibitor is a compound that may present antineoplastic activity by preventing activation of Raf-mediated signal transduction pathways, which may inhibit tumor cell growth.

In May 2023, an industry analyst was looking at the various players in the pan-RAF inhibitor space, reviewing in particular the players listed in a company presentation (Erasca, 2023a).

The player analysis established by the analyst is provided in Table 4.1. Notwithstanding best-in-class considerations, the table indicates that naporafenib represents a potential first-in-class pan-RAF inhibitor in NRAS-mutant melanoma, making this R&D area a strength for Erasca, Inc.

Execution Capacity Analysis

An execution capacity analysis considers two main resources: assets (tangible and intangible) and capabilities. The leadership team assesses the availability of such resources, especially if they are valuable, i.e., having the following characteristics: competitive superiority, scarcity, inimitability, appropriability, durability, and lack of substitutability.

Table 4.1 Pan-RAF inhibitor player analysis

Company (reference)	*Strategic intent*	*Realized strategy*	*Compound*	*Phase (est. completion)*	*Other information*
Erasca (2023b)	Commercialize in the United States and possibly Europe; explore partnerships in selected geographies	2022 in-licensing agreement with Novartis	naporafenib	Phase 1 (Feb. 2022) + Phase 1b (December 2023) + Phase 2 (July 2023)	License obtained in December 2022
Genentech (Genentech)	Target oncogenic and tumor suppressive pathways to achieve durable benefit and cure	2016 in-licensing agreement with Hanmi Pharma	belvarafenib	Phase 1 (November 2024)	Patients with NRAS-mutant advanced melanoma who have received anti-PD-1/PD-1 therapy
Kinnate (Kinnate)	Fight cancer by searching and developing novel programs that are differentiated, with validated drivers	In-house development	exarafenib	Phase 1 (June 2024)	Evaluated as monotherapy and in combination with binimetinib

Tangible assets are embedded in physical or financial company property. Intangible assets are immaterial elements that the company can leverage and typically belong to one of three categories: technology (patents, trademarks, corporate experience), human (individual skills, loyalty, and adaptability), and reputation (as for brands).

Capabilities differ from intangible assets in that they use the assets to produce services or products. They are a means to an end and not an input. Capabilities typically fall into three categories: operations, organization, or information.

Operational capabilities encompass the execution of company functions: scientific discovery, technical engineering, clinical development, marketing, purchasing, HR, accounting, finance, etc. Organizational capabilities involve the way the company is structured with respect to its tangible and intangible assets. Informational capabilities relate to the company's ability to leverage its information and related systems to enable a strategy. Informational capabilities can be related to control, intelligence, speed, responsiveness, coordination, or knowledge sharing.

Analyzing a company's execution capacity allows leadership to identify specific strengths and weaknesses that may support or hinder certain strategic approaches.

Case Example: Operational Capability

Vaxcyte, a clinical-stage vaccine company, built integrated operational capabilities such as advanced chemistry, manufacturing expertise, and a scalable cell-free protein synthesis platform exclusively licensed from Sutro Biopharma (Vaxcyte, 2023). These operational capabilities enable the company to overcome the limitations of traditional chemistry and develop novel broad-spectrum conjugate and protein vaccines to prevent or treat bacterial infectious diseases. This represents an opportunity for company to pursue challenging pathogen sub-markets using their strengths on "tough-to-make" protein antigens.

Environmental Scan – Opportunities and Threats

As with internal assessments, external assessments or environmental scans can be approached in various ways. These analyses must remain objective, fact-based, and focused on generating a short, relevant, and substantiated list rather than a long unactionable list lacking justification. Below are five frameworks that may be utilized to establish such a short list (see Figure 4.6):

- Trend analysis.
- Success factor analysis.
- Market analysis.
- PESTLE.
- Scenario planning.

DETERMINATION OF CORPORATE STRATEGY

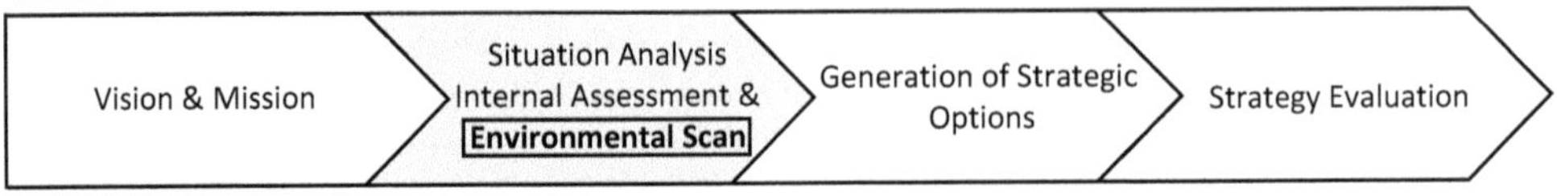

ENVIRONMENTAL SCAN FRAME WORKS – WHEN TO USE

Trend Analysis	Success Factor Analysis	Horse Jockey Race
• Identifying long-term market evolutions • Tracking patient and clinician behaviors and needs changes over time • Monitoring innovation	• Understanding critical drivers of competitive advantage • Identifying external opportunities that would align with internal capabilities • Identifying ways to enhance core competencies	• Understanding competitive threats and opportunities related to leadership, resources, and market conditions • Best for relatively stable market situations with low to medium complexity

5 Forces Analysis	DSR Squared Model	PESTLE	Scenario Planning
• Assessing competition level and company's leverage • Identifying potential threats	• Analysis of more complex markets (as is often the case in biopharma), possibly with customer fragmentation or different product access	• Ensuring comprehensive capture of environmental considerations • Focus on macro-environment	• Making assessments in situations of high uncertainty and complexity • Evaluating company's resilience to environment • Assessing flexibility required of strategy

Use of any of these frameworks provides different insights or perspectives and is at the discretion of the strategy team: custom frameworks or brainstorming might also be used instead.

Figure 4.6 Selection of environmental scan framework.

Trend Analysis

Biopharma leaders and analysts sometime keep virtual folders or organized notes with relevant industry information they collect over time to be able to discern trends and evolutions as they establish their next company plan. The quantitative and qualitative insights resulting from such a systematic review of credible industry sources are referred to as a trend analysis: all key evolutions observed for their industry segment. These might in turn result in threats or opportunities for the company.

Case Example: Research Trends

- NGS (Next Generation Sequencing) enabling gene therapy applications (Pervez et al., 2022).
  This technology opened opportunities in gene therapy applications by significantly reducing sequencing time and costs. The gains in time and costs have continued since the first generation of NGS solutions.
- CRISPR-Cas9 opening doors for new immunotherapy collaborations (Khurana et al., 2022).

The relative simplicity, speed, and low cost of then new editing techniques, like Clustered Regularly Interspaced Short Palindromic Repeat with and linked nuclease Cas9, enabled genome editing to be a standard part of research laboratories, thereby changing the landscape for collaborations. It also accelerated the pace of research and development in several therapeutic areas such as in immunotherapy.

Success Factor Analysis

One way to uncover opportunities and threats is to examine a company's critical success factors, i.e., the factors that exert a determining influence over value creation, be it for revenues, costs, funding levels, or another aspect. Critical success factors are activities and areas that are critical to value creation or to a successful strategy.

Case Example: Launch Success Factors

In 2022, Iveric Bio considered the following success factors for the US launch of Zimura, an investigational drug targeting Geographic Atrophy (Iveric Bio, 2022). Specifically, in order to ensure the broadest patient access to the medicine in a comprehensive and cost-effective way, three critical factors were identified:

- Commercial biopharma capabilities and infrastructure geared toward retina specialists, ophthalmologists, and optometrists.
- Promotion to retina specialists who perform most of the medical procedures involving diseases of the back of the eye in the United States.
- Adaptation of said promotion for balance of patients who see instead general ophthalmologists or optometrists.

Interestingly, Astellas Pharma acquired Iveric Bio in 2023 (Astellas, 2023), bringing its existing in-house commercial capabilities in the field of "Blindness and Regeneration" needed by Iveric Bio.

Horse Jockey Race Analogy

As a variant to the success factor analysis in the case of early-stage biopharma companies, venture capitalists might instead use an approach denoted as the horse jockey race analogy (Macmillan et al., 1985).

- The horse represents the biopharma products or technology, corresponding to IP, freedom to operate, platforms, and regulatory pathways.
- The jockey represents the leadership team and expertise, ensuring the best team possible is in place to the opportunities and threats considered.

- The race represents the market opportunities being pursued by the company along with their key characteristics concerning Patients, Physicians, Providers, Payers, and other Parties such as policymakers. These groups are sometimes collectively referred to as the 5 P's of Healthcare.

Market Analysis

When looking across industries, constructs like Michael Porter's Five Forces (Porter, 1980) provide a very helpful approach to conceptualize a market. Porter's model looks at five forces to understand the industry and inform a strategy:

1. Competitive rivalry between players.
2. Bargaining power of suppliers.
3. Bargaining power of buyers.
4. Threat of new entrants into the market.
5. Threat of substitutes to the product/service offering.

Biopharma markets tend to be comparatively complex, occasionally making the use of traditional market analyses challenging:

- Customer fragmentation: decision-maker, payer, and user roles reside with distinct groups as illustrated by the 5 P's of healthcare mentioned above.
- Access may vary depending on availability, reimbursement, contraindications, label, etc.
- Threat of new entrants is affected by customer fragmentation and affected by order-of-entry effects as early entrants are rewarded with higher market shares (Porath, 2016).

A market analysis framework helpful for biopharma is the DSR^2 model that addresses the complex characteristics of the industry. As shown in Table 4.2, it consists of six dimensions, with initials giving the model its name: DSR-DSR or DSR^2.

Table 4.2 DSR^2 model

Demand	*Supply*	*Regulations*
• Market size and growth • Customer/5 P's analyses • Market drivers and challenges • Demand funnel levers	• Current performance • Substitutes • Industry Pipeline • Order entry	• Expedited routes • Tax incentives • Regulatory evolutions

(Continued)

Table 4.2 (Continued)

Dynamics	*Sourcing*	*Risks*
• Competitive behaviors • Industry margins • New entrants	• Procurement • Accompanying products or services • Ancillary supplies & services • Logistics	• Market risk • Activity risk • Freedom to operate • Execution risk

Case Example: Illustrative Discussion Topics and Questions for the DSR² Model

Discussions on "Demand":

- Market size and growth estimates from syndicated research and other sources.
- Demand and preference analyses for the 5P's of healthcare.
- Epidemiology or scientific knowledge leveraged to understand demand evolutions or identify groups with higher needs.
- Information gathered from Key Opinion Leader network.
- Challenges that might arise regarding detection or diagnostics.
- Evaluation of biomarkers or tests that can help identify patients at risk.
- Is the disease burden similar between countries or specific to some regions?
- What specific factors might affect positively or negatively the funnel levers below?
- What levers can be controlled or impacted by the company or others? In what way?
    - Access lever: target markets to pursue and resulting population.
    - Disease lever: indications with resulting incidence and prevalence.
    - Segmentation lever: inclusion/exclusion – physician segments, certain disease states, or severity.
    - Awareness lever: percentage of patients diagnosed.
    - Treatment lever: percentage of diagnosed patients treated.
    - Penetration lever: percentage of treated patients treated with the company's product.
    - Effective pricing lever: net price per day of product × average number of days used for patient, adherence/compliance.

Discussions on "Supply":

- Existing competing platforms' quality and existing standard of care.
- Customers' (5 P's) current perceptions, unmet needs, and improvement priorities.

- Alternate process to platform or alternate treatment to standard of care and conditions of use.
- Industry pipeline of new technologies and products; information on expected performance and product profiles; information on market approval timing.
- Ideal market entry timing to meet. Expectations on order entry. Deadlines to watch.

Discussions on "Regulations":

- Possibility to take advantage of preferential regulatory pathways (e.g., Fast Track, Breakthrough Therapy, Priority Review).
- Options for localization and R&D avenues with preferential tax treatment (e.g., startup credits, tax incentives).
- New regulatory evolutions expected in targeted geographies, availability of new regulatory guidance.

Discussions on "Dynamics":

- How acute do we expect competition to be in this specific market segment?
- How large/small are current profitability margins?
- Are there many companies vying to be the next one to enter? What is the expected order entry and what are the corresponding advantages? See Table 4.3.

Table 4.3 Illustrative impact of order of entry for branded drugs

	Market share ratio (last entrant market share divided by first entrant market share)	*1st entrant market share*	*2nd entrant market share*	*3rd entrant market share*
After 1st drug enters the market	1.00	100%		
After 2nd drug enters the market	0.73	58%	42%	
After 3rd drug enters the market	0.61	43%	31%	26%

Kalyanaram (2008).

Discussions on "Sourcing":

- Are specific inputs required for the company's offering (e.g., ingredients, manufacturing equipment and services, patented components) that might be scarce and at risk of shortage or might otherwise significantly decrease offerings' profitability or availability?
- Are specific products (e.g., concomitant medications) or services (e.g., point of care diagnostic services) required with the company's offering? What do we know about the expected dynamics and availability of such services and products?
- Are other products and services synergistic with the company's offering? Options to optimize such synergies? Competitive actions to limit such synergies?
- Are certain mainstream geographies not likely to be timely served given import/export regulations? Is the company exposed to liabilities if it cannot deliver its offering in a timely manner with the required quality/condition? Do specific geographies represent a systematic challenge?
- What mitigations or differentiating approaches might be put in place from a logistics perspective (e.g., local depot, multiple production and manufacturing sites, temperature monitoring, controlled environment)?

Discussions on "Risks":

- Are there geographies with specific political, economic, or other risks? Can risks be managed?
- Should specific activities be avoided given their risk profile (e.g., financial investments for clinical development, commercialization activities outside of the United States)?
- What IP opportunities and threats should the company be concerned about?
- Specific operational opportunities or threats to consider (e.g., regulatory, personnel, quality assurance, information security, clinical trials, diversity equity, and inclusion)?

PESTLE Factor Analysis

PESTLE is a memory jogger to think about the various types of external factors that might result in threats or opportunities for the biopharma company. It derives its name from the initials of the factor types:

- **P**olitical factors, e.g., favorable R&D tax incentives or unfavorable trade restrictions.
- **E**conomic factors, e.g., manufacturing operations in high-inflation region might reduce profits.

- Social factors, e.g., favorable population growth rates that translate in higher disease incidence and thus increased product demand.
- Technological factors, e.g., NGS and CRISPR examples discussed above.
- Legal factors, e.g., labeling, patient protection, and safety regulations.
- Environmental factors, e.g., weather-impacting flu vaccine demand.

Scenario Planning

A scenario refers to a potential future evolution for the company and its environment; it describes the future state in response to a possible set of changes from the present situation.

The intent of scenario planning is to allow the leadership team to reflect upon possible evolutions, thinking through potential opportunities and threats, thereby establishing more robust strategic options.

The approach is sequential:

1. Selecting a defined and limited number of industry or business trends and uncertainties.
2. Assigning different options to each trend or uncertainty.
3. Selecting a set of coherent option combinations to define scenarios.
4. Thinking through the implications of each scenario.
5. Summarizing lessons learned from the aggregate scenario evaluations.

The main challenges for scenario planning usually consist of selecting:

- A reasonable number of input variables (i.e., trends and uncertainties).
- An appropriate set of values for each input variable.
- Insightful output variables (evaluation dimensions for each of the scenarios considered).

Ideally, the scenarios describe fundamentally different futures rather than variations on a theme.

Case Example: Commercial Opportunity Scenario Planning Based on Trial Outcomes

Cytokinetics, Inc (Nasdaq: CYTK) developed an investigational medicinal product, aficamten, targeting obstructive hypertrophic cardiomyopathy (oHCM). The New Drug Application for aficamten, is currently under review by the FDA, with blockbuster potential (i.e., peak sales above US$1B). It has the same myosin inhibitor mechanism of action as a BMS marketed drug, mavacamten, launched the previous year as first-in-class under a mandated Risk Evaluation and Mitigation Strategies (REMS) program.

Aficamten Phase 2 results indicated potential improved efficacy and safety versus reference product mavacamten, as measured by the following factors: half-life, speed to reach steady-state, withdrawal speed in case of adverse events, breadth of therapeutic window, and risk of drug – drug interactions.

The potential market opportunity represented by aficamten depended heavily on the confirmation of favorable Phase 2 signals in a successful Phase 3, now completed. Three illustrative scenarios as of June 2023 are listed in Table 4.4.

4.1.4 *Strategy Development and Strategic Choice*

Once complete, the SWOT analysis can help generate initial strategic options to be evaluated later:

- Opportunities.
    - Strategic options to seize opportunities while mitigating threats.
    - Strategic options that use selected strengths to provide a competitive advantage pursuing opportunities.
- Threats.
    - Strategic options to deflect or neutralize threats (e.g., partial market exit, repositioning on more attractive segments).
    - Strategic options to turn threats into opportunity (e.g., better response than competition).
- Strengths.
    - Strategic options for products or market segments that disproportionately prize the strengths.
    - Strengths that correspond to core competencies: strategic options that best use core competencies.
- Weaknesses.
    - Strategic options might eliminate or play down the weaknesses (e.g., complementary partnerships; products or markets where weaknesses are less relevant; weakness elimination through internal investment or external acquisition).

The strategy team may, at their discretion, generate strategic options based on the SWOT analysis or use alternate approaches (Figure 4.7). Alternate approaches include:

Table 4.4 Aficamten successful Phase 3 scenario planning analysis

	Scenario A *Downside scenario*	**Scenario B** *Base scenario*	**Scenario C** *Upside scenario*
Phase 3 variables		***Scenario outcomes***	
• Left ventricular outflow tract reduction • PK/PD curve	*Lower efficacy than mavacamten*	*Similar efficacy*	*Superior efficacy*
• Half-life • Drug–drug interactions	*Similar or lower safety*	*Better safety with REMS required by FDA*	*Better safety; no REMS requirement*
	⇩	⇩	⇩
		Product profile implications	
	Minimally marketable	Favorable	Best-in-class
	⇩	⇩	⇩
		Market implications	
Medical and treatment cost–benefits	No comparative advantage	Simplified therapy	Simpler therapy without costly REMS
Market share potential	Low: “me-too” drug	Challenger able to get a favorable sales ramp up	High market share and ability to expand the category

(*Continued*)

Table 4.4 (Continued)

	Scenario A *Downside scenario*	**Scenario B** *Base scenario*	**Scenario C** *Upside scenario*
	⇩	⇩	⇩
	Opportunity approach implications		
Manufacturing	Low-volume manufacturing	High-volume manufacturing	Flexible high-volume manufacturing
Sales & marketing	Launch strategy focused on early adopters; streamlined commercial organization	Early in commercial leadership investment, general marketing approach, commercial-scale salesforce	State-of-the-art commercial leadership organization and capabilities, with best-in-class positioning
Pricing	Outcome-based pricing to secure favorable drug formulary positioning. Discounts and rebates to pharmacy benefit managers.	Competitive pricing strategy used for positive signaling with clinicians	Price premium in line with superior performance. Rebates during launch phase
Reimbursement	Heavy investments in payor relationships to secure reimbursement	Standard reimbursement strategy to secure reimbursement parity with competitive options	Invest in value and health benefits publications highlighting product superiority; help payor organizations justify more favorable reimbursement than competitive drugs

DETERMINATION OF CORPORATE STRATEGY

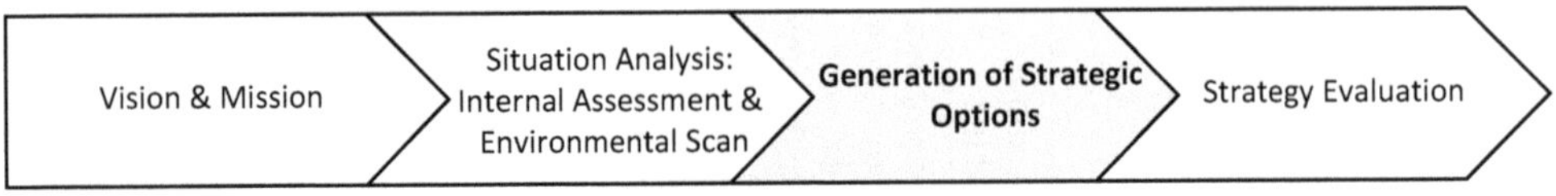

WHEN TO USE

Approach to generate strategic options	*Applicable situations include*
SWOT-based	• The company faces significant mission-critical pitfalls and opportunities. • Identified strengths correspond to core competencies well-aligned with the corporate mission & vision. • Market opportunities present strong company growth potential. • Identified threats and weaknesses put the company's vision and mission at risk.
Carveout	• The company has strong/unmatched capabilities in one critical area they decide to focus on, while carving out complementary or other areas that can be managed through external collaborations.
Ecosystem-sourcing	• The company operates in a strongly innovative and collaborative environment or location.
Voice of the Customer	• New markets, shifting markets, markets with conflicting requirements, or markets where customer (e.g., patient or clinician) experience is critical to adoption and use of company's products/services.
Goal-setting	• The company has very strong internal capabilities and is attempting to generate game-changing strategies for specific objectives.
Systemic inventive thinking / innovation	• The company believes it can challenge traditional industry approaches through innovation.
Analogous & translational thinking	• The company's market segment has not seen significant structural or strategic changes for a significant period, indicating potential opportunities for radically different thinking.

Use of any of these approaches provides insights into different strategic options and is at the discretion of the strategy team: custom approaches or brainstorming might also be used instead.

Figure 4.7 Approach selection to generate strategic options.

- Carveout.
  Reflecting on what activities or markets the company will not participate in, to focus instead on areas where it can compete effectively, and discuss the corresponding tradeoffs. Explicitly carving out areas the company will not play in can be extremely important to have a focused organization.
- Ecosystem input.
  Ask for ideas from thought leaders and innovative thinkers within a company's ecosystem (e.g., customers, former colleagues, suppliers, professional firms, convention attendees) can yield radically different ideas.
- Standard strategies.
  What could low cost, strong differentiation, or niche offering look like for a specific biopharma industry segment?
- Voice of the Customer (VOC).
  VOC is simply a process through which companies gather information on experiences and expectations from customers and potential customers. See Burchill and Brodie (2005). Reflecting upon VOC findings

from healthcare professionals and patients might generate additional strategic options

- Goal-setting.
  Setting drastically more ambitious objectives can challenge a leadership team to think differently. A platform company might ask what it would take to get 15 programs past Phase 1 in 2 years rather than three in the same period.
- Innovation frameworks.
  Given biopharma's R&D orientation, thinking through innovation takes care of one typical strategic expectation. Among the vast number of innovation frameworks, one might use Systematic Inventive Thinking (Boyd & Golderberg, 2014): for illustration purposes:
  - Offering subtraction – removing something from the current process or offering (e.g., removal of liquid to get to dry blood spot diagnosis test concept).
  - Offering multiplication – multiplying something in the current process or offering (e.g., provision of 10 rather than 5 mRNA sequence leads by platform company to pharma client).
  - Offering division – dividing something in the current process or offering (e.g., division of injection pen with six doses requiring use of multiple needles into six needle-equipped single-dose pens).
  - Offering unification – unifying something with the current process or offering (e.g., delivery system with progressive release for multiple drugs).
  - Offering dependency change – changing how attributes might relate in the current process or offering (e.g., repositioning drugs for new therapeutic applications, removing script requirement to create OTC drug version, or splitting vitamin supplements into men and women versions).
- Analogous and translational thinking.
  Such approaches consist in using abstract, common knowledge concepts or stories from other industries to challenge the leadership's thinking around potential strategic options. For example, one might ask how the concept of "Intel Inside" successful in the PC industry would apply to biopharma. The answer might be a discovery platform company that provides biopharma companies with drug candidates associated with higher success probability and shorter clinical developments.

Case Example: Strategic Option That Leverages an Identified Strength

Since its inception, BioNTech (Nasdaq: BNTX), a next generation immunotherapy company, has focused on its computational solutions strengths to create personalized immunotherapies. It has since in the same vein adopted a strategy to "build world-leading capabilities in AI-driven drug discovery and development" as evidenced by the 2023 acquisition of InstaDeep.

This acquisition allows BioNTech to incorporate rapidly evolving AI capabilities into their technologies, research, drug discovery, manufacturing, and deployment processes (BioNTech, 2023).

Synthesis of Strategic Options

Up until this stage, the goal was to define a reasonable number of strategic options without stopping at the first option the leadership team might like. Once the leadership team has generated a sufficient number of different strategic options, they should strive to consolidate those that are similar into a single one, while eliminating those that are clearly unrealistic, so that they can efficiently compare the remaining options.

Strategy Evaluation

Evaluation and selection of strategic options can be made via a wide spectrum of approaches from subjective ones (e.g., leadership team force ranks the strategic options in a workshop) to framework-based or quantitative evaluations that provide an explicit rationale. Three such framework-based approaches (designated as FMCO, VRIO, PSVF) are explained below. Each framework presents different perspectives and the strategy team should use the one they deem most appropriate (see Figure 4.8).

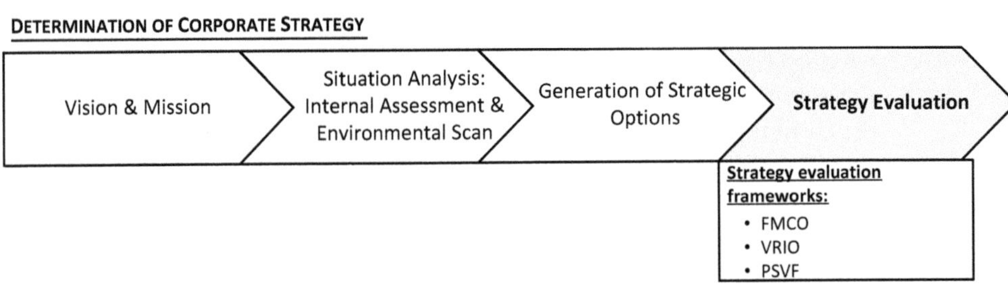

WHEN TO USE

FMCO: Finance, Market, Competitiveness, Operations	VRIO: Value, Rarity, Imitability, Organization	PSVF: Positioning, Sustainability, Valuation, Flexibility
• The company wishes to maintain an objective view on essential internal and external business factors, taking the standpoint of an investor • Best suited for rigorous strategic planning imperative that scrutinizes strategic options through the various dimensions needed to deliver superior value creation	• The company has significant core competencies or unique resources for its intended market(s) that should be reflected in its corporate strategy • Best suited for strategic resource allocation and competitive advantage assessment	• The company wishes to have a comprehensive in-depth evaluation of its strategic options, paying specific attention to resulting strategic dependencies • Best suited for corporate/division strategies with strong focus on long-term value creation and strategic adaptability

Although they share similar characteristics, each of these frameworks provides different insights and perspectives. Using onever sus the other is at the discretion of the strategy team; custom frameworks or simpler pros & cons evaluations might be used instead.

Figure 4.8 Selection of strategy evaluation framework.

FMCO: Finance, Market, Competitiveness, Operations

The FMCO framework views a strategy through the lenses of financial performance, markets, competitive advantage, and operating model to help companies make important strategic decisions while maintaining objectivity (Laczkowski et al., 2018).

Finance might be considered as the cost of entry for a strategy and the biopharma leadership team should ensure they can afford the option by discussing whether the strategy considered:

- Generates sufficient value (e.g., value inflection point expected at the next financing stage for a startup).
- Compares favorably to the value created by alternate strategic options with a similar risk level.
- Uses a financial runway the company can provide given benchmarks and margins for error.

The market dimension aims to validate that the strategic option is focused on the best "bet", compared with other strategic options, given the company's capabilities. Such validation would typically involve leadership discussions around the following:

- Continued attractiveness of targeted segments (size, growth, profitability, and market access).
- Competitive rivalry, risk of new market entries, technologies, and IP that might threaten current or planned levels of performance and profitability.
- Geographic implementation versus regulatory pathways, supply chain, manufacturing, market access, reimbursement, and epidemiology considerations.
- Adequacy of assets, expertise, and financial resources required.
- Coverage of best market opportunities available to the company.

With thousands of companies contributing to the industry R&D pipeline (IQVIA Institute for Human Data Science, 2023), evaluating the competitive dimension is paramount in biopharma. The leadership should validate that the strategy:

- Leverages competitive advantages for the company.
- Reflects a competitive environment in which the company can successfully maneuver (e.g., freedom to operate) in the most important regions for their therapeutic areas and products.
- Improves their ability to compete and aptly considers substitute products and competitive threats.

Lastly, ensuring operational execution can be crucial, as evidenced by the COVID pandemic that delayed the majority of clinical trials industry-wide and stopped a large number of them. The biopharma company's leadership's investigation of this dimension might include:

- Internal availability of required functional expertise and talent.
- Access to appropriate equipment, processes, and ecosystem.
- Adequate supply chain and manufacturing capabilities.

Case Example: FMCO for Collaboration and Licensing Strategic Option

In 2022, HOOKIPA and Roche announced a strategic collaboration and licensing agreement to develop a novel arenaviral immunotherapy for KRAS-mutated cancers (HOOKIPA, 2022). One might evaluate this strategic option afforded to HOOKIPA at the time by applying the FMCO framework and leveraging information from HOOKIPA (2023). An illustration of a favorable evaluation is provided in Table 4.5.

Table 4.5 FMCO for collaboration and licensing strategic option

Dimension	*Evaluation*	*Selected rationale*
Finance	Strongly favorable	• Immediate value from US$25M upfront payment plus significant upside (milestones, royalties). • Company has sufficient financial runway for collaboration areas under their responsibility (preclinical, half of Phase 1). • Deal, favorable compared with preclinical oncology licensing deals at the time, covers a single product with option for second one, while enabling funding of remaining company pipeline.
Market	Favorable	• Large unmet medical needs to treat KRAS mutant-driven cancers (pancreatic, colorectal, lung). • Agreement provides that commercially reasonable efforts will be devoted for development or commercialization, as applicable. • Many competitors pursing this indication.
Competitiveness	Strongly favorable	• Internal core competency in the discovery and generation of off-the-shelf arenaviral immunotherapeutics. • Proprietary arenaviral vector platform for engineering arenaviruses to carry and deliver tumor-specific genes directly in patients. • Both partners have immune-oncology development experience.

(Continued)

Table 4.5 (Continued)

Dimension	*Evaluation*	*Selected rationale*
Operations	Strongly favorable	• Robust manufacturing processes, reliable assays, and strong supply agreements for all of the components used in their product candidates to support ongoing and planned clinical trials. • Required platform expertise is available in-house.

VRIO: Value, Rarity, Imitability, Organization

Jay Barney established the VRIO framework to understand the return potential from exploiting a company's resources and capabilities (Barney & Hesterly, 2014). Applying this framework (Figure 4.9) to a potential strategy consists in probing each dimension sequentially to ensure that the strategic option really aligns with a sustainable competitive advantage by aptly using resources and capabilities that are valuable, rare, and costly to replicate.

Case Example: Evaluation of Strategy with VRIO Framework

In late 2022, Vaxcyte and Sutro established an agreement that gives Vaxcyte expanded rights to develop and manufacture cell-free extract in exchange for US$22.5M upfront payment and up to US$135M additional payments; cell-free extract is a key component of Vaxcyte's vaccine candidates (Sutro, 2022).

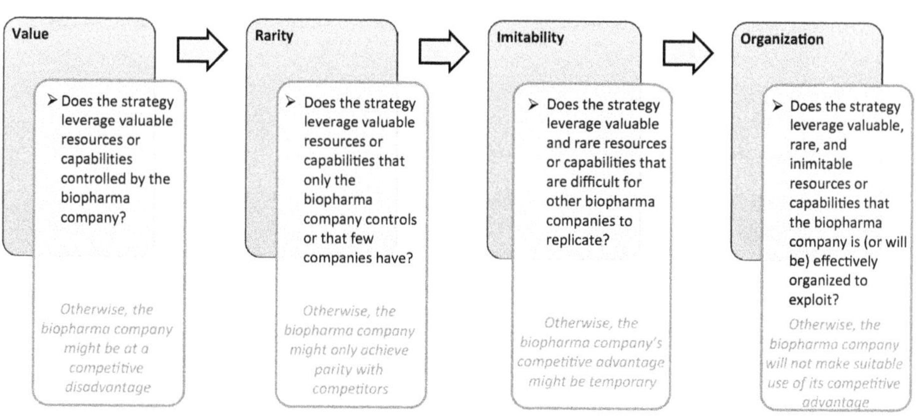

Approach derived from Barney & Hesterly, 2014.

Figure 4.9 VRIO framework application to biopharma company's strategy.

Sutro's strategy to trade these rights to Vaxcyte within the context of an expanded relationship can be reviewed using the VRIO framework to suggest it corresponds to a sustainable competitive advantage:

- Value – The agreement leverages valuable resources controlled by Sutro: it "underscores the value of Sutro's platform technology and the importance of cell-free extract as an essential element" (Sutro, 2022).
- Rarity – The rights correspond to unique Sutro capabilities encapsulated into their proprietary platform technology. Another company would need access to the rights owned by Sutro, which is rare. In fact, this is the "first time" that Sutro "has granted one of its partners for its licensed products rights to expand oversight and control related to the manufacture and development of cell-free extract" (Sutro, 2022).
- Imitability – Sutro's technology platform is made possible by the separation, into an extract, of the cellular components required to produce proteins from the process of protein generation. The extract includes all necessary biochemical components for energy production, transcription, and translation and can be used to support cell-free biochemical protein synthesis by the addition of the specific DNA sequence. This cell-free system is difficult for others to replicate.
- Organization – Sutro is organized to design, discover, characterize, and manufacture proteins for the treatment or prevention of diseases for itself and for partners using its proprietary platform technologies.

PSVF: Positioning, Sustainability, Valuation, Flexibility

The PSVF framework to evaluate a strategy has been developed by Ghemawat (1991). Let us illustrate with the bullet point list below, how a biopharma leadership team might use this framework to evaluate a strategy for their company.

- Positioning offered by the strategy should enable the biopharma company to have a favorable and profitable position.
    - Does the strategy leverage a unique competitive advantage using capabilities and resources that differentiate the company from its competition? Economies of scale resulting from using a salesforce across different products, high-end positioning of products with superiority claims (or at least non-inferiority), leading market access with competitive reimbursement approaches, superior distribution, etc.
    - Competitive advantages linked to R&D are particularly important (e.g., AI-enabled capabilities, innovative research methods, unique technologies or platforms)

- Sustainability of the strategy should enable the biopharma company to continue to benefit from its competitive position over time; that sustainability is contingent on three requirements:
  - Commitment – the firm needs to continue to deploy resources and capabilities to support the competitive position.
  - Scarcity – the capabilities and resources in question should remain relatively rare or difficult to obtain so that competitors cannot easily replicate what the company is doing.
  - Appropriability – the biopharma firm needs to be able to retain the financial benefits from such capabilities and resources. Said differently, there should not be any internal (e.g., required access to subject matter experts and equipment) or external factors (e.g., other company controlling complementary assets like the use of externally owned mRNA capping technology by an mRNA platform company) that that might prevent the company from doing so.
- Valuation – the value created by the strategy should be both favorable and meaningful for the company.
  - The value created is often measured using a quantitative, objective measure like Discounted Cash Flows (DCF) (see Chapter 2) that allows easy comparisons with other strategies.
- Flexibility of the strategy should enable the biopharma company to adapt to changes in its environment.
  - The expectation of a flexible strategic option is that the biopharma firm can adjust its strategic implementation in response to competitive reactions and evolutions in the environment.

After illustrating strategy evaluation approaches with three frameworks (FMCO, VRIO, PSVF), it is important to note that regardless of the evaluation framework a leadership team decides on, they should attempt to select their method of evaluation prior to brainstorming strategic options to avoid selection bias and leading answers.

While using an established strategy assessment framework is perfectly acceptable, certain companies might elect to build their own. Merck KGaA and the Boston Consulting Group (BCG) have defined a Sustainable Business Value framework (Buchholz et al., 2020).

Regardless of the evaluation and selection method used, the biopharma leadership will normally select the strategic option that objectively fared the best overall and seek clear endorsement and sponsorship by the CEO and the board.

4.1.5 Business Plan as Strategy Precursor

A quick word of caution mostly directed to early-stage companies in connection with the strategy selection we just discussed. Often times, biopharma startups begin with a business plan they show to potential investors rather than a strategic plan. They might even have focused that business plan around justifying the potential of a single molecule that would "make or break" the startup. In the context of such privately funded enterprises, it is important to review past investor documentation before drafting a new and improved strategic approach to ensure it takes into account past commitments and legal obligations that might arise from financing rounds. Also, looking at Figure 4.10, many elements of a business plan can inform a strategy and vice-versa.

From an investor's perspective, one must strike the right balance between control and innovation or even initiative. The more prescriptive the environment and investment control, the less the biopharma company leaders will take new initiatives and behave independently.

Figure 4.10 Typical business plan components.

As with any tradeoff, the key resides on selecting one dimension while taking measures to maximize success on the other dimension. As an illustration of this balancing act, Lifshitz-Assaf et al. (2018) took a page from hackathon organizers by recommending strongly setting the stage and then taking a step back:

1. Set the stage for filling knowledge gaps but do not manage learning.
2. Set the stage for experimentation but do not manage experiments.
3. Set the stage for early feedback on new ideas but do not supply it yourself.

4.2 Special Strategic Topics

4.2.1 *Managing Uncertainty*

The biopharma industry is known for its high levels of uncertainty and inherent risks as follows:

- Ability to attract and retain the cross-functional expertise required to develop truly innovative concepts and products.
- Equity ownership preservation and funding constraints versus long upfront R&D investments.
- Competitive and changing biopharma investment environment versus continuous financing needs.
- High R&D failure rates, varying by stage and therapeutic indication.
- Different regulatory pathways, evolving with new technologies that might not fit current frameworks.
- Tacit expectations that newer riskier avenues might yield new therapies or even new classes of therapies.
- Innovation IP might reside with different companies, adding uncertainty on the level of financial success.

Uncertainty might also be linked to the economy (e.g., high inflation and interest rates causing downturn in venture capital and private equity activity), political factors (e.g., targeted inquiries on price charged by biopharma companies), or country environment (e.g., mandatory discount applied to all medicines sales price).

Risk and uncertainty might be used interchangeably by various authors, sometimes depending on whether the described concept is measurable ("risk" terminology typically used) or not ("uncertainty" terminology typically used). In this section we do not distinguish risk from uncertainty but will refer to unmeasurable risk as "true uncertainty".

Conceptually, there are different ways to manage uncertainty:

- Protect: lower the risk probability.
- Insure: lower negative risk consequences.
- Diversify: generate a portfolio of activities with different risk profiles so that losses in one area might be offset by gains in another area.
- Capitalize on it: try and gain a competitive advantage as a result of the uncertainty faced. One avenue to do that might consist in building three abilities (Kuipers et al., 2020):
    - Signal: ability to detect, communicate, and assess risks and opportunities.
    - Decisiveness: ability to align around and execute the best strategy.
    - Resilience: ability to anticipate and recover from disruption.

Establishing a successful strategy will likely require different evaluation methods and approaches altogether depending on the level of uncertainty involved as illustrated by Figure 4.11 based on Courtney et al. (1997).

Traditional biopharma approaches will define parameters to characterize potential evolutions and attempt to "de-risk" the business by the next time incremental funding is required. The higher the uncertainty, the more flexible the strategy needs to be (making the last dimension of the PSVF strategy evaluation framework critical to consider – see Section 4.1.4).

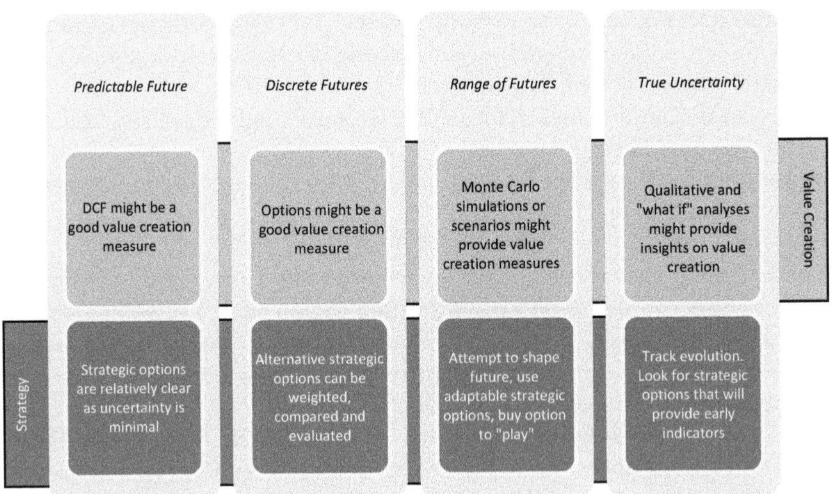

Based on Courtney et al. (1997).

Figure 4.11 Modeling increased levels of uncertainty.

4.2.2 *Knowledge Management*

How a biopharma company manages its knowledge has implications for the expertise and IP the firm depends on for its strategy. The processes used to create, communicate, use, and manage that knowledge can be de facto or formal depending on the company.

Figure 4.12 illustrates how one might conceptually approach knowledge management depending on where that knowledge resides ("diffusion") and on how explicit it is ("codification").

Given the dynamic and innovative nature of the industry, biopharma firms need to proactively define how they manage knowledge in a complex open innovation ecosystem, while safeguarding their intellectual property. The knowledge management approach used might vary depending on which quadrant of Figure 4.12 the knowledge falls into as a function of diffusion and codification.

Case Examples: Different Knowledge Management Approaches for Strategic Purposes

Table 4.6 provides illustrations and applications for each of the four knowledge management approaches.

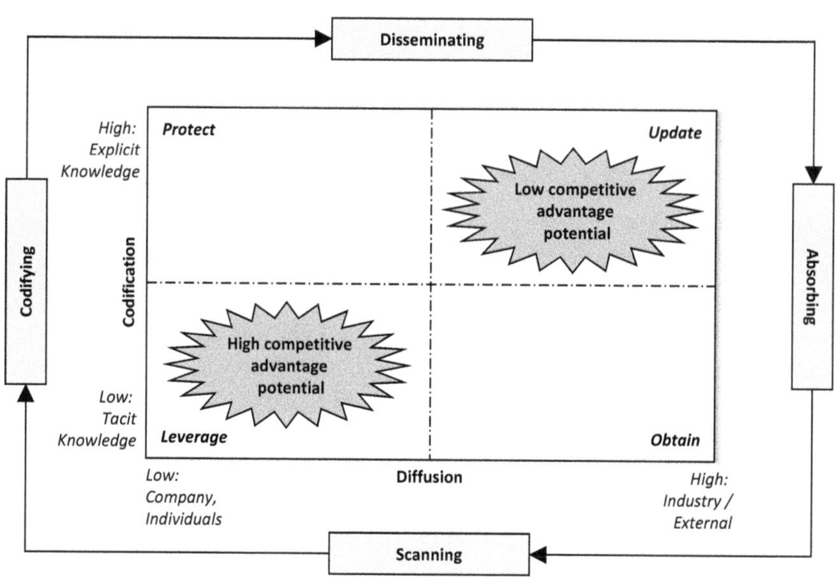

Figure 4.12 Knowledge management model.

Table 4.6 Illustrative knowledge management approaches

Approach	*Illustration*	*Application examples*
Protect	• Label information as confidential • Employee agreements protecting company confidential information • Information access restricted to specific employees • Mandatory compliance training	• Internal best practices and guidelines • Standard operating procedures • Case studies • Financial information
Update	• Review industry journals • Track supplier offering improvements and add-on offers • Check for potential practices that would improve competitive position	• R&D • Finance benchmarks • Workflow applications • Online database specification
Obtain	• Ensure training and capabilities parity • Obtain core competencies insights • Document and interpret market signals, patterns, and trends	• Industry forums and training • Collaborations and partnerships • Customer discussions • Analysis of competitors' results
Leverage	• Leverage core competencies in a cost-efficient way • Develop knowledge to address new markets/products	• Encouraged internal networks of resources and experts • Expertise-based processes and cross-functional approaches

Case Example: Collaboration Knowledge Management

In 2019, Voyager Therapeutics and Neurocrine Biosciences established a collaboration and license agreement, aimed at four separate programs, which emphasized knowledge management. The agreement required of each party complete, current, and accurate records for all development activities and documentation as codified by ICH (International Conference on Harmonization), GCP, GLP, and cGMP. (Voyager Therapeutics & Neurocrine Biosciences, 2019).

4.2.3 *Integrated Business Planning*

The true effectiveness of strategy resides in its successful implementation. The authors have unfortunately seen cases where a company goes through an annual "ritual" where they "dust off" the strategic plan from the previous year, make various updates and modifications, discuss the revision with the

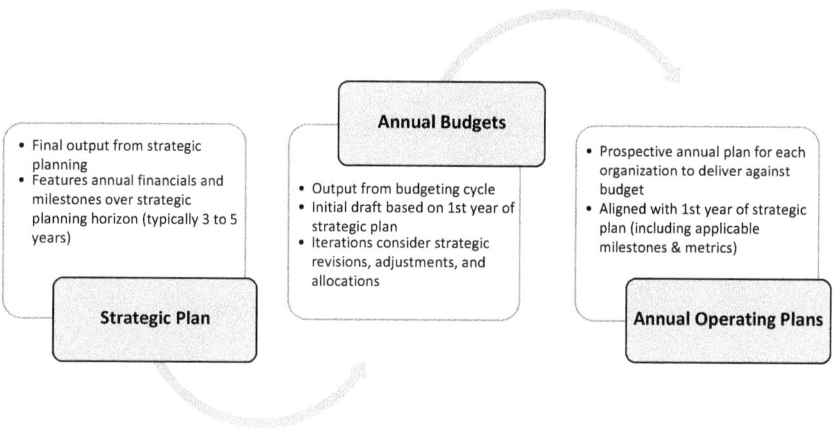

Figure 4.13 Integrated business planning.

leadership team in a well-orchestrated "dog and pony show", and then swiftly put the strategy documents back on their virtual shelves... Regardless of the potential entertainment value, such approach fails to constitute a meaningful strategy development and simply results in wasted time and efforts.

For a strategy to have real impact, it must be integrated into the organization's budgets and operating plans (Figure 4.13). The first year of the strategic plan financials should drive the next annual budget cycle. Aligning the strategic planning timing to precede the budgeting cycle is a best practice to ensure that cohesion.

Whereas budgets encapsulate measures related to value-creation expectations for the year, operating plans specify the actions used to drive strategic implementation during the current year. There is customarily one operating plan for each major budget holder (e.g., business units and functions). Such operating plan commonly includes:

- Approaches and outcomes to conduct the applicable parts of the strategic plan.
- Activities to be performed.
- A goal tree – the various goals against which the organization needs to deliver.
- Key Performance Indicators (KPIs) to gauge performance and monitor progress.
- Organization and resource planning.
- Gantt chart of major events, activities, and deliverables.

Once the operating plan has been finalized, the corresponding organization uses its regular day-to-day management tools and processes to implement it.

4.2.4 *Strategic Leadership*

Having a strategy is usually not sufficient; being successful at strategy takes specific leadership traits, in the biopharma industry as for other industries. Below are three capabilities considered at the core of strategic leadership ability (Boal & Hooijberg, 2000):

- Absorptive capacity (ability to learn).
- Adaptive capacity (capacity to change).
- Managerial wisdom (ability to perceive variation in the environment and understanding of the social actors and their relationships).

Related questions examined from a strategic leadership perspective, for the top team, CEO, or board of directors, may include the following aspects (Schaedler et al., 2022):

- Agency theory – are there any conflicts between the leadership goals and the required company strategy? Alignment is normally ensured via the company's governance system.
- Expertise – as leaders rely on their knowledge structure and bias, is there a need for training or new frameworks to successfully execute the strategy?
- Social evaluations – given stakeholders' perceptions (approval, legitimacy, reputation of the company, and its leadership) are there any critical adjustments to be made for the biopharma firm's strategy to be effective?
- Ethical leadership – how might ethical aspects be factored into the strategic approach and how might executives take the lead?

Successful strategy leaders often use, formally or informally, a strategic advisory group, i.e., a group of individuals that are experts, influencers, and out-of-the-box thinkers, who can challenge their thinking either through direct discussions or at least by reviewing their online posts and other publications.

Recognizing the significance of fostering strategic leadership within the executive team, founders commonly represent a primary consideration for venture capital companies to pursue deals (Gompers et al., 2021).

4.3 Biopharma Strategic Considerations

In addition to the general strategy concepts covered in Section 4.1, there are common biopharma industry situations faced by companies when pursuing their corporate strategy:

- Evaluation of new biopharma asset opportunities, developed internally or acquired externally through licensing and M&A.
- Portfolio management strategy.
- Asset strategy.

4.3.1 Biopharma Opportunity Evaluation

The FIRES (Financials – Interest from shareholders – Risks – Execution capability – Strategic fit) framework provided in Figure 4.14 can be used to evaluate an opportunity to invest in new assets from a strategic perspective. For presentation purposes, one would rather use SIREF as a sequence (instead of FIRES) although that acronym is unfortunately not as memorable... There are many strategic considerations that might identify a biopharma program as strategic:

- Differentiated target product profile.
- Unique MOA (Mechanism of Action).
- Best-in-class efficacy.
- Potential to replace Standard of Care.
- Improved side-effect profile or superior route of administration.
- Therapeutic area or indication with significant unmet needs.
- Attractive market and value-creation potential (e.g., high NPV, favorable IRR, large growth market, high peak sales potential).

The leadership team should evaluate opportunities along the FIRES dimensions as they progress opportunities from strategic options to modeled opportunities, to feasible high-level implementation plans, to a clear understanding of where the company might fall short.

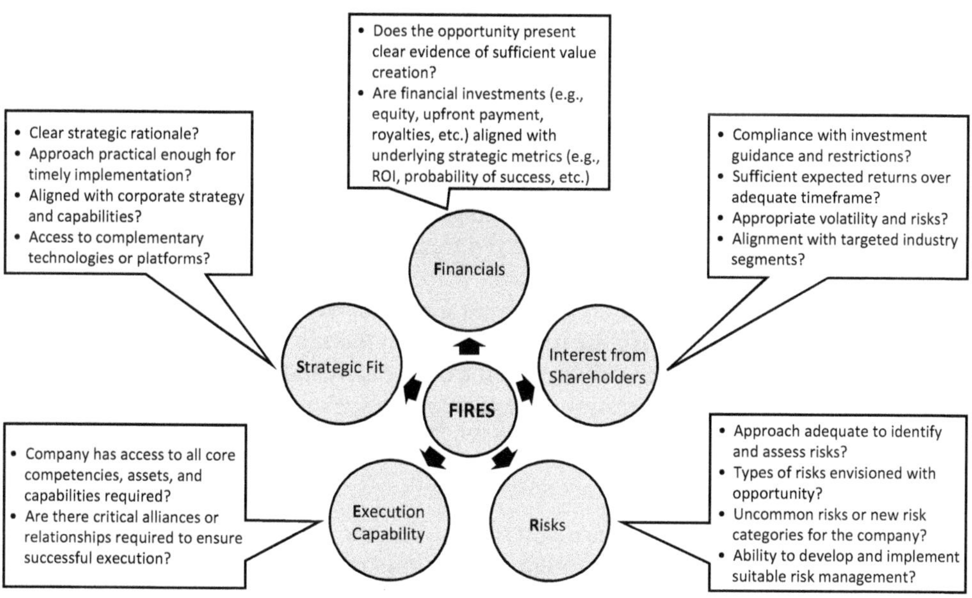

Figure 4.14 F I R E S framework.

Case Example: Company Acquisition Opportunity Evaluation with FIRES Framework

Merck announced the acquisition of Prometheus Biosciences in April 2023 (Merck, 2023). The opportunity could be evaluated at the time of the announcement with the FIRES framework:

- Strategic Fit.
  The acquisition accelerates Merck's growing presence in immunology and diversifies its portfolio given Prometheus' portfolio and 360 data sciences platform. The primary asset acquired, PRA023, completed Phase 2 favorably and represents a potential first-in-class and best-in-class product for immune-mediated diseases, including ulcerative colitis and Crohn's disease. This potential precision medicine treatment is expected to provide multibillion dollar peak sales. Merck's global scale and strong commercial capabilities can help accelerate and expand market access.
- Interest from Shareholders.
  The acquisition aligns with current capital allocation priorities to invest in the business while supporting the desired portfolio expansion. The lead asset, if successful, would provide significant revenue growth over the next decade, creating meaningful long-term value for patients and shareholders.
- Risks.
  Risks are still significant as PRA023 needs to demonstrate suitable efficacy in Phase 3 and clear global regulatory approvals. It faces potential competition from similar-stage products (e.g., Teva product or Roivant product) that might reach the market earlier or present a better product profile.
- Execution Capability.
  Given the specifics involved, the transaction is subject to the expiration of the waiting period under the Hart-Scott-Rodino Antitrust Improvements Act. One potential operational concern is that clinicians (rheumatologists and gastroenterologists) might not have the ability to perform the corresponding biomarker-driven treatments.
- Financials.
  The financials involved are significant given an offer at 75% premium and a total equity value of close to US$11B, even though Merck likely has the required financial capacity between existing cash and commercial paper. This said, the value-creation potential for the transaction depends mainly on PRA023's success tackling a US$23B ulcerative colitis and Crohn's disease market as of 2022.

Based on this evaluation, one might surmise that the strategic rationale played a prominent role in the acquisition decision, considering the significant upfront financial consideration and the remaining risks (e.g., Phase 3 not yet started at transaction time with competitors at similar development stage).

4.3.2 Portfolio Management and Optimization

Many biopharma companies with drug candidate portfolios assign a product and R&D-focused leadership team for each asset or asset group, in order to ensure strategic focus, effective implementation, and optimization at the asset level, while operating within the company's allocated resources and constraints. Nevertheless, shared production facilities and administrative and corporate functions are managed centrally to achieve economies of scope. In contrast, other companies adopt a different portfolio approach, establishing a corporate structure that oversees separate subsidiaries, one for each asset or asset group (Bleys et al., 2021).

Either way, portfolio management and optimization is the process through which a biopharma firm effectively decides on, and updates, its list of approved priority R&D projects. Making portfolio decisions requires structured, informed, and timely approaches to avoid costly or late decisions (resulting in unnecessary additional clinical trial costs), to optimize the drug pipeline, and to facilitate go-to-market strategies.

Portfolio strategy decisions also necessitate more extensive oversight expertise and experience than asset-specific strategy decisions (Jekunen, 2014). Different methods can be used to manage an R&D portfolio such as traditional portfolio strategic approaches and value-creation measures, but also algorithm-based, mathematically based, or even AI-based programming approaches.

Case Example: Use of AI for Portfolio Management

UK-based company Causaly Ltd developed an AI-powered platform helping researchers and developers to better drive projects and portfolio-level decisions. Specifically, the company offers AI-based solutions for more effective target selection, biomarker discovery, and disease biology. As explained by the company, such AI-enabled capabilities might allow to "terminate non-promising projects early" (Causaly, 2024).

Case Example: Use of Subsidiaries for Portfolio Management

As of 2022, Roivant Sciences Ltd. develops drugs and drug candidates in subsidiary companies they call "Vants" with a distinct approach to sourcing talent, aligning incentives, and deploying technology. The Vant model allowed Roivant to rapidly add capabilities in diverse therapeutic areas, including immunology, dermatology, and oncology, and modalities, including biologics, topicals, and bifunctional small molecules. Having launched and taken public multiple subsidiaries, the company has an aggregate ownership stake of approximately US$589M million as of March 31, 2022. The model also enables a modular therapy monetization as they progress through development, enabling independent product commercialization and partner selection (Roivant, 2022).

A biopharma company's portfolio is normally a direct result of the company's strategy, as illustrated by Figure 4.15. Strategic implementation for each asset then follows the organizational and operational constructs (e.g., clinical, data management) or processes established by the company across all assets, as illustrated in Figure 4.16. Projects with the highest strategic

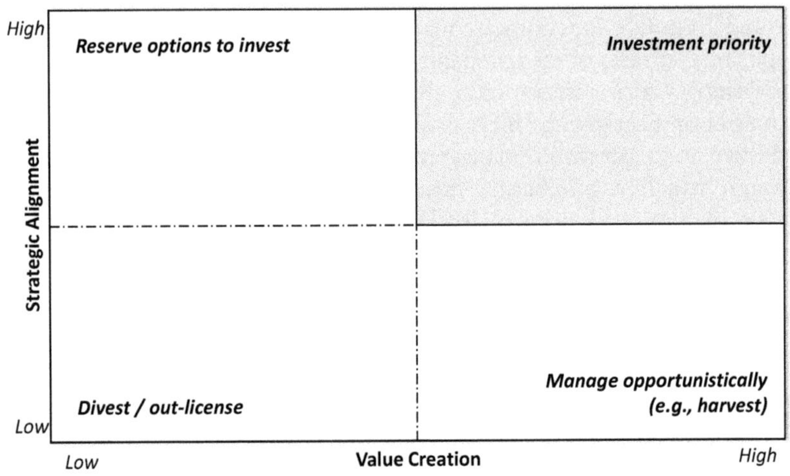

Figure 4.15 Illustrative portfolio prioritization matrix.

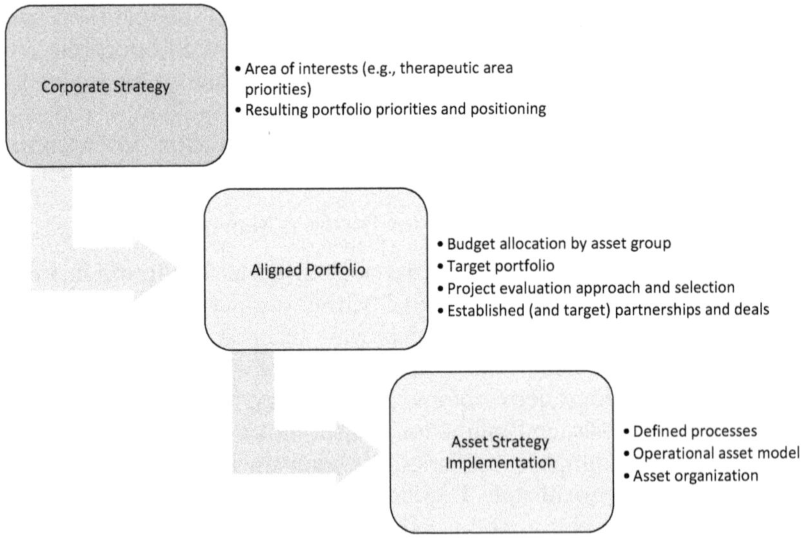

Figure 4.16 Practical portfolio strategic management approach.

alignment at each stage of R&D should rationally be prioritized based on greatest combined return and PoS expectations. rNPV, "C/I Ratio", or R&D productivity index are typically good measures to use; option value might also be used in certain circumstances – see Chapter 2. When very little information is available, companies sometimes resort to cost – benefits analyses: what will it cost to get to the next stage with what impact in either case (failure or success)?

Despite the simplicity of Figure 4.15, the inherent difficulty of portfolio management and optimization resides in part in the multiplicity of complex considerations to incorporate, which might explain the relative paucity of references on this topic and the natural tendency for some to use a subjective approach. Portfolio management and optimization might be described as a dynamic multi-criteria decision analysis problem, thereby emphasizing its analytical complexity and the interest in using AI solutions. A biopharma firm will typically not decide in favor of a development project in isolation of other projects that might be synergistic with it, or even represent a prerequisite. In addition, to execute the strategy defined by the company, it might be helpful to *enrich* the current portfolio with alternate research and development pathways beyond those already considered in-house, as well as with external options (such as in-licensing, acquisition, partnerships). With the typical time and financial pressures associated with the industry, exploring alternatives may not always constitute a prime focus.

An enriched portfolio approach as depicted in Figure 4.17 is sometimes implemented using practical performance metrics suitable for the

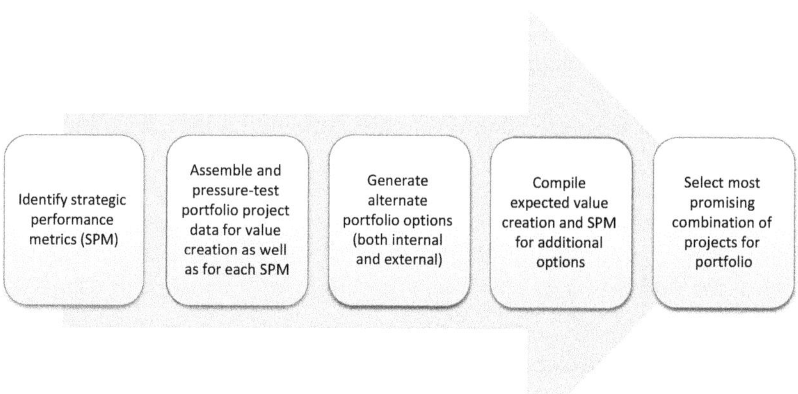

Figure 4.17 Enriched portfolio approach.

corporate biopharma strategy, denoted as SPM or strategic performance measures, e.g.:

- Suitable mix of projects at different stages considering success rates at each phase.
- Commercial forecast threshold, regardless of whether the company intends to commercialize (revenues from net sales) or out-license (milestones and royalty revenues).
- Balanced mix between different indications and therapeutic areas.
- Expected mix between different drug types (e.g., small molecules versus biologics, innovative MOA versus traditional route).

SPMs are specific to the biopharma company's strategy and the prioritization depends heavily on the reliability of the analyses conducted – see Gouglas and Marsh (2019) for an illustration of vaccine investments prioritization.

Alternatively, a specific strategic focus may be the main prioritization factor for in-house programs, along with ranking of programs by tiers: tier 1, tier 2, and tier 3 under predetermined criteria (e.g., R&D to spend, time to market, probability to obtain regulatory approval, peak sales potential, rNPV, R&D productivity index). Tier 1 programs would be generally managed with more frequent checkpoints.

In addition to the portfolio prioritization, it is common to group strategic portfolio management options by asset strategy, e.g.:

- Programs requiring a stage-gate assessment and decision (e.g., selection of clinical development options).
- Programs for which a renegotiation of existing contractual terms would be justified.
- Programs for which a partnership or an out-licensing transaction would be desirable.
- Programs for which the criteria for discontinuation have been met.

Given R&D costs, portfolio complexity can be expected to correlate with company size and funding. Companies with just one or two drugs, representing approximately one-fifth of the overall industry pipeline at the beginning of the 2020s, would have limited use for portfolio prioritization.

4.3.3 Biopharma Asset Strategy

Once an asset or asset group has been deemed a strategic priority for R&D, the biopharma firm will refine the asset strategy. That strategy will depend on the development stage and placed within the corporate strategy context:

a standalone strategy for a small biopharma company without alternate assets readily available, or guided by the company therapeutic area and modality approaches for a larger biopharma company.

Coming out of the exploratory research stage to be considered a development drug candidate, the asset will come with preliminary defined drug-like properties and a profile captured in a target product profile document (Figure 4.18).

The primary indication, if not already selected as part of the company's portfolio prioritization, is selected using available pharmacology data, competitive landscape, as well as expected speed of approval based on unmet needs and regulatory pathway.

The target product profile will guide the development of an integrated development plan combining preclinical or nonclinical studies, clinical studies, manufacturing aspects and the program regulatory plan.

As shown in Figure 4.18, establishing an asset strategy is an iterative process, going from target product profile with its associated value proposition (defined as therapeutic or treatment benefits expected versus risks with applicable mitigation strategy) and market analysis, to integrated development plan to a prospective product label that will drive commercial activities and

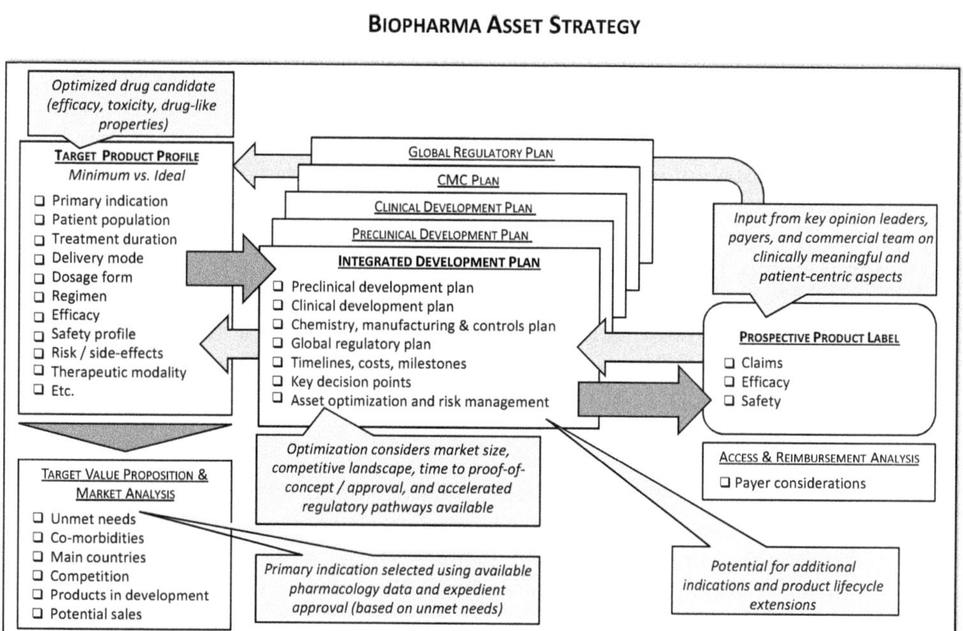

Figure 4.18 Biopharma asset strategy.

opportunities. The asset team will also work backward from the prospective product label, having collected input from experts and commercial teams, back to an optimized clinical development path that provides an optimal tradeoff between risks, speed, commercial returns on investment, and costs. Such tradeoff evaluation is often done with scenario planning or other decision support tools (see Chapter 2). Often, the asset team will define a baseline scenario representing a fairly standard development approach and explore more aggressive and more conservative "what if" scenarios from the baseline. Opportunities considered might include best-in-class and first-in-class scenarios, biomarker development, or simply an expanded therapeutic window. Alternative considerations might include the use of real-world evidence to optimize targeted populations or supplement clinical evidence. Specific technologies and AI solutions might also come into play.

Particular attention will be given to data requirements for the various regulatory approvals and to the order entry of the drug in competitive situations. Other considerations include follow-on products for additional indications as well as lifecycle extensions; note that follow-on might also represent backup options for development.

Overall, the asset strategy will consist of four main steps:

1. Establishing the vision for the asset, captured in the target product profile.
2. Define the development pathways, captured in an integrated development plan (covering nonclinical, clinical, regulatory, and manufacturing aspects).
3. Plan for prospective label, based on both efficacy and safety data for the primary indication, and resulting commercial approaches (e.g., marketing and distribution collaborations, licensing for specific region) as well as pharmacovigilance and applicable post-approval activities.
4. Iterate on the process as the program evolves, more data becomes available, and further approvals or funding are required.

Many of the general strategy concepts and tools presented in Section 4.1 (e.g., SWOT) can be leveraged to establish an effective asset strategy. Using the PSVF framework from that section, a biopharma company would typically steer its asset strategy in a direction that:

- Enables a favorable and profitable position, leveraging unique product advantages that differentiate the asset from its competition.
- Allows the company to retain program financial benefits with solid remaining patent life past launch with additional product lifecycle extension opportunities.
- Reflects favorable valuation prospects from commercial revenues or licensing.

- Offers reasonable flexibility for the company to adapt the approach as the program advances or the environment evolves (e.g., fallback indications, product extensions).

Case Example: Selecting the Best Clinical Development Pathway Considering the Intended Market

Table 4.7 provides two different development pathways depending on the target market.

Case Example: Selecting the Best Clinical Development Pathway Considering Partnership Opportunities

Table 4.8 provides two different development pathways a leadership team might consider.

Case Example: Early Asset Strategy Based on PK Profile

A team of researchers at the Broad Institute developed the BRD-810 oncology compound, a small molecule that inhibits the MCL1 protein and reactivates apoptosis in tumor cells, thus displaying therapeutic potential in animal models (Zusi-Tran, 2024). As the usual shortfall of MCL1 inhibitors is that they can impair heart cells, the team optimized BRD-810's pharmacokinetic

Table 4.7 Asset strategy considering target market

Scenario	*Clinical development plan*	*Target market*
Scenario A	One Phase 3 only to demonstrate efficacy in a core patient subgroup	Target market limited to the patient subgroup
Scenario B	Pursuing an additional Phase 3 study to demonstrate superiority versus current standard of care	Target market: broader patient population

Table 4.8 Asset strategy considering partnership potential

Scenario	*Scope of activities*	*Impacts*
Scenario A Full in-house asset strategy	Comparators purchased from a competitor	No cost savings, no commercial synergies provided by co-promotion
Scenario B Asset partially (or fully) partnered	Comparators supplied at cost (no mark-up) by the competitor in exchange for the right to co-promote	R&D cost savings, better marketing promotion

(PK) profile to maintain its apoptosis properties for tumor cells without negatively affecting heart cells. Such early endeavor might enable a superiority strategy for the asset downstream.

4.4 Strategic Support and Oversight

4.4.1 Biopharma Industry Monitoring

Once a biopharma firm has established a corporate strategy, a portfolio strategy and corresponding asset strategies, it is important for the company to monitor the assumptions and evolving data that support its various decisions to ensure that the approach is still valid. Ideally, they will identify an objective source of information, preferably independent from the company that will be used to monitor the data evolution. Sources of information typically combine industry associations, government resources, subscription services, and various free internet-based resources. Using such sources, the company will define metrics and leading indicators they can track to detect triggers to re-evaluate or adjust the strategy.

4.4.2 Searching for External Innovation Opportunities

Once a company's strategy is established, finding suitable external innovation opportunities is the first step in a corporate development journey, making it critical to success. Despite its importance, it is rarely a standardized approach but rather a mix of different avenues along which the company's strategy will outline interest areas such as key therapeutic area and disease indications, modalities, stage of research and development, and market potential.

Having designated professionals responsible for searching and locating external innovation opportunities is a common practice given the strong partnering activity in the industry, the prominent VC presence in biopharma funding, and the relative intertwined industry relationships inclusive of academia. Such designated professionals will typically build an opportunity pipeline or funnel by cultivating relationships at potential short-, medium-, and long-term target organizations. They scout opportunities:

- Through referrals from various contacts within their network, or the company's ecosystem (e.g., lawyers, accountants, consultants, research partnerships, and accelerators).
- By leveraging investment banker relationships and being on their distribution list for potential opportunities.
- Combing through industry association memberships, industry reports, journals, publications, and other forms of external credentialing.
- Walking the floors of trade shows, conferences, and similar venues.

- Using deal sourcing or deal origination platforms to identify potential targets they might not have considered.
- Facilitating incoming inquiries using the company's website to guide external interests and inquiries.

This last website point raises an interesting consideration: the larger and more visible the company, the more likely that will happen. Conversely, the smaller or less visible companies must be proactive to even get to see such opportunities. Equity firms refer to such deals that "come to your door" as "inbound" sourcing as opposed to "outbound" deals to designate those they must actively search and contact.

Lastly, internal business development teams will search through various industry signals and noise to identify potential targets to keep tabs on. This pursuit is rarely linear and involves parsing many different approaches.

Case Example: Sourcing of Partnering Opportunities

AstraZeneca launched an Open Innovation program in 2014, enabling better research links with academia, industry, non-governmental organizations, and governments. External scientists can access the program through a portal and submit proposals for collaboration on projects, share tools, technologies, and expertise, as well as explore partnering opportunities. As of September 2022, the company had reviewed "more than 1000 proposals from scientists in 40 countries across six continents" and collaborators had "been awarded $75 million in grant funding to support their research projects" using AstraZeneca's assets. The "Open Innovation portfolio now features 35 ongoing or planned clinical trials and more than 425 pre-clinical studies" (AstraZeneca, 2022).

It is important to note that impactful opportunities can be captured at early stages of development as mentioned by Wang et al. (2022). They mention pembrolizumab and other well-known drugs that were sourced at early stages of development. Pembrolizumab, perhaps better known under its brand name Keytruda, generated revenues in excess of US$20 billion for Merck & Co in 2022 and was obtained by Merck at the preclinical stage in 2009, via its acquisition of Schering-Plough. Indeed, although riskier, earlier-stage products might sometimes represent a valuable opportunity as company valuations rise significantly with the lead product development phase as established by Michaeli et al. (2022) in a study of over 300 US and EU biopharma company acquisitions from 2005 to 2020.

Partnering opportunities may also depend on the economic environment with increased opportunities for large biopharma companies at times when smaller companies have reduced access to public markets, narrowing their financing options.

Academia represents an interesting arena for biopharma business development teams to monitor. In fact, there are indications that deals with academia could generate higher value levels for biopharma companies: Shah et al. (2023) found academic licenses had lower royalty rates, deal size, and precommercial payments than corporate licenses.

Perspectives from a Veteran Business Development (BD) Leader at a Large Biopharma Company

Most Effective Ways to Generate a Deal Flow

There is no best source to identify deal opportunities, as the source for valuable opportunities may vary between investment bankers, conferences, colleagues, personal network, deal origination platforms, and so on.

Promising avenues to explore include:

- Looking for external innovations that align with the internal biopharma company strategy.
- Tracking relevant academic patent fillings, as indicators of early innovations to investigate.
- Tracking startup funding, especially Series A (often a proxy for innovation validation).
- Performing science-driven comparison analyses between companies.

To monitor progress of very promising technologies and build relationships to desirable innovation ecosystems, some large biopharma companies will finance startup labs, accelerators, or otherwise provide guidance and support in technology evaluations.

Ensuring Deal Flow Quality

At an early stage of research, ensuring opportunity quality is often done via Material Transfer Agreements (MTA). This is to ensure experiments can be reproduced to validate the claims made by the original research team. Typically, the originating biopharma company provides the materials and documentation for free, while the receiving biopharma company replicates the experiments at its own expense, normally over a few months. The **validation of research claims via MTA provides a solid relationship basis** for trust and credibility.

Seeking and establishing such relationships is usually done by scientific personnel, typically with PhD, at large biopharma companies with varying titles such as **External Innovation, Search & Evaluation, Technology Scouting**. These will function as ambassadors for the large biopharma company and involve various internal experts as needed to assess the value and potential of external innovations.

Maximizing Value from BD at a Small Biopharma Firm

In a small biopharma, it is often a CEO with a scientific background that fulfills the role of BD. Whoever plays this BD role in the small biopharma firm should in priority form relationships with biopharma business development contacts and establish MTAs as applicable. **It is a numbers game**: they should diversify contacts and work to identify companies with common interests as well as get to know scientists interested in the biopharma firm's technology. Usually, external innovation contacts at biopharma companies are straightforward to locate or identify, from a company's website or otherwise.

Unexpected Sources of Value Creation at Large Biopharma and at Small Biopharma Firms

The **most common unexpected source of value for small biopharma firms comes from** a more limited view or understanding on **longer-term benefits for their technology** – a large biopharma company can help them think **through an entire program from beginning to end** rather than focusing only on the immediate next steps or on the immediate next inflection point. This said, small biopharma leadership sometimes comes from large biopharma, in which case they would already have this long-term understanding.

The **most common unexpected value creation for large biopharma companies comes from the more aggressive perseverance of the small biopharma** in the face of adversity, which may or may not result in an unexpected win. A small biopharma firm will display scientific perseverance (e.g., expecting to manage higher than desired toxicity at clinical stage), have a "can do" attitude, and take what might be considered shortcuts in comparison with a process-driven large biopharma approach. While the outcome might be positive (or negative as expected), the unexpected part also comes from a speedier execution using a less stringent, and arguably less rigorous, process. This is often the result of the **small biopharma company single-minded "make or break" approach** compared with a large biopharma portfolio approach.

Value-Creation Opportunities Often Neglected

A small biopharma will typically **focus on only one or two disease indications, thereby neglecting other opportunities**.

Large pharma will typically **neglect acceleration opportunities** by using a slower gated decision-making process. They thus forgo the benefits of urgency that a small biopharma firm might bring to the table, by focusing instead on process management related to a large portfolio of programs.

Evaluation of Early Opportunities without DCF

Without DCF, there is no valuation, and at an early stage, it can be challenging to find meaningful comparable transactions (where an acquirer might or might not have overpaid), **so it comes down to what you are ready to pay to access the technology**. In my case, **I use a comparison with internal costs to determine what an acceptable price would be**. I would be ready to pay up to what it would cost me to develop the technology internally.

Good "Swiss Army knife" to Evaluate New Opportunity or Technology

My "Swiss Army knife" is a **three-part framework**:

1. **Rarity/Scarcity**
   How unique is this technology or innovation? Does this technology embody field leadership?
2. **De-Risking/Application**
   Has the platform or technology been de-risked? Have the data and claims been scientifically validated? Is there relevant applicability to the technology?
3. **Company Size**
   Typically in biotech, a company size of over 50 employees can be used as a proxy to validate that the company has enough critical mass to possess the expertise required for a well-established technology.

One add-on consideration is multiplicity of use: whether the technology is more of a single solution/single application or a platform technology that can be used for multiple products or applications.

Perspective on Platform Companies

A platform biopharma company **can be defined as** a company with **differentiated program-agnostic technologies for biopharma R&D** (e.g., drug discovery, drug delivery, drug development, optimized efficacy), **that are scalable and benefit from strong IP protection.**

There are **three main aspects to look at when evaluating a platform company:**

1. **Applicability of the platform.**
2. **Validation of the platform impact on R&D programs**, be it from data provision, MTA, or other approaches.
3. **The existence, or not, of internal platform company programs** that showcase the platform's value.

Views on Complex Licensing Approaches: Biopharma Equity Participation by Large Pharma & Risk-Sharing by Biopharma Firm

Equity stake as investment vehicle in the context of licensing typically comes with board access, which affects the independence of the biopharma representatives, due to the board fiduciary duties. It thus **requires a stronger strategic alignment** for such a deal to make sense. It is typically requested by the small biopharma firm (or their investors) **and represents additional management costs for the large biopharma company**. It may, however, be appropriate in some cases, e.g.:

- For important technologies where the large pharma is in competition with other companies, it might provide a competitive advantage through improved information access and possibly specific preferred shareholder's rights or other agreement terms (e.g., right of first refusal).
- It can help maintain aligned incentives toward successful developments.

The **expectation is that, even when requested by the biopharma company and negotiated, options for risk-sharing and profit-sharing clauses will never be executed**. The reason for these risk-sharing and profit-sharing option clauses is that they increase the value of the small biopharma company as they can claim to have an interest in commercial activities. **Such a request can**, however, significantly **increase agreement**

lead times by doubling negotiation time. Whether intended or not, it puts the company in a position to be acquired at a later stage by the biopharma company, to remove the profit-sharing encumbrance.

Final Advice to Biopharma Startup CEOs

My recommendation to small biopharma companies would be to **establish a business development function as soon as possible.** The ideal time to establish a business development function is **before Series A financing and after seed funding. BD is akin to a snowball** in that it takes a critical mass of BD activities before showing meaningful impact.

4.4.3 Board of Directors

Along with CEO replacement decisions and general oversight, strategy is one of the most important areas for boards to weigh in on.

Board composition and demands on board members can vary significantly depending on the type of organization, e.g., nonprofit versus private company versus publicly traded company:

- Nonprofit boards are typically larger (e.g., 15 directors) whereas private boards tend to be smaller (e.g., 6 directors) with public board in between (e.g., 9–12 directors).
- Nonprofit boards are typically not paid whereas private and public boards are.
- Oversight of private companies tends to be lighter whereas nonprofit boards and public boards face heavier oversight (e.g., 501c3 and SEC requirements respectively).
- The main board objective is to further the mission for nonprofits versus shareholder value creation for public board and owners' objectives for private boards.

Other types of organizations include governmental organizations.

Biopharma companies should ensure that the directors nominated to serve on their board collectively meet all the expertise, focus areas, diversity, and demographics requirements expected of the board as illustrated in Figure 4.19. While the dimensions evaluated vary from company to company, the biopharma firm should list its essential needs (considering specialized board committee requirements) to optimize its board capabilities and

FICTITIOUS BOARD OF DIRECTORS

Current Board	1	2	3	4	5	6	7	8	9
Company leadership experience	●			●	●		●		
Biopharma experience									
Medical		●		●			●		●
Finance / Accounting	●				●			●	
Regulatory			●					●	
Marketing		●			●				
Commercial			●						
R&D				●		●	●	●	●
Risk Management			●			●			
Technology	●	●						●	●
Strategy	●				●	●	●		
Broad international exposure		●	●	●			●		
Public relations experience					●				●
Social responsibility			●				●		
Independent	●	●		●		●		●	

Icon credits: Flaticon.com

Figure 4.19 Illustrative board composition versus requirements. Image credits: Flaticon.com

ensure all key expertise and focus areas are sufficiently represented. In particular, the board should have appropriate business and scientific expertise to review and approve major BD deals. Additional consideration are required for board members, e.g., no conflict in serving, ability to effectively work with other board members, aligning with diversity equity and inclusion objectives, suitable capabilities and characteristics for the role, availability, and within age limits.

Board committees represent an important governance aspect. Such committees are meant to make the board's workload more manageable by addressing specific topics in further depth and reporting to the larger board, especially for complex, specialized aspects. Other committees might also exist due to specific requirements making them mandatory. In the case of biopharma companies, an R&D-type committee generally supplements other standard committees found across industries like the audit committee.

The board is ultimately and collectively responsible to oversee the business on behalf of stockholders (or the public in case of a nonprofit) and ensure that the business has adequate resources to create value for said shareholders. That starts with setting a proper business course as defined by the company's strategy. In addition, the board is expected to positively challenge the biopharma leadership, to review major financial commitments and generally meet their fiduciary obligations through thoughtful application of governance principles, strategic thinking, financial acumen, and suitable risk management.

Biopharma startups often target physicians and more specifically Key Opinion Leaders for their board of directors, considering the collective medical, clinical expertise, and quality of care understanding they might require, or at the very least value, from their board. While physicians' medical or clinical leadership contributions to the collective board insights and perspectives are rarely challenged as long as they have the necessary financial and business training, the firm should consider potential conflicts of interest (e.g., medical ethics and resulting physician priorities, regulatory physician disclosures, healthcare leadership positions, and regulatory agency positions) that might result from such board membership and how to tackle them, would such potential conflict materialize. Academic and nonprofit leaders may have similar conflicts of interest.

When it comes to biopharma early-stage strategy, the following practical considerations may be helpful to the leadership team when interacting with their board of directors:

- Maintain perspective – leadership's focus should be on getting the company to its next value inflection point and de-risking the company rather than building fancy presentations.
- Concentrate on important fact-based discussions and decisions that require board involvement. What strategic framework will be effective to use with the board – what does a corresponding strategic and operational dashboard look like? What are the measurable targets and goals to measure progress?
- Adhere to relevant decision rights and engage the board accordingly in a timely manner.
- Be clear, transparent, and specific regarding board support sought and highlight deadlines so that the board can react accordingly.
- Cover lessons learned, next steps, and progress made even (and perhaps especially) against failed initiatives/pursuits.
- Send documents in advance of board meetings and seek buy-in before the meeting.
- Understand what matters to individual board members.
- Ensure process to regularly ensure the board is effective and of sufficient quality in light of the latest strategy.

4.4.4 *Advisors*

Advisors tend to be more common for earlier-stage companies whereas larger companies will tend to hire contractors or consultants, as they have the financial means to do so.

Early-stage biopharma companies will use advisors and often display them on their website or company documentation for three reasons:

1. Inspire confidence in the company through association with reputable advisors.

2. Fill critical gaps and access deep expertise that they do not need or cannot afford full-time.
3. Leverage the advisors and their network to "open doors" for the company.

Advisors typically receive a small share of company stock (e.g., 0.15%–1%) or stock purchase options (that vest over a predefined multi-year period, with or without a cliff period below which there is no payout) in exchange for their services depending on two main factors: the advisor's level of performance (e.g., how much time they spend and how fast they are available) and the company's stage (e.g., idea stage, startup stage, or growth stage). Advisors are different from mentors that characteristically do not get paid or from consultants that are normally paid in cash for a similar role (rather than the equity compensation used for advisors).

4.4.5 Governance and Operational Control

Given the board has ultimate responsibility for the company, it needs to define policies and procedures within which it will assign authority to the biopharma management to lead the business day-to-day. While general policies and procedures may be established to define the board expectations of the management team, the control and risk management framework used by the board is customarily encapsulated in the form of an Approval Authority Matrix.

As the name indicates, an Approval Authority Matrix is a document featuring the following to be able to clearly see which management level has the required authority to approve a given action or decision:

- The various actions and decisions the board intends to control in different lines.
- The board and key management levels in columns.

The entries might be simple check marks to indicate where the authority resides, or use a more sophisticated RACI approach (R in a column designates the responsible person, A designates the approver, C indicates the contributors, and I indicates those informed).

While the intent at the board level is to delineate what the CEO can authorize versus what needs to be approved by the board, larger companies sometimes use the same template with additional columns to indicate what can be decided by levels below the CEO such as a Division President or a General Manager. Using the same template can help in terms of consistency, as well as to ensure the various levels of leadership are aware of what the board would need to authorize. The Approval Authority Matrix should reflect the actual organization of the company as well as contractual obligations (Table 4.9).

Table 4.9 Fictitious illustrative example of approval authority matrix

Category	*Designated geographic leadership*	*Therapeutic Area Division (TAD) leadership*	*CEO*	*Board*
Acquisitions, equity investments	None	None	US$10M	>US$10M
In-Licensing or OutLicensing [a]	None	None	US$25M	>US$25M
Letter of Intent	TAD Leadership and Corporate Legal approvals			N/A
Strategic Plans	Out-of-cycle changes to CEO-approved plans need to be made in consultation with Head of Strategy			Company strategy
CapEx in annual operating plan	US$100,000	US$1M	Annual Plan Ceiling	Over Plan Ceiling
CapEx not in annual plan	US$25,000	US$250,000	Annual Plan Ceiling	Over Plan Ceiling
Real Estate commitment or disposal	US$50,000	US$500,000	US$20M	> US$20M
Insurance policies	CFO/Head of Risk Management Approvals			Premium >US$10M

[a] Documented consultation with, and evaluation by, Business Development Finance required.

Ensuring that the leadership team has visibility on, and access to, an Approval Authority Matrix or similar information helps the board control effective value creation and meet its fiduciary duties. Newly created biopharma startups should consider such an approach with their board to ensure alignment.

4.5 Last Word on Strategy

While strategy must be grounded in facts and demands thorough preparation and analysis (an aspect often underestimated), the level of effort varies significantly between companies and tends to increase as the company matures and grows. A biopharma company typically adopts a tailored approach, selecting a limited subset of frameworks from this chapter to best align with their strategic planning needs. Figure 4.20 provides an illustration of such selection for a small Series A biopharma firm.

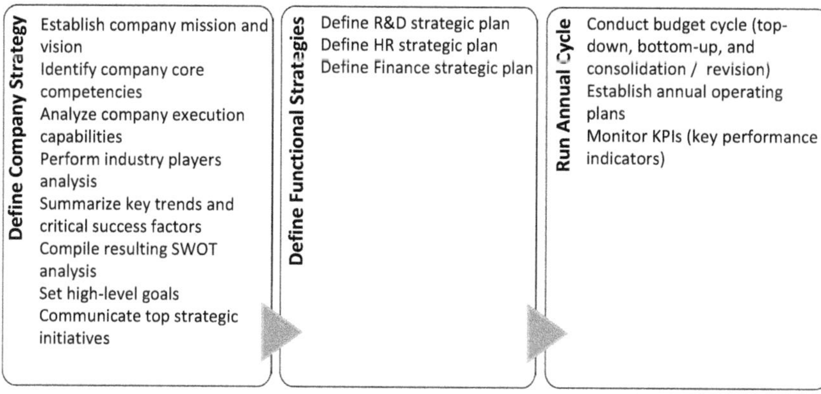

Figure 4.20 Illustrative biopharma startup strategic planning approach.

References

AbCellera. (2020). *Form S-1 Registration Statement.* SEC. Retrieved 5/26/2023, from https://www.sec.gov/Archives/edgar/data/1703057/000119312520299507/d29983ds1.htm

Adimab. (2009, January 1). *Adimab Company Website.* Retrieved 4/14/2023, from https://adimab.com/

Astellas. (2023, July 12). *Astellas Completes Acquisition of Iveric Bio.* Retrieved 10/27/2024, from https://www.astellas.com/en/news/28116#:~:text=Tokyo%20and%20Parsippany%2C%20New%20Jersey,ISEE%2C%20CEO%3A%20Glenn%20P.

AstraZeneca. (2022, September 28). *AstraZeneca R&D: Turning Science into Medicine.* Retrieved 11/1/2024, from https://www.astrazeneca.com/content/dam/az/r-and-d/pdf/turning-science-into-medicine.pdf

Barney, J. B., & Hesterly, W. S. (2014). *Strategic Management and Competitive Advantage: Concepts and Cases* (5th ed.). Pearson Education.

Biogen. (2021, September 21). *Investor R&D Day.* Retrieved 4/14/2023, from https://investors.biogen.com/static-files/f6d8ec6c-221d-43d5-914b-30fa48b90a48

BioNTech. (2023, January 10). *BioNTech to Acquire InstaDeep to Strengthen Pioneering Position in the Field of AI-powered Drug Discovery, Design and Development.* Retrieved 10/28/2024, from https://investors.biontech.de/newsreleases/news-release-details/biontech-acquire-instadeep-strengthen-pioneering-position-field

Bleys, J., Coravos, J., Fleming, E. & Quigley, D. (2021, January 29). *A New Portfolio Model for Biotech.* McKinsey & Company. Retrieved 5/19/2023, from https://www.mckinsey.com/industries/life-sciences/our-insights/a-new-portfolio-model-for-biotech

Boal, K., & Hooijberg, R. (2000). Strategic leadership research: Moving on. *The Leadership Quarterly, 11*, 515–549. 10.1016/S1048-9843(00)00057-6

Boyd, D., & Golderberg, J. (2014). *Inside the Box: A Proven System of Creativity for Breakthrough.* Simon & Schuster.

Bradley, C., Hirt, M., & Smit, S. (2011). Have you tested your strategy lately? *McKinsey Quarterly*, https://www.mckinsey.com/~/media/mckinsey/business%20functions/strategy%20and%20corporate%20finance/our%20insights/have%20you%20tested%20your%20strategy%20lately/have%20you%20tested%20your%20strategy%20lately.pdf

Buchholz, H., Eberle, T., Klevesath, M., Jürgens, A., Beal, D., Baic, A., & Radeke, J. (2020). Forward thinking for sustainable business value: A new method for impact valuation. *Sustainability, 12*(20). https://doi.org/10.3390/su12208420

Burchill, G., & Brodie, C. H. (2005). *Voices into Choices: Acting on the Voice of the Customer*. Joiner Associates Inc.

Causaly. (2024, February 29). *Drive More Effective Target Selection*. Retrieved 11/1/2024, from https://www.causaly.com/use-cases/target-identification-prioritization

Courtney, H., Kirkland, J., & Viguerie, P. (1997). Strategy under uncertainty. *Harvard Business Review*, https://hbr.org/1997/11/strategy-under-uncertainty

Cytokinetics. (2023a). *Putting Muscle Behind Our Mission*. Cytokinetics, Inc. Retrieved 10/25/2024, from https://cytokinetics.com/mission/

Cytokinetics. (2023b). *Vision 2025*. Cytokinetics, Inc. Retrieved 10/25/2024, from https://cytokinetics.com/company/vision/

Erasca. (2023a, April). *Corporate Presentation - On a Journey to Erase Cancer*. Retrieved 5/27/2023, from https://investors.erasca.com/static-files/91a2c17e-cc17-46b2-ad2a-e225ad628033

Erasca. (2023b). *Form 10-K for the Fiscal Year Ended December 31, 2022*. SEC. Retrieved 10/25/2024, from https://www.sec.gov/Archives/edgar/data/1761918/000095017023009496/eras-20221231.htm

Genentech. (n.d.). *Focus on Oncology*. Retrieved 6/2/2023, from https://web.archive.org/web/20240303093335/https://www.gene.com/scientists/oncology

Ghemawat, P. (1991). *Commitment: The Dynamic of Strategy*. The Free Press.

Gompers, P., Gornall, W., Kaplan, S. N., & Strebulaev, I. A. (2021, March 1). How venture capitalists make decisions: an inside look at an opaque process. *Harvard Business Review, 99*, 70. https://hbr.org/2021/03/how-venture-capitalists-make-decisions

Gouglas, D., & Marsh, K. (2019). Prioritizing investments in new vaccines against epidemic infectious diseases: a multi-criteria decision analysis. *Journal of Multi-Criteria Decision Analysis, 26*(3-4), 153–163. https://doi.org/10.1002/mcda.1683

Hamel, G., & Prahalad, C. K. (1996). *Competing for the Future*. Harvard Business School Press.

Hax, A. C., & Majluf, N. S. (1996). *The Strategy Concept and Process - A Pragmatic Approach* (2nd ed.). Prentice Hall.

HOOKIPA. (2022, October 20). *HOOKIPA Announces Strategic Collaboration and License Agreement with Roche to Develop Novel Arenaviral Immunotherapy for KRAS-Mutated Cancers*. Retrieved 10/30/2024, from https://ir.hookipapharma.com/news-releases/news-release-details/hookipa-announces-strategiccollaboration-and-license-agreement

HOOKIPA. (2023, March 21). *Annual Report 2022*. Retrieved 10/30/2024, from https://ir.hookipapharma.com/static-files/be15ed9e-9eda-4a62-b1a0-504c5fed40ee

IQVIA Institute for Human Data Science. (2023). *Global Trends in R&D 2023. Activity, Productivity, and Enablers.* Parsippany, NJ: IQVIA Institute for Human Data Science. https://www.iqvia.com/insights/the-iqvia-institute/reports/global-trends-in-r-and-d-2023

Iveric Bio. (2022). *Form 10-K for the Fiscal Year Ended December 31, 2021.* Retrieved 5/20/2023, from https://investors.ivericbio.com/static-files/bb26eb4e-ce36-4a9b-b13b-dea7ca4dc797

Jekunen, A. (2014). Decision-making in product portfolios of pharmaceutical research and development--managing streams of innovation in highly regulated markets. *Drug Design, Development and Therapy, 8*, 2009–2016. https://doi.org/10.2147/DDDT.S68579

Kalyanaram, G. (2008). The order of entry effect in prescription (Rx) and over-the-counter (OTC) pharmaceutical drugs. *International Journal of Pharmaceutical and Healthcare Marketing, 2*(1), 35–46. 10.1108/17506120810865415

Khurana, A., Sayed, N., Singh, V., Khurana, I., Allawadhi, P., Rawat, P. S., Navik, U., Pasumarthi, S. K., Bharani, K. K., & Weiskirchen, R. (2022). A comprehensive overview of CRISPR/Cas 9 technology and application thereof in drug discovery. *Journal of Cellular Biochemistry, 123*(10), 1674–1698. https://doi.org/10.1002/jcb.30329

Kinnate. (n.d.). *Science & Pipeline.* Retrieved 6/2/2023, from https://www.kinnate.com/science-and-pipeline/

Kuipers, H., Iny, A. & Sander, A. (2020, July 28). *Building Your Uncertainty Advantage.* Boston Consulting Group. Retrieved 5/15/2023, from https://web-assets.bcg.com/4b/35/bf8b0f1841cf94e14378a676aed7/bcg-building-your-uncertainty-advantage-july-2020.pdf

Laczkowski, K., Rehm, W. & Warner, B. (2018, November 29). *Seeing Your Way to Better Strategy.* McKinsey & Company. Retrieved 5/13/2023, from https://www.mckinsey.com/capabilities/strategy-and-corporate-finance/our-insights/seeing-your-way-to-better-strategy/

Lifshitz-Assaf, H., Lebovitz, S., & Zalmanson, L. (2018). The art of balancing autonomy and control. *Sloan Management Review,* https://sloanreview.mit.edu/article/the-art-of-balancing-autonomy-and-control/

Macmillan, I. C., Siegel, R., & Narasimha, P. N. S. (1985). Criteria used by venture capitalists to evaluate new venture proposals. *Journal of Business Venturing, 1*(1), 119–128. https://doi.org/10.1016/0883-9026(85)90011-4

Merck. (2023, April 16). *Merck Strengthens Immunology Pipeline with Acquisition of Prometheus Biosciences, Inc.* Retrieved 11/1/2024, from https://www.merck.com/news/merck-strengthens-immunology-pipeline-with-acquisition-of-prometheus-biosciences-inc/

Michaeli, D. T., Yagmur, H. B., Achmadeev, T., & Michaeli, T. (2022). Value drivers of development stage biopharma companies. *The European Journal of Health Economics, 23*(8), 1287–1296. https://doi.org/10.1007/s10198-021-01427-5

Moderna. (2014, December 31). *Moderna - About Us.* Retrieved 6/12/2023, from https://www.modernatx.com/en-US/about-us/our-mission

Moderna. (2023). *Moderna 2022 Annual Report.* Retrieved 6/18/2023, from https://s29.q4cdn.com/435878511/files/doc_financials/2022/ar/Moderna-2022-Annual-ReportvF.pdf

Oster, S. M. (1994). *Modern Competitive Analysis. How strategic planners can use powerful ideas from economic analysis in making business decisions; Emphasizes the competitive nature of strategy, the management of change, and coping with limited information in decision making.* (2nd ed.). Oxford University Press.

Park, A., Goudarzi, A., Yaghmaie, P., Thomas, V. J., & Maine, E. (2022). Rapid response through the entrepreneurial capabilities of academic scientists. *Nature Nanotechnology, 17*(8), 802–807. https://doi.org/10.1038/s41565-022-01103-6

Pervez, M. T., Hasnain, M. J. U., Abbas, S. H., Moustafa, M. F., Aslam, N., & Shah, S. S. M. (2022). A comprehensive review of performance of next-generation sequencing platforms. *BioMed Research International, 2022*, 3457806. https://doi.org/10.1155/2022/3457806

Pfizer. (2022, November 1). *Third Quarter 2022 Earnings Teleconference.* Retrieved 4/14/2023, from https://s28.q4cdn.com/781576035/files/doc_financials/2022/q3/Q3-2022-Earnings-Charts-FINAL.pdf

Pfizer. (2023, January 31). *Fourth Quarter 2022 Earnings Teleconference.* Retrieved 4/14/2023, from https://s28.q4cdn.com/781576035/files/doc_financials/2022/q4/Q4-2022-Earnings-Charts-FINAL.pdf

Porath, D. (2016). *Size and Dynamics of Order-of-Entry Effects in Pharmaceutical Markets.* University of Applied Sciences Mainz. https://EconPapers.repec.org/RePEc:zbw:uasmdp:42016

Porter, M. E. (1980). *Competitive Strategy - Techniques for Analyzing Industries and Competitors.* The Free Press.

Porter, M. E. (1985). *Competitive Advantage - Creating and Sustaining Superior Performance.* The Free Press.

Porter, M. E. (1996). *What is Strategy. Harvard Business Review*, 74(6), 61–78.

Rayport, J. F., & Sviokla, J. J. (1995). Exploiting the virtual value chain. *Harvard Business Review, 73*(6), 75–85. https://hbr.org/1995/11/exploiting-the-virtual-value-chain

Roivant. (2022, June 28). *Form 10-K for the Fiscal Year Ended March 31, 2022.* Retrieved 11/1/2024, from https://investor.roivant.com/sec-filings/sec-filing/10-k/0001193125-22-183362

Schaedler, L., Graf-Vlachy, L., & König, A. (2022). Strategic leadership in organizational crises: A review and research agenda. *Long Range Planning, 55*(2), 102156. https://doi.org/10.1016/j.lrp.2021.102156

Shah, P., Vaughan, G., & Ledley, F. D. (2023). Comparing the economic terms of biotechnology licenses from academic institutions with those between commercial firms. *PloS One, 18*(3), e0283887. https://doi.org/10.1371/journal.pone.0283887

Sutro. (2022, December 20). *Sutro Biopharma and Vaxcyte Enter into Option Grant Agreement for the Development and Manufacturing Rights of Cell-Free Extract.* Retrieved 10/30/2024, from https://www.sutrobio.com/sutro-biopharma-and-vaxcyte-enter-into-option-grant-agreement-for-the-development-and-manufacturing-rights-of-cell-free-extract/

Vaxcyte. (2023). *Form 10-K for the Fiscal Year Ended December 31, 2022.* SEC. Retrieved 10/27/2024, from https://www.sec.gov/Archives/edgar/data/1649094/000095017023004654/pcvx-20221231.htm

Viatris. (2022, February 28). *Viatris Investor Event.* Retrieved 4/14/2023, from https://investor.viatris.com/static-files/6a055dc2-4cd2-4d6c-91c9-c426ec1dcbce

Viatris. (2023a, January 11). *JP Morgan Healthcare Conference.* Retrieved 4/14/2023, from https://investor.viatris.com/static-files/700ce086-5fec-4d2d-948d-0d77a8a071a2

Viatris. (2023b, February 27). *Q4 and Full Year 2022 Earnings Presentation.* Retrieved 4/14/2023, from https://investor.viatris.com/static-files/99569352-e4a1-4aac-9fb9-9c59b9fa1439

Voyager Therapeutics, & Neurocrine Biosciences. (2019, January 28). *Collaboration and License Agreement by and Between Voyager Therapeutics, Inc. and Neurocrine Biosciences, Inc.* SEC. Retrieved 11/1/2024, from https://www.sec.gov/Archives/edgar/data/1640266/000155837019001105/vygr-20181231ex10284e899.htm

Wang, N., Burr, A., Dechter, A. & Powers, C. (2022, October 17). *Why Pharma Needs to Shift to an 'Innovation Constellation' Investment Strategy.* ZS. Retrieved 6/2/2023, from https://www.zs.com/insights/why-pharma-needs-an-innovation-constellation-investment-strategy

Zusi-Tran, K. (2024, October 29). *New Drug Triggers Rapid Cell Death in Cancer Models.* Broad Institute. Retrieved 11/5/2024, from https://www.broadinstitute.org/news/new-drug-triggers-rapid-cell-death-cancer-models

Chapter 5

Company Financing

As illustrated in Figure 5.1, the costs to develop a successful drug candidate can be in the US$200M to US$400M range. Estimates of typical drug development costs tend to have wide variances across publications for a variety of reasons:

- Accounting for cost of failure (e.g., a US$175M Phase III with a 50% probability of success would be valued at US$350M instead of US$175M if you consider it would statistically take two attempts at US$175M each to get a successful Phase III).
- Accounting for cost of capital. If a company spends US$1M two years prior approval and has a cost of capital of 20%, by the time the drug is approved, if the company accounts for the cost of capital, that US$1M will be treated as US$1.44M = US$1M $(1 + 20\%)^2$.
- Single versus multiple trials for a given clinical trial phase.
- Scope considerations spanning discovery and preclinical stages versus later stages only, with potential variations in starting points (e.g., in-licensed molecules).
- Inclusion of indirect costs versus direct costs only.
- Drug categories considered (e.g., orphan drugs versus non-orphan versus mix) and therapeutic areas considered (as costs vary significantly between different therapeutic areas).
- Different mix of companies that represent different geographies and regulatory environments.
- Different drug modalities with different cost structures.

Regardless of the methodology selected, drug development costs have consistently been high, making company financing a critical consideration for biopharma companies to be able to create value. Financing needs differ significantly between companies, depending on their type (e.g., nonprofit versus for profit), maturity, stage of development, positioning within the

DOI: 10.4324/9781003598046-5

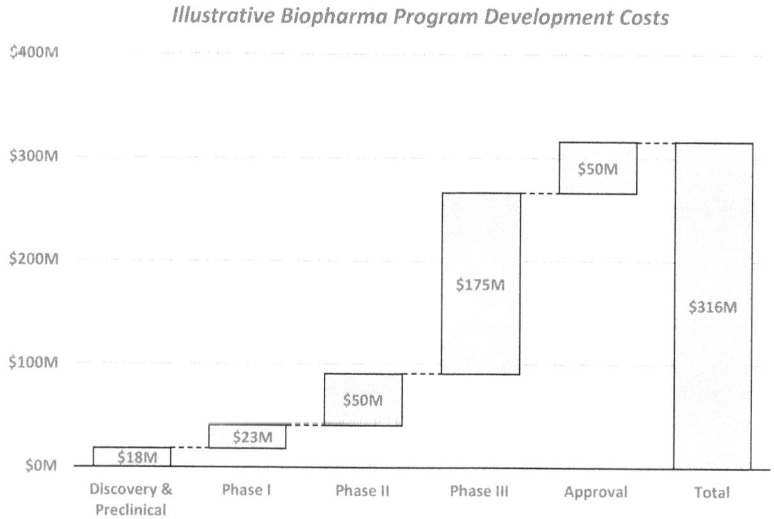

Figure 5.1 Illustrative drug development costs.

industry value chain (see Section 4.1.3), and ability to use AI and other technology-based solutions to optimize drug development costs or speed.

5.1 Determination of Financing Needs

As a biopharma company achieves major milestones in its business plan, its investment risk typically decreases and its equity value typically increases at each stage of development. A biopharma firm can analyze its business plan and identify those critical milestones that will result in significant increases in company value and result in a correspondingly lower investment risk profile – each such milestone referred to as a value inflection point. A value inflection point can be defined as a specific and meaningful change in risk concerning a program's evolution. Such a milestone is generally a data-driven outcome or event (e.g., data readout, regulatory feedback, clinical intermediate assessment).

Case Example: Illustrative Inflection Points

Below are selected examples of value inflection points considered by a biopharma startup:

- Achieving favorable toxicology results.
- Successful technology transfer.
- Financing round or partnership deal.

- Enrollment of a first patient in first-in-man trials.
- Completion of proof of concept studies.
- Marketing approval in a major country.

Investment rounds are usually timed on inflection points and provide the biopharma leadership with a sound financing roadmap since it typically results in higher company valuations. More established biopharma companies also benefit from such considerations: in the case of publicly traded companies, the stock-price impact of clinical trial outcomes for sponsor companies is characterized by the clinical trial phase, the sponsor company type, the clinical trial outcome, the therapeutic area or disease, the target trial accrual, and the clinical trial design (Singh et al., 2022). In particular, early positive outcomes tend to be associated with high abnormal returns (Singh et al., 2022).

5.1.1 *Cash Burn and Forecast to Inflection Points*

Rather than starting with a financial forecast, the company leadership team should consider the key milestones that represent a value inflection point and then estimate the cash needed to reach that inflection point (with a margin sufficient for execution slips and follow-on financing lead times).

Once inflection points have been identified and validated in relation to the company's strategy, the executive team should be able to ascertain the capabilities and resources necessary to reach the expected outcomes and demonstrate credibility to execute. They will have to estimate the timing and expenses required to reach each milestone.

The financial plan is a projection of cash inflows (e.g., financing, grants, out-licensing, revenue) and outflows (e.g., labor costs, equipment, supplies, outsourced activities) over a foreseeable period (e.g., 3 years), highlighting time and costs to reach each applicable milestone. A first round of biopharma startup funding (e.g., Seed or Series A) might typically correspond to achieving evidence of efficacy and safety along with a scalable manufacturing process for the investigational medicinal product. Subsequent rounds of financing (e.g., Series B) might focus on achieving clinical proof of concept (e.g., completion of Phase 1 studies in the target patient population or Phase 2 trials) and securing an incremental one-year runway.

The relevance of business assumptions and the quality of the financial framework inform investors and decision-makers on the credibility of the leadership team since the forecast reflects the team's understanding of, and ability to manage, underlying operations.

As most investors and finance professionals will have rules-of-thumb by which to gauge a financial forecast, the leadership team should attempt and validate their figures with industry benchmarks so they are prepared to justify any significant difference.

Case Example: Rule-of-Thumb Based on Labor Costs

Assume the rule-of-thumb for the biopharma cluster in which a startup operates is US$25,000 per employee per month. The startup, currently seeking financing, has ten employees and expects that number to average 12 employees over the following 2 years, the time needed to reach their next inflection point. With a typical 15% safety margin, experienced investors would typically expect the company to look for US$8.3M in financing calculated as US$25,000 per employee × 12 employees × 24 months × 1.15 safety margin factor.

Case Example: Series B Round Estimate

After very encouraging evidence of efficacy in in-vivo models for their lead program, a Series A biopharma leadership team has validated their strategic roadmap to start Phase I in 2 years and are preparing for their next funding round to get them past start of Phase I. Taking into account their currently available net cash of US$8M and the estimates they put together in Figure 5.2, including income they generate from testing services, they are planning to try and raise a Series B round of US$25M. That should leave them financial flexibility with US$1.5M of safety margin (US$8M current cash + US$25M raised – US$31.5M in cash outflows). As a word of caution, managing testing services and drug development programs might be challenging for a small company.

Development Timeline & Financial Plan		**Q3 N**	**Q4 N**	**Q1 N+1**	**Q2 N+1**	**Q3 N+1**	**Q4 N+1**	**Q1 N+2**	**Q2 N+2**
Lead Program Timeline	Compound optimization	■	■						
	GLP Toxicology Study	■	■	■					
	CMC / formulation costs			■	■	■			
	IND						■	■	
	Phase I								■
Financial Estimates (USD $ M)									
Direct Program Costs	Compound optimization	1.1							
	GLP Toxicology Study	1.0	2.0	1.5					
	CMC / formulation costs			0.8	2.0	2.0			
	IND						1.5	1.5	
	Phase I start								2.0
Costs of Ancillary Programs	Research Program 1	0.4	0.4	0.5	0.5	0.7	0.7	1.0	1.0
	Research Program 2	0.3	0.3	0.3	0.3	0.5	0.5	0.7	0.9
	Unallocated R&D	0.2	0.2	0.2	0.3	0.3	0.3	0.4	0.4
General & Administrative Costs	Support functions	0.1	0.2	0.2	0.2	0.3	0.3	0.4	0.4
	Professional & Legal Fees	0.1	0.1	0.1	0.1	0.2	0.2	0.3	0.3
	Office, Labs and IT costs	0.2	0.2	0.2	0.3	0.3	0.3	0.3	0.3
	Travel, Meetings, Conferences	0.1	0.1	0.1	0.1	0.1	0.1	0.1	0.1
- Service Revenue	Lab testing	-0.2	-0.2	-0.2	-0.2	-0.2	-0.2	-0.2	-0.2
Net Quarterly Cash Outflow		*3.3*	*3.3*	*3.7*	*3.6*	*4.2*	*3.7*	*4.5*	*5.2*
Net Cash to Inflection Point For the Year		***6.6***		***15.2***				***9.7***	
Net Cash to Inflection Point		**31.5**							

Figure 5.2 Illustrative timeline and forecast for fictitious biopharma firm.

5.1.2 *Planning for Contingencies*

Once a biopharma leadership has established their financing needs as illustrated by Figure 5.2, they will plan for contingencies around three dimensions: time, quality, and costs.

For instance, evaluating whether the safety margin is sufficient to address contingencies is important and may be assessed by running different scenarios (e.g., impact of stopping testing services and associated revenues to allow sufficient focus on the main program in the example above).

5.1.3 *Financing Macroeconomic Environment*

After establishing their financing plan, the leadership team will ordinarily turn to capital markets for financing. Capital markets designate the markets where securities (e.g., equity and bonds) are issued and traded; they represent the bulk of financing sources for non-financial firms (see Figure 5.3). Trading instruments used in capital markets include equity (also designated as stocks or shares, whether public or private), debt, digital assets (digital representation of value for securities), and shares of investment funds, i.e., investment vehicle pooling money from various investors (Congressional Research Service, 2023a). Capital markets are normally regulated; in the United States by the Stock Exchange Commission (SEC), state securities regulators and various organizations (e.g., securities exchanges, Financial Industry Regulatory Authority, Municipal Securities Rulemaking Board, and clearing agencies).

In the United States, private markets are significantly larger than public markets: registered offerings accounted for US$1.5 trillion of new capital compared with over US$3.0 trillion for private offerings (offerings falling

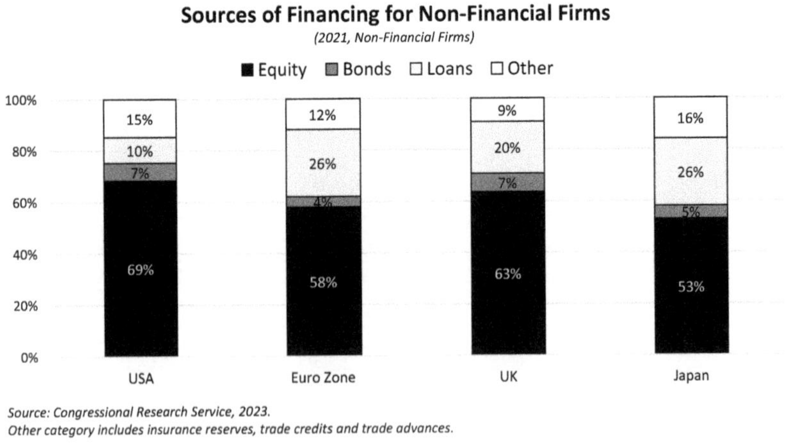

Figure 5.3 Sources of financing for non-financial firms.

under US Regulation D, Rule 144A, Regulation A, Regulation Crowdfunding, and other private offerings) in 2017 (Bauguess et al., 2018).

Understanding this macroeconomic backdrop is important as it significantly influences biopharma companies' ability to secure the financing they need.

5.2 Investor Landscape

In practice, biopharma companies looking for financing face a wide spectrum of investment stakeholders.

5.2.1 Founders, Friends, and Family

Founders, or cofounders, are those involved in the substantial activities required with starting a company, shaping its research and business foundations. Founders typically own at least 5% of an early-stage company, having received shares from the company (founder's stock) before the first financing round, and contribute to the biopharma company capital through efforts and commitments. Biopharma founders tend to be more experienced compared with other industries in the United States (Booth, 2018) with higher representation from top universities and built-in advantages when operating from a life sciences cluster like Greater Boston (Godfrey et al., 2020). During the startup phase, a founder typically works with an equity agreement, and may not receive a salary nor have established working hours.

Founders may gain rights over time or receive shares outright (most common), with a cliff period to ensure that founders do not receive anything if they do not stay at least past that cliff period. With a one-year cliff period, the founding team has one year to ensure team unity, bonding, and effectiveness. Founders sometimes establish preemptive rights allowing them to purchase the shares of a departing founder before letting someone else in. Founders will set up a restricted stock purchase agreement that details the rights and restrictions associated with the ownership of equity, such as vesting requirements, voting rights, transfer, or sale restrictions, as sometimes protection is attached to shares (related to voting rights or anti-dilution).

An important question is how to allocate shares between founders. Below are selected considerations that may help:

- Considerations to establish the founder equity split may normally include time invested, capital invested, intellectual property contributed, risk, and experience.
- CEO founders typically get the largest equity share. The expectation is that they work full time to build the new company. It is common for such founders to own most of the equity before a first round of financing.

- Additional key senior leaders (R&D, Business) are commonly added, in addition to scientific cofounders, before a first round of financing and receive shares or options.
- A biopharma startup will typically maintain an option pool representing approximately 15% of the total company shares (to be refreshed at each financing round).
- Vesting and share allocation should reflect past and expected contributions using rational justifications to ensure high-performing employees are recruited, motivated, and retained.
- Key scientific or business advisers may get equity as well (e.g., stock options or common shares representing a fraction of a percentage point of outstanding shares), based on time and critical expertise contributions.
- While all shares typically have voting rights, the CEO is often the only one to have a board seat unless others own a large percentage of company equity.

Friends and family are common sources of early investment in exchange for founders' equity or as a business loan.

When short on cash, a private startup might also use equity compensation for contractors and employees. In the United States, SEC Rule 701 allows private companies to grant and exempt certain sales of securities to compensate employees, consultants, and advisers; in the case of options, contractors would receive NSO or Non-qualified Stock Options (taxed on exercise) whereas employees would typically receive ISO or Incentive Stock Options (favorable tax treatment) assuming the company is set up as a corporation.

5.2.2 *Accelerators*

A typical accelerator will cater to small very early-stage startups (Bellucci et al., 2021) by providing them with capital, mentorship, and sometimes facilities for a specific duration in exchange for equity. Selected evidence suggests that the use of accelerators is correlated with higher growth trajectories for the corresponding startups (Davidson et al., 2021; Roberts & Kempner, 2017). Accelerators might have a cohort of companies that participate in a program designed to help the companies reach their next development stage, often in an immersive environment. In addition to providing economies of scale for the accelerator, a cohort approach allows startup participants to have peers with similar challenges that they can learn from and contribute to. Funding provided by accelerators might range from US$25,000 to US$150,000 (Drover et al., 2017).

The accelerator concept is traditionally attributed to Y Combinator, a company started in 2005. As of 2023, Y Combinator will typically invest US$125,000 in return for 7% equity under a Simple Agreement for Future Equity (SAFE) construct and standard terms, followed by a second SAFE investment of US$375,000 under a most favored nation clause (Y Combinator, 2013). Since Y Combinator's creation, the number of accelerators has skyrocketed to several thousands (Aljalahma & Slof, 2022).

5.2.3 *Angel Investors*

Angel investors, also referred to as seed investors, business angels, or simply private investors, are high net-worth individuals or networks of high net-worth individuals that provide startups with capital in exchange for company's equity or sometimes as convertible debt. They often focus on industries they have personal experience with, investing in high-potential startups at a very early stage when the risk of failure is very high (but also at later stages such as expansion stages). Their motivation might include getting innovative information on a specific R&D arena, a passion for certain areas, or maintaining a limited professional activity in the case of retired entrepreneurs and executives. They may also represent a useful resource for startups to tap into beyond the capital provided: experience in raising further capital, strategic and operational input, business advice, sounding board, or industry contacts.

There are over 400,000 angel investors in the United States; the average deal size was approximately US$340,000 in 2023, representing an average equity of 9.7% (Sohl, 2024).

Angel investors typically reject a majority of the deals they look at (e.g., two out of three) and expect high returns (e.g., above 20% annually).

5.2.4 *Grant Organizations*

Grants are awards made by an organization (e.g., governmental agency, company, or foundation) to the grant recipient with specific terms (e.g., toward a specific purpose and under specific conditions) under which the award does not need to be paid back, as long as its obligations have been met. Grants are usually considered income and taxed accordingly, unless otherwise exempt. They can be highly competitive with high rejection rates.

Grants do not affect the control or ownership of the company. They might however come with terms or processes that could be constraining (e.g., intellectual property or publication requirements, required complementary activities not financially supported by the grant, activities only tangential to the main company strategic direction, compliance with grant terms post-award).

	Pre-Award Stage	Award Stage	Post-Award Stage
Grant Organization	▪ Set grant requirements. ▪ Announce grant program, including eligibility, application process, timing. ▪ Manage questions, contact requests, and interactions with prospective applicants. ▪ Receive and evaluate applications.	▪ Communicate approvals and rejections to applicants. ▪ Complete legal contracts with grantees. ▪ Distribute initial funding to grantees within the defined timeframe. ▪ Provide title and access to assets as applicable.	▪ Supervise compliance (e.g., audits, reports, remediation, etc.) ▪ Continue to disburse funding and assets as applicable. ▪ Close out grant after all terms have been fulfilled.
Biopharma Company	▪ Establish grant strategy. ▪ Operationalize and secure required resources (e.g., grant writer). ▪ Research grant opportunities, interface with grant program contacts. ▪ Review and select specific grant opportunities to pursue. ▪ Prepare, complete, and submit applications.	▪ Receive approvals and rejections from grant organizations. ▪ Negotiate and discuss with grant organization before accepting or declining. ▪ Complete required documentation and contracts. ▪ Receive applicable funding and assets.	▪ Manage administrative grant aspects and carry out activities required to comply with grant terms (e.g., research, reporting, audits, publications, etc.) ▪ Use grant funding and assets within grant constraints.

Figure 5.4 Generic grant process and phases.

Ensuring the biopharma company is eligible for a specific grant is a key part of the process (Figure 5.4) and might depend on a wide variety of factors such as company location, company ownership, field of activity, non-profit versus for-profit status, or financial need. Lastly, grants might be in kind (e.g., drug supply and use of laboratory facility), financial, or a combination thereof.

There are many different grant types (Figure 5.5), some of which may involve a significant learning curve and require the support of a grant writer with specific experience with the grant.

Case Example: Foundation Grant

Grants from the Breast Cancer Research Foundation (BCRF), with a typical size below US$250,000, are aimed at clinical and translational breast cancer research in need of seed funding. These grants produce significant impact, including company creations, patent filings for 20% of recipients surveyed, and over 35% getting to clinical trials, besides favorable non-commercial impacts (Vasileva et al., 2019). In addition to spending over 90% of funds raised on research programs, BCRF discourages unsolicited requests but rather uses its scientific advisers to seek out promising investigators and invite proposals from them during their annual grant process (BCRF, 2018).

Figure 5.5 Illustrative selection of different grant types.

Case Example: Government Grant

The NIH provides a wide array of grants and has a policy statement of over 400 pages, ranging from application information and processes to peer review process, pre-award process, terms and conditions, public policy requirements, and administrative requirements. NIH grants may impact intellectual property:

> It is NIH policy that the results and accomplishments of the activities that it funds should be made available to the public. PD/PIs and recipient organizations are expected to make the results and accomplishments of their activities available to the research community and to the public at large.
>
> (National Institutes of Health, 2022)

5.2.5 *Venture Capital (VC)*

VCs are organizations (typically limited partnerships) that independently manage dedicated capital, in one or several funds, by making financial investments in privately held high-growth companies in exchange for equity in such companies (typically preferred shares with certain rights and privileges).

In the United States, to be technically deemed a venture capital fund and benefit from the corresponding Investment Company Act of 1940 (ICA) exemptions, the fund must meet several conditions, as provided by 17 CFR § 275.203(l):

- Represent to investors that it pursues a venture capital strategy.
- Hold no more than 20% of the fund's aggregate capital contributions in assets that are not qualifying investments.
- Not incur debt in excess of 15% of the fund's aggregate capital contributions nor incur leverage for a term longer than 120 calendar days.
- Only issue securities that do not provide holders with withdrawal rights.
- Not be registered as investment company nor elected to be treated as a business development company.

At the fund level (an important distinction as different funds may have different investment strategies), VCs typically invest in startups and smaller companies, taking mostly minority stakes, often with a specific industry focus, and possibly at different stages of evolution for such companies (from Series A until IPO). VCs often play an active role in mentoring and advising the companies they invest in, taking seats on the board of directors or on the advisory board. The capital the VCs manage is typically raised from institutional investors and high-net-worth individuals, referred to as "Limited Partners", as opposed to the "General Partners" who actively manage the VC fund and make investment decisions. VC funds' term for limited partners is typically 10 years with possible extension periods. Congressional Research Service (2023b) estimates the number of VC funds in the United States at over 2,000 managing over US$330 billion in assets as of 2022, based on SEC data. VCs typically operate in syndicates, meaning that they make investments with peer VC firms, one of them being the lead investor. They tend to operate in R&D-intensive industries (e.g., biopharma) where startup firms face a higher cost of capital than their larger competitors due to the perceived high risks of failure of the industry (Hall & Lerner, 2009). They thus play a key role in funding biopharma startups.

Geographically, the United States represents the primary region for VC (Figure 5.6), concentrated in San Francisco, New York, and Boston (Congressional Research Service, 2023b).

VCs scrutinize the management team, the quality of the assets under development, the significance of the next key value inflection points, and the time and assumed probability to reach them. Their returns are based on future liquidity events and exit opportunities. The expectation is to gain exceedingly high returns from companies that survive and compensate for those that do not: 80% of a VC fund might typically be generated by 20% of its investments, as such investments might provide a 10× return over 5 years.

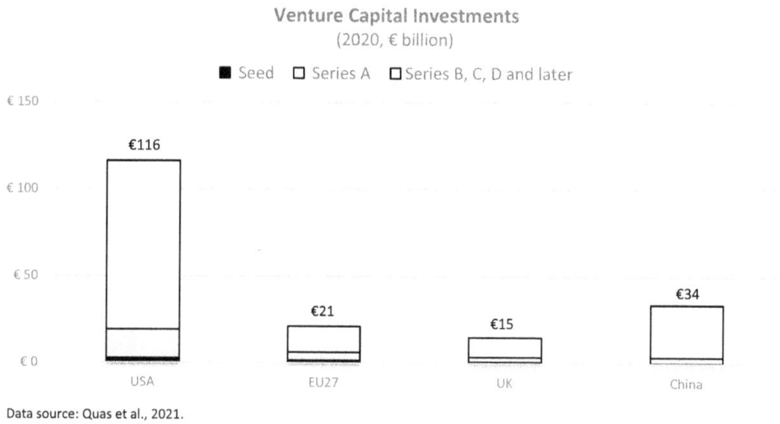

Figure 5.6 VC investments by region (Quas et al., 2021).

When seeking VC financing, prospective companies should understand competing investments the VC might have in their portfolio as such potential conflicts between pharmaceutical startups may result in VC involvement aimed at redirecting innovation away from the startup less advantageous for the VC (Li et al., 2023).

5.2.6 *Private Equity (PE)*

Similarly to VCs, PE firms (PEs) are investment management companies that raise capital from accredited investors referred to as Limited Partners (as opposed to the general partners that run the investment company) for different PE funds and then invest that capital (at the fund level) in private companies in exchange for equity before selling that equity ownership years later at a significant profit. For LPs, the PE fund typically has two phases: an investment phase of approximately 5 years during which investments are made and managed, followed by an exit phase of similar duration during which proceeds are distributed. Unlike VCs who primarily deal with minority equity investments, PEs characteristically use a combination of debt and equity for investments. PEs also target mature private companies (or public companies then taken private) and seek to obtain a majority ownership to control the company and improve its operations. Acquiring that controlling stake is usually done at a premium, representing larger investments, and the increase in value comes from financial and operational performance improvements (as opposed to the substantial company growth and evolution in the case of VCs), holding investments over shorter durations than VCs (e.g., 5 years versus 5–10 years for VC). The PE approach for each company they acquire is usually captured in a "value creation plan" that provides the PE strategy to increase its value, typically combining financial structure optimization, operational improvements, and specific strategic actions. Leveraged buyouts, defined as the purchase of a controlling share in a company by its management using outside capital, are often overseen by PE firms. In some cases, PEs might also invest at earlier stages or also expect significant company growth, blurring the dividing line with VCs. Similarly, some VCs might also propose debt financing to their portfolio companies, as this makes their equity more valuable by delaying the next priced financing round. Still, PEs use a combination of debt and equity to manage larger investments with substantial operational involvement and aim for a majority stake in the companies they invest.

5.2.7 *Corporate Biopharma Investors*

Larger biopharma companies also invest in other companies in the industry through different means: access to their facilities (e.g., laboratories, workspace, or equipment) and expertise to stay on top of certain research domains, funding in exchange for equity, IP out-licensing, or co-development and co-commercialization partnerships.

A large biopharma company's investment can have a large impact on the success of a biotech startup (Melchner von Dydiowa et al., 2021) making corporate biopharma investors an attractive investor segment to pursue. Indeed, corporate-venture-backed startups have higher rates of innovation than independent venture-backed counterparts (Shuwaikh & Dubocage, 2022). In addition, corporate venture capital provides for strong market signals by legitimizing biotech startups in a manner unlike other venture types (de Lange & Valliere, 2020).

Biopharma company investments often take one of two main forms:

- Corporate venture capital (CVC) where the company makes minority stake investments in innovative young companies, generally still in an early stage of technology validation. IP and technology might not be sufficiently advanced to justify a licensing agreement but still warrant moderate equity investments to enable future development options. With an observer seat or board seat, the biopharma company can continue to build relationships and stay on top of a company's progress in a highly strategic area. CVCs can seed deals, but often invest as member of a syndicate with institutional VCs and other CVCs. As an example, Sanofi CVC assessed startups in Consumer Healthcare based on eight factors: team, market, product, business model, financial indicators, traction, medical fit, and regulatory fit (Rivera et al., 2021).
- Corporate equity investment where the company makes a tactical investment in more mature companies to optimize future potential licensing

deals, or might be part of an upfront licensing deal. Taken as a step to secure a future licensing or purchase option, such investments typically include a right of first negotiation, allowing the pharma company to wait for an upcoming milestone (e.g., Phase II results) before exercising its right to enter into a license agreement or to acquire the company. Although tactical, such relationships are often announced as strategic relationships, strategic alliances, or strategic partnerships.

A corporate equity investment by a large biopharma company may involve different partnering teams than the CVC team. A higher percentage ownership than a CVC deal might be considered, as well as a deeper due diligence process. The due diligence process is cross-functional and involves both financial and operational teams. In addition, external service providers may be used to assess the value of the startup portfolio. Such an approach provides for early-stage investments with lower time pressures.

Case Example: Corporate Equity Investment

Provention Bio, a biopharmaceutical company dedicated to intercepting and preventing immune-mediated diseases, announced in early 2023 a US$35M equity investment from Sanofi. The investment was made to complement their co-promotion agreement in support of Provention's commercial launch of TZIELD (Sanofi, 2023a). Interactions with Provention were led on Sanofi's side by Corporate Business Development. Sanofi later acquired full ownership of Provention for US$2.9B (Sanofi, 2023b).

5.2.8 *Banks and Associated Intermediation Organizations*

Banks and associated intermediation organizations provide debt financing (borrowing money and paying it back with interest over a certain time frame) to companies. Debt typically has a number of covenants (document defining obligations, restrictions, and commitments) and may use assets as collateral (assets that are forfeited if the debt is not repaid). Debt interest might be tax deductible depending on location and regulations. Often used as complementary financing to equity funding, it is typically faster to obtain and might involve a simpler legal process in comparison. Debt financing may not be appropriate for all financing needs nor for all companies, as it may restrict a company's activities or require certain collaterals a company might not have or reasonably use (e.g., critical pipeline asset or intellectual property would not be reasonably used as collateral).

While debt normally does not directly impact stock ownership, a company still needs to have the cash flows necessary to effect repayments with interest and meet the various corresponding obligations. This typically requires being able to generate sufficient commercial or licensing revenues considering expected future equity financing available.

Case Example: Venture Debt

Venture debt can be used as complementary funding to VC equity financing, thereby extending a company's cash runway to reach a value inflection point and enabling capital equipment purchases or program funding. In 2018 Absci Corporation, a generative AI drug creation company, signed a Loan and Security Agreement (LSA) with Bridge Bank to provide long-term financing with 6% annual interest rate through term loans available in three tranches up to US$3M through December 2019 upon reaching defined milestones. Substantially all tangible assets of Absci were used as collateral, with the notable exclusion of intellectual property (still subject to a negative pledge). After several amendments, Absci paid off the remaining US$2.4 million outstanding balance of the LSA in 2022 (Absci, 2023).

Forms of debt commonly used by companies include:

- Lines of credit (revolving debt financing providing funding up to a defined limit; as a company pays back what it used, it can borrow up to that same limit). Functioning as short-term business loans, lines of credit might typically be used to cover operating expenses.
- Business credit cards function as very short-term financing and expense reimbursement. Prompt payment is required to avoid high interest payments.

Small biopharma companies and startup might also use specific forms of debt:

- Personal loans from family or personal relations – those need to be documented in a legal contract with a suitable amount of information, such as lender's name, borrower's name, principal amount, interest amount, minimum payments, payment periodicity, term, and a loan default clause. Personal loans may have tax implications, e.g.: charging an interest rate below Applicable Federal Rates (AFR are minimum acceptable interest rates published monthly by the IRS) might give rise to gift taxes in the United States and interests might be considered as taxable income for the lender.
- Government agencies like the U.S. Small Business Administration (SBA) facilitate loans for small businesses. SBA supports different types of loans, including 7(a) loans (most common SBA loan program), 504 loans (long-term fixed rate financing for fixed assets), and microloans (US$50k or less).

5.2.9 *Public Markets*

Companies can obtain financing from the public and possibly higher company values than private markets, due to increased transparency, visibility, and liquidity.

Public financing is often first accessed through an Initial Public Offering (IPO) whereby the company first makes some of its equity available for purchase by the public, receiving funding in exchange for shares. An IPO represents significant work and requirements. The process typically takes 6 months, the large majority of which consists in an IPO preparation phase of 3–4 months, followed by the IPO execution over a few weeks, a settlement over a few days, and a post-IPO completion phase of 1 month. Given the length of that process, some companies will resort to crossover funding prior to completing an IPO. Crossover funds invest in IPO-ready companies before they go public, gaining company shares at a discount compared with IPO pricing expectations; the private company receives operating cash to build financing confidence ahead of the IPO. Crossover investors often invest at series C or later and might be considered a quality signal to IPO investors.

Most biopharma companies conduct their IPO to be listed on a stock exchange (the place where the company stock will be traded) in their local market, but cross-border registration is possible. Registering cross-border might be motivated by various factors, such as enhanced industry positioning in the chosen exchange, improved or more favorable access to targeted capital, or more suitable listing terms.

Once publicly traded and listed on a stock exchange, the firm has easier access to future equity financing (by offering additional securities to the public), market value is easily determined with much higher equity liquidity, and correspondingly, fluid equity compensation approaches become feasible for employees. All these benefits come at the expense of the administrative costs associated with being a public company, the potential control loss, and the resulting quarterly and annual financial performance focus.

For private companies not ready to commit to an IPO, crowdfunding (defined as funding by raising small amounts from many people, typically via the internet) might represent an alternative access to public funding. Crowdfunding is still subject to specific rules and regulations. In the United States, all related transactions need to be conducted online through a SEC-registered intermediary, either a broker-dealer or a funding portal. In addition to specific information disclosure requirements and limits on non-accredited investor investment, the maximum amount raised over 12 months is limited to US$5M. Typically, securities purchased through crowdfunding cannot be resold for 1 year. Similar regulations exist in Europe, namely the European Crowdfunding Service Provider Regulation.

For public companies, private investments in public equity (PIPE) might represent a streamlined alternative to a registered public offering to raise additional financing. In a PIPE, the public company issues restricted equity in bulk quantities in a private placement to accredited or institutional investors, usually at a discount compared with the current stock price. The company also agrees to file a resale registration statement so investors can resell the shares to the public. As the regulatory requirements are lower, the public company is able to quickly and efficiently raise financing. PIPE regulatory requirements vary depending on geography and stock exchange, including for preemptive rights, discount limitations, company takeover, and implementation hurdles.

Although technically the opposite of financing, it should be noted that public companies might at times attempt share repurchase, also known as stock buyback or stock repurchase, where the company purchases some of its shares outstanding, using its cash to do so. As the shares purchased by the company become treasury shares or are simply canceled, the number of outstanding shares for the company is reduced by the number of shares effectively repurchased. It usually signals that the stock is undervalued in management's opinion. This could be done if the difference between the stock intrinsic value (see Chapter 2) and its price is greater than potential gains the company might derive from alternative investments (Jacobs, 2006).

5.3 Dilutive Versus Non-Dilutive Versus Hybrid Financing Approaches

Financing approaches can be divided between dilutive and non-dilutive (Figure 5.7). When an approach calls for issuance of additional company shares, thereby increasing the number of shares outstanding, each share will represent a lesser percentage of the company than before the issuance. Such equity-impacting approach, which reduces the relative ownership of a stakeholder, is called dilutive (like adding water to a soup and getting less nutrients per cup). By opposition, funding approaches that do not necessitate the issuance of company stock are called non-dilutive.

Some approaches described as hybrid may or may not end up being dilutive: they do not involve upfront stock issuance but might later trigger it depending on specific events.

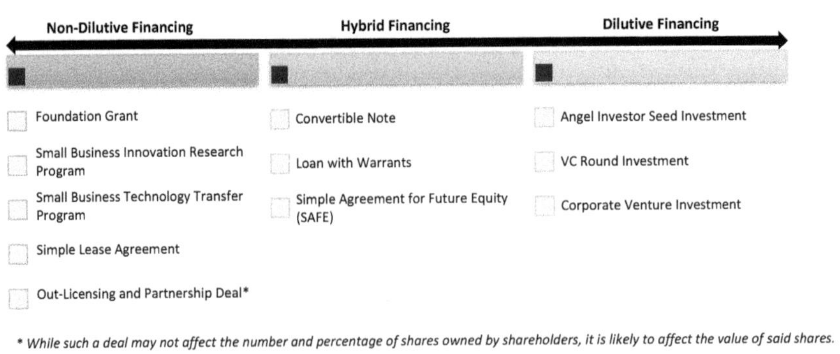

Figure 5.7 Illustrative spectrum of financing approaches.

By definition, dilutive approaches will require evaluating the value of the stock price while non-dilutive approaches and hybrid approaches may not. Equity investors might include anti-dilution clauses to shield their investment from losing value. Such clauses try and avoid the impact of future equity financing transactions that might result in a lower value per stock ("down round") than the one established in the current funding round. Common anti-dilution clauses:

- Weighted average anti-dilution provision. This provision uses a formula, in case of future down round, to increase the rate at which the preferred shares convert into common stock. The new conversion price NCP is obtained as follows: NCP = OCP × (SA + SB)/(SA + SC) where:
  - OCP is the original conversion price.
  - SA can be defined either broadly or narrowly (more favorable to original investor) as follows:
    - For the broad-based version of the provision, SA is the fully diluted number of common shares outstanding prior to the new stock issuance, including conversion of preferred shares, options, and warrants.
    - For the narrow-based version of the provision, SA is only the number of common shares equivalent to the investment protected.
  - SB is the investment value of the new stock divided by the old conversion price.
  - SC is the number of new fully diluted common shares.
- Full ratchet anti-dilution provision. As opposed to the previous weighted average anti-dilution provision, full ratchet allows the preferred shareholder to convert at the lower price per share of the new stock issuance. This clause offers greater protection to the investor.

Case Example: Simplified Weighted Average Anti-Dilution Provision

During Series A round, the term sheet includes a narrow-based weighted average anti-dilution clause and VC company VCA receives 100 preferred shares at US$1.00 in biopharma company BioInc with a 1:1 original conversion. BioInc has 300 common shares at US$1.00, no stock options, no warrants.

Later in Series B, BioInc issues 400 new preferred shares (1:1 conversion) to a new VC company VCB at $0.60 in a "down" round. As a result, VCA obtains a new conversion price of US$0.68 (Figure 5.8).

The value of VCA's stake goes from the original value of US$100 down to approximately US$83 rather than down to US$60 if it had been fully

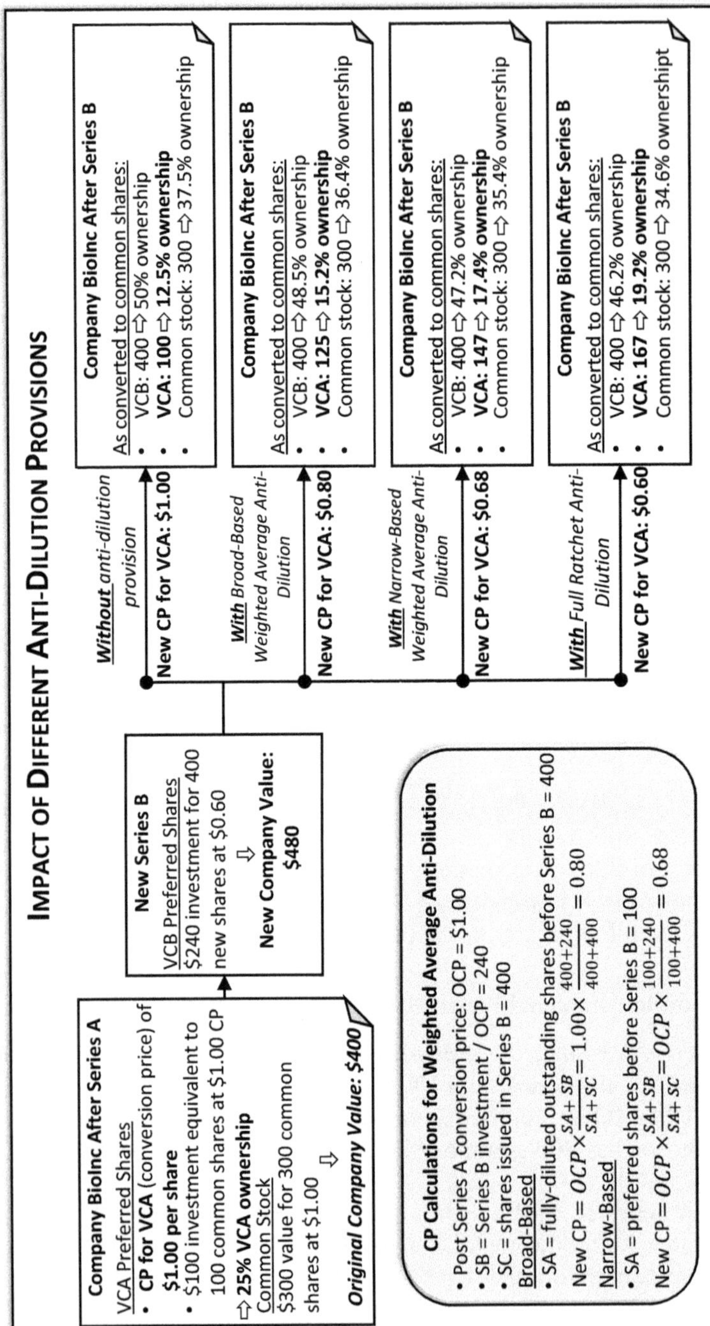

Figure 5.8 Impact of different anti-dilution provisions for BioInc.

diluted with the new round. Common shareholders are correspondingly further diluted, representing a disincentive for the biopharma leadership and founders to undergo a down round.

As the biopharma company pursues different sources of financing, they also need to keep in mind their liquidation preference implications for the company's capital stack. Liquidation preference refers to the pecking order with which various groups have access to proceeds from a sale or liquidation of the company: it answers the question of "who gets paid in what order". Groups with a higher liquidation preference get repaid for their investment before other groups can receive proceeds, which is especially important when the sale or liquidation value is lower than anticipated. Non-dilutive funding typically receives higher liquidation preference compared with dilutive funding (Figure 5.9).

Such basic concepts can become more complex with the use of additional qualifiers or modifiers, e.g.:

- Participating versus non-participating liquidation preference.
  With the non-participating version, the investor has the option to either exercise their liquidation preference, or to convert to common shares and receive participation in proceeds remaining to common shareholders in pro rata of their common shares.
  With the participating version, the investor receives their liquidation preference and also receives participation in proceeds remaining to common shareholders in pro rata of their ownership.

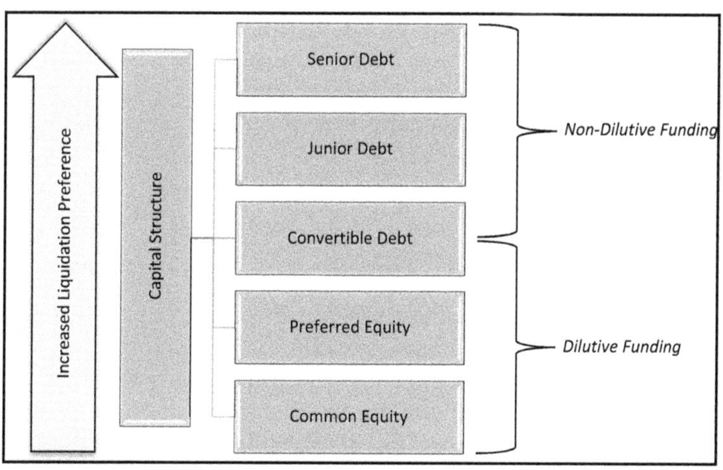

Figure 5.9 Capital stack and liquidation preference.

- Liquidation preference multiple: the multiple designates the number of times the investor needs to be paid back their investment before investors with lower liquidation preference can be paid. An investor that invested US$2 million with a 1.5× multiple would need to be paid US$3 million (i.e., 1.5 times the initial investment of US$2 million) before investors with a lower liquidation preference can be paid.
- Cap: the limit on how many times the investor will receive in return the amount of capital invested, without converting to common shares. An investor that invested US$2 million with a 3× cap will receive maximum proceeds to US$6 m; to be able to receive more than that cap, they would need to convert their shares to common shares, assuming that it would make sense based on company value and pro rata ownership.
- Seniority structure: how different sub-groups are ranked for liquidation preference within a group. With standard seniority, the last investment has seniority or higher liquidation preferences than previous investment rounds (e.g., Series C would have higher liquidation preference than Series A and B). In contrast, with Pari Passu seniority, all rounds have the same seniority (e.g., Series C would have the same liquidation preference as Series A and B).

Between dilutive and non-dilutive funding, a biopharma company usually raises more capital than its short-term R&D needs, investing the rest in short-term instruments and looking like an investment company with the risk of being exposed to corresponding rules and regulations. In the United States, they are exempt because Rule 3a-8 (under 17 C.F.R. 270) provides a safe harbor for R&D-intensive companies defined as:

- Having substantial R&D expenses as a percentage of total expenses.
- Having net income lower than twice the R&D expenses.
- Having low expenses for investment activities.
- Focusing investments on capital preservation with corresponding board policy.
- Not being primarily engaged in investing activities.

5.4 Financing from Out-Licensing and Partnerships

Out-licensing and related partnerships constitute another way to finance a (licensor) company as intellectual property assets are converted into revenue streams. In addition to being non-dilutive, this may provide a valuable alternative during economic downturns that make alternate avenues like VC less likely or more competitive. It is crucial to emphasize that while out-licensing does not technically dilute shareholder ownership, it typically impacts the overall value of the company. On the licensee's side, they gain access to new products, technologies, or platforms in addition to faster time to market, competitive advantages, or lower early development risks.

The renegotiation of an existing out-licensing agreement can also provide accelerated financing, in instances where the licensor negotiates with the licensee to buy out the future royalty obligations in exchange for an upfront payment based on agreed-upon fair market value of said obligations. This type of royalty buy-out transaction provides immediate and de-risked funding for the licensor.

Another non-dilutive financing avenue loosely related to licensing is revenue interest financing or revenue-based financing. The principle consists in creating additional royalties in exchange for upfront funding (that might be used toward R&D costs). A portion of revenues in the form of royalties is paid back to the investor (typically a specialized financial venture fund) until a predefined multiple of the initial investment has been repaid.

5.5 Equity Financing

Using the US Federal Register (67 FR 19673) as of July 2023, an equity security might technically be defined as:

> Any stock or similar security, certificate of interest or participation in any profit sharing agreement, preorganization certificate or subscription, transferable share, voting trust certificate or certificate of deposit for an equity security, limited partnership interest, interest in a joint venture, or certificate of interest in a business trust; any security future on any such security; or any security convertible, with or without consideration into such a security, or carrying any warrant or right to subscribe to or purchase such a security; or any such warrant or right; or any put, call, straddle, or other option or privilege of buying such a security from or selling such a security to another without being bound to do so.

Simply stated, equity securities represent partial ownership claims on the company's net assets (assets that remain once debt and liabilities have been paid). Equity financing exchanges such ownership claims for capital or financing.

Private companies raise financing in successive equity rounds conventionally designated with iterative names: Series A, followed by Series B, and so on. Series A might be preceded by a seed financing event and even a pre-seed financing event, making designations somewhat variable.

Equity financing comes with its own "language" and terminology, as illustrated by Figure 5.10.

409A valuation: US concept designating common stock valuation. The term is related to US internal revenue code section IRC 409A regulating nonqualified deferred compensation in which a stock price valuation is required	**Cashless exercise:** provision allowing the holder of options in the money to exercise them without paying the strike price in cash, thereby receiving the difference between stock price and strike price.	**Convertible preferred stock or nonparticipating preferred:** preferred stock that can either receive liquidation preference or convert to common stock. Participating version gets both conversion & preference.	**Down round:** financing round in which the value of the company is lower than that of the previous round.	**Information rights:** right for investors to have access to financial company information as well as updates on major company activities and evolution.	**No-shop or exclusivity:** term sheet clause preventing company from seeking further investors for a defined period after term sheet signature.	**Overhang or liquidation preference overhang:** convertible note holders purchasing stock at a discount, for both the value of principal and accrued interest, receive a correspondingly higher preference	**Pre-money valuation** : the agreed-upon value of the company's stock prior to a financing round. It is a negotiated dollar value!	**Registration Rights** : stipulates the conditions and timing for the owner to register shares in the context of an IPO	**Stock options:** instruments providing the right to buy shares of the company's common stock at a set price during a given period.
83b Election: IRS election to pay income tax on stock purchases prior to vesting	**Change of control preference:** multiple of the principal to be paid to the owner of a convertible note, would the convertible note not have the time to convert	**Capped Participating Convertible Preferred:** same as participating preferred but with limit (cap) on maximum proceeds.	**Drag-Along:** provision preventing a shareholder minority from blocking an action approved by a majority of shareholders.	**Keep It Simple Security (KISS):** financial instrument created by accelerator 500 Startups in 2014.	**Option pool:** shares of common stock reserved for employee or contractor stock option grants.	**Participation rights or Pro rata rights:** right for investors to participate in future rounds to maintain their pro rata ownership percentage.	**Protective provisions:** clause listing activities requiring board approval; might also entail veto rights.	**Restricted Stock Units (RSU):** common stock subject to a vesting schedule and additional restrictions –typically offered to employees in lieu of Stock options	**Term sheet:** generally nonbinding agreement that shows the basic terms and conditions of a financing agreement. Some aspects might be binding.
Accelerated vesting: unvested shares to be vested immediately in the case of the corresponding trigger, typically when the company is acquired	**Cliff:** minimum time before options or shares can vest	**Co-sale rights or tag-along rights:** right for investors to sell their shares as part of a transaction.	**Dry powder:** money raised by VCs that has not yet been deployed or cash reserves a company has.	**Key Person Insurance:** clause whereby company must take life insurance payable to the company for designated personnel	**Option pool refresh:** act of increasing the size of the option pool, done either before (pre-money) or after financing round (post-money).	**Pay-to-Play:** stipulates that investors need to maintain their pro rata ownership by investing in future rounds if they wish to avoid certain penalties	**Qualified Small Business Stock:** US C corporation with less than $50 million in assets (capital gains might be tax exempt If held 5 years or more)	**Right of First Refusal:** opportunity to first purchase in the case of a specific sale	**Vesting:** process by which the underlying asset rights pass onto the owner or recipient.
Anti-dilution: reduces dilution of investors in down round	**Confidentiality provision:** Confidentiality of a term sheet signed by the parties	**Counsel & expenses:** term sheet clause indicating company pays for investor's legal & administrative costs.	**Fully diluted shares outstanding:** common shares outstanding given all possible conversions are made and options exercised.	**Liquidation preference:** order of precedence over net proceeds.	**Out of the money:** unfavorable situation where current stock price is lower than option strike price.	**Post-money valuation:** value of the company after a financing round (sum of investment and pre-money valuation)	**Redemption rights:** right to redeem shares for the sum of original purchase price and accrued unpaid dividends	**SAFE:** standardized financing agreement created in 2013 by accelerator YCombinator	**Voting rights:** allowance to participate in company's decision-making based on pro rata of total votes.
Authorized shares: shares authorized by the company's board of directors, whether already issued or still available to be issued in the future	**Convertible note / loan / debt:** debt that can be converted to common or preferred shares	**Dividends** (cumulative vs non-cumulative): payments to stockholders that do not impact ownership.	**In the money:** favorable situation where current stock price is higher than option strike price.	**Mandatory conversion:** forces preferred shares or convertible debt to convert to common stock, under specific triggers	**Outstanding shares:** total number of issued common and preferred shares (not counting authorized shares not yet issued)	**Preferred shares or preferred stock:** separate class of shares with special pre-negotiated rights	**Redemption value:** sum of the liquidation preference and unpaid cumulative dividends	**Security interest or secured note:** note backed up by company's collateral assets and / or intellectual property.	**Warrants:** type of option that may be issued as part of a company financing arrangement.

Figure 5.10 The equity financing "Language" – Selected examples.

Case Example: Overhang

A company takes on a convertible note of US$100,000 with 10% interest and 20% discount to the priced round (see Table 5.7 for selected pros and cons of convertible debt).

One year later, they pursue a Series A with a price per share of US$1 and a liquidation preference of 1×. The note holder receives 137,500 shares in conversion of principal and accrued interest of US$110,000 purchased at 20% discount or US$0.80 per share.

The noteholder now has a liquidation preference for US$137,500 (number of shares times price per share for Series A) – this represents a 1.375× preference compared to their investment of US$100,000 rather than a 1× preference – hence the term "overhang", referring to the much higher liquidation preference.

5.5.1 *Capitalization Table, a Fundamental Building Block for Equity Financing*

Simply stated, a capitalization table, commonly referred to as "cap table", is a record of all investments in the company: capital investment, equity (stock, options, warrants), convertible debt instruments, SAFE, etc. The cap table quantifies the ownership structure for each security class.

The cap table clearly answers the question of who owns a stake in the company and what they paid.

An accurate and complete cap table is necessary to effectively run a company and to stay abreast of securities laws. It is also used to support valuation and ownership discussions with potential investors or to evaluate related considerations, such as granting new options, tracking options, and adjusting the option pool for new or existing employees before a round of funding.

While there is no standard format that a cap table needs to adhere to, recommended practices might include:

- Keeping the table as simple as possible.
- Maintaining the table as "auditable", i.e., current, and strictly aligned with supporting legal documentation for every shareholder and investor. E.g., preferred stocks, warrants, and option grants should be tracked in detail with their various terms (vesting period, etc.)
- Aligning the table with final authorizations and corresponding legal documentation; new entries should be made in the official table only after they are completely authorized through internal governance (i.e., board of directors signed off on all issues) and effective. As a result, attorneys are often involved in keeping a cap table accurate.
- Safeguarding the table with appropriate access permissions.

The cap table will be particularly helpful to the biopharma leadership seeking further financing to:

- Simulate future financing rounds: size of financing, dilution effect, shares per investor, valuation scenarios.
- Model different exit scenarios and financial returns to investors.
- Justify expected valuation and share pricing in upcoming round.
- Optimize the financial decisions taken by the company (e.g., decision to raise a convertible debt financing prior to a key value inflection point, equity transaction with a new category of investor).
- Analyze and negotiate with investors the size of the option pool necessary to facilitate employee recruitment and retention.

Case Example: Cap Table Evolution Over Fictitious Company 7-Step Lifecycle

In step 1, founders Jean-Noël and Alain create company Bio-Therapeutics Inc. Each founder contributes capital and intellectual property to the company; each is issued 500,000 common shares. A securities attorney provides support for the initial corporate documents and the two stock certificates. The simple cap table is provided in Figure 5.11.

In step 2, before raising funds from friends and family, the founders add an option pool to be able to use equity compensation for critical new employees, key advisers, and consultants. The new personnel option pool is formalized according to an employee stock incentive plan established with their attorney. Planning on an upcoming dilution and targeting 15% ownership for the option pool post-dilution, they allocate 20% to the option pool based on their best dilution estimate. The founders have

BIO-THERAPEUTICS CAPITALIZATION TABLE

STEP 1: FOUNDERS ROUND

	Founders	
	Common Shares	Ownership %
Jean-Noël	500,000	50.0%
Alain	500,000	50.0%
Total	1,000,000	100.0%

Figure 5.11 Step 1.

BIO-THERAPEUTICS CAPITALIZATION TABLE
STEP 2: ADDITION OF OPTION POOL

	Founders Shares		Option Pool Round			
Founders	Common Shares	Ownership %	Options	Existing Shareholders	Total Shares	Ownership %
Jean-Noël	500,000	50.0%		500,000	500,000	40.0%
Alain	500,000	50.0%		500,000	500,000	40.0%
Options			250,000		250,000	20.0%
Total	1,000,000	100.0%	250,000	1,000,000	1,250,000	100.0%

Figure 5.12 Step 2.

been equally diluted, with their ownership reduced by 20% as shown in Figure 5.12.

In step 3, after 8 months as research activities progress, Jean-Noël and Alain need additional resources to complete important in-vitro testing and purchase lab equipment. Based on their latest business plan, they decided to raise US$400,000 from family, friends, and trusted acquaintances to reach these objectives. They build a presentation to share with this audience, showing the scientific progress of Startup Bio-Therapeutics, goals per program, and initial budget forecast.

Using comparable startups and own estimates, they establish a pre-money valuation of US$1.2M representing US$0.96/share and thus a post-money value of US$1.6M, which aligns with the option pool step estimate.

Cynthia, a family relative, decides to fund the entire US$400,000 amount for the targeted equity ownership of 25% (Figure 5.13). Founders' control has been reduced from 80.0% to 60.0%, their combined shares are worth US$960,000, and the company has now received a US$400,000 investment for the 25% stock ownership given to Cynthia. The option pool has been diluted from 20.0% to 15.0%, as planned.

In step 4, Bio-Therapeutics is facing growing challenges (in-vivo testing encountered characterization issues and delays; with a staff of 4, they still miss critical biomarker expertise and face rising outsourcing expenses; only 14 months of cash runway left). The founders decided to raise a seed round to reach the next milestone (completed in-vivo efficacy testing in selected indications) by recruiting the required expertise and developing biomarker assays. They reach an agreement with North England Angels for an investment of US$800,000 in common stock at a negotiated pre-money valuation of US$2.4M (Figure 5.14). Price per share is now US$1.44.

In step 5, after encouraging efficacy evidence from animal models, the executive team is further persuaded of Bio-Therapeutics' success. Their Board however wants to minimize dilution and require short-term milestones to

Bio-Therapeutics Capitalization Table
Step 3: Friends & Family Round

Price / share $0.96

	Pre-money	Investment	Post-money
Valuation	$1,200,000	$400,000	$1,600,000
Shares	1,250,000	416,667	1,666,667

	Founders Shares		Friends & Family Round				
Founders	Common Shares	Ownership %	Options	Existing Shareholders' Shares	New Investors' Shares	Total Shares	Ownership %
Jean-Noël	500,000	50.0%		500,000		500,000	30.0%
Alain	500,000	50.0%		500,000		500,000	30.0%
Other Individuals							
Cynthia					416,667	416,667	25.0%
Options			250,000			250,000	15.0%
Total	1,000,000	100.0%	250,000	1,000,000	416,667	1,666,667	100.0%

Figure 5.13 Step 3.

Bio-Therapeutics Capitalization Table
Step 4: Seed Financing Round

Price / share $1.44

	Pre-money	Investment	Post-money
Valuation	$2,400,000	$800,000	$1,600,000
Shares	1,666,667	555,556	2,222,222

	Founders Shares		Seed Round				
Founders	Common Shares	Ownership %	Options	Existing Shareholders' Shares	New Investors' Shares	Total Shares	Ownership %
Jean-Noël	500,000	50.0%		500,000		500,000	22.5%
Alain	500,000	50.0%		500,000		500,000	22.5%
Other Individuals							
Cynthia				416,667		416,667	18.8%
Seed Round							
North England Angels					555,556	555,556	25.0%
Options			250,000			250,000	11.3%
Total	1,000,000	100.0%	250,000	1,416,667	555,556	2,222,222	100.0%

Figure 5.14 Step 4.

be met before preparing a larger round. They are convinced that the more validations they can achieve, the higher the valuation and equity they can preserve for themselves. A convertible loan should help them meet these objectives, which VC investor VCI agrees to fund under the following terms:

- Cash amount of US$1M.
- 10% interest rate accrued over the term of the loan.
- Term of 12 months maturity, preferred shares conversion.
- "Conversion trigger" defined as next equity round (Series A expected within 12 months).
- Discount rate of 20% on next round price per share.

As this is a convertible note, they do not need to agree with VCI on an explicit pre-money value. The cap table is updated in Figure 5.15.

In step 6, Bio-Therapeutics has reached its next milestone and validated several targets in specific therapeutic indications. The company has ongoing out-licensing agreement discussions with several potential pharma partners. However, Startup Bio cash burn rate increases fast resulting in an expected runway of less than 10–12 months. The company is seriously considering a large size Series A, which would enable them to scale up development activities and start first-in-man studies in 1–2 years.

BIO-THERAPEUTICS CAPITALIZATION TABLE
STEP 5: CONVERTIBLE NOTE

Price / share not required

	Pre-money	Investment	Post-money
Valuation	Not required	$1,000,000	Not required
Shares	2,222,222	-	2,222,222

	Founders Shares		Convertible Note Round				
Founders	Common Shares	Ownership %	Options	Existing Shareholders' Shares	Convertible Note Shares	Total Shares	Ownership %
Jean-Noël	500,000	50.0%		500,000		500,000	22.5%
Alain	500,000	50.0%		500,000		500,000	22.5%
Other Individuals							
Cynthia				416,667		416,667	18.8%
Seed Round							
North England Angels				555,556		555,556	25.0%
Convertible Note							
VCI					Fixed next round		Next round
Options			250,000			250,000	11.3%
Total	1,000,000	100.0%	250,000	1,972,222		2,222,222	100.0%

Figure 5.15 Step 5.

They decide to organize a Series A to raise US$8 m. After 4 months of meetings, roadshows, and pitches to VC firms, they reach an agreement with VC ScienceCapital on the following term sheet:

- Pre-money valuation of US$20M plus the US$1.1M from the convertible note, which is converted as part of Series A.
- ScienceCapital investment of US$8M in preferred stock, representing 27.5% of the post-money valuation of US$29.1M and a US$7.79 share price.
- 10% dividends cumulative, payable upon an exit event.
- Liquidation preference at 1× of invested capital.
- Governance restrictions (protective rights).
- Replenishment of option pool to 15% on pre-money basis (no dilution for ScienceCapital).

The revised cap table is provided in Figure 5.16. The company now has a new class of shares: preferred shares. The option pool, totaling 15% post-round, was replenished with 310,000 additional options. VCI receives 176,517 preferred shares corresponding to US$1.1M paid-in capital (original US$1M convertible note plus 10% interest) and a 20% discount. Price per share after the transaction is now US$7.79.

In step 7, 2 years after Series A, very promising clinical outcomes prompted a US$40M acquisition offer for Bio-Therapeutics by a large biopharma company. Options will be exercised at closing (all options modeled at a uniform

BIO-THERAPEUTICS CAPITALIZATION TABLE
STEP 6: SERIES A ROUND

Price / share $7.79

	Pre-money	Option refresh	Note conversion	Series A	Post-money
Valuation	$20,000,000		$1,100,000	$8,000,000	$29,100,000
Shares	2,222,222	310,000	176,517	1,027,010	3,735,750

	Options	Existing Shareholders' Shares	Converted Note Shares	Series A Shares	Total Shares	Ownership %
Founders						
Jean-Noël		500,000			500,000	13.4%
Alain		500,000			500,000	13.4%
Other Individuals						
Cynthia		416,667			416,667	11.2%
Seed Round						
North England Angels		555,556			555,556	14.9%
Convertible Note						
VCI			176,517		176,517	4.7%
Series A						
ScienceCapital				1,027,010	1,027,010	27.5%
Options	560,000				560,000	15.0%
Total	560,000	1,972,222	176,517	1,027,010	3,735,750	100.0%

Figure 5.16 Step 6.

"in the money" strike price of US$1.20 for simplicity); proceeds from the options exercise (560,000 shares at US$1.20) are paid to Bio-Therapeutics according to the Incentive Stock Option Plan. Stock option exercise proceeds are included in the net cash balance at closing and thus added to the US$40 m purchase price representing a total of US$40,672,000 to be paid by the buyer and allocated to shareholders. The cap table is used to calculate such allocations.

Holders of preferred shares will receive cumulative dividends totaling US$1,911,000:

- VCI: US$231,000 of interest based on US$1.1 m paid-in capital and 10% dividends compounded over 2 years.
- ScienceCapital: US$1,680,000 based on US$8.0 m paid-in capital and 10% dividends compounded over 2 years.

The total net proceeds of US$40,672,000 go in priority to preferred shareholders as presented in Table 5.1.

The remaining balance of US$26,273,569 after paying preferred shareholders goes to common shareholders as pro rata of their common share ownership (Table 5.2).

Table 5.1 Bio-therapeutics – preferred shareholder proceeds from sale

Preferred shareholders	*Dividends*	*Preferred shares*[a]	*Total*	*% Total net proceeds*
VCI	US$231,000	US$1,831,487	US$2,062,487	5.1%
ScienceCapital	US$1,680,000	US$10,655,944	US$12,335,944	30.3%
Total Preferred	US$1,911,000	US$12,487,431	US$14,398,431	35.4%

[a] Note that the liquidation preference of 1× paid-in capital minimum (US$1.1 m for VCI and US$8.0 m for ScienceCapital) was met and did not require further adjustment to this column.

Table 5.2 Bio-therapeutics – common shareholder proceeds from sale

Common shareholders	*Proceeds*	*% Total net proceeds*
Jean-Noël	US$5,187,848	12.8%
Alain	US$5,187,848	12.8%
Cynthia	US$4,323,207	10.6%
North England Angels	US$5,764,276	14.2%
Options Holders	US$5,810,390	14.3%
Total Common Shareholders	US$26,273,569	64.6%

5.5.2 *Typical Private Company Funding Rounds*

The typical amount a company might expect from a given financing round may depend on the geography, business environment, and other considerations, such as therapeutic area, modality, or clinical phase. Funding levels may also evolve over time as illustrated in Table 5.3.

It is also important to note that a company's structure might affect their ability to secure financing. In the United States, VCs might typically only invest in C corporations as opposed to Limited Liability Companies or S Corporations.

Table 5.3 Typical funding per round in the United States (Chang, 2022)

Round	*2021 median in USD*
Seed	US$3m (+67% from 2016)
Series A	US$10m (+100% from 2016)
Series B	US$25m (+101% from 2016)
Series C	US$50m (+273% from 2016)
Series D	US$74m (+307% from 2016)
Series E-H	US$105m (+946% from 2016)

5.5.3 *Spin-Off, IPO, SPAC, APO, and Other Public Equity Financing Approaches*

There are different mechanisms through which a new public biopharma company will emerge. They include spin-offs (the creation of a new public company created by separating a part of an existing public company in this context), initial public offerings (a private company becoming public by selling shares on a public exchange), and special purpose acquisition companies or SPACs (most commonly the merging of a private company with a listed shell company already established for such purpose). Another possible mechanism to start accessing public investment is a direct listing, in which a private company becomes public without raising new funds but rather by allowing existing shareholders to sell shares directly to the public, without using an underwriter as would be the case with an IPO. As financial markets continue to innovate, new offerings occasionally used that are derived from direct listing might entail financing avenues (e.g., direct listing with capital raise). However, since direct listing is technically not financing as no new capital is raised, we will not discuss it further.

Spin-Offs

Alternate terminology to spin-offs might be encountered, such as spinouts, split-offs, carve-out, or starburst, and distinctions are typically made through different models assigned to each term.

A spinout might designate a new company in the same space started by former employees while a spin-off would be a decision by the company to create a new and separate entity. Starburst might designate multiple separate new companies being created while a spin-off focuses on one instance only. Split-off represents a difference in share assignments: while with a spin-off, shares of the new company are typically provided to existing shareholders, in a split-off, shareholders must choose between the shares of the former company and the shares of the new company. Carve-out may yet represent another model where the new company shares are sold through an IPO.

For simplicity, we will focus solely on the corporate creation of a single company, with shares provided to existing shareholders, and accordingly use the term spin-off.

Spin-offs represent complex transactions as they require separating leadership, talent, operations, assets, and liabilities previously managed under one roof. They also require an effective transition plan, separate strategies (one for the parent, one for the new company), and respective implementation plans.

In any case, a spin-off may represent the means to secure financing for a part of the business with different characteristics, needs, and dynamics from the remaining parent company. Downsides might include a de facto lower revenue level, lower visibility, and reduced economies of scale.

Despite the simplified process provided by Figure 5.17, each spin-off may be unique with specific strategic and regulatory contexts. The spin-off

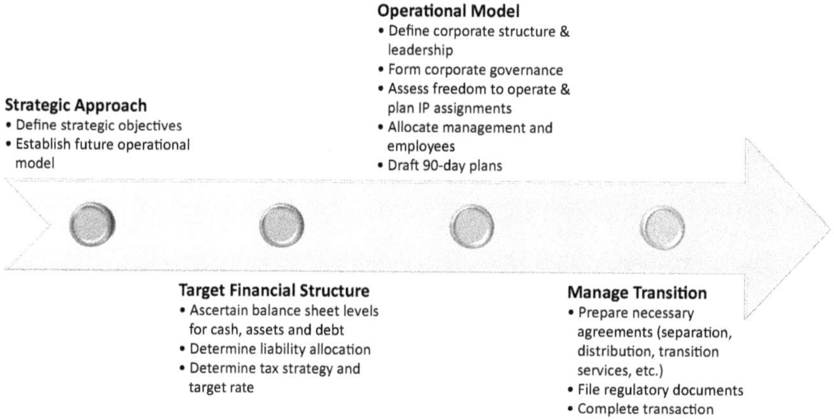

Figure 5.17 Illustrative spin-off process.

company typically uses a different equity and debt structure than the original parent company, with new debt commonly issued in addition to the different equity structure.

Case Example: Spin-Off

In January 2021, bluebird bio announced the separation of the oncology business into an independent company, Oncology Newco, later renamed 2seventy bio. The result was two independent publicly traded companies, each with specific operational and financial priorities, in a transaction designed to be tax-free to shareholders. bluebird bio retained the severe genetic disease business while 2seventy bio focused on oncology (bluebird bio, 2021).

2seventy bio's spin-off process followed major steps, including the following (2seventy bio, 2023):

- April 2021: 2seventy bio incorporated as a Delaware Corporation.
- September 2021: bluebird bio's board of directors approved the distribution of 2seventy bio common stock, distribution recorded on October 19, 2021.
- November 3, 2021: signing of a separation agreement with bluebird bio. Additional agreements included a tax matters agreement, an employee matters agreement, an intellectual property license agreement, and respective transition services agreements.
- November 5, 2021: 2seventy began trading on Nasdaq under ticker symbol "TSVT" while bluebird bio continued to trade under ticker symbol "BLUE".

IPOs

An IPO is the traditional route for a company to go public and obtain equity financing from public markets. With this approach, the company raises new capital, selling shares to underwriters who then sell the shares to various investors but predominantly to institutional investors. Underwriters are normally investment banks and help the company to market the new shares and manage trading volumes initially. It is important to note that transaction fees are relatively high since they include investment banking fees.

For previous investors, an IPO typically represents an attractive exit option compared with a private company sale to the extent that the general IPO market environment is reasonably favorable.

Before proceeding with an IPO, the biopharma company leadership should validate that the advantages of doing so outweigh the disadvantages of becoming public compared with staying private. In addition, they should ensure that the timing is suitable for both the market and the company's strategy. The market for biopharma IPO needs to be sufficiently favorable to enable a favorable initial stock price and generate sufficient proceeds for the company to achieve the next value inflection points it is counting on in its strategic plan. Market dynamics can vary significantly over a relatively short period of time: the median raised in 2021 for biopharma companies was US$126 million compared with US$190 million the previous year (Morrison, 2022).

舒服

Case Example: The Long IPO Journey in the Form of an Illustrative and Completely Fictitious "IPO Fairytale". (All Company Names Are Fictitious.)

Once upon a time, there was a biotech named Shūfu, Inc. located in the greater Boston area. Shūfu, written 舒服 in Mandarin Chinese, means comfortable. With 117 employees, the company focuses on immuno-oncology and relied on outsourcing to keep headcount and costs to reasonable levels. Founded five years ago, the company has a solid R&D and funding track record. With a lead asset in Phase 2, Shūfu raised a US$45M Series A three years ago and a US$75M Series B round one year ago. To continue delivering against their strategy, they need to raise another US$140M. Having weighted several alternatives, the leadership team firmly believes an IPO represents the best path forward (having sufficient financing ahead of the IPO, possibly with an additional crossover financing).

Day 1. As Shūfu's leadership starts its strategy review at the board meeting and reviews an IPO base case scenario, they feel it is the right time to consider "pulling the trigger" on the IPO and embark on the corresponding 6-to-12-month journey, which they get the board to approve, having maintained a systematic transparency and "no surprise" approach with their board.

Given IPO demands, the leadership temporarily increased resources (especially in project management) to try and compensate for their focus away from the day-to-day. After auspicious results for their lead asset (SHF001) in a pivotal clinical study, the company has submitted an NDA to the FDA and expects a review in the current year. The company also expects favorable outcomes from a second asset (SHF003) entering Phase 2, given very promising results to date.

With its fast positive trajectory, Shūfu also conducted recent 409A valuations that have shown consistently favorable estimates – a good omen for an upcoming IPO. In addition, the environment seems positive as biotech IPOs over the last 4 months have brought in reasonable IPO proceeds, in light of favorable biotech industry conditions and a strong underlying general market. Last, but not least, they expect sufficient pipeline progress and announcements in the 6 months following the target IPO time frame to maintain stock performance and trajectory. Still, Shūfu is prepared to alter its IPO timing, should the need for flexibility arise.

The leadership team selected Nasdaq as exchange platform for their IPO given the exchange's reputation for technology and innovation, its growth orientation, and its reasonable listing fees. As an emerging growth company (EGC) under SEC regulations, Shūfu will benefit from reduced public company requirements both for the IPO prospectus (S-1) and for future filings. The EGC status will also allow the company to keep the financial and business information provided during the SEC submission and review confidential until Shūfu has decided to complete the IPO process.

As Shūfu is looking for a reasonably sized IPO, a syndicate (team of several underwriters) is assembled. In Shūfu's case, the syndicate is composed of three well-known companies with whom the leadership team has established relationships since they feel that these companies have solid experience in marketing Nasdaq biotech stocks. Gold LLC, Rhenium Partners LLC, and Iridium Group LLC will be joint book-running managers for the Shūfu IPO. (Bookrunners designate the primary underwriters who oversee the overall process).

For legal services, the company is planning to use Latinum LLP with whom they have an existing relationship, since they are typically acknowledged to be in the top five law firms in the Boston area for biotech IPOs. They will use Palladium Osmium Californium (POC) for external auditing and accounting services. They retained Copper Trust Company as stock transfer agent and registrar; they will provide all the needed administrative services associated with Shūfu's stock trading (e.g., stock certificate issuance, transfer, and cancelations) once the company goes public.

Shūfu also tightened the collaboration with its public relations firm to include more specific strategies around the company's institutional image rather than the past tactical execution focus on scientific press releases. The new approaches will be starting 40 days after the IPO so as not to run afoul of "gun jumping" laws. In addition, they have embarked on a non-deal roadshow program to start building relationships with potential investors, manage expectations, and learn about specific areas of interest. Lastly, in anticipation of the IPO and required infrastructure, the company has established a new agreement with a specialized document management, financial printing, and distribution company, Boston-based Wicked-GoodEdgah, which can be leveraged for SEC filings among other services.

Day 15. Shūfu's leadership set up an IPO Project Management Office (PMO) and assign an IPO leadership team as well as a separate working group charged with working on the remaining gaps and challenge areas identified in its recent IPO readiness assessment.

Day 20. Shūfu organizes an all-hands meeting including all members of the IPO team, such as company IPO leadership team, PMO, independent auditors, accounting advisers from POC, underwriters from Gold LLC, Rhenium Partners LLC, and Iridium Group LLC, company's attorney, and representatives from Latinum LLP. In addition to formally kicking off the IPO process, Shūfu's objective is to discuss the offering, the SEC registration form, and the plan to get there (e.g., who will fill out which section, time frame, targeted filing date).

During the all-hands meeting, the various team members get to know one another and packed discussions occur throughout the day covering many aspects, including for example:

- IPO playbook.
- Immediate restriction of all external communications and required approaches during pre-filing stage, quiet period, and overall IPO period (to avoid violating the communications restrictions stipulated under Section 5 of the Securities Act).
- Registration statement approach.
- Offering minimum size and composition.
- Price range targeted.
- Various fees and expenses considered.
- Existing shareholders registration rights, especially Series A and B.
- Intended use of funds raised through the IPO.

Day 25. Now it is time for Shūfu Inc. and the IPO team to prepare and start filling out Form S-1 (SEC Form S-1 is a filing required under the US Securities Act of 1933 to register the securities of companies that want to become public). Completing this form, especially the first time around, will be a significant endeavor requiring hundreds, if not thousands, of hours of preparation and entries, typically using a wide variety of sources.

Beyond the basic information included on the cover pages (exact company name, registration jurisdiction, proposed sale date, etc.), Form S-1 registration statements have two main parts:

- The first part is referred to as the "prospectus". It is named that way as it corresponds to the legal offering document that must be delivered to any party receiving an offer to buy the securities offered by the company. This prospectus must cover many facets of the business so potential investors can make an informed decision regarding the investment opportunity represented by the IPO. Its content includes detailed information about the company: description, operations, financial performance with audited financial statements, risk factors, and management among other considerations.

- The second part includes various additional exhibits and information required by the SEC that do not have to be provided to potential buyers of the offered securities.

Independently Shūfu's IPO team assists with the underwriters' due diligence process on the company and works on the roadshow presentation, as explained below. The underwriters need to conduct a thorough due diligence not only to fulfill their duties and safeguard their reputation but also because they can be liable in case of material misrepresentations or meaningful omissions.

Day 26. Shūfu's underwriters collaborate with the company to conduct their due diligence in earnest, e.g.:

- Visit of the company locations.
- Review of R&D operations and essential documents.
- Examination of intellectual property and freedom to operate.
- Review of material agreements.
- Evaluation of financial statements, audit reports, tax returns, and board meeting minutes.
- Request of comfort letters from auditors (within the scope previously agreed with Shūfu to keep costs manageable).
- Fairness opinions from independent third parties.

The underwriters also requested extensive information around statements and facts used in preparation of, or within, the registration statement. Shūfu's leadership is now assembling the time-consuming trove of information requested, including justifications for market opportunities and industry overviews.

While due diligence is ongoing, Shūfu's team continues to work on the registration statement preparation, including producing the following parts:

- The Summary, sometimes referred to as "the box" since it is framed to make it stand out. Shūfu's team and the underwriters consider it to be a critical piece as it sets the tone for the investment story and value proposition that Shūfu represents. For now, Shūfu is planning on the following headings within this section, an approach not dissimilar from many biotech IPOs.
    - Overview (covering Shūfu's mission, key clinical assets, and main markets).
    - R&D pipeline.

  - Clinical development focusing on lead asset (SHF001) as well as brief points on SHF003.
  - Corporate information.
  - Company and team.
  - Strategy.
  - Risks associated with our business.
  - Implications of being an emerging growth company.
  - Offering summary.
  - Summary financial data.

- Business. As Shūfu well understood, the objective of this section is to provide potential investors with a solid basis from which to appreciate Shūfu's operations and the general development of the business.
- Risk Factors. As explained in 17 CFR Part 229 (item 105), Shūfu is providing within this part "a discussion of the material factors that make an investment in [Shūfu's] offering speculative or risky". This is where Shūfu gets to "caveat all the potential bad news", sound negative, and position important legal protections for the company.
- Management's Discussion and Analysis. This section is where Shūfu's management explains its financial statements and how to evaluate the business.
- As explained in 17 CFR Part 229 (item 303), the objective of that section is to provide potential investors with the material information required to assess the financial condition and the operations results of Shūfu.

Shūfu has extensively trained its leadership team and employees on what the "quiet period" means (i.e., a time where company executives, employees, and representatives must not promote the company as explained further down). This quiet period approach started immediately after the IPO all-hands meeting and since then, unless preapproved through the IPO PMO, all have refrained from interviews, inquiry responses, public relations statements, external meetings and conferences, postings on social media, and press coverage.

Day 80. As it managed to substantially complete the first draft of the registration package, Shūfu makes its first confidential submission to the SEC and has 30 days to wait for the first round of SEC comments. Shūfu selected this confidential approach since it safeguards their information from its competition: would they not proceed further with the IPO, none of this sensitive information would be made public. Also, expert and auditors' consent are not yet required at the confidential submission stage. Lastly, because it is technically not a filing, Shūfu has no filing fee to pay to the SEC – the filing fee will be due when Shūfu first files publicly.

Concurrently, discussing with its various advisers, Shūfu has been working to confirm its choice of the Nasdaq as its choice of stock exchange to pursue, having made sure it would be able to meet the requirements of the exchange. Also, it worked with Nasdaq to confidentially reserve a potential four-letter ticker symbol; Shūfu's team was eager to do so as there were few ticker symbols left to choose from with Shūfu's spelling.

As an EGC, Shūfu will still engage in oral or written communications with qualified institutional buyers during the quiet period to "test the waters" and gauge interest in their offering. This refers to meeting with institutional investors to solicit preliminary indications of interest in their coming IPO. Nevertheless, as is customary, Shūfu waited to start testing the waters until it made its first confidential submission to the SEC and set its investment thesis straight (especially since they know that the SEC is likely to ask for copies of the materials they used for these meetings). While they were greatly confident in their IPO prospects, they discussed with Gold, Rhenium Partners, and Iridium to decide whether to test the waters. Collectively they felt there was value in doing so and decided to invest time and effort in making it happen.

Day 110. Shūfu's team works diligently to address the first round of SEC feedback and issues they are starting to receive. Since their first confidential submission, the SEC assigned a team (consisting of lawyers, accountants, examiners, and supervisors) to review Shūfu's submission and assess its compliance with the various SEC registration and disclosure rules – they also scour data sources (e.g., industry and competitors' websites, press coverage, information research tools) to check for information that Shūfu would need to add to, or modify in, their registration statement.

Day 120. Shūfu makes its second confidential submission to the SEC, with suitable amendments taking into account all SEC feedback and issues received at this stage. Part of the interactions with the SEC have resulted in Shūfu's needing to provide the SEC with unredacted sections of various exhibits (they were redacted to protect confidentiality and privacy), which the SEC then destroyed after completing their assessment.

The underwriter syndicate and Shūfu have had ongoing discussions around valuation and price range since even before the all-hands meeting and, considering the company's valuation, concluded that a stock split was not required to get to the targeted range given the latest performance of publicly traded comparable companies.

Lastly Shūfu's PMO has ensured that lock-up agreements (agreements by existing stock and option holders not to sell shares during the 180 days following the IPO) have been delivered to Gold, Rhenium Partners, and Iridium, as agreed and planned before the first filing with the SEC.

Day 145. Shūfu receives a letter from the SEC asking a limited number of additional questions and concerns regarding their second confidential submission. Most of the points had to do with clarifying some of the descriptions and graphics used by Shūfu in the registration statement, one concern required additional intellectual property details, another issue required supporting information on positive evidence for a clinical trial, and the last point asked for results for a clinical study still ongoing. Shufu's team was able to respond on all fronts within a day.

Day 150. Shūfu makes its first public filing with the SEC.

As Shūfu files its registration statement, the so-called "Waiting Period" starts. This waiting period goes from the time Shūfu files its registration statement until the time the SEC declares that registration statement effective. The legal team has explained to Shūfu's leadership team the byzantine considerations for permitted communications, including Rule 164 and Rule 433. They continue to engage in minimal external communications activities as required and allowed by SEC rules and after consultation with their IPO lawyer (e.g., release of factual business information, limited participation in conferences and industry meetings they have consistently participated in the last few years, normal ongoing medical science activities that would not affect the registration statement information in any way).

Day 180. Using Form S1/A to file amendments to an existing form S-1, Shūfu makes its second public filing with the SEC, having amended the previous public filing, and added many exhibits. Based on the latest interactions with the SEC, they expect this amendment to be the final one, pending SEC's confirmation.

Shūfu and their underwriters have timed their road shows to start at least 15 calendar days (the required "seasoning period") after their initial submission and all amendments have been publicly filed with the SEC. US Securities Act Rule 433 defines a road show as

> An offer (other than a statutory prospectus or a portion of a statutory prospectus filed as part of a registration statement) that contains a presentation regarding an offering by one or more members of the issuer's management [...] and includes discussion of one or more of the issuers, such management, and the securities being offered.

During the quiet period, road shows constitute the legally compliant and predominant approach to present information to potential investors – they are typically performed by key company management.

The syndicate has planned an optimal live road show schedule over two weeks, combining virtual meetings covering several time zones with face-to-face meetings in three cities (Boston, New York, San Francisco) to meet with potential investors across the United States. Shūfu's leadership (CEO, CFO, Chief Medical Officer & VP Clinical R&D, and the new VP of Investor Relations) has prepped and rehearsed the presentation many times to be effective – the four of them feel they can deliver the 30-minute company pitch with their eyes closed at this point!

Day 185. Shūfu starts on the road show. During the road show, the syndicate builds an order book consisting of the various indications of interest received. The road show is conducted flawlessly although by the end the team was a bit spent and out of voice after so many presentations, despite the significantly reduced travel compared with what it would have been without the virtual option! On a positive note, there seems to be tremendous demand for Shūfu's stock at this point, including international investors.

Day 196. As all SEC staff comments have been addressed by Shūfu, the SEC declares Shūfu's registration statement S-1 effective, meaning the SEC has cleared Shūfu to sell its securities covered in the S-1 registration statement. Shūfu also becomes subject to the Securities and Exchange Act of 1934 reporting requirements (e.g., file quarterly statements with unaudited financial statements and annual audited financial statements).

Based on their order book model generated during the road show, the underwriting syndicate was able to make a pricing recommendation to Shūfu they expect will be well received. Shūfu's leadership and board approved the recommended price, as it is ultimately Shūfu's responsibility to determine the price of the offering. Now that the registration statement is effective, Shūfu and the underwriting syndicate execute the underwriting agreement. They are now one day before the IPO closing date and Shūfu's leadership has had to negotiate and agree to many clauses on the underwriting agreement. Below are some of the selected considerations that were included in Shūfu's final underwriting agreement.

- Firm commitment underwriting in light of the very well-received road show: the underwriters have committed to purchase all the securities offered by Shūfu as opposed to best effort underwriting agreement where they would be able to return unsold shares to Shūfu.
- Greenshoe option: this option allows the underwriters to sell more shares than planned and increase the supply of stock to investors if an IPO attracts higher than expected returns. Like in most cases, this overallotment clause is for an additional 15% of shares to be exercised within 30 days of the IPO.
- Representations and warranties. Although the subject of negotiation between the parties, most of these used relatively standard language typical for "reps and warranties" such as the company representing that the S-1 registration statement being effective, that it is eligible to act as a security issuer, that there has not been any material adverse change in the company, etc.
- Conditions and obligations of the underwriters such as receiving a negative assurance letter from the auditors or various legal attestations.
- Covenants of Shūfu: these essentially pertained to obligations the company agreed to regarding future activities.

Day 197. Since the offering price has been set, the underwriters have been working on deciding how to allocate shares to the institutional investors that bid for Shūfu's shares. As the aggregate bids for Shūfu's shares exceed the number available, they are making allocations by trying to find a balance between expected longer-term holders and expected short-term holders to ensure both robust pricing (increased by long-term holders) and liquidity (increased by short-term holders). In addition to being critical to the IPO performance, this activity greatly matters to the underwriters as their share assignment also determines the commission they receive.

The underwriters release the shares on the primary market on the morning of the IPO: investors who have subscribed or registered their interest with the underwriters receive their allotment of shares before the market opens. Once the lock-up period has passed, the investors in question will be able to trade their Shūfu shares on the secondary market, like any public company shares.

Later that day, trading begins on the open market and Shūfu's underwriters may start stock-price stabilization activities. Shūfu's leadership team gets to participate in the "ring the bell" ceremony at the beginning of the trading day that morning at the Nasdaq stock exchange and celebrate this significant milestone achievement! Shūfu's stock starts trading for the first time under ticker symbol SHUU a little bit later after the opening, after the exchange determines an opening price for SHUU. Once Nasdaq has set the opening price, Shūfu's stock begins to trade in earnest and the underwriters have to smooth out price fluctuations by increasing the number of shares available (taking advantage of the greenshoe option).

The first day trading return is relatively high (around 18%) but not unreasonably so, indicating Shūfu's offering pricing was well positioned to offer potential returns to institutional investors without compromising IPO proceeds for Shūfu.

Day 200. Three days later, the offering closes and Shūfu receives the net proceeds from the IPO.

Overall Shūfu's IPO costs came remarkably close to 10% of the deal, between the underwriters, lawyers, accountants, registration and listing fees, printing fees, and others. The bulk of these costs were constituted by the underwriting fees representing approximately three-fourths of the total costs, followed by the legal fees representing slightly over one-tenth of the total. Despite the relatively high costs and the grueling past months, Shūfu's leadership is thrilled with the IPO outcome.

The underwriters continue to stabilize Shūfu's shares using the entire greenshoe allotment to eliminate imbalances. They publish Shūfu's resulting valuation and the company transitions to regular market competition and public company activities.

Day 227. The difference between offering price and the stock price one month later is still favorable.

Initiating coverage by various research analysts, published the month following the IPO, have pegged Shūfu as a growth stock with 12-month upside in the 45%–65% range based on a current stock price already more than 20% above the IPO price. The floating shares or stock float (i.e., shares available to public investors) now represent 65% of the company's total equity.

The End (of Shūfu's Fairytale)

As this fairytale demonstrates, while the outcome can be exhilarating, doing an IPO represents numerous months of ongoing, complex, grueling, expensive work and distractions away from the day-to-day business. The steps involved (Figure 5.18) are characterized by inherent financial, legal, regulatory, and process intricacies notwithstanding the business dynamics between the numerous parties involved and the need to build out governance or reporting capabilities.

SPACs

Simply stated, a Special Purpose Acquisition Company, or SPAC, is a company structure formed to raise financing through an IPO (without assets) and later merge with a target company with actual assets (or "de-SPAC" as it is called – see Figure 5.19). Although they may designate a target industry or target segment that they wish to pursue in their IPO prospectus, SPACs are also called "blank check companies" given their relatively unspecific

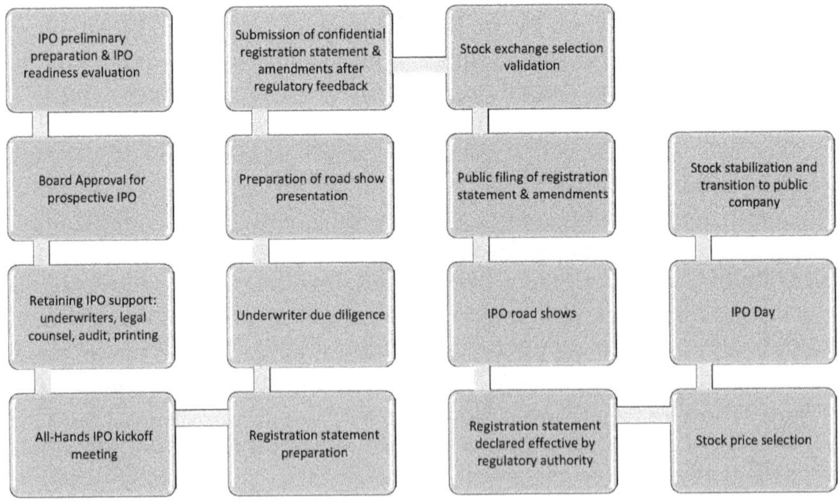

Figure 5.18 An illustrative road to IPO.

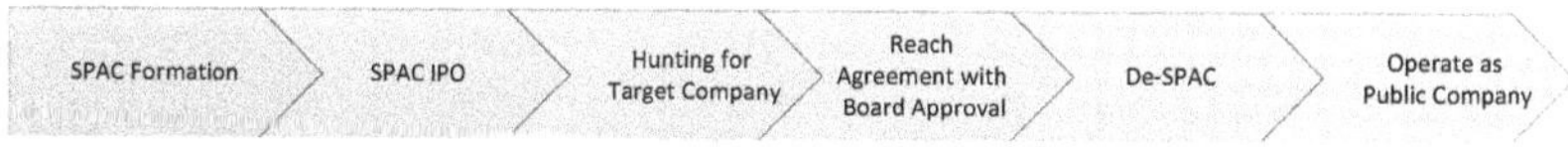

Figure 5.19 Typical successful SPAC process.

initial nature. Note that underwriting fees are correspondingly set differently to those of an IPO: e.g., one-third of underwriting fees payable upon IPO with the balance paid only upon an effective merger.

SPACs represent a vehicle to take private companies public: as the SPAC is publicly traded, a private company merging with it becomes de facto public. Some "market participants believe that, through a SPAC transaction, a private company can become a publicly traded company with more certainty as to pricing and control over deal terms" compared with the normal IPO approach just discussed (U.S. Securities and Exchange Commission, 2021). Also, going public via a SPAC can typically be twice as fast for the target company and represent a timing of 3–6 months, compared with the 6–12 months (and sometimes up to 24 months) typically required for a traditional IPO.

As a SPAC is only a "shell company" (i.e., a company without actual business operations) and as the target company becomes public when merging with the SPAC, the target company still needs to undergo many of the maturing evolutions required to operate publicly as for an IPO (e.g., readiness assessment, process and infrastructure improvements, and management upgrades).

At time of publication, SPACs have mostly been a US phenomenon outpacing other regions by an order of magnitude. In the biopharma space, results for SPACs seem to have been mixed: as coined by Elmhirst and Brown (2023), a "poor track record at delivering strong companies into investors' laps has not helped the so-called blank-cheque space". They also noted some brighter spots in those "gloomy stats": a few companies like Roivant Sciences (Nasdaq: ROIV) and Cerevel Therapeutics (Nasdaq: CERE) have been doing well and have significant enterprise values.

Additional Public Offerings

Once public, a company may decide to issue additional shares to the public through a registered follow-on offering, called additional public offering (APO), or seasoned equity offering, to raise additional capital. Since it is used in the context of raising additional capital, such offering will be dilutive, reducing the portion of the company owned by existing shareholders as well as earnings per share. Note that follow-on public offerings may be non-dilutive when existing investors sell their shares to the public in a secondary offering as no new shares are issued; in that scenario, no proceeds go to the company.

The APO timeline (e.g., 1–3 months) is typically much shorter than that of an IPO. The process varies depending on the structure used by the company and typically includes due diligence, filing a registration statement using the applicable process (e.g., Form S-3 versus Form S-1 in the United States), waiting for that registration to become effective, making various additional filing requirements (e.g., final offering prospectus), and closing the offering once complete.

APOs can be structured in many different ways, e.g.:

- At-the-market offering (ATM), where the company sells new shares at market rates, controlling timing and size of the various sales. These are more suitable for relatively smaller offerings. In the United States, those typically require a registration on SEC Form S3 (either a universal shelf registration for ATM programs or a specific one).
- Traditional underwritten public offering where an underwriter or syndicate markets the offering, similarly to an IPO.
- Direct public offering is a transaction where the company markets the new shares directly, usually to a small investor group. The investors receive registered shares with favorable terms.
- Block trades, also called "bought deals", where an investment bank or institutional investor buys a block of new shares (e.g., over 10,000 shares) from the company at a discount and takes on the market risk of the new shares. This is a process used for well-known seasoned issuers that in the United States would be able to use a registration statement Form S-3 automatically effective without SEC review. The process is fast: the company contacts several banks after markets close, gets a response within a few hours, selects the most favorable, and completes the deal that day or night.

Note that Private Investment in Public Equity transactions, or PIPE, discussed in Section 5.2.9, would not be an APO since they are not public as the name indicates. Under such issuance, private investors make a sizable investment in the public company and receive stock at a discount in addition to registration rights for the securities in question. In the United States, PIPEs are exempt from registration. Another private follow-on offering sometimes used is the equity line of credit, or ELOC, which is a specific financing agreement with an institutional investor allowing the company to issue shares over time and sell them to the investor under predetermined conditions (e.g., up to US$50M at 5% discount on volume weighted average price over three business days for a duration of three years).

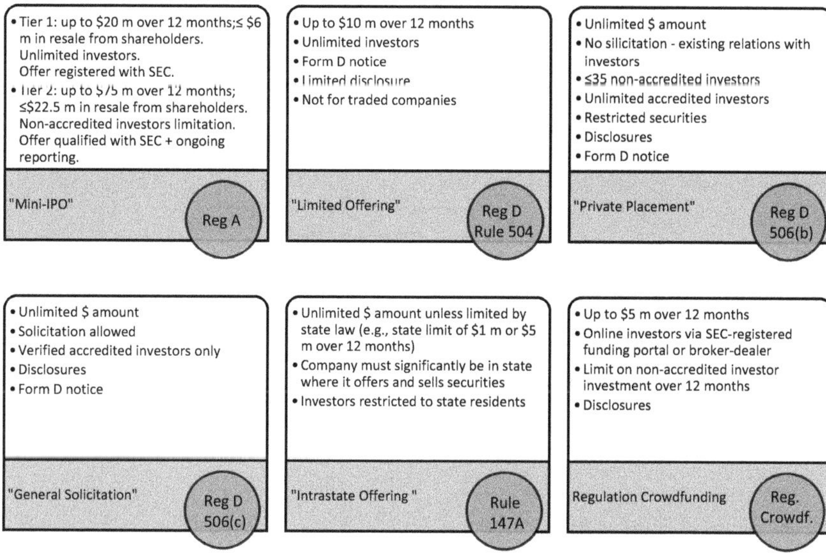

Figure 5.20 US exempt equity financing approaches.

Other Public Equity Financing

In addition to emerging concepts like the direct listing with capital raise briefly mentioned at the beginning of the section, there are other public equity financing avenues depending on the jurisdiction.

In the United States, a company cannot normally offer securities without registering the offering with the SEC. There are, however, well-defined exemptions: Figure 5.20 illustrates the main exempt equity financing approaches. Differences between these US exemptions revolve around financing amounts, investor restrictions, resale limitations, and disclosure requirements.

5.6 Debt Financing

As examined by Lo and Thakor (2023), debt financing might be underutilized to finance biomedical R&D, in part due to the early-stage challenges associated with more limited collaterals than in other industries. Debt financing is a critical source of capital to consider for biopharma companies when manageable as it typically results in a lower overall cost of capital for the company (see debt lower risks and returns depicted in Figure 5.21 as well as WACC calculations in Chapter 2).

Like equity financing, debt financing comes with specialized language. Debt is usually segmented between senior debt and subordinated debt.

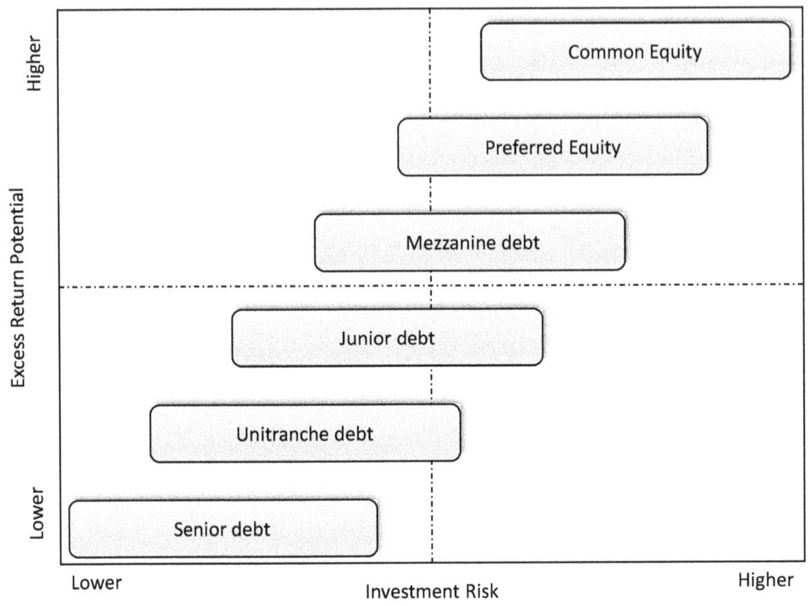

Figure 5.21 Capital stack's illustrative risks and returns.

"Senior" means that it has liquidation preference over other forms of debt in the capital stack: it gets paid first before lower preference debt (subordinated debt also called junior debt). Unitranche is a hybrid between junior and senior debt described in Section 5.6.3.

Debt can be referred to as public or private, depending on the funding source. Public debt designates debt raised via a public transaction, similarly to equity, and can be later publicly traded, like in the case of a bond. Private debt designates debt raised via a private transaction between the company and lender(s), like in the case of a loan; the lender(s) could be a bank, a group of institutional investors, or a syndicate of banks.

Senior debt can be secured with collateral or unsecured. When public, senior debt is normally issued as notes (short-term or medium-term debt) or bonds (long-term debt). Bonds are typically considered securities and regulated as such (e.g., required registration under the Securities Act of 1933 in the United States unless exempt) while notes might not always be.

Bonds, or loans for that matter, might be organized in tranches (tranche means slice in French), tranches being portions of the debt instruments but with different preferences, interest rates, maturities, and risks. In terms of preference, tranches are paid in sequence from senior to junior, characteristically resulting in senior tranches having a stronger credit rating in the case of bonds. Different debt instrument tranches are usually referred to by letters in alphabetic order starting with the seniormost tranche, e.g., A Tranche, B Tranche, etc.

Depending on the issuer's credit rating, bonds can be either investment grade (meaning high grade) or non-investment grade (and in that case either high yield for the most favorable rating, or junk for the least favorable rating).

Unless otherwise specified, debt subscribed earlier has a higher precedence compared with debt taken on later. Secured debt tends to be senior to unsecured debt since by definition, specific collateral assets were identified. Similarly, a first lien debt (indicating the debt corresponds to first priority claim on certain assets serving as collateral for payment in case of default) will be senior to a corresponding second-lien debt (indicating the debt corresponds to second priority on the same assets).

Senior debt tends to have fixed interest rates while subordinated tends to have a variable interest rate.

As shown in Figure 5.22, there are many different types of debt offerings that might be involved in a biopharma company's capital structure, and that composition will vary as a given company will typically have only a subset of the various debt products depicted, possibly some with different seniority levels.

While senior and secured debt allow for lower interest rates, they typically also incorporate certain restrictions. Operational restrictions might preclude additional debt, asset sales, M&A activities, and so on, barring the approval of the Board and the restricted debt holders. In addition, debt

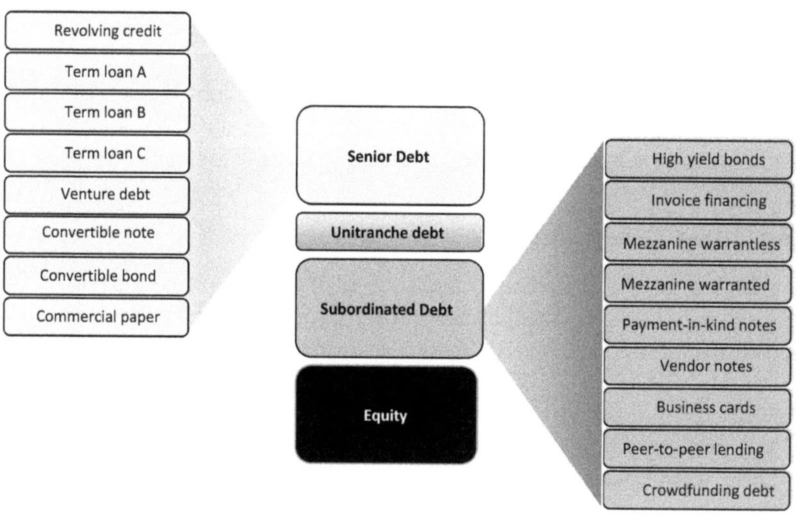

Figure 5.22 Numerous debt building blocks that may appear in a capital stack.

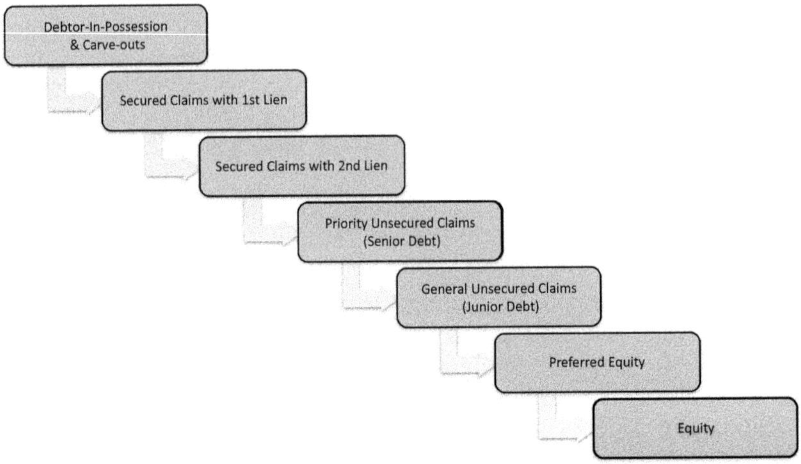

Figure 5.23 Company liquidation precedence.

offerings may include financial covenants to ensure greater lender protections. This usually means that the company needs to report and meet certain financial performance criteria on a periodic basis. Failing to comply with its various requirements may have significant adverse effects on the company (e.g., increased interest rates, accelerated repayment). Also, debt taking precedence over equity, company management, and equity holders in general might be left with limited residual company value, or no value at all, after years of investments pursuing a business venture, as illustrated in Figure 5.23, providing successive priorities on proceeds in case of a company liquidation.

As a note of caution, pledging IP as collateral for debt is very risky, as IP is the most important asset of the company. Losing the IP to a noteholder would severely compromise future value and returns for equity holders.

5.6.1 *Debt Classification*

In addition to the differences discussed at the beginning of Section 5.6, debt securities can be classified based on maturity (i.e., when it needs to be repaid), e.g.:

- Short-term notes with maturities of up to 1 year.
- Medium-term notes with maturities between 1 and 10 years.
- Long-term bonds with maturities above 10 years.

The conditions under which debt is established initially as well as whether and how it can be subsequently traded depends on the debt. In the United

States, debt facilities generally need to be registered with the SEC. Specific debt facilities might, however, be exempt from registration but restricted; Rule 144A issues, while not registered, are only tradable to qualified institutional buyers.

Public Debt

Public debt is used to designate debt facilities that can be publicly traded as opposed to being restricted. Note that public debt is sometimes used to designate government issues, which is not what is meant here. Public debt securities may be issued by publicly traded companies or privately held companies. Although subject to the same regulatory requirements, there are, however, indications that privately owned companies incur a higher cost of public debt than their publicly held counterparts (Badertscher et al., 2019).

Public debt securities are categorized depending on the credit classification of the issuing company. In the United States, agencies providing such classifications include Moody's and Standard & Poor's (S&P). The ratings are divided between investment grade (top ratings) and speculative grade or high yield as they are associated with higher interest rates (thus riskier). In the case of long-term investments, using Moody's or S&P, investment grade is further segmented into four categories while speculative grade is further segmented into six categories (Table 5.4).

Table 5.4 Long-term debt classification (Moody's, 2022; S&P Global Ratings, 2023)

Credit quality classification (long-term investments)	*Moody's*	*Standard & Poor's*
Investment grade		
Highest quality (lowest credit risk)	Aaa	AAA
High quality (very low credit risk)	Aa	AA
Upper medium grade (low credit risk)	A	A
Medium grade (moderate credit risk, possible speculative traits)	Baa	BBB
Speculative grade		
Somewhat speculative (substantial credit risk)	Ba	BB
Speculative (lacks characteristics of desirable investment)	B	B
Highly speculative (poor standing)	Caa	CCC
Most speculative (poor prospects)	Ca	CC
Imminent default (extremely poor prospects)	C	C
Default	C	D

Table 5.5 Moody's short-term debt classification (Moody's, 2022)

Credit quality classification (short-term investments)	*Moody's*
Investment grade	
Prime-1: Superior ability to repay short-term obligations.	P-1
Prime-2: Strong ability to repay short-term obligations.	P-2
Prime-3: Acceptable ability to repay short-term obligations.	P-3
Speculative grade	
Not prime	NP

Table 5.6 S&P short-term debt classification (S&P Global Ratings, 2023)

Credit quality classification (short-term investments)	*Standard & Poor's*
Investment grade	
Extremely strong capacity to meet its financial commitments on the obligation	A-1+
Strong capacity to meet its financial commitments on the obligation	A-1
Satisfactory capacity to meet its financial commitments on the obligation, somewhat more susceptible to the adverse effects of changes in circumstances and economic conditions	A-2
Capacity to meet its financial commitments on the obligation more likely to be weakened by adverse effects of changes in circumstances and economic conditions	A-3
Speculative grade	
Current capacity to meet its financial commitments with major ongoing uncertainties that could lead to inadequate capacity	B
Capacity to meet its financial commitments dependent upon favorable business, financial, and economic conditions	C
In default or in breach of an imputed promise	D

In contrast to the long-term investment classification, Moody's and S&P have different short-term debt classification approaches that do not align as well as those of long-term investments (see Tables 5.5 and 5.6).

Private Debt

In contrast to public debt, private debt designates debt instruments that are not registered nor publicly traded (e.g., private placements placed directly with institutional buyers that keep the debt to maturity). In addition to restrictive features that might be set by the issuing lender, private debt is still regulated by the SEC in the United States:

> Under the federal securities laws, every offer and sale of securities, even if to just one person, must be either registered with the SEC or conducted under an exemption from registration. This is true for companies of all sizes, private and public alike, and includes debt secured from anyone, including friends, family, angel investors, and venture capital funds.
>
> (U.S. Securities and Exchange Commission, 2023)

Offers of securities are broadly defined and broadly interpreted in the United States: securities may include stock, restricted stock, membership interests, stock options, convertible instruments, and debt (U.S. Securities and Exchange Commission, 2023). Reporting compliance, therefore, represents a critical aspect for the debt-issuing company to ensure it has met all the necessary requirements before, during, and after the sale of its debt securities.

Like public debt, private debt can be rated for its credit quality. Generally speaking, private debt has lower ratings than its public counterpart, everything else being equal. It is worth noting that periods with low interest rates and less favorable equity financing environments (as was seen in 2021) might result in higher private debt demand and volumes.

5.6.2 *Use and Typology of Debt Products*

There are many different types of debt instruments; they typically differ in terms of maturity, complexity, size, and seniority. Such typology includes convertible debt, venture debt, revolving credit, term loans, mezzanine debt, unitranche debt, Payment-in-Kind (PIK) notes, commercial paper (CP), crowdfunding debt, vendor notes, and small debt instruments.

In general, complexity tends to increase with maturity. Debt complexity may result from various product characteristics, e.g.: use of a syndicate, significant covenants, collateral requirements, hybrid nature (e.g., use of warrants or convertible options), disclosure and registration requirements, as well as the need for complex financial considerations (e.g., rates, conversions, returns).

Expected return from debt products might also vary depending on numerous factors, e.g., changing market conditions, company creditworthiness, and specific debt attributes (size, duration, covenants, collateral, liens, convertible options, leverage range, amount of existing senior debt, capitalization, fees). In the United States, CP maturity and returns are constrained by their 270-day limit. Overall, expected returns are generally inversely correlated to debt seniority, which makes sense since expected returns are usually correlated to the counterparty risk or overall risk involved. The cost of debt might thus be lowered by improving the business credit score, providing collateral assets, or becoming a better known entity by building an ongoing relationship with a specific lender.

Notwithstanding covenants and other constraints, when evaluating debt offering, it is also important to understand the various fees charged to the company as borrower and how they might affect analyses. Those fees might or might not be factored into interest rates. Annual percentage rates (APR) will include fees associated with a loan whereas annual interest rates (AIR) will not. Additional fees to consider might include origination fees (cost of processing a loan), guarantee fees, servicing fees, underwriting fees, closing fees, and so on. Fees might be charged as a flat fee or as a percentage of the debt. A discussion with the lender is often required to understand which fees apply and how they are calculated. Even with the APR approach just mentioned, the APR may or may not capture all the applicable fees.

In general, debt product availability tends to increase with the maturity of the company. Managing the debt structure, an activity typically led by the Chief Financial Officer of the company, is an essential aspect to balance risk and to optimize value creation in biopharma as it affects the company in many ways.

Selecting the right debt composition (see description of various options in Section 5.6.3) between short-term instruments and longer-term ones allows the company to optimize its cost of debt and avoid unwanted financial exposure (e.g., interest rate exposure) and align its financial strategy to its cash flow projections and anticipated market evolutions.

In addition, debt structure can have important consequences for operational flexibility and adaptability to evolving environments. Some debt offering might allow for easier refinancing, others might allow the company to trigger conversion to equity, while others might allow prepayment at a premium. Barring negotiations with lenders, a lower flexibility might prevent the company from taking advantage of improving economic conditions on the one hand, or increase the challenges associated with degrading economic conditions on the other hand.

Covenants associated with certain debt products might also limit the company's operational flexibility. There are three main types of covenants to consider in that respect:

1. Financial covenants that require the company to meet certain financial performance objectives on an ongoing basis.
2. Negative covenants that prevent the company from undertaking certain activities, such as mergers, acquisitions, additional indebtedness (except for permitted incurrences), new bank accounts, new encumbrances or pledges, dividends.

3. Affirmative covenants that require the company to undertake certain activities such as delivering regular financial statements or meeting specific requirements.

5.6.3 Overview of Selected Debt Products

Convertible Debt

Convertible debt is a loan that converts to future equity.

One of the complexities of convertible notes is that they combine debt interest with a call option. When the convertible note holders exercise their call option to convert the note into preferred stock, they forego future debt interest payments (since after conversion, there is no debt left and the principal is repaid). As a result, convertible debt is often converted close to maturity, not to lose the remaining time value of the conversion option. Given that time value, convertible debt may come with a "make-whole fundamental change" clause indicating that the convertible note holder gets some form of financial compensation, would the convertible note holder significantly erode the option value or time value because of a major change in the company stock (e.g., company acquired for cash, public company delisted from stock exchange). Alternatively, convertible debt instruments might use an automatic conversion rather than a call option.

Table 5.7 provides selected pros and cons of using convertible debt instead of equity as illustrated in the private company case example of Section 5.5.1.

Table 5.7 Selected pros and cons of convertible debt over equity

Advantages	*Drawbacks*
• Relatively early use in startup lifecycle. • Extending financial runway prior to the next funding round. • No negotiated company valuation as stock price and terms are set by next funding round. • Streamlined transaction with simpler documents and lower legal fees. • Flexibility of closing at different times with different investors.	• Senior form of debt that takes precedence over equity and subordinated debt. • Risk that conversion triggers do not happen, necessitating repayment or roll-over. • Could complicate the company' future funding plans given interest, discount, caps on conversion price. • Possible tax implications (e.g., interest payment might constitute a taxable event).

Convertible debt can be complex and uses specific terminology, which may require the involvement of Finance and Investment experts. Convertible note technicalities might include the following:

- Dilution protection approaches typically stipulate an adjustment to the conversion ratio in the event of capital increase, attempting to maintain the pro rata of outstanding shares the convertible debt converts into.
- Conversion triggers indicate which events must occur in order for convertible debt to be allowed to convert into equity. Conversion triggers typically include equity raises above a certain threshold (e.g., closing a priced round of financing over a minimum amount, or IPO). Triggers might also include stock-price threshold, convertible price ceiling, corporate events (e.g., redemptions), and transactions (e.g., M&A). Conversions are usually mandatory but under special circumstances would be optional and can have significant accounting implications.

Venture Debt

Venture debt is a loan-type offering typically made by banks and venture capital firms that is very often combined with, follows, or precedes an equity round of financing. It is designed for earlier-stage venture-backed companies with solid growth potential.

Venture debt has the effect of extending the company's runway as well as the value creation or returns associated with the equity round. It might be set up as loans secured by the next round of funding. A loan size representing 30% of the previous equity round might be considered typical, and since venture debt is secured by the next financing round, the VCs that invested in the last round might be a decisive factor as their past performance and approach might be indicative of the next round's likelihood and expected performance. While potential dilution might come from a portion of the venture debt payoff in the form of warrants (e.g., 5%–15% of loan amount when included), venture debt otherwise provides for minimal equity dilution, an important aspect between VC rounds.

Venture debt is often repaid as lump sum and typically comes with warrants and variable interest rates – these terms draw a distinction from traditional senior debt that typically has fixed rates, installment payments, and no warrants.

Revolving Credit

Revolving credit is also called a "revolving loan facility" or "revolver". Revolving credit constitutes senior debt and, as the names indicates, it is a line of credit that the company can borrow against up to a certain ceiling, pay back the debt, and borrow up to that ceiling again. It is arguably one of the most flexible debt instruments as the company can normally borrow against it and repay it at any time for any reason.

Revolving credit is often used to fund working capital or guarantee a letter of credit. Revolving credit characteristically uses two separate rates:

- The unfunded rate (e.g., 0.50%) used to calculate commitment fees due to compensate the lender for making the line of credit available. The commitment fees are calculated by multiplying the unused portion of the credit by the unfunded rate.
- The funded interest rate, usually indexed on a well-known benchmark such as the US prime rate plus a spread adapted to the financial rating of the company receiving the line of credit.

A revolving credit is typically provided by a bank and is negotiated based on the company's expected cash flows and working capital needs. Revolver interests may be lower when secured with future cash flows (e.g., accounts receivable).

Term Loans

A term loan is a lump sum of money the company borrows from a lending party that the company will pay back with interest at regular intervals over a defined time frame. The time frame can vary from several months to more than 10 years.

Key Loan Terms and Conditions

- Amount
- Interest
- Maturity or term
- Repayment schedule
- Various covenants
- Representations
- Seniority & collateral
- Rating

Term loans are typically used for acquisitions, equipment purchases, and real estate. They normally carry a floating interest rate based on a well-known benchmark such as the US prime rate or the UK LIBOR plus a spread that depends on the financial rating of the company taking on the loan.

Installments, i.e., combined interest and principal payments, are normally paid quarterly for a period between 5 and 7 years. Such loans might be resold on secondary markets with a discount on their original issuance (called OID or original issuance discount).

Term loans are normally established as senior debt and might be structured in different tranches, e.g., term loans A through C, each tranche with its own maturity and schedule.

A particular type of term loan is a "second-lien term loan". As the name suggests, this is a term loan that has a subordinated or second-lien claim to a collateral used to secure a term loan. Since the claim is subordinated to the senior term loan, second-lien term loans represent a higher level of risk and have correspondingly higher rates than term loans (e.g., 1% or 2% higher).

Another particular case is what is called a bridge loan. Commercial bridge loans are short-term loans that are used to cover a specific company's transitional period. As the name suggests, they are used to bridge the gap between the current company's need for capital and a longer-term financing solution. They are common for commercial real estate, where the real estate typically serves as collateral. Repayment terms typically do not exceed three years.

Mezzanine Debt

In architecture, a mezzanine floor designates an intermediate floor between two main floors, and thus not factored in the official number of floors. Mezzanine financing, placed between equity and senior debt, was given a similar name.

Mezzanine financing is typically structured as a hybrid approach between debt and equity financing; it may for example combine cash interest, PIK interest, warrants, and participation payout based on specific company performance measures.

Mezzanine financing represents a much higher level of risk than senior debt and is priced at correspondingly higher and fixed interest rates (e.g., 15%–22%). The maturity used for mezzanine financing is traditionally set at five years or longer (e.g., longer than senior debt), with a norm in the 5–8 year range.

Mezzanine financing is normally used to replace part of the equity financing required in an acquisition. One particularity of mezzanine financing is that it relies on the company's cash flows for repayment. As a result, mezzanine financing covenants might include limitations to preserve such cash flows (e.g., incurrence of further debt, asset sales, change of control).

Although second-lien loan components are possible, most mezzanine financing takes the form of subordinated unsecured debt, complemented by equity participation represented by warrants, options, or conversion triggers.

Unitranche Debt

Unitranche loans are a hybrid blend of senior debt and subordinated debt combined under a single loan structure with an overarching issuance agreement and a syndicated approach (multiple lenders with different term structures syndicated behind a single lender). Unitranche interest rates are correspondingly set at an average cost of debt in between those of senior debt and subordinated debt. In simpler terms, a unitranche combines multiple loans into a single one with a single interest rate and repayment structure.

Compared with multiple loans, a unitranche provides simplicity and increased certainty given the single lender (an aspect essential when planning a time-sensitive company acquisition), increased predictability in terms of setting a payment structure, and arguably a more cost-effective administrative oversight requirement, albeit less diversified in light of the single agreement.

Typically, the company issues unitranche debt by working with an investment bank or investment bank syndicate that will structure the unitranche debt in an underwriting process. Unitranche debt providers can include debt funds and institutional lenders.

In biopharma, unitranche loan users might include small to mid-size companies, as unitranche loans may represent an alternative credit market for companies that may access the same credit facilities enjoyed by larger companies. A typical unitranche loan size might be considered to be US$100 million. Typical terms include a call protection (no early prepayment) for 1–2 years, a maturity between 5 and 7 years, and lump sum repayment at maturity. This minimum period lock-in with lump sum or bullet repayment is considered one of the drawbacks of unitranche loans.

PIK Notes

PIK notes, or Payment-in-Kind notes, are debt instruments that allow the company not to pay interest in cash but rather to have the option to capitalize them, to be accrued and paid later. True PIK notes refer to the version where all interest is capitalized and added to the principal, whereas with another version called PIYC notes or Pay If You Can notes, interest is paid if certain conditions are met and added to the principal otherwise. A third kind, called PIK toggle notes or Pay If You Want notes, lets the company decide.

PIK notes are junior debt with higher interest rates (e.g., issued by companies without a rating or with a low rating). Interest rates may be floating or fixed depending on the issue. Some may have call protection (no early repayment before a certain time frame).

Given their characteristic of allowing interest capitalization, PIK components in a financing mix might help with situations where companies face liquidity challenges or accommodate interest coverage ratio objectives.

CP

Commercial paper refers to short-term, unsecured debt (promissory notes), exempt from SEC registration in the United States and issued by a company. CP represents an affordable short-term source of financing and is typically issued by large companies or by financial institutions. CP is sold at a discount to its face value (payable at maturity) to provide investors with a return on their investment. Expected returns depend on the issuer's credit rating. Although situations vary, CP may be considered on par with senior unsecured debt in case of company default.

CP may be used to finance activities like payroll, inventory, or accounts payable. The maturity by which CP needs to be repaid is 270 days or less (with an average of one month) in the United States. Maturities do not extend beyond 270 days to avoid coming under the SEC's regulations. In non-US markets, CP maturity might be slightly longer but typically remaining below 365 days.

Crowdlending

Crowdfunding debt, also called crowdlending, constitutes a peer-to-peer lending or P2P lending. Peer-to-peer lending in the United States is regulated by the SEC and requires registration unless exempt, as is the case with crowdfunding regulation. Crowdlending works like crowdfunding through an online platform where third parties can assess the opportunity and decide to lend in exchange for repayment with interest under specified conditions.

Vendor Notes

A vendor note, also known as seller note or vendor loan note, is defined as a short-term loan from a company's vendor, using the vendor's services or goods provided to the company as collateral, when applicable. Such debt is often considered vendor financing. A vendor note is essentially a deferred loan (i.e., a loan that postpones interest payments until a certain time after which interests start to accrue) and subordinated debt.

5.7 Debt Financing for Challenged and Distressed Companies

Given that debt sits at the top preference of the capital stack, when a company faces financial difficulties, it might be necessary to take corrective actions and secure the financial means for the company to continue to operate. Distressed debt financing approaches might be required.

5.7.1 *Debt Refinancing*

Debt refinancing and debt consolidation refer to replacing existing debt with new debt featuring more favorable terms. The company is still held to all applicable contract terms and to all applicable securities laws without specific judicial oversight.

5.7.2 *Debt Restructuring*

Debt restructuring involves more dire situations than debt financing, in that it focuses primarily in avoiding defaulting on the debt by making the obligations more manageable, e.g., extensions (lengthened repayment schedule) and compositions (lower amounts).

Debt restructuring involves negotiating with creditors to take on revised debt facilities with improved overall characteristics in lieu of existing debt commitments: different interest rates, addition of PIK options, standstill periods, maturity date changes, as well as revised covenants and representations.

Creditors might prove responsive to restructuring given the alternative could be bankruptcy proceedings with associated litigation costs as well as an automatic stay of payments. Senior debt may constitute a priority as its covenants might be more constraining to the company.

5.7.3 Debt for Equity Swaps

In a debt for equity swap, the company offers the creditor(s) company shares in exchange for writing the debt off. This alternate form of debt restructuring can be a useful consideration for a viable company in financial difficulty with debts expected to bring the company into insolvency or bankruptcy.

On the creditor's side, a debt for equity swap might provide a way to avoid debt recovery processes and associated risks while participating in potential future upsides, would the company indeed be viable. However, since debt holders have priority over equity holders in case of liquidation, viability assessment represents a pivotal consideration to move forward.

Major considerations in debt for equity swaps may include:

- Company viability post swap.
- Underlying company valuation used.
- Discount on debt value versus discount on price per share.
- Type(s) of equity with attached rights or restrictions.
- Deal approach and approval process along with other applicable rules or regulations.

Let us turn to debt financing avenues available to a company in bankruptcy or reorganization.

5.7.4 DIP Financing

Debtor-in-possession financing, or DIP financing, is designed as short-term debt to enable the liquidity (e.g., payroll, rent, operating expenses) required in the context of a reorganization or bankruptcy.

When a company gets to a stage of financial distress, they might no longer have access to their previous short-term financing and associated liquidity for various reasons (e.g., the company's assets existing liens, remedies for existing debt). In such a situation, DIP financing might become necessary during the bankruptcy process.

In the United States, Chapter 11 of the US Bankruptcy Code allows the company (more specifically the trustee) to "obtain unsecured credit and incur unsecured debt in the ordinary course of business allowable under section 503(b)(1) of this title as an administrative expense" (11 U.S.C. § 364). In addition to giving the resulting debt priority over unsecured claims, section 364 provides a path for increasingly senior debt (up to priming existing liens) if more junior-level debt cannot be obtained (U.S. Securities and Exchange Commission, 2023).

Independent of its ultimate seniority, DIP financing typically comes with higher interest rates and might provide a way for existing lenders to safeguard their existing debt with the company (notwithstanding the incentive for senior lenders to offer DIP financing in order to avoid seeing their existing lien primed by another DIP financing offer).

5.8 Grants and Other Financing Approaches

Biopharma companies can also seek alternative financing avenues, such as grants, lease financing, royalty monetization, synthetic royalties, and factoring.

While each of these alternative arrangements will be instrumental in securing financing for the company, each may come with its own limitations, e.g.:

- Grants are frequently used in earlier-stage companies, and will often require the company to undertake activities or operate under certain constraints that may not align with the company's strategic value creation objectives or timelines.
- Royalty monetization and synthetic royalties are appropriate for late-stage development programs. They provide upfront funding at the expense of future cash flows and thus the company's future self-funding capacity.
- Factoring (loans against near-term revenue) reduces short-term revenues in exchange for upfront funding.

5.8.1 *Grants*

Following up on concepts discussed in Section 5.2.4, a grant is typically an award, usually financial, that a government, corporation, nonprofit, or other party gives an individual, company, or organization for a particular purpose such as research or small business support.

To pursue grants successfully, a biopharma company needs to have an effective and ideally well-defined grant development process, as illustrated by Figure 5.24, as well as the appropriate personnel or support to develop, prepare, submit, and execute on the grant.

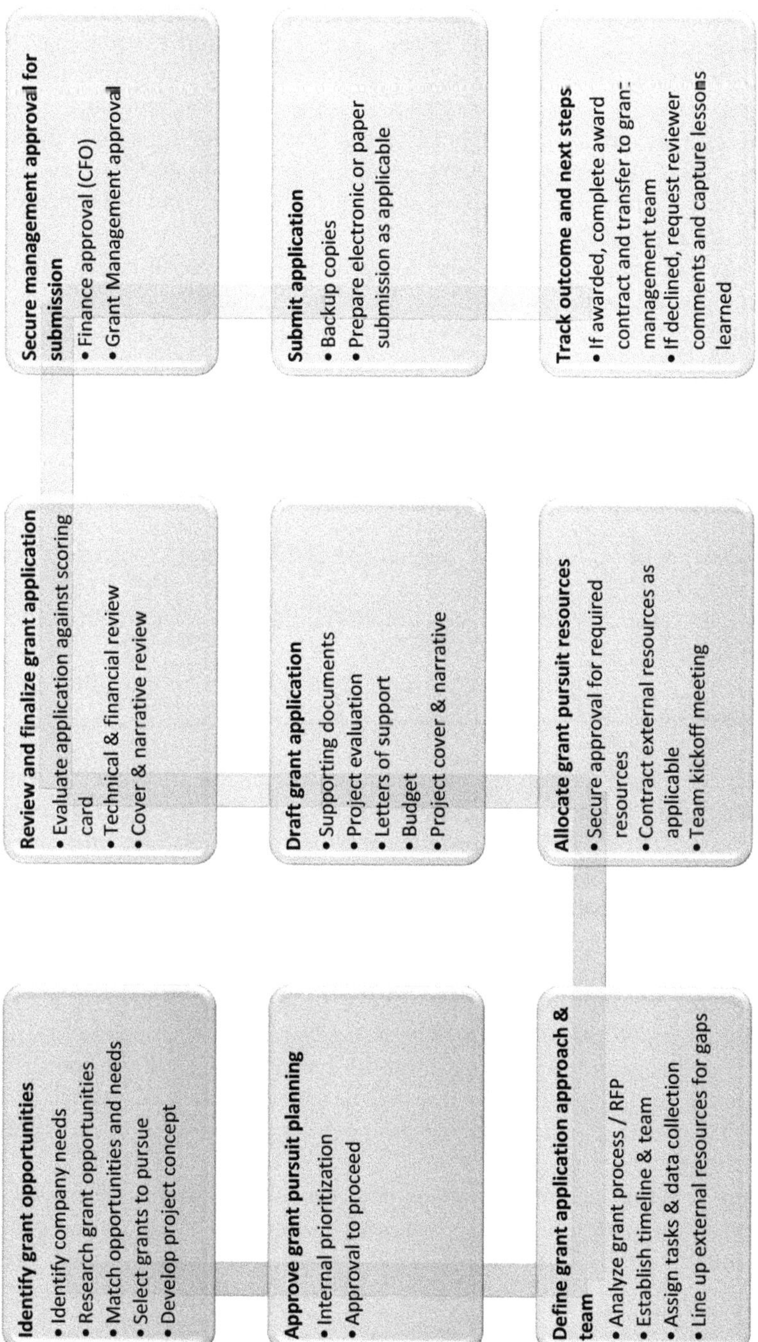

Figure 5.24 Illustrative grant development process.

Understanding where and how the company might benefit from grant opportunities is essential as the grant submission process may be time-consuming, with high rejection rates, and may divert effort from the company's approach and priorities. Possible reasons to undertake such challenges may include value positioning or expertise signaling, public relations and marketing objectives, ensuring key opinion leader involvement, improved resource utilization, or financial performance improvement (e.g., revenues).

As the grant process can be competitive, resource-intensive, time-consuming, complicated, and features exacting eligibility requirements, it is important for the company to evaluate the adequacy of specific grant pursuits for the company's needs (e.g., grant cycle, average grant amount, success rate).

Although straightforward to avoid, common pitfalls resulting in grant rejections include poor:

- Selection process (not being aligned with the grantor's objectives and priorities).
- Completion (not following the complex and extensive grant application directions).
- Review (not providing a coherent approach throughout the grant response).

Most grant proposals end up in rejections and taking the time to learn from that is an integral ingredient of future successes for grant development (Sohn, 2019). An average grant application success rate often mentioned across grant sources being one in ten, grant development represents a non-negligible resource investment and possibly a significant opportunity cost for the company: with this success rate, if one application took an arbitrary average 200 hours of collective preparation, it would statistically take the equivalent of one year full time for one person to get one grant award. von Hippel and von Hippel (2015) surveyed grant applications submitted to NASA, NIH, and NSF and found an average of 171 hours per proposal between Principal Investigator (PI) hours and Chief Investigator (CI) hours. They also recommended focusing on grant opportunities with at least a 20% success rate.

Grant application budgets can represent a substantial investment for a biopharma company and should thus not be undertaken lightly as a financing avenue.

Case Example: NIH Grants

From 2018 to 2022, approximately one in five grant applications submitted to the NIH is successful on average. In 2022, the average research proposal size was approximately US$600,000 consistent with the prior year (NIH, 2023). And it can take between 8 and 20 months after the due date to get an award (NIH, 2019). "Overall timing from planning to award may take as long as two years" (NIH, 2019).

5.8.2 Lease Financing

An asset lease is a contract providing the lessee (i.e., the biopharma company) the right to use an asset (owned by the lessor) under specific conditions (e.g., a specific amount of time) in exchange for payment. Lease provides for an alternative means of financing that is not based on equity or debt. It can typically be used in lieu of upfront capital for property, plant, and equipment. Indeed, leases distribute the corresponding costs over time, making cash flow requirements more manageable for the company.

There are two types of leases: finance leases (previously called capital leases) and operating leases. A major difference between the two is the ownership of the asset at the end of the lease: the operating lease does not transfer ownership rights of the asset whereas a finance lease transfers (or provides the option to transfer) ownership after the lease period has been completed and all contract obligations have been met. Typical US differences between the two types of leases are captured in Table 5.8.

Note that accounting approaches may vary depending on the jurisdiction: in contrast to US GAAP, the IFRS lease approach is unified as IFRS 16 has introduced since January 1, 2019, a single lessee accounting model without differentiation between financial and operating leases.

5.8.3 Royalty Monetization

Royalty monetization, or royalty buyout, requires a situation where the biopharmaceutical company has out-licensed intellectual property to another party and is entitled to royalties on the sales generated by a third party using the intellectual property in question. With that prerequisite, royalty monetization refers to receiving an upfront payment in exchange for the future royalty revenue stream.

This royalty monetization approach that requires a prior change in access to intellectual property is referred to as "traditional" as opposed to synthetic royalties, discussed next, that do not involve a change in access to intellectual property.

As there is no equity (or debt) involved, royalty monetization represents a non-dilutive financing approach for the biopharmaceutical company, enabling short-term financing in exchange for lower self-financing potential in the future.

From 2018 to 2022, royalty monetization represented an annual average of US$3.1 billion with a US$1.1 billion standard deviation (Dokomajilar, 2023).

Table 5.8 Comparison between financial and operating leases in the United States

Features	*Financial lease*	*Operating lease*
Ownership	Option for ownership to be transferred to the lessee at the end.	Ownership stays with the lessor at the end.
Term	Longer: spans most of the asset's useful life.	Shorter: useful life remaining at lease end.
Approach	Resembles a financed purchase.	Resembles a rental agreement.
Maintenance	Managed by the lessee.	Managed by the lessor.
Obsolescence risk	Lessee is bearer.	Lessor is bearer.
Tax Treatment	Lessee owns the asset and deducts depreciation and interest expenses.	Lessee deducts rental payments as they do not retain ownership of the asset.
GAAP Accounting (ASC 842)	Balance sheet. Lessee records: • ROU (Right-of-Use) asset (total lease liability + initial direct costs + prepaid – incentives) • Lease liability equal to present value of unpaid lease payments Income statement. Lessee recognizes: • Amortization of ROU asset (straight line). • Interests on lease liability. Cash flow statement: • Interest cash payments in operating section • Principal cash payments in financing section	Balance sheet. Lessee records: • ROU (Right-of-Use) asset (total lease liability + initial direct costs + prepaid – incentives) • Lease liability equal to present value of unpaid lease payments Income statement. Lessee recognizes: • Single lease cost (straight line). Cash flow statement: • Overall cash payments in operating section

5.8.4 *Synthetic Royalties*

Synthetic royalty is the "seller's obligation to make payments, typically quarterly, based on net sales of the relevant products in exchange for an upfront payment and, sometimes, future milestone payments". Habitually, the products in question benefit from various patents and regulatory exclusivities (Schwartz et al., 2022).

One particular feature of synthetic royalty deals is that there is no intellectual property ownership change involved nor any change in development and commercialization approaches. A pre-existing royalty payment stream is not required. Still, intellectual property strength and related market potential are critical to secure a synthetic royalty deal.

Synthetic royalties, unsecured or secured with collateral, with or without restrictive covenants, do not technically constitute a debt facility since there is no principal repayment nor interest. Rather the buyer gets a percentage (royalty rate) of the relevant products' net sales made by the company. Royalty rates are typically in the mid-single-digit range over a defined time period (e.g., 5 years). A cap (e.g., 2 × multiple of invested capital) might be added, fixed, or variable depending on cumulative returns within a defined time period (Schwartz et al., 2022).

5.8.5 Factoring

With factoring (also called invoice factoring or accounts receivable factoring), the company sells its outstanding invoice amounts to a factoring company at a discount. The factoring company is then responsible for collecting payments: the company's debtors pay the factoring company directly instead of paying the company. Factoring might thus be considered a source of alternative short-term financing for companies with recurring receivables.

Typically, the factoring company will pay a percentage of the face value of the total invoice amounts (e.g., a specific percentage between 70% and 90%) to the biopharma company upfront, work on collecting outstanding payments, and send an additional payment to the biopharma company net of the factoring company's fees when they collect an invoice. Factoring can be expensive as the factoring company's fees typically range from 1% to 10%, depending on various factors, one of which is typically the number of weeks the customer took to pay their invoice. In addition, payment guarantee (this type of factoring is called non-recourse factoring where the factoring company retains the responsibility for unpaid invoices) when possible will significantly increase the factoring company's fees. Without payment guarantee (recourse factoring), the biopharma company has to buy back unpaid invoices.

Alternate approaches to factoring might include invoice financing and credit insurance. With invoice financing, the biopharma company borrows an amount against its accounts receivable (e.g., 90% of face value), still collects its own invoices, and repays the financing company the principal of the accounts receivable with interest as they get paid. If for some reason, a biopharma company is concerned about its debtors' ability to pay on time, credit insurance covering accounts receivable might be an alternative to evaluate.

One important metric to consider in this respect is the accounts receivable turnover ratio, obtained by dividing net sales by average account receivables; that metric is used to measure how effective a business is at collecting debt and managing credit. The higher the ratio, the more adept the company is at managing credit. An accounts receivable turnover ratio for the biopharmaceutical industry is typically around 6. An accounts receivable turnover ratio of 6 translates to approximately 60 days of accounts receivable outstanding (the days receivable figure is calculated as 365 days divided by the ratio of 6). If customers are typically supposed to pay in 60 days (net 60 terms), that 60-day receivable figure corresponds to a performance many would qualify as particularly good.

References

2seventy bio. (2023, March 16). *Form 10-K for the Fiscal Year Ended December 31, 2022.* 2seventy bio. Retrieved 11/11/2024, from https://www.annualreports.com/HostedData/AnnualReportArchive/2/NASDAQ_TSVT_2022.pdf

Absci. (2023, March 30). *Form 10-K for the Fiscal Year Ended December 31,* 2022. Retrieved 11/11/2024, from https://www.sec.gov/Archives/edgar/data/1672688/000162828023014188/a202210k330asfiled2.pdf

Aljalahma, J., & Slof, J. (2022). An updated systematic review of business accelerators: Functions, operation, and gaps in the existing literature. *Journal of Open Innovation: Technology, Market, and Complexity, 8*(4), 214. https://doi.org/10.3390/joitmc8040214

Badertscher, B. A., Givoly, D., Katz, S. P., & Lee, H. (2019). Private ownership and the cost of public debt: Evidence from the bond market. *Management Science, 65*(1), 301–326. https://doi.org/10.1287/mnsc.2017.2935

Bauguess, S., Gullapalli, R., & Ivanov, V. (2018). *Capital Raising in the U.S.: An Analysis of the Market for Unregistered Securities Offerings, 2009–2017.* Washington D.C.: U.S. Securities and Exchange Commission. Division of Economic and Risk Analysis. https://www.sec.gov/files/dera-white-paper_regulation-d_082018.pdf

BCRF. (2018, January 25). *Grant Guidelines.* Retrieved 11/9/2024, from https://www.bcrf.org/grant-guidelines/

Bellucci, A., Gucciardi, G., & Nepelski, D. (2021). Venture capital in Europe. Evidence-based insights about venture capitalists and venture capital-backed firms. (KJ-NA-30480-EN-N (online)) https://doi.org/10.2760/076298

bluebird bio. (2021, January 11). *bluebird bio to Separate Oncology Business into Independent Company.* bluebird bio. Retrieved 11/11/2024, from https://investor.bluebirdbio.com/news-releases/news-release-details/bluebird-bio-separate-oncology-business-independent-company

Booth, B. (2018, February 26). *Grey Hair in the C-Suite: Experience, Age, and IPOs in Biotech.* Life Sci VC. Retrieved 7/30/2023, from https://lifescivc.com/2018/02/grey-hair-c-suite-experience-age-ipos-biotech/

Chang, L. (2022, February 15). *State of Private Markets: Q4 2021 and Year in Review.* Carta. Retrieved 7/27/2023, from https://carta.com/blog/state-of-private-markets-report-q4-2021/

Congressional Research Service. (2023a). *In Focus - Introduction to Financial Services: Capital Markets.* In Focus. https://sgp.fas.org/crs/misc/IF11062.pdf
Congressional Research Service. (2023b). *In Focus - Venture Capital Operations and Regulation.* https://crsreports.congress.gov/: In Focus. https://sgp.fas.org/crs/misc/IF12412.pdf
Davidson, A., Roberts, P. W., Guttentag, M., & Hume, V. (2021). *A Rocket or a Runway? Examining Venture Growth during and after Acceleration.* GALI. https://www.galidata.org/assets/report/pdf/Rocket%20or%20Runway_EN.pdf
de Lange, D., & Valliere, D. (2020). Sustainable firms and legitimacy: Corporate venture capital as an effective endorsement. *Journal of Small Business Management, 58*(6), 1187–1220. https://doi.org/10.1080/00472778.2019.1681880
Dokomajilar, C. (2023, April 3). Biopharma Deals and Funding Trends – Review of 2022 and Updates through Q1 2023. https://dealforma.com/blog/biopharma-deals-and-funding-trends-review-of-2022-and-updates-through-q1-2023/
Drover, W., Busenitz, L., Matusik, S., Townsend, D., Anglin, A., & Dushnitsky, G. (2017). A review and road map of entrepreneurial equity financing research: Venture capital, corporate venture capital, angel investment, Crowdfunding, and Accelerators. *Journal of Management, 43*(6), 1820–1853. https://doi.org/10.1177/0149206317690584
Elmhirst, E., & Brown, A. (2023, March 8). *Evaluate Vantage - The Ink Dries on the Blank Cheque Craze.* Retrieved 9/3/2023, from https://www.evaluate.com/vantage/articles/insights/other-data/ink-dries-blank-cheque-craze
Godfrey, P. C., Allen, G. N., & Benson, D. (2020). The biotech living and the walking dead. *Nature Biotechnology, 38*(2), 132–141. https://doi.org/10.1038/s41587-019-0399-1
Hall, B., & Lerner, J. (2009). The financing of R&D and innovation. *Handbook of the Economics of Innovation, 1.* https://doi.org/10.3386/w15325
Jacobs, T. (2006). Biotech buybacks—good or bad? *Nature Biotechnology, 24*(10), 1207. https://doi.org/10.1038/nbt1006-1207
Li, X., Liu, T., & Taylor, L. A. (2023). Common ownership and innovation efficiency. *Journal of Financial Economics, 147*(3), 475–497. https://doi.org/10.1016/j.jfineco.2022.12.004
Lo, A. W., & Thakor, R. T. (2023). Financial intermediation and the funding of biomedical innovation: A review. *Journal of Financial Intermediation, 54,* 101028. https://doi.org/10.1016/j.jfi.2023.101028
Melchner von Dydiowa, G., van Deventer, S., & Couto, D. S. (2021). How large pharma impacts biotechnology startup success. *Nature Biotechnology, 39*(3), 266–269. https://doi.org/10.1038/s41587-021-00821-x
Moody's. (2022, May 24). *Moody's Investors Service - Ratings & Regulatory - Ratings Definitions.* Retrieved 9/11/2023, from https://ratings.moodys.com/rating-definitions
Morrison, C. (2022). No shortage of fresh IPO capital in 2021. *Nature Reviews. Drug Discovery,* 21(2). https://doi.org/10.1038/d41573-022-00018-0
National Institutes of Health. (2022, December). *NIH Grants Policy Statement.* Retrieved 8/4/2023, from https://grants.nih.gov/grants/policy/nihgps/nihgps.pdf

NIH. (2019, December 30). *Illustrated Application and Grant Timelines.* Retrieved 9/14/2023, from https://www.niaid.nih.gov/grants-contracts/timelines-illustrated

NIH. (2023, February). *Research Project Grants: Competing Applications, Awards, and Success Rates.* Retrieved 9/14/2023, from https://report.nih.gov/nihdatabook/report/20

Quas, A., Mason, C., Compañó, R., Gavigan, J., & Testa, G. (2021). *Tackling the Scale-Up Gap.* (No. JRC127232). Luxembourg: European Commission - Joint Research Centre. 10.2760/982079 https://publications.jrc.ec.europa.eu/repository/handle/JRC127232

Rivera, L., Jain, A., Iserin, G., Pak, S., Vallee, I., & Chan, J. (2021). *BCG & INSEAD - Corporate Venture Capital. How CVCs Contribute to Corporate Strategy. How CVCs Affect Deals and Exits. Key Learnings for Successful CVCs.* INSEAD. https://www.insead.edu/sites/default/files/assets/dept/centres/gpei/docs/corporate-venture-capital.pdf

Roberts, P., & Kempner, R. (2017, October 2). Startup accelerators have become more popular in emerging markets — and they're working. *Harvard Business Review,* https://hbr.org/2017/10/startup-accelerators-have-become-more-popular-in-emerging-marketsand-theyre-working

S&P Global Ratings. (2023, June 9). *S&P Global Ratings Definitions.* Retrieved 9/11/2023, from https://disclosure.spglobal.com/ratings/en/regulatory/article/-/view/sourceId/504352

Sanofi. (2023a, February 13). *Provention Bio Announces Completion of $35 Million Equity Investment from Sanofi US.* Retrieved 11/9/2024, from https://www.news.sanofi.us/2023-02-13-Provention-Bio-Announces-Completion-of-35-Million-Equity-Investment-from-Sanofi-US

Sanofi. (2023b, March 13). *Sanofi to Acquire Provention Bio, Adding to Portfolio TZIELD, the First Disease-Modifying Treatment for the Delay of Stage 3 Type* 1 *Diabetes (T1D).* Retrieved 11/9/2024, from https://www.sanofi.com/en/media-room/press-releases/2023/2023-03-13-06-00-00-2625367

Schwartz, P., Wright, J., Beeler, M. & Simon, A. (2022, November 16). *Your Guide to Synthetic Drug Royalty Dealmaking.* Covington & Burling LLP. Retrieved 9/12/2023, from https://www.cov.com/-/media/files/corporate/publications/2022/11/your-guide-to-synthetic-drug-royalty-dealmaking.pdf

Shuwaikh, F., & Dubocage, E. (2022). Access to the corporate investors' complementary resources: A leverage for innovation in biotech venture capital-backed companies. *Technological Forecasting and Social Change, 175,* 121374. https://doi.org/10.1016/j.techfore.2021.121374

Singh, M., Rocafort, R., Cai, C., Siah, K. W., & Lo, A. W. (2022). The reaction of sponsor stock prices to clinical trial outcomes: An event study analysis. *PloS One, 17*(9), e0272851. https://doi.org/10.1371/journal.pone.0272851

Sohl, J. (2024, July 3). *The Angel Market in 2023: An Inflection Point for Women Angels?* Retrieved 11/9/2024, from https://www.eban.org/wp-content/uploads/2024/07/2023-Full-Year-Analysis-Report-Final.pdf

Sohn, E. (2019). Secrets to writing a winning grant. *Nature, 577*(7788), 133–135. https://doi.org/10.1038/d41586-019-03914-5

U.S. Securities and Exchange Commission. (2021, May 25). *Investor Alerts and Bulletins: What You Need to Know About SPACs – Updated Investor Bulletin.* Retrieved 9/3/2023, from https://www.sec.gov/oiea/investor-alerts-and-bulletins/what-you-need-know-about-spacs-investor-bulletin

U.S. Securities and Exchange Commission. (2023, June 22). *What Does the SEC Have to Do With My Private Company?* Retrieved 9/12/2023, from https://www.sec.gov/education/capitalraising/building-blocks/sec-have-do-my-private-company

Vasileva, D., Norton, L., Hurlbert, M., & Lo, A. W. (2019). *Measuring the Economic and Academic Impact of Philanthropic Funding.* SSRN. https://doi.org/10.2139/ssrn.3395019

von Hippel, T., & von Hippel, C. (2015). To apply or not to apply: A survey analysis of grant writing costs and benefits. *PloS One, 10*(3), e0118494. https://doi.org/10.1371/journal.pone.0118494

Y Combinator. (2013, June 11). *Y Combinator - Make Something People Want.* Retrieved 11/9/2024, from https://www.ycombinator.com/

Chapter 6

Pitching Your Company

Several years ago, one of the authors' colleagues (let's call him Jack to maintain anonymity) cynically used "going rodeo" to qualify the back and forth personally experienced (for as long as the business unit leader is able to last) in public companies between corporate and business units during budget discussions. Jack's mordant analogy pointed out one of the fundamental rules when pitching a business proposal or direction: if you do not manage to keep control or if you have not developed the right reactions to changes in direction, you are very unlikely to stay on top and win! And in Jack's environment, staying on top, rather than being ignored or worse treated as a "sandbagger", was indeed important to receive more achievable financial performance objectives. Perhaps more importantly, as may be the case with such financial proceedings, the "Go Rodeo" session was another chance for Jack (and other leaders) at a story narrative to demonstrate his passion for a specific business direction and convince the corporate executive team of its legitimacy in a way that would otherwise be lost through a sheer financial budget or analysis.

We felt such "go rodeo" analogy might apply well to the many intensely experienced company pitch presentations biopharma leadership teams need to make to investors and other parties.

Regardless of the context in which a biopharma company leadership needs to pitch their ideas and business (be it to VC for a new Series, to institutional investors for an IPO roadshow or a 506b private placement, to banks for debt issuance or convertible debt, to a grant organization committee, or simply to a potential partner), there are some common practices and considerations they should leverage.

And while many of these might seem somewhat obvious in hindsight, the authors have been repeatedly surprised at the overwhelming proportion of otherwise brilliant entrepreneurs they have met in the biopharma space that did not (initially) avail themselves of such practices and considerations during their startup phase.

DOI: 10.4324/9781003598046-6

The importance of developing an effective pitch is arguably reflected by the astronomical number of seminars, training, and online references available on this topic.

Authors' Favorite Online Search Tool

Search > business pitch training

About 118,000,000 results (0.42 seconds)

And even though some lessons can be learned the hard way during "Go Rodeo" sessions, the authors felt it useful to devote a small chapter on the topic of company pitches.

Given the extensive number, and wide variety, of references on pitches, it is humanly impossible to follow them all, notwithstanding the fact that some of them might simply not align perfectly with one another. Ultimately, the biopharma company's leadership team needs to find an approach that works for them, a storyline that they can deliver with aplomb, and an iterative process that allows them to test new approaches, keep learning, and improve.

There are two main types of pitches we will discuss: a very brief one, typically referred to as an elevator pitch, covered in the next section, and a longer one, typically referred to as a presentation, or simply pitch, discussed thereafter. Depending on circumstances, a short pitch may not be needed (e.g., IPO roadshow).

6.1 Elevator Pitch

A business elevator pitch is a very brief speech used to get your business noticed for its potential. The name was derived from delivering it in the time taken by an elevator ride with someone. The rules for an elevator pitch can be deceptively simple: you have to be compelling and spark interest in your audience in the limited time allotted.

To spark interest, the pitch will typically need to be tailored to your audience, be it a potential investor, a prospective colleague, or a prospective partner. Ideally, your elevator pitch will be a prompt to (the anticipated) action for your intended audience.

Given their short delivery imperative, elevator pitches typically benefit from being simple and unique in order to be memorable by most. Expected durations typically range from 30 seconds to a couple of minutes, with possibly a few more minutes if your audience asks you to elaborate further. In the authors' experience, presenting a concise and attractive overview of a business is harder to pull off, and more effective, than longer elevator pitches. We will thus use a 30-second duration by default for elevator pitches. A shorter duration may also give the presenter greater control over the information retained by their audience.

Riding a one-ton bucking bull		Delivering an elevator pitch
Understand the rules! The performance should last at least 8 seconds without touching the bull or equipment with free hand.	⟹	Understand the rules! The performance should last at most 30 seconds and strike a chord with your audience.
Lasting longer will score you points.	⟹	Being quicker will score you points.
Minimal gear required. Wear the basic gear!	⟹	No materials required. Dress the part!
Understand how scoring works! Maximum score is 100 points: 2 judges with 50 points each, 25 for level of difficulty and 25 for skills.	⟹	Understand how scoring works! Score is one single point – being invited to discuss further – regardless of the number of judges, difficulty, or skills.
Learn from experienced riders. Develop strength.	⟹	Learn from experienced pitchers. Develop strengths.
You don't just hold on for dear life: train to perfect your technique!	⟹	You don't just hold on for dear life: train to perfect your technique!

Figure 6.1 Elevator pitch lessons from bull-riding.

Being able to deliver an elevator pitch for the company is a standard leadership expectation. Below are a few additional thoughts on the matter (Figure 6.1), derived by analogy to bull-riding (Valdez, 2010; wikiHow, 2020), an activity that also requires intense training and is sometimes depicted as the most dangerous eight seconds in sport (Valdez, 2010; wikiHow, 2020).

6.2 Pitch Story Components

We already discussed the importance of stories, and how to organize and present them, at the beginning of the book, in Chapter 1. It is an aspect we cannot emphasize enough – notice we used the term "story" in this section heading here as well!

There are countless books and articles on what investors may want or not want in a pitch or presentation. They may come as a list with some random number in front of it (e.g., the 23 "stuffs" you need in your pitch), be organized in a somewhat clever framework (e.g., "ABC" of pitches for Anchored with a story, Based on facts, and Compelling offering), or simply be presented as a prescriptive recipe (e.g., the 11 "tenets" of pitch presentations).

The authors' only recommendation in that respect would be simply to keep an open mind: if you find an approach that resonates with you and that resists the acid test of experience (meaning you do well in terms of pitch outcomes), just use that. If you find that the "23 stuffs" should really be a list of "9 stuffs" in your case, just adapt it accordingly and as needed until it becomes your own and resists the experience test!

The audience might be made of risk-takers or risk-avoiders but generally speaking to get to the level where a company seeks them out to invest, they typically have had a number of successes under their belt and stand to lose both capital and face if they make a predictably unsavory investment with your company. They will thus be looking out for signs, even gut feelings, which might later, in hindsight, constitute indicators of a poor company bet.

6.2.1 *Points That Undermine Pitch Credibility*

Before even getting into major narrative aspects, to avoid opening themselves to unwarranted hasty judgment, there are some basic "blocking and tackling" aspects presenters ought to consider irrespective of any audience. These points might include the following non-exhaustive list, distilled from suboptimal biopharma startup pitches.

- Avoid using acronyms or jargon unless you are absolutely sure every single person in your audience will understand the acronym correctly.
- Show your energy and enthusiasm for your company, especially at the beginning to provide a high note.
- Understand the rules of engagement: if you have not worked directly in your audience's world, seek the advice and perspective of people who did so you understand how your message might come across, what might be missing, and what might need to be removed or changed.
- Make your message and story as clear, consistent, and simple as possible so it is easy to follow for anyone. In the author's experience, biopharma startups that execute pitches well are those companies that have managed to distill the usual complexity of their solutions and processes to an easily understood solution.

> From *The Art of Poetry* (1674)
> by Nicolas Boileau-Despréaux
> "Ce qui se conçoit bien s'énonce clairement et les mots pour le dire arrivent aisément."
> (Whatever is well conceived is clearly said, and the words to say it flow with ease.)

- Ensure the solution works for the market considered and its specific stakeholders (e.g., the advantages and commercial approach suitable for a single-payer European market may not readily translate into a multi-payer environment like the United States).
- If your pitch includes a presentation document, ensure it meets the ART (Accessibility, Readability, Transparency) requirements – see below.

Accessibility

- Ensure contact information is included and extremely easy to access (phone number and email typically at the beginning) – do not bury it in the middle!
- For electronic documents, make it easy to locate by including the company name in the filename (and perhaps the presenter's last name and date as well).
- Footnote your sources so they can easily be found in case someone has a different set of numbers or perspective. Ensure your sources are credible.

Readability

- Proofread for typos and spelling – sometimes it is helpful to have someone new look at it with fresh eyes.
- Formatting – use legible fonts and appropriate font sizes to ensure a crisp and clear document. Limit the number of bullet points to a manageable number (e.g., 2–5).
- Do not crowd the slides or document sections. You typically do not need every single detail or technicality – instead, you can reference other documents.
- Only use graphics that contribute to your story rather than detract from it, even if it is a "pretty picture".
- Go back through each slide or document section to validate that you have been as concise as possible.

Transparency

- Only use charts that are intelligible without deep technical expertise. That usually means having a meaningful header, tied to your storyline, as opposed to a purely scientific header (e.g., a chemical concentration evolution).
- Try to be fact-based as often as possible. As an example, if a proposed solution is more effective, justify it with one compelling data point or fact so you avoid a debate in the mind of your audience or in the room. Again, you do not need every single detail here either – just the most expedient to quickly support your point without any time for debate (internal or otherwise).

Issues exemplified in the list above often stem from the incredible time pressures biopharma startups and executives are under. Ultimately, thinking through as simple and logical an approach as possible will typically make stronger impressions but also save time by limiting the message to practice, limiting the number of slides or pages to review, and reducing the questions to field at a later date. Investing in planning upfront might very well pay off down the road.

Now that we have covered the basic blocking and tackling, let us go over typical information to cover in a biopharma company pitch. Unfortunately, a large majority of the biopharma firms we have seen had pitches that were missing key information or took forever before clearly, if at all, painting a picture of what they do and why it made sense. Below are the key pieces of information the authors like to see as concisely and as quickly as possible in a pitch or presentation (more or less in the following sequence).

- Company purpose – brief company overview in one sentence or insights on why the company was created.
- Problems, challenges, and pain points the company addresses.
- Solution(s) offered by company – who receives what value or benefit?
- Why does this make sense for the current market?
- Market – what is this worth? Who will pay for what in each of the specific markets considered?
- Competition versus your unique selling points – What is it that they missed? What traction or validation have you already demonstrated?
- Business model, intellectual property, barriers to entry – what makes your business model sustainable against competition? Have you established and justified clear revenue streams?
- Team – what makes you uniquely qualified to tackle this and why the team can hack it.
- Revenue and financial model.
- Clear investment requirements (e.g., budget time and steps to the next value inflection point) and exit options.
- Company timeline with a clear future vision and key value inflection points (tied to investments).

While the points above might be considered to be generic since applicable across various industries, for each point, there are specific biopharma aspects to include when relevant, e.g.:

- Company purpose.
  - Are there specific aspects of the company's purpose, such as therapeutic areas, current stage, or business model that align well with investors' specific focus and should be emphasized?

- Solution(s) offered by company.
  - Value and benefits may not be strictly limited to patients: consider the 5 P's of healthcare: patients, physicians, providers, payers, and partners.
- Why this makes sense for current market:
  - Does it improve greatly upon standard of care?
  - Are there specific patient populations that should be targeted as a priority?
  - Has the company received noteworthy external validations (e.g., publications, conference presentations, industry awards, and recognition)?
- Market.
  - Is the market size significant enough (e.g., large size or suitable orphan drug)?
  - Are there significant unmet needs?
  - Can epidemiology measures (such as incidence and prevalence rates) meaningfully serve as indicators of the market value?
- Competition versus your unique selling points.
  - When dealing with complex scientific aspects, are there simplifications or analogies or even graphics that might help clarity?
  - What preclinical and clinical data (safety, efficacy, benefits) can support the case?
- Business model.
  - What patents, trademark, and proprietary technologies has the company already secured? When early in the process, what steps have already been taken?
  - Has the company already established strategically significant collaborations or licensing deals with payments or royalties?
- Team and ecosystem.
  - Does the team (management, board, advisers) include Key Opinion Leaders for the therapeutic area and indications considered?
  - Does the company have privileged access to a scientific ecosystem, hub, cluster (e.g., university, institutional organizations)?
- Financial model.
  - Will the R&D run rate reinforce recognition by being in line with standard R&D timing per stage as well as with industry averages and expectations both in dollar terms and percentage of total company burn rate?

- Are there specific functional projections important to mention given modality and therapeutic area (e.g., staying away from areas representing high protocol uncertainty and lack of adequate biomarkers, avoiding prohibitive and non-scalable manufacturing approaches that would compromise downstream commercial potential)?

- Investment requirements and exit options.
  - What research outcomes and clinical development milestones does each funding step take the company to? How do the various steps increase the overall probability of success?
  - Are there relevant comparable valuations or recent transactions worth mentioning for this specific therapeutic area, platform, or modality?
- Company timeline.
  - How does this relate to the intended regulatory process, pathway, and milestones?
  - Has the company established partnerships indicative of scientific validation and potential company acquisition interests?

6.3 Audience Viewpoints

In addition to varying cultural perspectives, in the context of business pitches, audiences normally come with specific viewpoints tied to their profession or investment profile. To convince investors, a company should cover the aspects required by the audience to make an informed decision, especially if that decision is to be positive.

Aspects important to potential investors might include upfront filters (e.g., some funds might invest principally in certain therapeutic areas or only at certain company stages) as well as performance metrics they will be looking to ascertain.

Upfront filters can be helpful to ensure that the company has the right audience to start with (e.g., for a VC, does the company fit with their usual investment mandates, criteria, portfolio, and track record).

Performance metrics can be helpful to ensure that the company incorporates favorable underlying data or information in its presentation. Below are selected examples of key performance metrics from an investor's viewpoint.

- Equity financing.
  - Return on Equity (ROE) – ROE is the ratio of net income by the average shareholder's equity.
  - Internal Rate of Return (IRR) – see definition in Chapter 2. An IRR above 30% might be favorable for a high-risk investment.

- Cash-on-cash Return (CoC). CoC is simply the amount of money the investor gets after exit divided by the amount of money invested. It is often expressed as a multiple (e.g., 50×).
- Multiple Of Invested Capital (MOIC). MOIC is similar to CoC and it is the ratio of the total value (realized and unrealized) by the initial investment.

- Debt financing.
  - Debt Service Coverage Ratio (DSCR). DSCR is the ratio of net operating income to the total annual debt service (principal and interest payments). Figures above 1.25 are typically considered strong.
  - Loan-To-Value Ratio (LTV). LTV is the ratio of a loan by the underlying asset or collateral value. Figures below 0.8 are typically considered good.
  - Interest Coverage Ratio (ICR). ICR is the ratio of the company's earnings before interest and taxes (EBIT) to its interest expense for the period. A ratio of 2 is typically acceptable while 3 or above is typically preferred.
  - Debt to Equity Ratio (D/E). D/E is simply the ratio of the company's financial liabilities to the total shareholder equity. A D/E below 1.0 is typically good.
  - Debt to Enterprise Value (D/EV). D/EV is simply the ratio of the company's financial liabilities to the enterprise value. D/EV is sometimes used instead of D/E. Enterprise value is calculated as total shareholder equity + total debt – cash and cash equivalent.

Performance metrics used by potential investors can normally be found in their annual reports, performance reports, or marketing information, or alternatively equivalent materials produced by competitive firms. For a loss-making venture-backed biopharma company, focus might typically be on IRR, CoC, and MOIC offered by exit options.

6.4 Cultural Awareness

When pitching a business, biopharma leaders need to be aware of the country's expectations or regional paradigms for the location in which they are pitching so they can adapt their approach accordingly. While globalization has had convergence effects, differences might still remain. There are facets of a pitch that may be dependent on the cultural context such as:

- Presentation lead time.
- Investor-independent review time.
- Pitch length.
- Sequence of presentation components.
- Formality and interactivity.

- Body language.
- Expectations on forecast aggressiveness.
- Contextual and relative references (e.g., US budgets might be larger than those in a single European country, use of audience-specific units can be important such as using yen for a Japanese audience).
- Pitch feedback positive or negative emphasis.

Depending on the country, the pitch audience may have different ways to establish business relationships, different decision-making approaches, and different thought processes.

Let us take the case of two countries where individuals in one country typically feel knowledgeable about the other country: United States and France, even though they might not always be aware of the cultural differences involved. Establishing a connection in the United States tends to be based on transactional activities with direct explicit communications compared with relationships evolving over time with implied understanding in France. The United States tends to be a lot more individualistic in contrast to arguably more pronounced group identities in France. Likewise, a US environment will be more risk-tolerant than France in making decisions. Similarly, a French thought process will be likely to be more conceptual and context-dependent than the US counterpart. On average, pitch delivery in France will be as calm, modest, and neutral as it will be enthusiastic, confident, and positive in the United States. Finally, feedback in a French environment will be much less emphatic than its US equivalent: a French "it is not bad" ("ce n'est pas mal" in French) might correspond to a US "it is amazing".

Being culturally aware is essential when pitching internationally – using the examples above, it is important for a French presenter in the United States to be overly enthusiastic and positive compared with normal, to avoid coming across as lacking both confidence and interest. Correspondingly, an American presenter in France might want to tone down the positive and the enthusiasm not to be perceived as hypocritical and overexcited. The cultural differences might be so pronounced in some cases that it might take an entire book to provide a solid perspective – there is for instance a book on France comprising over 200 pages devoted to this topic: "Au Contraire! Figuring Out The French" (Asselin & Mastron, 2010).

If the company does not already have individuals in-house that can guide through a specific cultural context, it is advisable to run the pitch approach and content by someone who can.

6.5 Legal Caveats

Like for any correspondence dealing with information that could be considered an offering or linked to an offering, it is important to understand the legal framework within which the company is operating when making a pitch.

For instance:

- Which acts, regulations, or other legal limitations might govern what you are allowed to present or say?
- Are there multiple jurisdictions to consider (e.g., Federal and State in the United States)? Are there potential or adverse implications under additional jurisdictions and contexts?
- Are there restrictions on the audiences you are allowed to present to (e.g., accredited investors only, in-state investors only)?
- Are there documents, agreements, or information you need to obtain from your audience, perhaps before the presentation (e.g., US Regulation D Rule 506 c)?
- Are there any registrations, qualifications, disclosures, submissions, or publications required for what you intend to present, prior to or after the presentation?
- Are there restrictions on what you can present (e.g., IPO roadshows) or time periods during which you are not allowed to present?
- Even if you are free to present any information you want, is the company exposed to potential liabilities as a result, vis-à-vis the audience or others outside the audience?
- Are there safe harbor clauses the company can leverage and what requirements need to be fulfilled in that context?
- What legal disclaimers and requirements, if any, should be included or factored in your pitch?
- Does the company carry sufficient and appropriate insurance coverage in the context of company pitches (e.g., liability, directors, and officers)?

These are essential matters to bear in mind – in the United States, as explained by the SEC, even when a registration is not required,

> the government enforces the federal securities laws through criminal, civil and administrative proceedings. Private parties also can bring actions under certain securities laws. Also, if all conditions of the exemptions are not met, purchasers may be able to return their securities and obtain a refund of their purchase price.
>
> (U.S. Securities and Exchange Commission, 2023)

On a related note, unless helpful to your audience, including legal language in a pitch when it is not required and not customary may generate negative perceptions in your audience.

Below are illustrative legal considerations for inclusion in relation to business pitches:

- Confidentiality – this might be helpful in connection with intellectual property and trade secrets. Another related consideration is a prior non-disclosure agreement.
- Investment advice – this might be helpful (as disclaimer) if there is an unwanted possibility that your pitch be considered as investment advice.
- Forward-looking statements – this might be helpful for example to avoid potential future claims and explains that there are risks and uncertainties, that results might vary from what is presented, etc.
- Legal disclaimer – this might be helpful to try and avoid, under certain circumstances, having the pitch be construed as a legally binding agreement and make the company liable as a result.

As illustrated above, it is important to consult a legal professional if the company is not sure of the legal restrictions and protections it should take into account.

Disclaimer: this section and this book do not constitute professional advice. The information is illustrative and general in nature, based on the authors' understanding and is written for informational purposes only. The content provided is not intended as, and does not constitute, legal or financial advice, nor a source thereof, nor is it a solicitation to offer legal or financial advice, and no attorney–client relationship is formed. This book should not be used as a substitute for the advice of a competent attorney authorized to practice in your jurisdiction nor as a substitute for the advice of a competent financial adviser. The publisher and the authors make no warranties, no guarantee, no other promises, as to any results, financial, legal, or otherwise, that may be obtained from using this book. To the maximum extent permitted by law, the publisher and the authors disclaim any and all liability in the event any information, commentary, analysis, opinions, advice, and/or recommendations contained in this book prove to be inaccurate, incomplete, or unreliable, or result in any investment or other losses. The publisher and the authors are providing this book and its contents on an "as is" basis. Your use of the information in this book is at your own risk.

6.6 Back Pocket Materials

We designate as "back pocket materials" those extra notes, presentation slides, links, or information, you can pull out and use with little to no advance notice, such as slides you might include just in case at the end of a presentation but not present unless needed.

Depending on the audience the company is pitching to, presenters might want to come prepared with background materials to leverage for questions or during follow-up discussions.

Investment considerations typically fall into three key categories:

- Economic terms (valuation, dividends, conversion, anti-dilution, liquidation preference).
- Control terms (board representation, participation rights, employee retention, etc.).
- Exit terms (co-sale, drag, redemption, registration rights).

For VC discussions, the pitch team might want to be prepared with a typical term sheet they might be looking to negotiate – see Chapter 7.

6.7 Conclusion – Something to Remember You By

A company's pitch might be one among many such pitches when the VC companies in the audience might have received several thousand pitch decks in a year and seen a couple hundred in person. In such a situation, making sure a company is memorable is a critical success requirement.

Getting into a pitch, the company's presenter should have a strategy on how the pitch will be memorable, e.g.

- Markman (2015) suggests building ways to affect the audience and give them opportunities to think about the presentation content.
- While speakers should still look and sound natural in their pitch, there is data suggesting (Morett & Fraundorf, 2019) that gestures and voice contrasts impact memory of what is said. Using voice contrast and gestures to emphasize critical words the audience should remember from the pitch can thus help with recall. This aligns with previous research, including Zant and Berger (2019), which found that communicators who speak louder and vary their volume convey confidence, thereby enhancing persuasion.
- Use a bull-riding analogy so people remember to practice and keep pitches short! ☺ 🐂

Grit is another "must have" quality when seeking financing – as VC companies reject the vast majority of pitches they see, they end up saying no very often and do so very quickly. Facing quick rejections is thus something to be expected. Even when invited to pitch in person, the vast majority of companies still get rejected.

When it comes to business pitches, there are more books and references than we could list here, and not all of them necessarily consistent – which is one of the reasons we intentionally kept this chapter short and encouraged readers to keep an open mind. With that caveat, below are three references with very different perspectives that readers in search of additional background materials on pitches may find interesting.

- Klaff, O. (2011). *Pitch Anything: An Innovative Method for Presenting, Persuading, and Winning the Deal* (1st ed.) McGraw-Hill.
    - Written with an investment banker's style and perspectives, this book has a relatively unique pitch framework drawn from the author's experience and may provide contrasting views on how to pitch.
- Coughter, P. (2012). *The Art of the Pitch: Persuasion and Presentation Skills That Win Business* (2012th ed.) Palgrave Macmillan.
    - Written in a conversational style from the perspective of an ad agency.
- McGowan, B., & Bowman, A. (2016). *Pitch Perfect: How to Say It Right the First Time, Every Time* (Reprint ed.) Harper Business.
    - Written from a general communication perspective and organized around a number of principles to observe.

Lastly, never waste an opportunity to learn, e.g., even if the investor says "no", ask if there is anything that would get them to "yes" and whom they can think of that might say "yes".

References

Asselin, G., & Mastron, R. (2010). *Au Contraire! Figuring Out the French.* (2nd ed.). Nicholas Brealey Publishing.

Markman, A. (2015, September 21). Getting an audience to remember your presentation. *Harvard Business Review.* https://hbr.org/2015/09/getting-an-audience-to-remember-your-presentation

Morett, L. M., & Fraundorf, S. H. (2019). Listeners consider alternative speaker productions in discourse comprehension and memory: Evidence from beat gesture and pitch accenting. *Memory & Cognition, 47*(8), 1515–1530. https://doi.org/10.3758/s13421-019-00945-1

U.S. Securities and Exchange Commission. (2023, April 6). *Frequently Asked Questions about Exempt Offerings - Do Anti-fraud Provisions Apply?* Retrieved 9/23/2023, from https://www.sec.gov/education/smallbusiness/exemptofferings/faq#faq1

Valdez, A. (2010, December). How to ride a bull. *TexasMonthly*. https://www.texasmonthly.com/the-culture/how-to-ride-a-bull/

wikiHow. (2020, October 19). How to ride a bull. *wikiHow*. Retrieved 10/19/2024, from https://www.wikihow.com/Ride-a-Bull

Zant, A., & Berger, J. (2019). How the voice persuades. *Journal of Personality and Social Psychology, 118*, 661. https://doi.org/10.1037/pspi0000193

Chapter 7

Understanding the Art of the Deal in Biopharma

When externally sourced new molecular entities represent two thirds of the total industry revenues (Berghauser Pont et al., 2022; 2021 data), successful deal-making is a critical competency to have. Making such deals, i.e., executing a transaction to exchange interest or ownership in assets or companies in exchange for financial and in-kind values, is a complex multidimensional endeavor, often conducted under time constraints. Although processes and approaches to manage deals vary from company to company, Figures 7.1 and 7.2 illustrate that complexity, covering buy side and sell side, respectively (straight collaborations represent yet another model).

While deal-making uses many concepts discussed in Chapter 5 (Company Financing), the deal-making operational focus and strategic intent is markedly different from financing.

Deals are expectedly subject to supply and demand as well as evolving market dynamics. Unmet needs in therapeutic areas with adequate demographics will tend to result in higher valuation, especially with clinically well-tolerated and efficacious newer technologies with a long remaining patent life. Deal value, measured by shareholder returns, depends on therapeutic

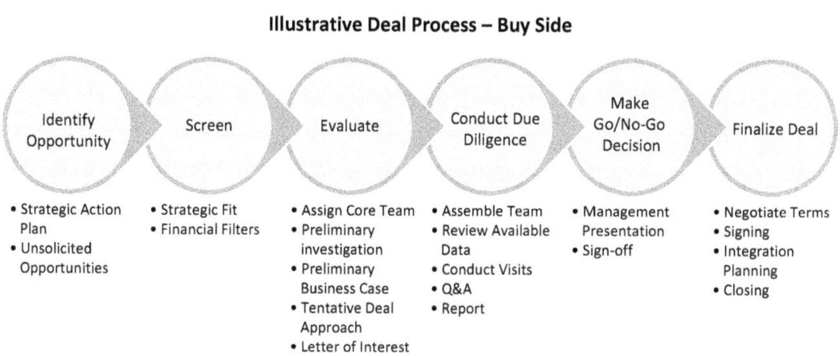

Figure 7.1 Illustrative deal process – buy side.

DOI: 10.4324/9781003598046-7

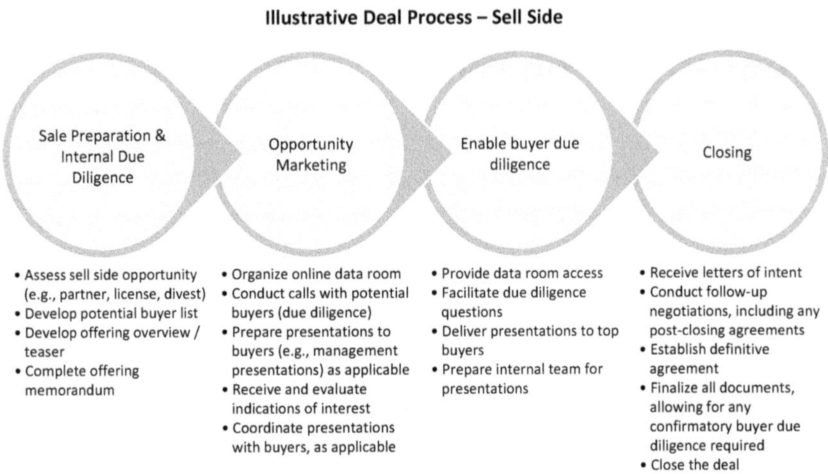

Figure 7.2 Illustrative deal process – sell side.

area, clinical considerations, and strategic development approaches used. US and EU company acquisition data showed certain indications (e.g., oncology with its characteristically high demand for drug innovation) are valued significantly higher at later development stages (Michaeli et al., 2022). Similarly, orphan-designated drugs or multiple indication drugs represent higher returns (Michaeli et al., 2022).

The drug lifecycle also plays a significant role on deal returns for the buyer: deals made by large pharmaceutical companies for early-stage assets may provide for higher returns than late-stage assets (Wang et al., 2022). Recent years appear to feature an increasing percentage of early-stage deals in outperforming deals (Berghauser Pont et al., 2022).

7.1 General Concepts

7.1.1 Deal Team

The deal team is a group of individuals assembled to define, negotiate, and execute a transaction on one side of the negotiation table (buy side, sell side, or one of the two collaboration sides). It is common for a deal team to include a combination of internal members (e.g., executives, functional experts) and external members (e.g., bankers, lawyers, consultants, subject matter experts).

The constitution and effort intensity of the deal team depend on the nature and specifics of the deal. While some functions tend to be systematic deal team pillars (e.g., corporate development, legal, IP, finance), other functions might play a less pronounced role depending on circumstances (e.g., commercial operations will require stronger involvement for a marketed

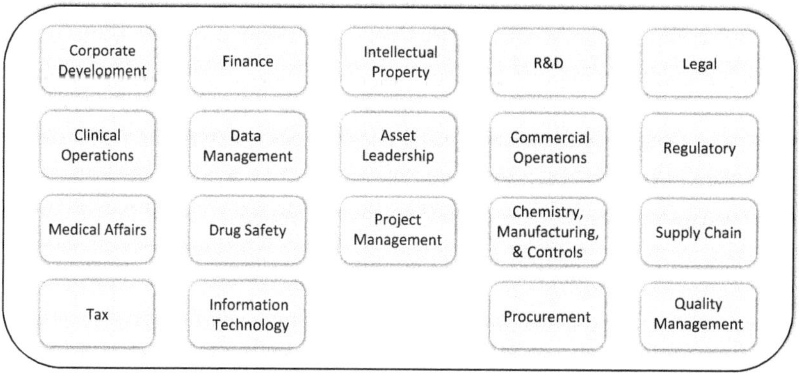

Figure 7.3 Possible biopharma deal team functional representation.

or even a Phase 2 drug than for early discovery compounds). Figure 7.3 provides an illustrative list of possible functions to be included as part of the deal team.

In addition, the composition of the deal team typically evolves over time in order to ensure efficient use of company resources. The time spent by, and the size of, the team is typically minimized early on when the deal's probability of going through is still low, increasing with the closing probability as well as the specificity of points to elucidate and clarify as part of the deal (typically in the due diligence and integration planning phases).

As a best practice, a deal leader (or "deal sponsor"), accountable for deal performance and empowered within the limits of the company's authority matrix (decisions are typically subject to board approval), is assigned to manage the efforts of the deal team. The deal leader (or by default, the main executive involved) defines and communicates deal objectives and expectations to the deal team. Objectives are multifaceted (e.g., scientific, strategic, financial, and operational) and outline how the deal will create value for the company. Expectations encompass a wide variety of aspects ranging from confidentiality, governance, or team processes, to success factors, budgets and deal costs tracking, work quality and reporting, resource allocations, timelines, schedules, and milestones.

Another common role, especially for larger deals, is that of the project manager working under the deal leader to monitor progress and facilitate teamwork, including information submission and capture. For smaller opportunities, the project manager role is typically taken on by the deal leader. An experienced project manager will have a strong understanding of the various functions to involve in due diligence.

Each deal team member should clearly understand their role within the deal team, the team organization (e.g., so they can refer specific findings or concerns to the correct person), the deal context and objectives, aspects they are responsible for, including risks and challenges, as well as their specific deliverables. The more critical deliverables are to a deal's value, the more expertise and knowledge is expected of the team member; when such expertise is not readily available inside the company, external contractors are typically added to the deal team.

Case Example: Large Pharma Deal Team Approach

A large pharma company defined the following organization principles for deal teams:

- The business leader (e.g., Head of Oncology or Rare Diseases) impacted by the potential transaction designates the deal leader or "Sponsor" who will decide on the strategic interest of the transaction, supervise the transaction, and be accountable for its execution post-closing.
- Depending on the transaction type (company acquisition, acquisition of minority shares, licensing deal), a project manager will be assigned to the transaction. The project manager will typically be a specialized professional in the domain of business development or M&A, as appropriate, and will manage all aspects of the transaction tied to corporate development:
    - Relationships with the other party.
    - Due diligence organization.
    - Coordination of all functions involved.
    - Business valuation and deal terms structuring.
    - Opportunity presentation to internal governance committees.
    - Deal coordination and negotiations.
- The project manager assembles a team of internal and external functional experts as relevant to the characteristics of the transaction, with input or guidance from the deal leader. In addition to the project manager, core team members typically include legal and finance plus functions deemed critical to the evaluation:
    - A licensing deal related to an early-stage asset will involve scientific experts knowledgeable of innovative modalities, and the commercial aspects will be typically evaluated by new product planning experts.
    - A deal related to marketed products will involve commercial experts but may or may not involve R&D representatives.
    - The acquisition of shares in a biopharma company will require the support of corporate experts able to perform due diligence, valuation, and contractual activities.

7.1.2 *Due Diligence*

Due diligence refers to how a company will fulfill its duty of care by conducting a comprehensive appraisal of the relevant dimensions and aspects via various reviews, audits, and investigations, before proceeding with a transaction. It encompasses the various steps a savvy buyer would be expected to take before proceeding with a binding agreement. Typically, due diligence is conducted by appropriate experts, as illustrated by the possible deal team members in Figure 7.3.

Often functional leads use standard checklist for due diligence to cover the basics, using further discretion to investigate aspects specific to an opportunity. As they refine their understanding and views (Figure 7.4), functional leads will typically provide input back to the deal leader, the project manager, and other team members on:

- Recommendations and observations.
- Documents reviewed and interactions.
- Opportunities and value contributions to be considered.
- Specific expenses and risks to be considered.
- Concerns and issues uncovered, criticality, and potential mitigations.
- Information gaps remaining, outstanding questions, and suggested assignments as applicable.

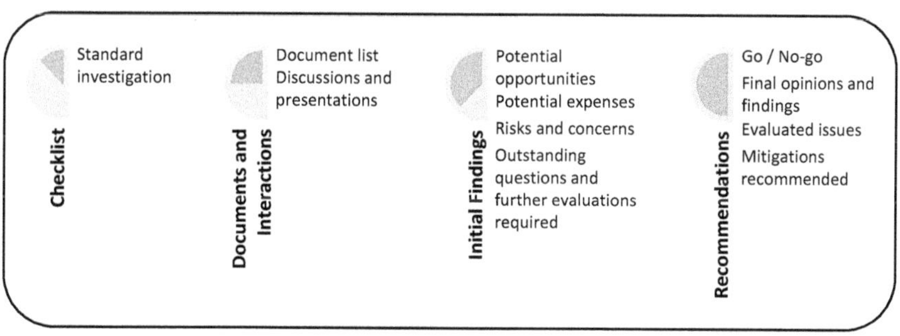

Figure 7.4 Buyer's due diligence – refinement of functional lead's perspective.

Functional due diligence checklists tend to differ from one company to the next as they cannot be exhaustive; they should, however, be sufficient for the general functional understanding expected by the company to effectively evaluate potential opportunities, issues, and risks.

Often, the buy-side deal leader will require the use of a standardized reporting template from all due diligence team members to make consolidation manageable as well as to ensure consistency and to ease sharing of findings with other team members. The deal leader will also make sure that each piece of information provided by the seller (e.g., virtual data room sections and documents) is reviewed by at least one due diligence team member.

7.1.3 *Deal Lifecycle*

A deal lifecycle (Figure 7.5) is typically measured in months (six months to a year is commonplace) and depends among others on the number of competitive parties involved in the process as well as on the sense of urgency of individual parties involved. Table 7.1 provides further factors that might influence the pace of a deal.

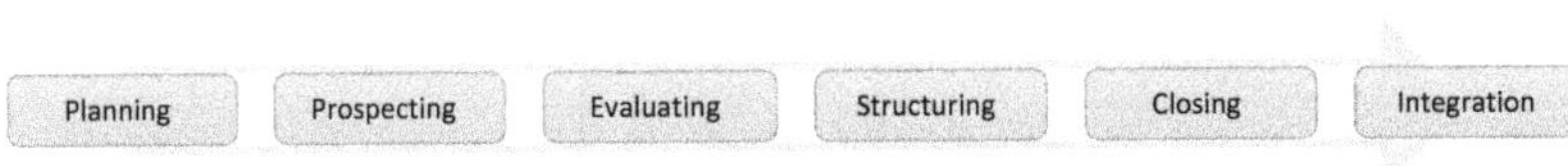

Figure 7.5 Deal lifecycle.

Table 7.1 Illustrative time factors for biopharma deals

Potential accelerators	*Potential decelerators*
• Experience of parties with deal-making. • Pre-existing trusted relationship or prior deals between involved parties. • Mutual understanding of other party's processes, templates, and sensitivity. • Well-organized virtual data room anticipating buyers' needs for an informed decision. • Competitive process (or perceived as competitive) with clearly communicated timeline and steps. • Specific deal rationale conveyed to other party. • Set of potential buyers with demonstrated intent, strategic fit for the opportunity, and solid deal track record. • "Bolt-on" nature of a deal. • High buyer interest and willingness to overpay.	• Undefined or uncommunicated process. • Large opportunity size. • Underlying complexity (e.g., complex intellectual property landscape, multiple markets and geographies, multiple indications). • Involved buyer's process (e.g., reproducing research parts or material transfer agreements). • Heterogeneous set of potential buyers. • Lack of seller's preparedness. • The seller is not spending sufficient time or effort to understand the buyers' position. • Regulatory uncertainty or approval requirements.

This said, both parties might be interested in moving things along. The buyer tries to eliminate from consideration as early as possible in the process those potential deals that will ultimately not be a fit. The seller tries to eliminate potential buyers that will ultimately prove not to be viable as early as possible in the process, unless they need them for the process, e.g., as a "rabbit" to bid on the proposed transaction and maintain a competitive situation for the targeted buyer(s).

7.1.4 *Deal Elements and Term Sheet*

Term sheet designates a non-binding document that provides the context and major elements of a deal or business transaction under discussion (Figure 7.6). It serves to negotiate and document mutual understanding between parties so the legal teams on each side can later capture the various aspects in a legally binding document. The deal elements themselves typically belong to one of three categories: economic, control, or process. Economic elements clarify the allocation of benefits from the deal, covering aspects such as purchase price or working capital. Control elements help define decision approaches over certain activities in the context of the transaction such as information rights or board seats. Lastly, process elements guide the manner in which the deal may evolve such as closing conditions

TERM SHEET AND DEAL ELEMENTS

This term sheet provides the main terms regarding the acquisition of ____________________

[term sheet context, parties involved, and deal structure added here, indicating asset purchase versus asset license versus company purchase for instance.]

Object of Acquisition

[description of license / asset / company]

Provisions

- *[itemization of provisions such as "No material changes to the business" or Transition services.]*

Considerations

- *[itemization of the main various considerations.]*

Purchase Price

[specification of the overall purchase price along with the different price elements such as upfront payment, royalties, milestones payments, equity, etc. Discussion of key assumptions such as working capital.]

Payment Terms

[various terms such as holdbacks, earnouts, research funding, etc.]

Due Diligence

[options for, and contingencies related to findings from due diligence.]

Conditions to Close

[all conditions required to close such as verification of reps & warranties, satisfactory due diligence outcomes, etc.]

Various Clauses

- Governing Law
- Fees and Expenses *[who pays for what in the transaction.]*
- Non-Compete
- Confidentiality
- Survival period *[time after closing during which breach of reps & warranties claims may still be made.]*

Process

- Closing Date *[specific deadline by which close should occur.]*
- Expiration Date *[date until which term sheet is valid.]*
- Binding Terms *[e.g., exclusivity or time during which seller may not negotiate with another party.]*

Figure 7.6 Illustrative term sheet and deal elements.

or confidentiality. On a related note, despite the traditionally non-binding nature of term sheets, some elements like confidentiality and exclusivity (of negotiation) might still be binding. Certain terms used in the context of equity financing (see Figure 5.10) might also be used in a term sheet.

Some elements might be more common than others depending on the deal type (e.g., licensing versus asset purchase) and later dispute may be more common for certain aspects (e.g., earn-out provisions) rather than for others. Being informed about common practices is thus critical when negotiating a term sheet to reach appropriate outcomes and adequately plan for contingencies.

7.1.5 Negotiation

A proven ability for negotiation, often supported by professional training, is a basic requirement to successfully close deals. A structured approach, such as "Anticipate, Initiate, Manage" or AIM (Figure 7.7), is also recommended.

As the AIM acronym suggests, the goal for the deal negotiation is to navigate toward the goals the team has identified during the preparation stage, and to keep refining a path that leads there as effectively and advantageously as possible as the negotiations progress and as the deal team uncovers further information and potential options to move forward and avoid bottlenecks.

The "Anticipate" step is sometimes considered the most important negotiation step, e.g.:

- Context: recurring (relationship) versus one time negotiation (transactional).
- Various terms to be discussed and agreed upon.
- Modeling potential outcomes (with cap table discussed in Section 5.5.1).
- Defining objectives upfront (success definition, "must have" versus "nice to have").

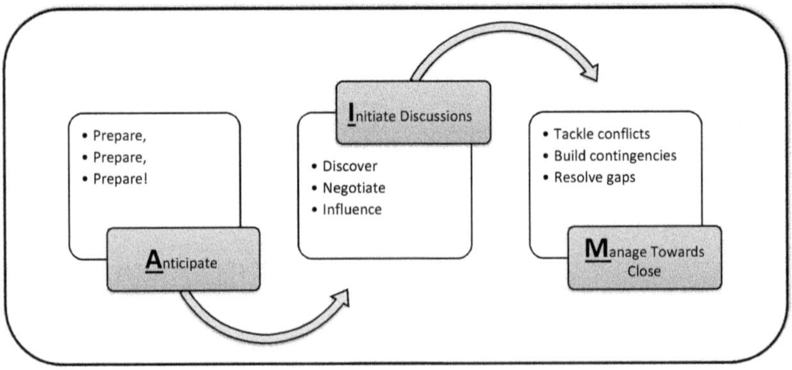

Figure 7.7 AIM negotiation framework.

- Recognizing the facts, associated perspectives, and BATNA (Best Alternative To a Negotiated Agreement: what the next best option is if an agreement is not reached).
- Requirements to ensure effective, organized, coordinated, professional negotiations (possibly in a dynamic and competitive environment).

Given biopharma industry's characteristics (e.g., high research and development risks, uncertainties on development costs or demonstrated clinical benefits, expertise and information asymmetry between parties), as the team enters the "initiate" step, discovery may play a central role for that step. Finding information helps the team define better positions and negotiation strategies. Aspects particularly important to uncover are sometimes referred to as the 4 C's of negotiation: Common interests, Conflicting interests, Compromise, and Criteria.

- Common interests apply to both parties and can be used to help move negotiations along.
- Conflicting interests help identify deal-breakers, or barring that, areas where the team might need to be creative to overcome reservations.
- Identifying possible compromises or other party's "nice to have" and their relative importance may provide for some win-win approaches where one party gets an important "nice to have" that ranks low for the other party and vice-versa.
- Criteria are frequently identified during the "anticipate" step but additional ones might crop up during discussions and negotiations. Summarizing and asking for any missing considerations might sometimes uncover potential additional criteria not yet discussed.

With the last step (manage toward close), it is important to cover all the angles defined as important success factors during the "anticipate" step. A successful outcome might hinge on:

- Timing leverage – does delaying or accelerating the deal benefit one party?
- Payment timing objectives.
- Critical resources: will critical resources remain under the control of one party in a way that might affect economic benefits?
- Risk allocations between the parties.
- Locking in specific options versus having the flexibility to decide later.
- Deal experience and relationship maturity.
- Responsibility for deal-related expenses.
- Closing conditions (e.g., agreements with third parties, regulatory approval, financing, board validation, and reps & warranties confirmation).

7.1.6 *Value Sharing*

A feasible agreement between the negotiating parties means they have an overlapping bargaining range – that range is sometimes referred to as the region of possible agreements. That possible agreement region can have several dimensions (e.g., royalty rate, upfront payment, earn-out, board seat, licensing field of use) or a single dimension when the only real variable negotiated is a purchase price entirely paid upfront. As various dimensions may have different values between two negotiating parties, value sharing offers the potential to further increase value on both sides.

Let us illustrate this value-sharing concept with a valuation analysis. A biopharma program valuation range resulting from one of the parties' analysis may look like Figure 7.8. Each of the valuation approaches (see Chapter 2) depicted in the plot typically depends on specific dimensions (e.g., field of use for licensing agreement) within the region of possible agreements. Making concessions on certain dimensions of lower interest for the conceding party may result in much higher value for the other party (e.g., geographical rights for a region in which the other party already has an existing sales and distribution network).

Successful value sharing depends on understanding the other party's interests and perspective as well as on the trust that can be leveraged for the discussions (see arrows in Figure 7.9). This highlights the importance of relationship building, which is often an essential responsibility for corporate development professionals in biotech and pharma. The greater the trust and the more objective the arguments are, the better the ability to significantly influence valuation outcomes.

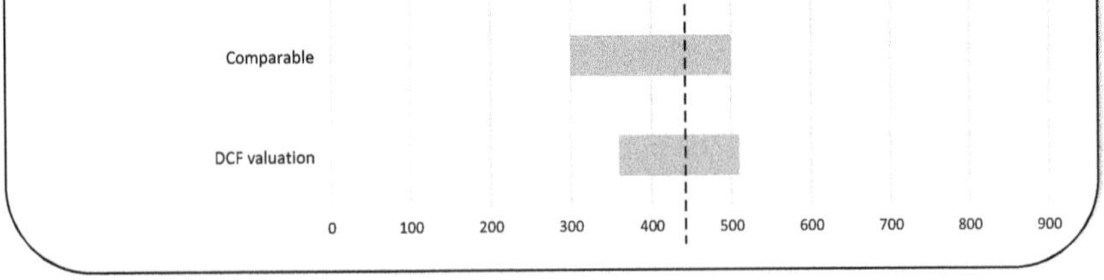

Figure 7.8 Program valuation "football field" graph.

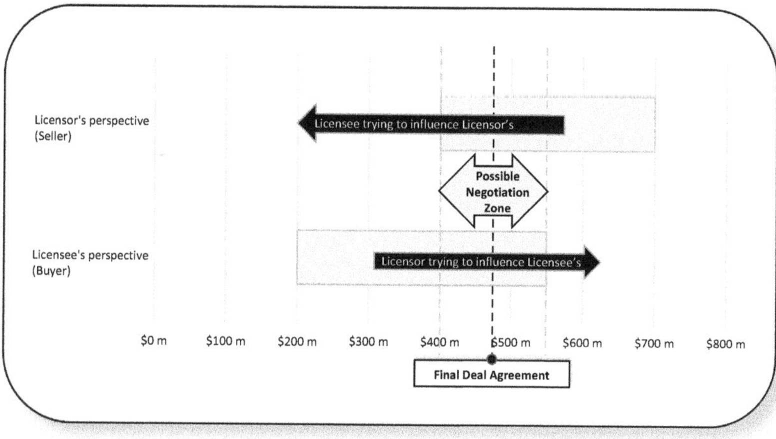

Figure 7.9 Influencing value creation potential of licensing transaction.

7.1.7 *Regulatory Considerations*

Regulatory factors represent a multidimensional challenge for biotech and pharmaceutical deals (Figure 7.10) and require utmost consideration:

- Although the seller's country of incorporation plays a determinant role, multiple jurisdictions need to be considered for governance, tax, foreign investment restrictions, possible company structures, and so on.
- Evolving regulatory perspectives from FDA, EMA, and similar regulatory agencies might put a dampener on some potential acquisition considerations or result in different valuations as buyers factor in the corresponding uncertainty.
- The type of company (e.g., private versus public) may have implications on the requirements to follow in the context of a transaction (e.g., Form 8-K requirement for US public company).
- The transaction structure (e.g., asset purchase versus stock purchase versus statutory merger) may have significant tax as well as other implications.
- Likewise, transaction characteristics can have a significant regulatory impact such as the payment used in a transaction (e.g., stock versus cash) impacting the taxable nature of the deal.
- Antitrust and trade regulations (e.g., Hart-Scott-Rodino Antitrust Improvements Act of 1976 in the United States) are typically an important consideration for large deals.
- Tax regulations (e.g., 26 U.S. Code § 368, commonly referred to as Section 368 discussed in Section 7.1.8) are almost always critical to consider.

- While accounting standards may typically not, per se, prevent deals or transactions that might otherwise be made, they can materially impact their financial performance metrics.
- Drug development and marketing regulations may result in one party seeking to exclude risk-shifting from the other party, or a carve-out. More importantly, understanding possible regulatory pathways and regulatory commercial constraints are critical to securing appropriate deal outcomes.
- Other regulatory factors may also play an important role depending on deal specifics (e.g., pricing and reimbursement).

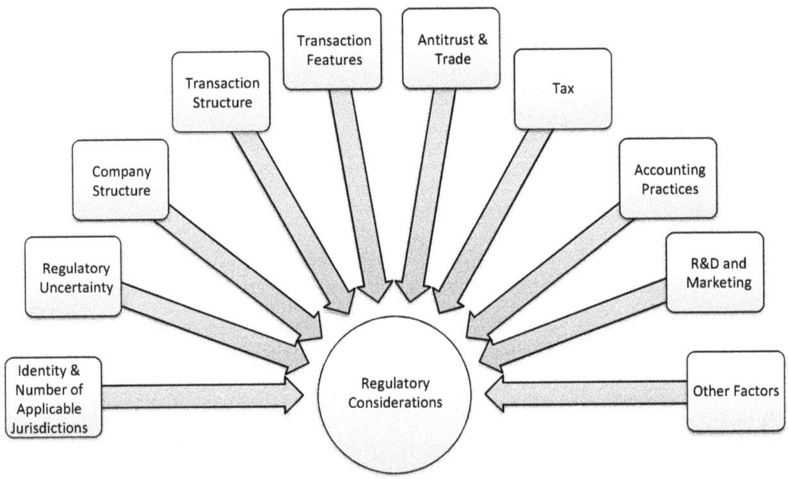

Figure 7.10 Biopharma multidimensional regulatory considerations.

7.1.8 *Tax Considerations*

Tax considerations can affect many transactional aspects of interest to both buyer and seller in addition to the transaction structure, including acquisition price, tax indemnification agreement with escrow account, reps and warranties, or transaction timeline.

From a seller's perspective, taxable transactions create the expectation of a higher purchase price to compensate this tax effect while allowing cash payment for the transaction. Tax-exempt transactions on the other hand may require the buyer to use stock as payment and thus face potential dilution prospects.

While tax details and regimes can vary from country to country, notwithstanding cross-border considerations, we take below the case of Mergers & Acquisitions in the United States to illustrate possible options. M&A

Table 7.2 Taxable M&A transactions for the United States

M&A type	*Description*
Taxable Merger	Merger where most of the consideration is paid with cash (thereby not meeting the continuation of interest described further below). In a merger, only one of the two companies (buyer for a straight merger or seller for a reverse merger) survives.
Taxable Sale of Stock	Sale of substantially all the target company stock purchased with mostly cash consideration; the company sold typically becomes a subsidiary of the buyer. Seller shareholders recognize capital gains equal to the difference between the per stock purchase price received and their base when they purchased/received the target company stock price.
Taxable Sale of Assets	Target company sells assets to the buyer for a consideration that includes a substantial cash part (e.g., significantly over 20% of fair market value). The selling corporation recognizes gains between assets transferred to the buyer and purchase price. Both the selling corporation and the buying corporation remain as independent operating entities at the end of the transaction. When substantially all its assets are sold, selling corporation is then liquidated, with proceeds to be provided to seller shareholders, who will then be taxed on proceeds received.

transactions are taxable in the United States (Table 7.2) unless they qualify as one of the defined types of tax-exempt transactions (Table 7.3). The designation for the various tax-exempt transaction types (e.g., "Type A") is derived from the paragraph numbers used to list the various instances of reorganization defined in 26 U.S. Code § 368.

Note that additional more complex US reorganizations are also discussed in Section 368, e.g.:

- Forward subsidiary merger – Section 368(a)(2)(D). This designates a statutory merger in which the target is merged into a subsidiary of the acquiring company whereby the shareholders of the target company receive stock of the acquiring company.
- Reverse subsidiary merger – Section 368(a)(2)(E). This designates a statutory merger in which a subsidiary of the acquiring company is merged into the target whereby the shareholders of the target company receive stock of the acquiring company.

Table 7.3 Tax-free M&A transactions for the United States

M&A type	*Description*
Type A	Statutory Merger or Consolidation or Type A Reorganization Covered under Section 368(a)(1)(A) Type A reorganizations designate mergers or consolidations under law (e.g., State or Country Law). Continuity of interest required (stock of acquiring company used as sufficient percentage of the purchase price).
Type B	Stock for Stock Acquisition or Type B Reorganization Covered under Section 368(a)(1)(B) B reorganizations cover the acquisition of enough stock of the target to constitute control (usually 80%) of that target company, solely in exchange for voting stock of the acquiring company.
Type C	C-Reorganization or Practical Merger or Stock-for-Assets Deal Covered under Section 368(a)(1)(C) C reorganizations cover the acquisition of substantially all assets (90% of net assets, 70% of gross assets) of the target in exchange for voting stock of the acquiring company (80% of gross fair market value should be paid with stock; assumption of liabilities permitted only if stock is the only other consideration).
Type D	1) Acquisitive D-Reorganization or Liquidation Covered under Section 368(a)(1)(D) The corporation transfers its assets to another controller corporation and distributes stock in controlled corporation in an acquisitive § 354 transaction. Control usually means 50% of voting rights and 50% of stock value. 2) Divisive D-Reorganization or Division Covered under Section 368(a)(1)(D) Often used under the designations of split-up, split-off, and spin-off discussed in Chapter 5. The corporation transfers its assets to another controller corporation and distributes stock in controlled corporation in a divisive § 355 transaction.
Type E	***Out of scope and included for reference only.*** Recapitalization Covered under Section 368(a)(1)(E) A typical use of type E reorganization is a situation where certain classes (preferred stock and debt issues) are exchanged for common stock.
Type F	***Out of scope and included for reference only.*** Simple Corporate Change Covered under Section 368(a)(1)(F) This is intended to cover simple changes such as a change in identity, and change in form, or a change in place of incorporation (e.g., moving from Massachusetts to Delaware).
Type G	***Out of scope and included for reference only.*** Bankruptcy Reorganization Covered under Section 368(a)(1)(G) This type of reorganization is typically used by insolvent companies to transfer assets under Title 11.

These two more complex Type A merger approaches may sometimes be helpful in the biopharmaceutical industry where it is not uncommon to have a top holding company managing investor relations and financing with one or more intermediate holding companies underneath and one or more operating companies below each intermediate holding.

Case Example: Taxable Stock Sale

In 2023, Mindset Pharma Inc. and Otsuka Pharmaceutical entered into an agreement whereby Otsuka acquires Mindset in an all-cash transaction for CAD$ 0.75 per share, after which Mindset would become a wholly owned subsidiary of Otsuka. As explained to Mindset's resident shareholders, as a result of the transaction, they "will realize a capital gain (or a capital loss) equal to the amount by which the cash payment exceeds (or is less than) the aggregate of the adjusted cost base to the Resident Holder of such Mindset Shares and any reasonable costs of disposition" (Mindset Pharma, 2023).

Case Example: Exempt Reorganization

In 2021, AstraZeneca acquired Alexion Pharmaceuticals to enhance its immunology presence and obtain critical size in rare disease medicines. As explained to AstraZeneca's shareholders, AstraZeneca and Alexion would not be obliged to complete the transaction unless it qualified as a reorganization under Section 368(a) and would not result in gain recognition to Alexion stockholders, as provided by independent legal opinion (AstraZeneca PLC, 2021).

As this Section 7.1.8 illustrated, tax considerations can be intricate and complicated. In the United States, while biopharma companies typically are C corporations, different tax rules and constraints might apply to other structures (e.g., S corporation or limited liability company).

7.2 Sell Side

Overall Process

Making a deal from a seller's perspective is often a step-by-step exercise with upfront resource allocation to prepare once the sale decision (or out-licensing, or equivalent decision) has been made (Figure 7.11). The priority at each step is to maximize the probability of closing, e.g.:

Figure 7.11 Illustrative sell-side deal process.

- Understanding, as part of the strategic analysis, the type of buyers that would maximize the value and understanding the setting in which such value would be maximized is critical to help identify those strategic buyers likely to offer the seller a favorable deal value.
- Anticipating changes and preparing due diligence information toward a favorable buyer evaluation is important. This might mean disclosing more information on certain favorable aspects or putting in place short-term improvement plans on aspects that might otherwise detract from the buyer's valuation if not fixed.
- Selecting and executing well the approach that will best optimize the interests of the seller is important to ensure a successful deal outcome. There are two traditional M&A approaches used to market opportunities effectively.
  - Targeted approach.
    Developing a well-thought-out but limited potential buyer list along with an effective teaser that accurately portrays the opportunity to potential buyers represents another important step to ensure enough credible strategic biopharma buyers with extensive knowledge of the products are looped into the process.
  - Broad approach.
    Developing an extensive list of knowledgeable potential buyer list to ensure the company can play the odds and the numbers ensure there should be sufficient interest from financial buyers or strategic players to secure an appropriate deal for the company in the end.
- A buyer can try and maximize the likelihood of a deal by selecting credible leading bidders based on the evaluation of the received letters of interest that include a favorable indication of the intended purchase price as well as aspects around strategy, financial elements, transaction timeline, approval process, and due diligence elements.
- Keeping at least two buyers in the running might increase competition, even if the least favored of the two only serves as a "rabbit" to get the most favored potential buyer to pursue the deal more aggressively. Keeping a runner up might also be helpful in case the deal unexpectedly falls through with the lead buyer.

We now discuss different sell-side situations sequentially: company sale, asset sale, out-licensing, minority equity sale, and option sale.

7.2.1 Negotiating a Company Sale

Buyers' intent may vary but higher company purchase offers tend to be associated with buyers that view the acquisition as strategic, aligned with its therapeutic areas or portfolio focus areas or responding to an important strategic gap (e.g., replacing products facing loss of exclusivity and obtaining important new modality or platform capability). Current or expected market dynamics also play a significant role, with stronger valuation conferred by regulatory advantage (e.g., orphan drugs), potential superiority claims, and large indications with recurring or ongoing medical needs. Lastly, a seller should emphasize freedom to operate and progressive de-risking for research and development programs.

General Approach

Notwithstanding commercial potential, telling that story of progressively de-risked company assets with suitable freedom to operate and growth opportunities through the various sell-side documents (Figure 7.12), with increasing details and confidence-building facts, is a critical element to negotiate a successful company sale.

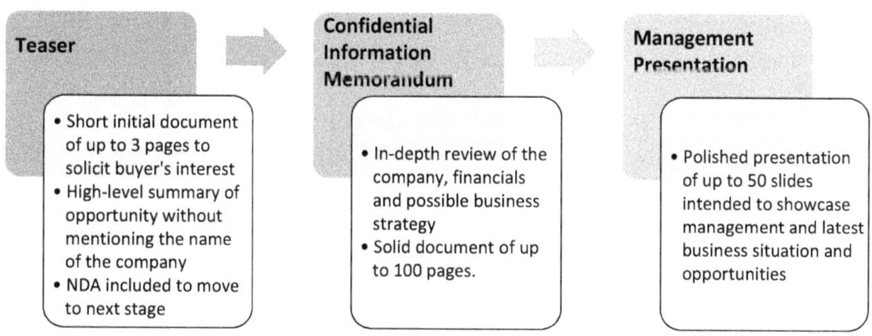

Figure 7.12 Major sell-side documents.

The first document, the "teaser"", will typically cre-dibly and concisely cover the following:

- Company code name (used to replace the actual company name). A code name is used in order to avoid people contacting employees or clients as there is typically no non-disclosure agreement at this stage.
- Legal notice with appropriate caveat to be specified by a lawyer (e.g., restriction of use, not an offer to sell, no warranty or representation, and

Illustrative Teaser Outline

Project XYZ – Opportunity Overview

I Important Notice
Legal language to guide document use and communications regarding the opportunity.

II Transaction rationale, approach, and scope
Explains what is for sale, what is excluded from the sale, why it is for sale,

communication restrictions), even though a teaser is typically not binding.
- Investment rationale and company potential (e.g., compelling investment overview, opportunities, growth avenues).
- Industry overview and business description.
- Business location(s).
- Products and services provided by the company.
- Management and organization.

and how to take things to the next step by when if interested.

III Key Investment Highlights
Concisely and crisply articulates the differentiation the business provides, the value it brings, what the growth potential is, and what further investments or cash runway might represent an opportunity.

IV Markets, Products, and Services
Uses fact-based information as evidence that these are good markets and offerings to be in.

- Information on market, competition, and customers.
- Selected company financial highlights and metrics (e.g., revenue, profitability, and trends that would not be deemed critically confidential).
- Process information (e.g., transaction structure, non-disclosure agreements to proceed to the next step, contact details).

If the seller uses an investment banker for the transaction, the banker typically takes the lead in putting the teaser document together. The goal is to generate interest in the opportunity, emphasizing the positives and usually preventing an easy identification of the business not to alarm current employees, partners, or customers.

The Teaser, like the Confidential Information Memorandum afterward, is usually sent with a cover letter or process letter that helps potential buyers understand the process steps and requirements. The teaser process letter might cover the following points:

- M&A process timeline, including key dates and milestones.
- Submission criteria and evaluation criteria.
- Information on Confidentiality Agreement or Non-Disclosure Agreement.
- Complete contact information to relevant party/parties.
- Legal disclaimer.

Upon reviewing the teaser, potential buyers may express interest in learning more, return an executed non-disclosure agreement, and fulfill other requirements highlighted in the process letter. After that, they will, at the discretion of the seller, receive a Confidential Information Memorandum (CIM). The CIM is commonly done with a slide editor like Microsoft

PowerPoint, and shared with selected potential buyers using appropriate restricted access approaches (e.g., virtual data room tool).

Depending on their prior knowledge of potential buyers, the seller might ask potential buyers to return with the non-disclosure agreement:

- A cover letter clarifying the potential buyer's identity, contact information, and full disclosure of principals, direct and indirect.
- A form of financial disclosure and credit quality that will allow the seller to make a reasonable determination for the potential buyer's financial and general capabilities to consummate such a transaction.

A CIM might feature seven sections:

1. Disclaimer and transaction team.
   Section intended to recap the legal context in which the information might or might not be used as well as to specify authorized transaction contacts.
2. Executive summary.
   Section intended to provide the major points of the transaction at a glance, highlighting what makes it attractive. It may span several pages but should always remain concise and impactful.
3. Company and capabilities.
   Section intended to provide company's history, its offerings, and so on. The section might have subsections like specific competencies, a business model, or innovative offerings that warrant further explanations.
4. Company programs and R&D pipeline.
   Section intended to provide information on the various company programs, data generated, development plans, regulatory submissions, and other critical information regarding biopharma assets.
5. Market opportunity.
   Section intended to provide an understanding of the company's markets, as well as of company's advantages that are different from the competition.
6. Customers and growth.
   This section should provide evidence of the value to customers and how the business might grow or improve further.
7. Operations and personnel.
   Section intended to highlight employee demographics, organizational chart, locations, and other company descriptions. This section would normally highlight specific competencies, intellectual property, scientific capabilities, and opportunities related to facilities and other aspects that make operations and personnel a desirable asset to have.

8. Financials.
   This section should gather all the financial aspects and set expectations on the financial evolution of the business, a critically important element as it often drives the valuation of the target company. Common subsections include:
   - Key highlights.
   - Basis used for financials.
   - Management discussion.
   - P&L with at least two years of actuals, current year estimate, and three years of projected financials. P&L is at least down to EBITDA level.
   - Adjustments, revenue recognition approach, and assumptions.
   - Balance sheet.
   - Capital expenditures.

Once a potential buyer has reviewed the CIM, if they are still interested, they will issue a non-binding letter of interest, including an indication of value as well as process information (e.g., ready to move fast, strategic fit, or integration envisioned). The non-binding letter of interest may also be referred to as Non-Binding Offer or NBO.

At that point, the seller and its representatives will conduct a management presentation with the most attractive potential buyer(s) that are still interested. Similarly to a company pitch (see Chapter 6), that management presentation's objective is to sell the investment to potential buyers. To justify an acquisition premium, the presentation should be engaging and make a clear investment case rather than rehash the CIM information. Storytelling and financial savviness are two important ingredients to keep in mind at this stage. For the record, the management presentation will still include the following elements as part of the story:

- Disclosure and legal caveats.
- Company and market overviews.
- Strategy and opportunities.
- Offerings vis-à-vis competition.
- Leadership, intellectual property, and operational effectiveness.
- Financial performance.

It is important to ensure consistency between the various documents presented to a potential buyer, starting with the teaser, continuing with the CIM, and finishing with the management presentation and data room information. This can typically be achieved by preparing all transaction marketing materials upfront.

Case Example: Data Room Structure

Note that the structure is usually indexed to make it easier to reference folders and documents.

Project [CODENAME]

Note that the transaction project code is usually indicated at the top of the data room architecture.

1. **Investment Opportunity**
   1.1 Teaser
   1.2 Non-Disclosure Agreement
   1.3 Confidential Information Memorandum
   1.4 Management Presentation
   1.5 Anonymized Q&A
2. **Business Overview**
   2.1 Company Overview
   2.2 Governance
   2.3 Corporate Records
   2.4 Market Data
   2.5 Positioning and Competitive Analysis
3. **Products and Services**
   3.1 Discovery
   3.2 Preclinical
   3.3 Clinical
   3.4 Approved and Exempt Products and Services
   3.5 Regulatory Information
4. **Sales and Marketing**
5. **Legal**
6. **Human Resources**
   6.1 Organizational Chart
   6.2 Management Bios and Key Employee Profiles
   6.3 Employment Agreements
   6.4 Employee Stock Option Plan
   6.5 Policies
   6.6 Other HR Information
7. **Intellectual Property**
   7.1 IP Strategy
   7.2 Patents
   7.3 Trademarks and Domains
   7.4 Licenses
   7.5 Other IP
8. **Information Technology**
9. **Contracts and Agreements**
   9.1 Customers
   9.2 Suppliers
   9.3 Partners
10. **Quality Management, Manufacturing and Facilities**
11. **Chemistry, Manufacturing, and Controls**
12. **Regulatory Affairs**
13. **Financial Information**
    13.1 Financials
        13.1.1 Balance Sheet
        13.1.2 Income Statement
        13.1.3 Cash Flow Statement
        13.1.4 Projections and Forecast
        13.1.5 Audit Reports
        13.1.6 Debt Schedule
        13.1.7 Other Financials
    13.2 Capitalization Table
    13.3 Stock Purchase Agreements
    13.4 Valuation Information
    13.5 Tax

Figure 7.13 Example of data room structure.

Figure 7.13 provides an illustrative virtual data room structure in the case of a medium-size US biotechnology company with multiple pipeline assets.

It is important to note that virtual data room application providers will typically offer specific functionalities that allow the seller to manage which information a given potential buyer has access to (e.g., visibility of a given folder or not) as well as restricted rights (e.g., download versus not). Such software options typically allow the seller to evolve the folder structure as due diligence progresses.

Although individual situations may vary significantly (e.g., public company deals might be faster), information progression and the company sale is typically a 6-month process after banker and adviser selection (Figure 7.14).

Price

The payment for the company, or total consideration, may be a straightforward cash for stock payment or include several components combining upfront and contingent payments. On a related note, executives and more importantly the board of directors, need to ensure they have met the threshold of the "business judgment rule" in view of the enhanced scrutiny that may accompany the sale of a company, especially for public companies. In the United States, this "business judgment rule" is the typical standard used in courts: "the business judgment rule protects a director of a corporation from liability for business decisions made in good faith if the director is informed to the extent he or she reasonably believes to be appropriate under

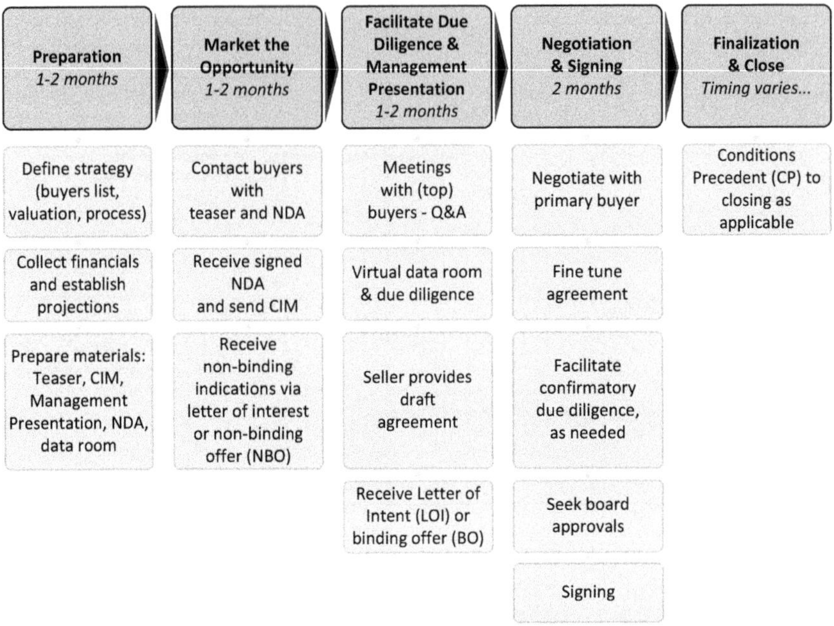

Figure 7.14 Typical timing for sell-side process.

the circumstances and reasonably believes that the decision is in the best interests of the corporation" (Ramos et al., 2020).

Especially for private companies, earn-out, retention, and other performance-based provisions can be used to palliate information asymmetry or deal with situations where buyer's expectations are more conservative or misaligned with the seller's expectations. Such performance-based clauses can also motivate management staying with the buyer post-closing by providing them with potential upside value. Generally speaking, sellers will prefer objective criteria for earn-out payment while more buyer-driven subjective criteria might be more advantageous to the buyer who at this stage runs the company.

Although simultaneous signing and closing is possible for straightforward transactions without regulatory approval requirements or third-party consents, in other cases, there might be a significant lag between signing a deal and the close of the deal, and several underlying factors that affect a company's valuation, and thus the purchase price, might evolve during that time frame. Such factors may include cash levels and working capital. The total consideration paid for the acquisition may thus include post-closing purchase price adjustments to reflect the updated actual financial situation observed by the buyer at the closing date but typically available several weeks after the closing date. This is one of the reasons that closing normally occurs at the end of an accounting period to avoid further allocations and accounting challenges. It is also good practice to clarify the approach expected for the buyer to deliver suitable financial statements to the seller, how they will be reviewed by the seller, and what accounting and valuation methods will be used for the post-closing adjustments. For both the seller and the buyer, it is important to consider how adjustments might be influenced between signing and closing and to add covenants preventing actions or activities that would be deemed undesirable. Unless precluded by a suitable covenant, a seller with marketed drugs might be within their rights to offer special sales incentives short term that would result in higher working capital and thus a higher purchase price.

One should also note that adjustments may not always be the norm. One common approach without post-completion adjustment is referred to as "locked box". When the deal uses a locked box approach, both parties agree on a purchase price using audited financial statements and there is no purchase price adjustment. However, the parties may negotiate additional terms to ensure there is no substantial value decrease between the date of the locked box and deal completion (from a buyer's perspective) or on the other hand to ensure benefits from significant appreciation are shared (from a seller's perspective).

Contingent value rights (CVR) can represent an important tool for biopharma mergers and acquisitions in the case of the sale of a public company. CVR are analogous to the earn-out considerations used for private company sales. Normally, the value of CVR is estimated using financial models that incorporate the probability of the underlying milestones, the term or duration allowed, the discount rate for equivalent investments, and the expected underlying forecasts. CVR are more common in life sciences than in other industries and represented approximately 30% of the M&A deals conducted from May 2022 to April 2023 included (Wagner Partin et al., 2023). CVR are also more common with smaller public M&A transactions; the typical CVR is event-driven, non-transferable, and settled in cash (Wagner Partin et al., 2023).

Case Example: Contingent Value Rights

In early 2023, Ipsen made the acquisition of Albireo, a leading innovator in bile-acid modulators to treat pediatric and adult cholestatic liver diseases (Ipsen, 2023). Shares of Albireo were acquired at a price of US$42.00 per share plus one non-transferable CVR of US$10.00 per share. The deferred cash payment of the CVR is payable upon FDA's approval of Albireo's lead asset Bylvay in the Biliary Atresia indication, no later than the end of 2027.

Intellectual Property

In biopharma, it is not uncommon for a significant part of the company's valuation to be derived from few products or even a single lead product.

In such situations, the due diligence on the IP related to these products will be an utmost priority to the potential buyer. Having correspondingly robust assignment of IP as well as actionable representations and warranties will be a "must have" aspect of the deal. Aspects evaluated on major product patents include remaining term, pending application, strength of patent claims, potential for additional claims and patents, infringement allegations, third-party rights, and freedom to operate. For products in development, the potential for patent-term extensions applicable to key geographies (e.g., 35 U.S.C. § 156 for the United States) also plays an important role.

Continuity of Operations

To ensure operations run smoothly during and soon after the sale of the company, a transition service agreement might be put in place. Such agreement provides a legal structure enabling a successful transition of operations between transaction close and the effective separation of the company from its original setup. Transition service agreements typically have a duration between 6 and 24 months and are relevant when the company sold is part of a larger organization, as opposed to a standalone company sale.

As specifics depend on both buyer and seller, the agreement is drafted only after a deal is expected. The seller and the buyer will typically agree in general terms on the type of services provided to one another, their scope and duration, before letting lawyers nail down specific language and agreements while retaining a level of flexibility to avoid numerous amendments.

For both sides, transition service agreement objectives are to minimize risks, enable a smooth transition, optimize value, and be pragmatic on what might be required as a result of the transaction. Pragmatism is important to emphasize as effective collaboration requires realistic expectations on a limited time frame during which good (not perfect) support will be provided, ideally based on quantifiable and auditable performance metrics.

In biopharma, transition service agreements may possibly include one or several of the following areas:

- Contract manufacturing.
- Facilities (sharing or support arrangement).
- Finance and accounting.
- Human resources and payroll.
- Information technology and data sharing.
- Intellectual property (e.g., temporary license).
- Procurement and use of third-party vendors (e.g., CRO).
- Quality.
- Regulatory affairs and regulatory consulting.

- Sales support (e.g., distribution, billing, collection) or medical science liaison support.
- Supply chain.
- Tax and Legal support (e.g., importer of record).
- Technical services and R&D.

Legal Considerations

Legal clauses can cover a wide variety of aspects and may come up at various steps of the deal process, either as expectations, representations, or legally binding (Figure 7.15). Critical aspects end up being captured in covenants. Covenants are an important part of the company purchase agreement and represent promises to ensure certain conditions or perform certain activities on the one hand, or to limit or prevent certain activities, conditions, actions,

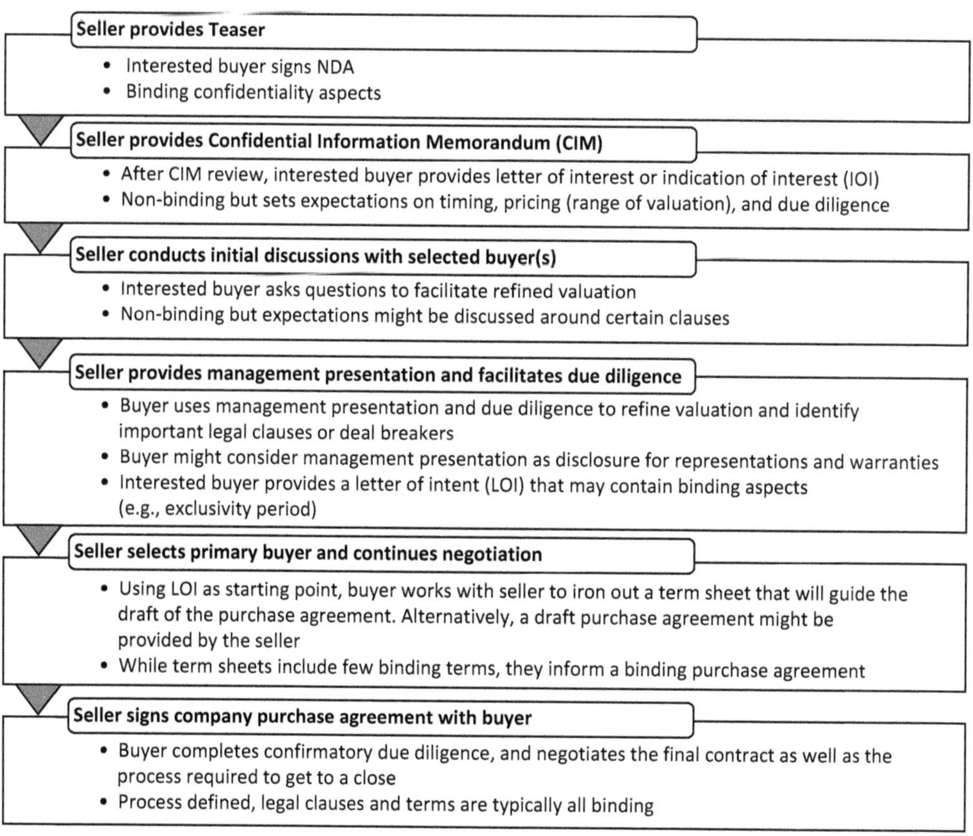

Figure 7.15 Evolution of legal considerations throughout a deal.

or situations on the other hand. The former are referred to as obligations, requirements, or positive covenants while the latter are sometimes referred to as limitations or restrictive covenants.

Seeking legal counsel opinion is highly recommended as even non-binding documents such as a letter of intent (sometimes called a memorandum of understanding or MOU) or a term sheet might possibly be claimed by one party to be binding, e.g., if both of the following conditions were met:

- The parties intended to be bound by the obligations described.
- The document is sufficiently clear and certain around the obligations described.

For the avoidance of doubt, it might thus be prudent to clearly indicate in the document what terms are legally binding versus not.

The non-disclosure agreement is usually the first legally binding document within the company sales process. NDAs are relatively straightforward and typically cover the following elements:

- What is meant by confidential information?
- What restrictions are placed on using the confidential information the potential buyer will receive, along with any applicable obligations?
- How long does the non-disclosure agreement last (term of the agreement)?
- What can and must be done with the information (information safeguards, disclosures, return and destruction, cease using after deal termination, etc.)?
- What the agreement does not provide (e.g., no grant of intellectual property, no obligation to proceed with a deal)?
- How the agreement will be enforced (e.g., jurisdiction, dispute resolution)?

The point of the non-disclosure agreement is to establish a legal obligation for potential buyers to only use the information provided for the deal itself. In transactions such as the acquisition of a publicly listed company, a non-disclosure agreement will also be signed by individuals involved in the transaction (i.e., employees of acquiring company involved in the transaction, advisers). The non-disclosure agreement is typically drafted by the seller and ideally kept consistent across potential buyers for simplicity.

Despite the name, NDAs may contain restrictive covenants dealing with aspects other than confidentiality (e.g., non-solicitation of employees or customers). These other aspects may be pertinent for potential buyers that already compete in the same markets.

The letter of interest is typically non-binding, as validated by legal counsel, but might set expectations on aspects that might later be binding such as pricing range, deal time frame, transaction structure, and other terms that might be relevant to the buyer or seller. In addition to allowing the seller to get an impression of potential buyers (e.g., capabilities, professionalism, and strategic interest for the deal), aspects like an intended deal structure, if mentioned, may have significant implications (see Table 7.4 using only two parties for simplicity as opposed to multiple buyers).

The letter of intent (LOI) is generally much more comprehensive, indicating price, deal structure, various process points, and possibly selected binding aspects. The LOI serves as backdrop for the term sheet negotiation and the negotiation of the draft purchase agreement. Most large corporations will have a two-step approach for offers, a first general one that serves as a framework and is clearly non-binding (non-binding offer or NBO or letter of interest), and a second one (e.g., LOI) that is considered binding pending applicable confirmatory due diligence and related offer adjustments.

Table 7.4 Illustrative deal structure comparison for company sale

Statutory merger		*Stock purchase*	
Definition: combination of two corporations – merger agreement where one of the two corporations survives.		*Definition: purchase of all/most of the stock of the company, the acquirer of the stock becoming owner of the company (at least in majority). When the acquirer is a corporation, the acquired company becomes a subsidiary.*	
Selected potential pros	Selected potential cons	Selected potential pros	Selected potential cons
• Simple title transfers. • Flexibility in use of preferred stock. • Elimination of minority interests. • Option available for reverse merger.	• More complicated process (e.g., shareholder meeting required for each set of shareholders). • The surviving entity assumes all liabilities. • Potential regulatory constraints.	• Simple process with purchase and transfer of stock certificates. • Speed of execution (no shareholder meetings required, no board approval). • Seller liabilities remain with the acquired entity.	• All liabilities remain with the acquired entity. • Minority stockholders might remain (unless sale can be forced through a "squeeze-out"). • No value adjustments for assets. • Potential constraints and obligations from stock transfer regulations.

Finally, the purchase agreement is a binding document that supersedes previous documents and provides all the important considerations for the transaction: price, process and timing, parties, conditions, reps and warranties, fees, and payments. Terms and clauses that a seller negotiates in the context of a company purchase agreement negotiation may include:

- Management retained post-closing and retention agreements.
- Deal structure.
- Acquisition payment and tax implications.
- Representations and warranties (R&W), including carve-outs.
- R&W insurance policy.
- Survival period for R&W compared with intellectual property life and regulatory milestones.
- Warranty against materially misleading or omitted information in light of country practices for acquired company headquarters (such warranty might be common in some countries but uncommon in others).
- When R&W apply (e.g., at signing, both at signing and close, at all times in between).
- Applicability of non-compete (this might vary depending by country).
- Employee non-solicitation.
- Customer non-solicitation.
- Use of waterfall or blue pencil methods (common US practice of modifying, reducing, or deleting a clause or provision that is not enforceable to ensure the remainder of the agreement is enforceable).
- Restrictions imposed on the target business between signing and closing.
- Access to management, accounting, and records between signing and closing.
- Product liability clauses for GMP issues and other liabilities that occurred pre-close.
- Tying/offsetting indemnification claims to deferred considerations (seller would want to consider the two separately whereas buyer might not).
- Carve-outs and exclusion to material adverse effects clauses (seller wanting to restrict what might constitute a material adverse effect for which they would be responsible, like impact of FDA actions, government actions regarding pricing, and generic competition). Such changes in circumstances can significantly reduce the value of the company for sale and unless carved out, they might allow the buyer to walk away from the deal if such a change occurs prior to closing.
- Condition precedent to closing – conditions without which the other party is not obligated to close (e.g., antitrust, third-party consent, confirmatory due diligence, pre-closing restructuring).

- Responsibility for payment of stamp duty (tax levied on legal documents if applicable).
- Use of setoff against claims (i.e., cancellation of mutual financial obligations between two parties).
- Buyer's obligation to mitigate damages.

Case Example: Seller's Representations and Warranties

Pfizer Inc. acquired Biohaven Pharmaceutical Holding Company Ltd in 2022 for US$148.50 per share in cash plus assumption of debt. Pfizer was to retain the calcitonin gene-related peptide (CGRP) programs in the acquired company and spin off a new company formed for the non-CGRP development stage pipeline compounds. The agreement included both representations and warranties by the seller, Biohaven, and the buyer, Pfizer. Seller's representations and warranties were broken down into 33 different categories covering many different aspects, including the following (Pfizer Inc. et al., 2022):

- Organization, registration, and capitalization.
- Governance and authority.
- Liabilities.
- Asset ownership and compliance with all applicable laws.
- Regulatory compliance.
- Company sale process.
- Aspect specific to the expected spin-off.

Case Example: Condition Precedent

The closing of Pfizer's acquisition of Biohaven was subject to a number of condition precedents listed in the Agreement and Plan of Merger (Ibid). There were in particular conditions related to each of the following categories:

- Regulatory compliance (e.g., antitrust clearance).
- Seller's pre-closing corporate obligations (e.g., Biohaven shareholders approval).
- General conditions and closing certificates (e.g., no material adverse effect; all merger agreement conditions have been met).

Regulatory Considerations

Depending on buyer and seller, a company sale might fall under multiple jurisdictions. A company sale involving multiple countries or cross-border transactions can present additional challenges, opportunities, and compliance considerations. Such aspects might include language selection for the transaction, tax considerations, access to capital and commercial markets, governance considerations (e.g., different threshold at which control can be obtained), national security concerns, foreign investment restrictions or limitations, identification of the governing laws and applicable international treaties for the specific type of company structure at hand (e.g., private versus public), political risk, cultural differences, as well as possible acquisition mechanics (e.g., what entity survives, which entity is merged with or acquiring which one), sequence of events, and competent authority rulebook and regulatory approvals required (such as obtention of market authorization at country and product level). Most determinations generally remain, however, driven first by the law of incorporation of the company for sale. And while the buyer's country standards definitely play a role, considering the standards and norms typically applied by the country of the company for sale might help optimize efficiency and timelines.

Cross-border transactions can indeed represent a significant percentage of the global M&A deal volume: 32% in 2022, in line with the 35% average of the prior 10 years (Emmerich & Panovka, 2023).

Case Example: Selected Matters for Cross-border Transactions for the United States (Alvarez et al., 2022; Baker McKenzie, 2022; Sibbett & Kim, 2022)

Key considerations for a cross-border transaction include the following in the United States:

- The acquisition structure is driven by various characteristics such as entity type under state law, tax classification, jurisdiction, capital structure and shareholders, as well as strategic objectives.
- The SEC imposes regulatory requirements and review for US public companies.
- Using US subsidiary/company to make a US acquisition allows for simplified tax filings whereas a non-US subsidiary/company will need to take into account the various tax treatments and tax treaties applicable to its specific situation.
- CFIUS, also known as Committee on Foreign Investment in the United States, can review transactions involving the acquisition of US businesses by non-US persons. CFIUS is relevant for the biotech industry as it is deemed critical to the US national security.
- Transactions above certain thresholds require notification to the Department of Justice and the Federal Trade Commission (HSR ACT of 1976 regarding antitrust).

- Lastly, many other aspects and requirements are tied to companies doing business in the United States, e.g., Foreign Corrupt Practices Act of 1977, fiduciary duties of company board, intellectual property, multidimensional data protection (federal, state, standards), allowed choice of governing law (Delaware and New York are most common), common use of representation and warranty insurance for M&A transactions.

Another important regulatory consideration for a company sale to a specific buyer is whether it might violate applicable antitrust laws. The goal of antitrust laws is to prevent transactions that might result in significantly lessening industry competition or in creating a monopoly situation. In the United States, if an acquisition meets certain criteria based on size (of sales, assets, or equity value), the parties must file a premerger notification notice to the Federal Trade Commission and the Department of Justice, according to the Hart-Scott-Rodino (HSR) Antitrust Improvements Act of 1976. In such a situation, the parties must wait for a specified period of time (e.g., 15 or 30 days), allowing the regulatory agencies in question to review the proposed transaction. During the review, the regulatory agencies may require additional information and extend the waiting period. If the regulatory agencies find the intended transaction to violate antitrust laws, they can seek an injunction and prevent the transaction.

There might be other regulatory requirements well-known by M&A professionals that might impact the timeline and validity of a contemplated transaction. Publicly traded companies normally face additional regulatory requirements, e.g.:

- Form 8-K is a report that public companies need to file with the SEC to notify the public of major events they should know about. Form 8-K is to be filed within 4 days of the triggering event. Such events include M&A, bankruptcy, board resignations, new officers, and so on.
- Form S-4 is required by the SEC for public companies offering new securities in connection with a merger, acquisition, or stock exchange offer.
- Schedule 14A of the Securities Exchange Act of 1934 provides the regulatory requirements for proxy statements, an aspect important for shareholder meetings in connection with M&A transactions.

7.2.2 *Negotiating an Asset Sale*

An asset sale refers to a transaction in which the selling company transfers all or selected assets to a buyer.

Asset Sale as Alternate Approach to Company Sale

An asset sale process might serve as an alternative to a company sale, when all, or at least substantially all, the balance sheet assets are sold to the buyer. Once the transaction is completed, the seller is left with the company shell, i.e., the legal entity with any liability that was not explicitly included in the sale, and any leftover assets and rights not included in the sale. At that point, the empty shell company is typically liquidated with proceeds going to the shareholders. In contrast to a statutory merger or a stock purchase approach, it is important to note that an asset sale is technically not a company sale since the company shell remains the property of the original shareholders. Also, still from a technical perspective, the seller is the company itself and not its shareholders. On a related note, a stock sale might be treated as an asset sale in specific situations: see IRC section 338(h)(10) in the United States covering such a scenario referred to as a "338 sale".

The main asset sale characteristic often mentioned (the asset in question being a business as codified by ASC 805 in the United States) in contrast to a company sale is that liabilities passed onto the buyer can be designated in the purchase agreement. This might not be favorable to the seller since, barring exceptions, the buyer does not take on any undisclosed or unspecified liability (these normally stay with the seller). Asset sale may still present advantages from a seller's perspective, e.g.:

- The purchase price can be allocated to specific assets with appropriate justification (e.g., independent appraisal): assets are written up if their carrying value is below fair market value prior to the transaction. The stepped-up value and its associated higher depreciation and amortization amounts may represent a tax benefit advantage for the buyer and may be reflected in the purchase price they are willing to pay. Under US GAAP (accounting standard code ASC 805-50-30-3), goodwill is not recognized for asset acquisitions: the excess purchase price consideration over the fair value of the net assets is allocated to the identifiable assets on a pro rata of their market value. Avoiding goodwill, by using an asset purchase structure, might allow the seller to obtain a higher purchase price and avoid goodwill-associated risks (e.g., risk of impairment charges if the goodwill fair value estimate decreases, risk of overvaluation, amortization decreasing earnings). In the case of a bargain purchase (i.e., purchase price is below the net fair market value), the "negative" excess purchase would be allocated the same way as a positive one.
- The transaction process might encompass one less stockholder meeting if a meeting of the buyer's stockholder is not required. Also, the

transaction may not be regulated by securities laws to the same level as stock transactions.

- Minority interest concerns may be eliminated for the seller since 100% of the business can be sold in an asset sale transaction, even if minority shareholders dissent as long as they are paid a fair market value for their shares. In such a scenario, all shareholders are subsequently eliminated through the company dissolution.
- Other technical aspects may or may not constitute an advantage for the seller: accounting differences, varying tax treatments, capitalization of transaction costs, reps and warranties, asset and liabilities scope, etc.

On the negative side, asset purchase transactions tend to be more complex, typically requiring significant processes and documentation (e.g., explicit list of assets and liabilities transferred, consents to obtain or negotiations with third parties especially for the assignment of contracts to the buyer, potential loss of confidentiality, various title transfers or new titles depending on the various types of assets). Contracts, including necessary manufacturing or licensing agreements, might have to be renegotiated by the buyer: an aspect that might possibly be a deal-breaker or make transition services by the seller more difficult. Asset purchase transactions may also present different legal challenges (e.g., conflict with credit or loan agreements that feature covenants preventing major asset sales). Lastly, in addition to the tax cost to the seller being typically higher than with a stock sale, the seller is left to liquidate any aspect that was not included in the asset purchase transaction (e.g., retained liabilities). It is, however, important to note that in certain situations (see Type C-reorganization in Table 7.3), an asset sale might qualify as a tax-free reorganization.

Case Example: Service Level Agreement in Case of Asset Sale Transaction

When an asset sale transaction is used to purchase a biopharma company (without the original company "shell"), temporary support might be required by the buyer, e.g.:

- Buyer's use of seller's National Drug Code (NDC) numbers (see Figure 7.16) until the buyer can obtain their own numbers.
- Centers for Medicare & Medicaid Services price reporting unless the corresponding data comes across with the business sold.
- Federal and governmental contracts and relationships.
- Commercial calculations (e.g., chargebacks, rebates, credits).
- Receivable collection by the seller on behalf of the buyer during a short period of time post-closing.

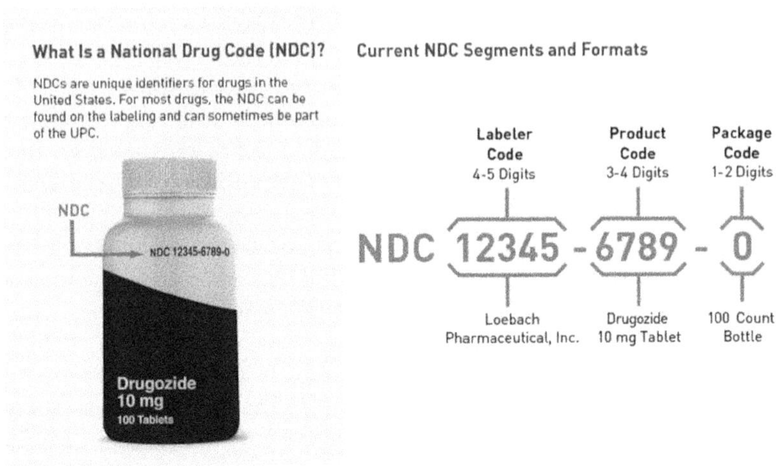

Figure 7.16 NDC serves as identifier for drugs for the FDA (FDA, 2022).

Divestitures

Notwithstanding its approach for company sales, an asset sale or divestiture can be a way to realign the organization with the latest corporate strategy and streamline the company's product portfolio and facilities resulting from corporate history and acquisitions. The divestiture of specific assets and businesses might also be mandated after a merger or acquisition in order to comply with antitrust agencies' requirements, or when a company executes divestitures under Chapter 11 of the United States Bankruptcy Code. Lastly, a divestiture might represent a way for the seller to secure sufficient financing for its other activities.

Whether they result from strategic, financing, or regulatory imperatives, divestitures might designate a wide variety of transactions, e.g.:

- Sale of a business (using ASC 805 definition for the United States), including the rights to sell and develop a product or a portfolio of products as well as employees and facilities. A large pharma company might sell an entire division with personnel and facilities working in a therapeutic area they have decided to exit.
- Sale of assets that do not qualify as a business, e.g.:
    - Sale (or assignment) of rights to sell and develop a product or a portfolio of products (no employee or facility transfer).
    - Sale of a manufacturing plant.

The same considerations as before (when selling substantially all company assets) still apply: the purchase agreement will need to list in detail any transferred asset (such as patents, trademarks, domain names), any exclusion or carve-out, every assumed liability (while non-specified liabilities might typically stay with the seller, it is good practice to spell out excluded liabilities to avoid any uncertainty or differences of opinion). Likewise, any third-party agreement that cannot be readily assigned to the buyer would likely need to be renegotiated.

The overall steps of an asset deal will typically follow the same approach as described in Figure 7.14. Depending on the deal complexity, the preparation phase may be longer for an asset sale due to the itemization of assets.

Case Example: Asset Sale Transaction for a Business

In 2024, 2seventy bio and Regeneron entered into an asset sale agreement whereby Regeneron acquired 2seventy bio's "oncology and autoimmune research and development programs, clinical manufacturing capabilities, and related platform technologies" (2seventy bio, 2024). The scope of this transaction corresponds to a business as codified by ASC 805 in the United States, e.g., it is not restricted to a single asset but includes the transfer of a complete activity with a team of approximately 160 members, infrastructure, R&D programs, and discovery platforms.

7.2.3 Negotiating an Out-Licensing

Out-licensing is an agreement where the seller, or licensor, grants the buyer, or licensee, the right to use a specific intellectual property (e.g., development, manufacture, and distribution of resulting products) in exchange for payment. Out-licensing may require significant upfront strategic considerations as the rights granted are typically based on geography (e.g., United States and Canada), field of use (e.g., oncology or preclinical research stage only) or specific diseases (e.g., Alzheimer's), within the jurisdiction in which the intellectual property is applicable. Non-exclusivity, field of use, and geographical limitations might enable the seller to retain higher levels of control over, as well as to optimize the value of, the intellectual property.

Specific terms and provisions may be added to the out-licensing deal to refine how conferred rights might be used, how collateral assets or licensor know-how might be used, or what might happen in case of company's change of control (on the part of the licensor or the licensee).

A primary consideration for a biopharma licensor is that the licensee makes active use of the license to secure licensing revenues. The seller will want to negotiate best efforts terms (e.g., "commercially reasonable efforts") to ensure that the buyer exercises a reasonable level of activity in pursuing the use of the license, and to have a way to terminate the agreement in case of breach. Best effort terms are especially important when the license is exclusive (giving the licensee full control for the defined field of use and geography). Similarly, governance and respective company contributions should be clarified to ensure optimal development and commercial activities. Non-compete limitations or covenants are another important negotiation topic and need to be considered in the context of company affiliates as well as in the context of future mergers and acquisitions, whether the company is the acquirer or the acquiree. Lastly, the seller should validate with its legal counsel that as a company, it has the appropriate consent of all relevant parties to the patent or intellectual property, as required to out-license the corresponding rights.

Case Example: Out-Licensing with Best Efforts Clause

In late 2022, Novartis out-licensed naporafenib, a Phase 2 pivotal-ready pan-RAF inhibitor, to Erasca. The exclusive license agreement included a "Commercially Reasonable Efforts" clause, under which Erasca will deploy such efforts to develop and commercialize at least one licensed product and Novartis will provide answers and clarifications to support the knowledge transferred to Erasca (Novartis & Erasca, 2022). Having deployed such efforts, two years later, Erasca was announcing strong momentum for naporafenib, with favorable preliminary Phase 1b data for potential of naporafenib plus trametinib in NRAS-mutant melanoma and potential for approval following ongoing Phase 3 trial or tissue-specific indication in melanoma (Erasca, 2024).

Overall, typical out-licensing deals will cover the following terms:

- Designation of transaction parties, including affiliate language and transferability in case of mergers and acquisitions, as applicable.
- Description of the technology licensed, fields of use (e.g., geographical, therapeutic area, disease, commercial, or development stage), extent of granted exclusivity, rights to sublicense, as applicable.
- Time frame and milestones, including termination and renewal language, as applicable.
- Payment structure (Table 7.5).
- Expenses reimbursement and expenses allowed.
- Obligations and consideration to maintain intellectual property licensed.
- Respective roles, activities, and responsibilities afferent to the licensed property, as applicable (e.g., relevant knowledge or equipment, research, development, commercialization, and regulatory authorities).
- Best efforts (e.g., benchmarks, development, production, sales, and marketing).
- Indemnification and liability clauses.
- Governance, jurisdiction, and dispute resolution.

Table 7.5 Advantages and drawbacks of different out-licensing payment structures

	Pros from licensor's perspective	*Cons from licensor's perspective*
Upfront payment	• Immediate non-dilutive funding. • Certainty of payment.	• Such income is normally taxable.
R&D milestone payment	• Can be set independently for different therapeutic indications. • Applicable to near-term events (e.g., clinical study start). • It can be aligned with derisking along the development plan timeline.	• Risk of low near-term milestones (that decrease licensee's financial risk). • Lack of control on licensee's efforts to reach milestones.
Commercial milestone payment	• Completely aligned with licensee's interests. • Can be set to desired granularity levels or thresholds (e.g., first sale in a given territory or US$500M of annual net sales).	• Remote timing and low probability for early-stage programs. • Lack of control on licensee's efforts to reach commercial stage.
Royalties	• Adequacy of payment to licensee's value created. • Normally based on net sales, thus not subject to licensee's manufacturing or commercial costs. • Might be sold to a third party to increase liquidity.	• "Net sales" might include various adjustments or reductions. • Administrative burden (calculations, reporting, specialized terms).
Cost and profit sharing	• Possibility to actively help drive development and success. • Higher reward potential than straight licensing deal. • Cost sharing can be customized, so can profit sharing. • Can build options to stop cost sharing.	• Higher financial risks than straight licensing. • Might require proof of financial capacity. • Complex governance and reporting, especially for multiple countries (although such approach may be restricted to key countries, leaving rest as standard royalties).

A licensing deal follows similar key steps to those described in Figure 7.14, with a typical overall timing of 6 months to 1 year.

Out-licensing lets the seller receive upfront payments and contingent cash inflows (such as milestones and royalties) while allowing the buyer to avoid or at least defer the purchase of the underlying asset. An out-licensing deal might also enable the seller to monetize the value of an asset without proceeding with an upfront asset sale.

7.2.4 Negotiating a Minority Equity Sale

For the seller, negotiating a minority share sale is similar to VC and corporate VC funding discussed in Chapter 5 although the buyer will be a biopharmaceutical company in this case.

When selling a minority share to an industry player, the seller typically benefits on multiple levels:

- Industry validation of their technology and commercial prospects.
- Funding and extended cash runway for research and development activities.
- Potential operational guidance and support from buyer.
- Possible strategic complement to out-licensing agreement.
- Buyer typically less focused on exits opportunities and dilution risks than VC investors.

In addition, these various benefits are often associated with an increased company valuation.

There are various reasons a seller might be able to entice a buyer to pursue a minority acquisition (as opposed to a straight acquisition), e.g.:

- Reinforcing alignment of strategic collaboration.
- Preserving key personnel incentives.
- Learning before you jump (e.g., as target company board member) especially if the progress of a lead program is uncertain or if valuation is challenging to establish.
- Securing, along with minority acquisition, a right of first refusal or first negotiation for technology or products of interest.
- Overcoming short-term financial obstacles to full acquisition (e.g., negative earnings impact in case of an M&A deal, unfavorable financing environment, or liquidity considerations).

Case Example: Collaboration with Minority Acquisition

In April 2024, Regeneron and Mammoth Biosciences announced a collaboration to pursue next-generation CRISPR-based gene editing in multiple disease areas. The collaboration includes a minority equity sale to Regeneron for US$95M at signing. "By leveraging Regeneron's expertise in AAV and antibody engineering and Mammoth's expertise in ultracompact gene editing systems, the teams will endeavor to create disease-modifying medicines that can be delivered to tissues beyond the liver, to which most gene editing treatments are currently limited" (Regeneron, 2024).

Notwithstanding the need to manage the expectations of new board members and new industry investors, one of the downsides of a minority acquisition is that the seller might have a lower upside for a later-stage deal, since the minority acquisition lessens the potential for a controlling stake to be sold and might complicate or even block the sale of certain assets upon which the minority acquisition buyer may have obtained certain rights (e.g., board seat, right of first refusal, veto rights, redemption, conversion and voting rights, information rights, no shop clause). As a result, the type and class of securities as well as drag-along rights and minority shareholders' rights (e.g., appraisal rights) represent critical considerations for minority acquisitions.

7.2.5 *Negotiating an Option to Sell*

In such a transaction, the owner of an option to sell (see Chapter 2 for valuation model) might typically pursue investments in R&D activities with the expectation to be able to sell the resulting underlying asset at a predetermined price until a fixed expiry date. This is not a common approach in the authors' experience; however, major considerations might include the following:

- Scope.
- Option premium and premium structure.
- Option period and expiration date.
- Exercise price, terms, and conditions.
- Triggering events.
- Option buyback/cancellation/termination conditions.
- Other rights (e.g., information, board observer).
- Ensuring enforceability.

7.3 Buy Side

To close on one deal, a buyer might need to evaluate many more, allocating increasing levels of resources to a specific opportunity as the probability of success increases along the deal-making process. A ratio of hundred to one

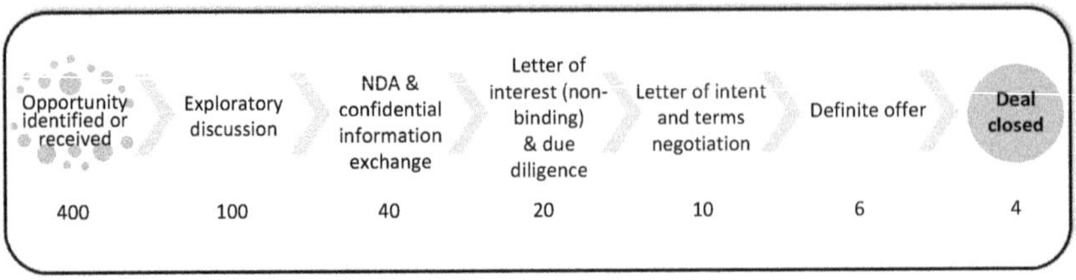

Figure 7.17 Illustrative buy-side deal funnel.

might not be uncommon (Figure 7.17), especially for large companies that tend to receive more opportunities and be present in multiple therapeutic areas. This sobering ratio also shows the importance for buyers to have an effective triage process that discards unlikely and unattractive deals as early as possible while minimizing resource investments early in the process. It also emphasizes the need to "keep several irons in the fire" in key strategic areas.

Important note:
In Section 7.3, we cover only incremental concepts from the perspective of a buyer, as opposed to the concepts already covered in Section 7.2 using a seller's perspective, or in Section 7.1 using a general perspective. Note that Section 7.3 uses a mirror structure of Section 7.2.

7.3.1 Negotiating a Company Purchase

When negotiating the purchase of a target company, a buyer will need to consider additional aspects specific to the buyer's perspective, e.g.:

- Competitive M&A environment, risk of interlopers in the process.
- Intrinsic uncertainties around target company products.
- Potential target's significant liabilities (e.g., litigations, tax issues).
- Deal financing and potential impact on credit rating.
- Antitrust issues (e.g., risk of divestitures imposed by the antitrust authorities).
- Transaction expenses (purchaser's expenses as well as seller's expenses, which, typically, will be borne by the target company and, as such, will reduce its cash position or increase its liabilities).
- Potential class actions (for listed companies).
- Acquisition integration plan and implementation.
- Cultural fit with internal team.
- Any required third-party consents.
- Potential opposition by the target's board of directors.

- Risk of a major inflection point occurring during the transaction process (either related to the target's products or related to competitors' products).
- Timing of the transaction until closing.
- Deal process and legal clauses.

Many of these points are discussed below in further details.

Competitiveness of M&A Environment

Understanding the context of a prospective deal can help gain insights into the level of competition to expect. Favorable economic conditions with limited interest rates, low inflation, and a favorable IPO market will typically result in less acquisition opportunities and therefore increased competition. Notwithstanding promising development at a target company, high levels of cash reserves at relevant large pharma companies, favorable regulatory pathways, and upcoming loss of exclusivity with revenues that need to be replaced might also augur of increased competition.

Product Uncertainty

Uncertainty around biopharma products might represent areas where the buyer is at an information disadvantage compared with the seller, thereby negatively affecting company valuation estimates. New modalities and new technologies often represent a material source of uncertainty that might compound the risks generally encountered in the biopharma industry. In the early 2020s, AI and machine learning represented an area of relative uncertainty with discrete pockets of expertise, despite significant growth and investments (Figure 7.18). Whether or not linked to new technologies or product types, evolving biopharma regulations have likewise the potential to affect company valuations.

Case Example: Impact Potential of Evolving Regulations

The Inflation Reduction Act was passed into law in the United States in August 2022. It stipulated price renegotiations for most expensive drugs under Medicare, starting in 2026 and 2028 for small molecules and biologics respectively, negotiations 13 years post approval for biologics versus 9 years for small molecules, outcome measures taken across all patients, and exemption for single-indication orphan drugs. When passed, the Act raised concerns on its impact on portfolio prioritizations and program valuations since it impacts biologics and small molecules differently. A small molecule product in development with an expected approval date in 2028 for patients under the Medicare coverage would be eligible for price negotiation in 2037.

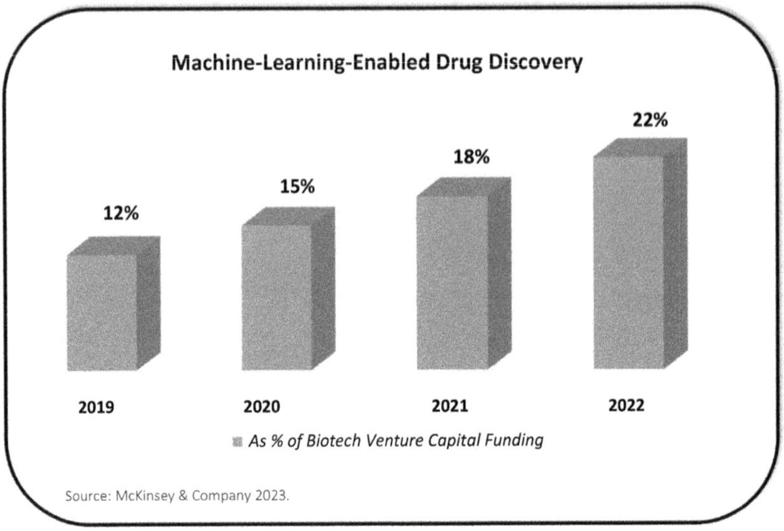

Figure 7.18 AI and machine learning in VC-funded drug discovery (see Capra et al., 2023).

Deal Financing and Tax Aspects

The buyer should not only ensure that they have sufficient capital for the transaction but also to develop acquired assets. In addition to cash on hand, deal financing is achieved through debt and equity, with a mix between the two that typically impacts the taxable nature of the transaction. Authorities might elect to reclassify such mix, depending on the jurisdiction. In the United States, Internal Revenue Code Section 385 authorizes the IRS "to prescribe such regulations as may be necessary or appropriate to determine whether an interest in a corporation is to be treated for purposes of this title as stock or indebtedness (or as in part stock and in part indebtedness)".

In addition to cash, debt, and equity considerations, earn-outs (in the case of private companies) or contingent value rights (public companies) might constitute complementary financing avenues for the buyer in addition to providing incentive alignment with the seller. Lastly, taxes or tax credits might lower or increase the acquisition cost of the transaction and upcoming operations.

Case Example: Acquisition Financing

Jazz Pharmaceuticals acquired GW Pharmaceuticals in 2021 in a taxable transaction. The deal between the two Nasdaq-traded companies was financed mostly through debt. The total deal consideration of US$7.2B was paid with US$6.6B in cash and US$0.6B in newly issued Jazz common shares. Jazz debt financing approach featured the following debt facilities: a 7-year US$3.8B term loan, US$1.5B of 4.375% senior secured notes due 2029, and a US$0.5B revolving credit facility (Jazz Pharmaceuticals, 2022).

Acquisition Integration Plan and Implementation

For the buyer, immediate steps after closing the deal also need to be anticipated. The way the company will be integrated into the buyer's organization is informed by what motivated the deal in the first place, i.e., the buyer's corporate strategy. Does the acquisition represent a completely new area for the buyer, in which case keeping the new acquisition relatively independent might make sense? Are there major synergies or strict control imperatives, in which case a full consolidation within existing buyer company's operations might make sense? Or is it more ambiguous where relative independence makes sense for certain steps but not for others? In any case, even in situations where the buyer has standard integration approaches, the integration plan may not always be a "one size fits all" approach (e.g., stage of development, use of buyer's organization, alignment with existing therapeutic areas, nimbleness and cultural alignment, relative sizes of buyer and target).

In all cases, the buyer should typically start and plan early on what the post-transaction integration will look like, identifying potential challenges to be tackled (Figure 7.19).

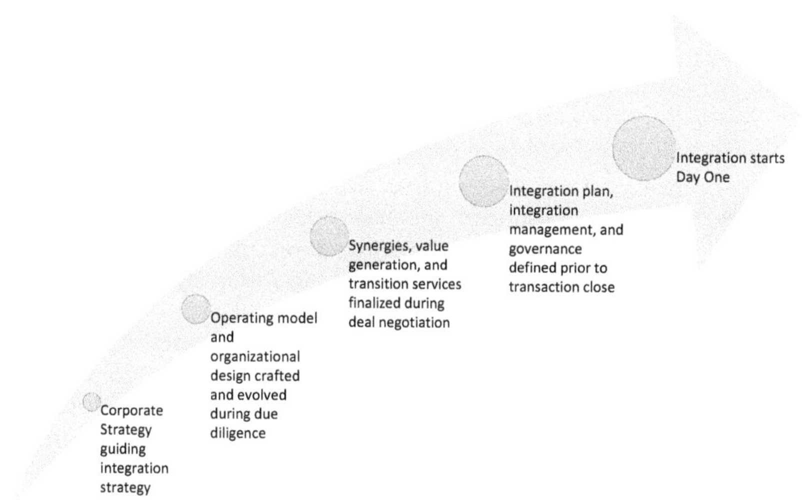

Figure 7.19 Steps toward day one readiness – integration planning.

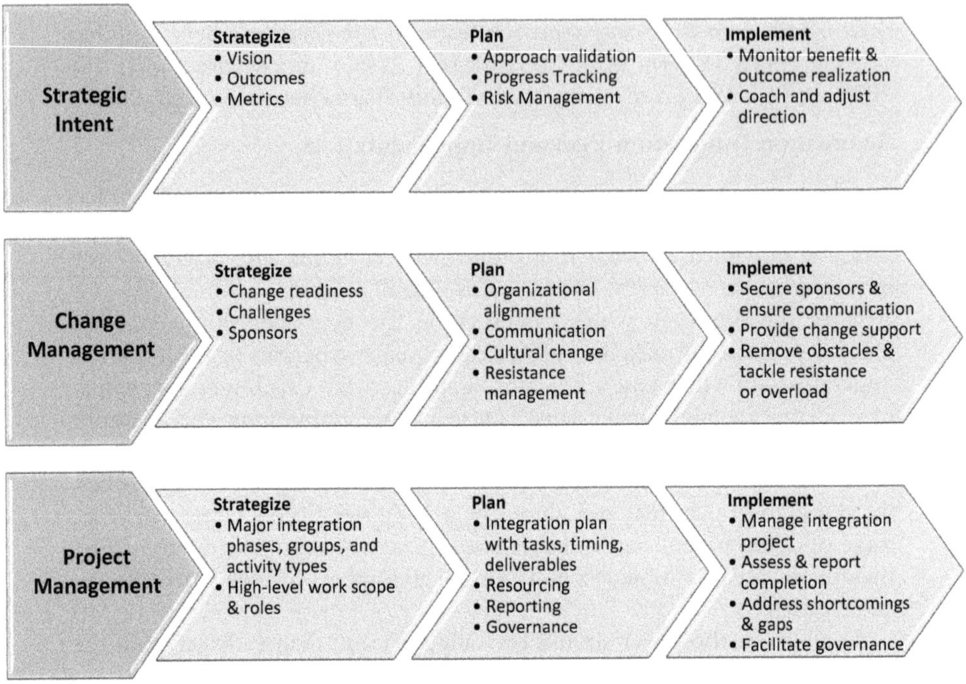

Figure 7.20 Conceptual elements of company integration.

There are three conceptual elements (Figure 7.20) to integrating a company after the transaction has closed:

- Intent: ensuring that the acquisition delivers the outcomes envisioned by the strategy.
- Change management: ensuring that disruptions are kept to a minimum and that required adjustments are made smoothly.
- Project management: ensuring that integration tasks are performed effectively and efficiently on time, on budget, and within allocated resources.

If one were to use a navigation analogy, strategic intent concerns itself with ensuring arrival at the intended point B (and not C) starting from point A; change management concerns itself with making sure people actually get on the boat and stay on; project management concerns itself that there is a boat, not only seaworthy but also equipped and steered to get everyone from A to B (taking appropriate vectors and under proper captaincy, i.e., in an appropriate time and budget).

Given the highly regulated nature of the biopharma industry and differences in practices, integration could vary by region and happen at different times within the overall integration plan. Integration planning and implementation can be complex and often makes suitable expertise and previous experience desirable.

Process and Legal Clauses

Prominent legal aspects for a buyer to consider arguably include post-closing adjustments as well as representations and warranties.

For post-closing adjustment considerations, working capital should be such that it allows the buyer to optimally operate the business within its future environment. The buyer will typically want to make sure that, under the agreed-upon price, they will not have to further increase their investment in the company by supplementing an unexpectedly underfunded operating capital. For such discussions, it is important to understand the periods considered, any adjustment or exclusion made, the accounting standards used, the use of actuals versus estimates, the consistency of the approach at closing with that of deal signing, and so on. While working capital is often a primary focus, other aspects might need to be considered such as debt, cash level, and other metrics.

Overall, the buyer should ensure that potential downward price adjustments may not exceed the cap defined for the transaction by the amount in escrow, as applicable, to avoid overpaying for the acquisition. This means adequate due diligence, analysis, and preparation, in addition to ensuring they receive appropriate substantiation or documentation for any seller's estimate.

Representations and warranties most often treated as fundamental in biotech and pharma deals include the following, starting with the most common (American Bar Association, 2024):

- Authority: party has the authority and capacity to enter into the transaction agreement.
- Enforceability: agreement has the elements necessary to constitute a legal contract.
- Organization: company is properly organized and in good standing in its jurisdiction.
- Approval: no additional party's approval or consent is required for the transaction.
- Capitalization: ownership interests for the company have been properly provided.
- Broker's fee: names of applicable brokers have been provided as well as whether their fees or commissions have been paid or will be paid.

- Subsidiaries: subsidiaries are properly organized, and ownership has been clearly laid out (including any options, warrants, or other applicable instruments).
- Financial adviser's opinion: opinion of third-party financial adviser indicating that the consideration for the acquisition is fair.
- Takeover statutes: indication that takeover statutes are not applicable to the transaction given the specifics of the contemplated transaction.

Such representations are typically expected to be accurate both at signing and closing, although in some cases, they might be at closing only.

Case Example: Buyer's Representations and Warranties

Using the same Pfizer's acquisition of Biohaven example from Section 7.2.1, buyer's representations and warranties were broken down into 12 different categories covering many different aspects, including the following (Pfizer Inc. et al., 2022):

- Organization and qualification.
- Governance and authority.
- No conflict or liabilities.
- Brokers and financial capacity.
- Ownership of subsidiary to be used for the contemplated merger transaction.
- Company purchase process.
- Taxes.

These buyer's representations and warranties organized into 12 categories are characteristically "less dense" than the seller's counterpart broken down into 33 categories (see Section 7.2.1).

7.3.2 *Negotiating an Asset Purchase*

An asset purchase can be used either as an alternate mechanism to a company purchase, or as a way to purchase a subset of company assets with a narrower scope.

Asset Purchase as Alternate Approach to Company Purchase

There are two noteworthy differences for the buyer compared with a regular purchase transaction (see Table 7.6):

1. Lower-risk transaction given ability to cherry-pick specific assets and liabilities.
2. Adjusted tax basis (down or up) for the assets to align with the purchase price minus assumed liabilities.

Table 7.6 Considerations for asset purchase transaction versus company purchase

What the buyer gets	*What the buyer does not get*
• Assets explicitly listed as part of the transaction. • Only liabilities explicitly agreed to. • Third-party contracts without anti-assignment clause assigned by seller. • Adjusted asset tax cost basis (down or up): new basis equals purchase price adjusted for assumed liabilities and other factors. • No complications from securities laws or minority shareholder opinions since there is no security involved in the purchase (unless paid with buyer's stock).	• The actual legal entity shell in which the various assets and liabilities reside. • Any asset not identified as part of the transaction. • Any liability not explicitly assumed by the buyer. This encompasses any undisclosed or unknown liability. • Any contract that contains an anti-assignment clause unless consent is obtained from the third party and seller.

Asset purchase transactions require in-depth attention to processes, consents, and approval aspects. While filings might be lighter, obtaining third-party consents might be time-consuming and could result in conditions less favorable than what was available to the original entity. The buyer also needs to understand, and specify in the asset purchase agreement, how assets, including IP, will be transferred from the seller and secure the appropriate documentation for assignments. Specific attention should be given to how the seller's legal entity was operating to ensure all necessary assets are transferred as part of the transaction (e.g., if an asset cannot be transferred as part of the transaction, a new license might be required). Lastly, for time-consuming asset transfers (e.g., active pharmaceutical ingredient and product manufacturing, market authorizations), transition service agreements might be necessary.

Case Example: Asset Purchase in Lieu of Company Purchase

In 2024, STEMCELL Technologies acquired substantially all the assets of SQZ Biotechnologies, including its entire portfolio of over 400 patents and trademarks, equipment, and a primary licensing agreement with MIT. After the transaction, SQZ filed for dissolution (SQZ, 2024).

Regular Asset Purchase

Asset purchase transactions might be used to purchase:

- A specific business or division (e.g., specific therapeutic area) of a larger corporation.

- A biopharma program.
- A specific technology platform.

Intellectual property and freedom to operate are particularly important to consider since rights and third-party agreements (e.g., licenses) are not automatically transferred with the transaction. Like any acquisition, asset purchases might be impacted by antitrust regulations.

Case Example: Asset Purchase of Biopharma Program

Novartis purchased Avrobio's cystinosis program in 2023 for US$87.5M. The asset purchase cash transaction also included an exclusive license to related know-how, assets and intellectual property, as well as a transition service agreement (Avrobio, 2023).

7.3.3 *Negotiating an In-licensing*

Typical motivations for a buyer to negotiate an in-licensing deal may include:

- Gaining access to new technology outside their core competencies.
- Securing freedom to operate in a given area.
- Obtaining exclusivity for specific applications.
- Bypassing the time and resources required to produce equivalent research.
- Share development and commercialization risks.
- Secure potential future revenues to replace decreasing revenue streams or to secure future financial growth.

The benefits the licensee (or buyer) receives from accessing the intellectual property come with corresponding costs and liabilities, governance, and processes, notwithstanding information-sharing with the seller to fulfill the obligations resulting from the in-licensing transaction (Figure 7.21). In each applicable jurisdiction, the buyer should pay attention to field of use, time bounds, confidentiality, ownership of inventions that result from the in-licensing and its associated collaborations or support, right of use by original licensor, right to sublicense by licensee, duration of the various obligations, survival questions for rights and obligations, etc.

To the extent possible, the licensee or buyer will want to ensure the deal to be structured to help manage their risk and reward expectations (Table 7.7). On a related note, in-licensing deals tend to focus more heavily on the discovery stage that arguably represents a large majority of big pharma deals as of 2023, with preclinical and clinical representing less than 15% and 30% respectively (J.P. Morgan, 2023).

COLLABORATION AND LICENSE AGREEMENT

This collaboration and license agreement (the Agreement) is entered into effective as ____________
[license context such as parties involved, recitals, definitions added here.]

Research phase
[description of research phase, including goals, research conduct approach, obligations of respective parties, what each party supplies, subcontracting approaches, oversight, rights of each party such as additional toxicology studies, and various terms]

Development and commercialization
- *[Independent activities by Licensee.]*
- *[Co-development options between Licensor and Licensee.]*
- *[Results & reporting: by Licensee, for co-development, pharmacovigilance]*
- *[Manufacturing & supply for each applicable phase / stage, subcontracting, technical development, manufacturing approach for additional products.]*

Co-development and co-commercialization
- *[Description of approach such as options available to each party, obligations and responsibilities for each step, including filing, worldwide and country approaches, branding and sales booking, audit rights, rights related to product transfers, etc.]*

Exclusivity
[Exclusivity during research phase and during commercial phase, and other related information.]

Financial provisions
[Description of payments: upfront, milestones, royalties, offsets, equity, option exercise, special cases, reporting and terms, exchange rates to be used, expenses reimbursement and expenses allowed, etc.]

Intellectual property
- Ownership rights
- Licenses *[who gets access to what under what conditions (sublicense).]*
- Patent approaches
- Assignment of inventions
- No implied license *[restriction of agreement to explicit list.]*

Other clauses
- Confidentiality
- Representations & warranties
- Indemnification and limitations of liabilities
- Governance
- Agreement term
- Jurisdiction, dispute resolution, termination
- General provisions, including change of control

Various schedules or appendices
[Supplementary information such as milestone information, research plans, supply agreements, technology details, termination process, etc.]

Figure 7.21 Illustrative collaboration and license agreement.

As platforms, AI, and software technology have become increasingly important to biotech and pharma endeavors, it is important to note that in-licensing such elements might introduce additional complexity, e.g.: is the licensee allowed access to the source code, can the licensee modify said source code, or in case source code is not accessible, what are the expectations for bug corrections?

Case Example: In-licensing to Secure Freedom to Operate

A large pharma company is considering a biotech company acquisition. During due diligence, given the crowded and complex landscape of therapeutic field, the freedom to operate determination identified IP risks: to avoid potential IP infringement and litigations, contracting a separate licensing agreement with an identified third party (or obtaining a waiver) is considered as a required step. The pharma company will try and negotiate listing the separate licensing agreement as a condition to closing.

Table 7.7 Advantages and drawbacks of different in-licensing payment structures

	Pros from licensee's perspective	*Cons from licensee's perspective*
Upfront payment	• Tax deductibility.	• Payment at closing so least aligned with buyer's risks. • Tax deductibility may be not fully immediate but amortized.
Research & Development milestone payment	• It can be set to specific key events and de-risk the deal structure.	• Documentation of the triggering events has to be specific to avoid misinterpretations or disputes.
Regulatory milestone payment	• Uses official program validation and easy to track. • Ability to be specific to target product profile (e.g., best in class profile) or jurisdiction (EMA, FDA, etc.)	• Often commensurate with development stage and increase significantly with regulatory progression. • Do not account for commercial risks (e.g., market access, pricing).
Commercial milestone payment	• It can be tailored per product, per geography and can significantly de-risk a deal structure.	• Usually represents significant payment amounts and might be challenging to negotiate with licensor.
Royalties	• They can be tailored per product, per geography.	• Careful definitions needed for net sales and duration of obligations. • Negative impact of royalties on gross margin.
Cost and profit sharing	• Cost sharing allows the licensee to de-risk and reduce the R&D investment.	• Program might not align with licensor's financial capacity or strategic priorities. • Higher governance demands, especially for multiple countries.

Case Example: In-licensing Agreement

Astellas Pharma (through wholly owned subsidiary Xyphos Biosciences) and Poseida Therapeutics entered into a research collaboration and license agreement in 2024 to develop novel allogeneic cell therapies in oncology: Poseida focuses on the research phase (reimbursed for such costs by Xyphos) while Xyphos is responsible for development and commercialization. As a result of the licensing, Poseida received an upfront payment of US$50M plus development and sales milestone payments of up to US$550M, as well as tiered royalties in the low double-digit range as a percentage of net sales (Poseida, 2024).

Antitrust Considerations

In-licensing transactions are subject to the same antitrust considerations as M&A transactions. Indeed, in the United States, under a Federal Trade Commission (FTC) Rule released in November 2013, both parties to a proposed exclusive license agreement that meets the size thresholds of the HSR Act must notify the FTC before the closing date of the transaction. The FTC has 30 days to decide and can request additional documentation. Clearance by FTC would be made public on the FTC website. Parties to the agreement may decide to terminate the transaction before closing.

Case Example: In-licensing and Antitrust Considerations

Sanofi announced in December 2023 that it opted to terminate a licensing agreement with Maze Therapeutics for a Phase I investigational program targeting Pompe disease after the FTC announced that it was seeking a preliminary injunction against the proposed licensing agreement (Sanofi, 2023).

7.3.4 Negotiating a Minority Equity Purchase

Different reasons might motivate a buyer to make a minority acquisition, i.e., a stock purchase transaction resulting in ownership of less than 50% of the voting stock of the target company:

- Improving partnership incentive alignment.
- Obtaining a regular board seat, a board observer seat, or shareholder information access to learn more about the target company and its industry segments.
- Gaining participation in the company's scientific advisory board.
- Securing an initial foothold in a new risky market segment.
- Facilitating target company financing while signaling target's value to other investors.
- Obtaining limited rights through a minority investment vehicle while leaving control to the target company leadership.

Before proceeding with a minority acquisition, the buyer should evaluate its benefits and drawbacks: target's current financial constraints, extended cash runway resulting from minority acquisition and impact on ability to reach a subsequent value inflection point, shareholder rights, company valuation for minority shareholders in case of a company sale, control, or influence conferred by the minority acquisition, and exit options. Minority acquisitions are primarily used to efficiently relieve financial constraints for the target company, maintain appropriate target leadership stock-based incentives, and for the buyer to collect information about the business; conversely, compared with other options, minority acquisitions are not ideally suited to ensure full benefit realization for the buyer (Ouimet, 2013).

A buyer's approach might differ depending on whether the target is public (e.g., PIPE investment discussed in Section 5.2.9) or private (e.g., invest jointly with other investors). A minority acquisition might also be paired with certain terms or contingent rights as a precursor to a follow-up transaction, such as a right of first negotiation or right of first refusal at a later-stage event (e.g., read-out of Phase 2, M&A offer received from another party). Similarly to any equity financing, the buyer should negotiate:

- The type and mix of company securities purchased, including considerations relevant to the security class such as liquidation preference, dividends, conversion, voting rights, restrictions, registration, lock-up, and redemption.
- The investment amount, purchase price, implied company valuation, and accounting implications (e.g., premium not supported by fair value might require booking overpayment as expense under IFRS).
- Other rights (e.g., information, right of first refusal, drag along, board seat).
- Other clauses (e.g., no shop, anti-dilution, pay to play).
- Option pool size and vesting considerations.
- Coverage of deal expenses.

Case Example: Minority Acquisition with Right of First Negotiation

In 2023, Sanofi made a US$30M PIPE minority equity investment in MeiraGTx Holdings, a gene therapy company with a broad pipeline of late-stage clinical programs. As part of the deal, Sanofi secured a right of first negotiation for the use of riboswitch gene regulation technology in certain therapeutic areas and diseases and for the xerostomia program, plus representation rights in the Science and Technology Committee of MeiraGTx' Board of Directors (MeiraGTx, 2024). The transaction provided Sanofi with potential rights to multiple programs of interest and a close strategic relationship with MeiraGTx. The transaction provided MeiraGTx with immediate funding in a challenging environment and validated its technology, notwithstanding a favorable stock price impact from the deal.

Under US GAAP, as an example, there are three ways to account for an ownership stake in another company:

- Consolidated method – used when the buyer owns over 50% of the voting interest of the target company or is shown to have control over the target in a different way (e.g., control of the board of directors). Under the consolidated method, financials from the target are recognized as part of the buyer's financials as if it were one single entity.

- Equity method – used when the buyer owns more than 20% but less than 50% of the voting rights of the target company and does not otherwise have control over the target. Under the equity method, the initial investment is recorded at cost, and investment profits or losses are assessed quarterly; the buyer then has to record their share of the target company's profits or losses in its own financials.
- Fair value method – used when the buyer owns less than 20% of the voting rights of the target company and when the investment does not lead to significant influence over the company. Under this method, the minority acquisition is recorded on the balance sheet of the buyer as a non-current asset based on the historical transaction purchase price. Under US GAAP, the fair value change of shares would be recognized in the P&L. Note that under IFRS, an election for treatment as equity instruments (IFRS 9) may be done, avoiding the impact on the P&L. This election is not available under US GAAP. Dividends are recorded on the income statement as financial income and taxed accordingly.

As a result of the financial impact considerations highlighted above, it might be desirable for a minority acquisition to remain below a 20% voting right level post transaction and avoid terms that might be interpreted as having significant influence over the target company. A board observer seat might be preferable to a regular board seat (board observers do not have board member voting rights and thus exert no significant influence or control).

Likewise, the buyer might not necessarily be exempt from antitrust considerations, as regulators will typically evaluate transaction aspects that might confer control of the company to the buyer. In any case, to avoid gun-jumping cases, when in doubt, a minority acquisition buyer should seek informed expert opinions on any regulatory approval or notification that might be required based on the specifics of the transaction and corresponding jurisdictions.

After the transaction, the buyer becomes a minority shareholder of the target. In many jurisdictions, minority shareholder rights are protected by law and through various regulatory bodies. Depending on the jurisdiction, advantages for the minority stake buyer might include:

- Ability to influence a subsequent company purchase or sale of strategic assets.
- Possibility, as minority shareholder, to independently seek higher valuations per share from a deal in certain circumstances.
- Protection conferred by anti-dilution mechanisms.

7.3.5 *Negotiating an Option to Purchase*

With an option to purchase, the buyer agrees to pay the company a fee in exchange for the exclusive option to buy a targeted company or financial asset under predetermined conditions (e.g., specified strike price and time to maturity of the option). An option to purchase might be used for an entire company, a business or division, a technology, a platform, a compound, equipment, or intellectual property such as a license. The fee may encompass different elements such as option fee payment, option extension fee, and milestone payments to reflect possible evolutions. The purchase agreement that would be used if the option is exercised is typically established and agreed upon at the time of the option transaction. The agreement normally includes conditions, covenants, representations, and warranties. For the option to have value to the buyer, the agreement needs to be enforceable and the buyer will keep abreast of the performance of the underlying company, business, R&D, or assets, with the expectation to exercise the option when deemed most attractive before it expires. The option maturity might be fixed in time or relative to a specific event (e.g., clinical trial completion or regulatory milestone). The option provides a way for the buyer (and seller) to fix the valuation in advance; however, the buyer may have limited control over how the company runs underlying operations. When the buyer wants to evaluate an external innovation, technology, or molecule at an early stage, they might use the option in lieu of doing an evaluation and then separately negotiating an in-licensing: with the option to license, they bundle the evaluation agreement and the licensing agreement into one single agreement negotiated upfront that gives the buyer exclusivity while they evaluate the underlying assets' value.

Case Example: Option to Purchase a Company

In 2022, Boehringer Ingelheim negotiated an option to acquire Trutino Biosciences, a preclinical immuno-oncology biotech company, with which it already had a collaboration and licensing agreement. The undisclosed deal amount at signing included an upfront payment and a convertible note funded by Boehringer Ingelheim, in exchange for the option to acquire Trutino under predetermined purchase price terms, once pre-defined milestones are achieved (Trutino Biosciences, 2022).

Case Example: Option to Purchase a License

In late 2023, as reproxalap was under the FDA new drug application review, AbbVie entered into an exclusive option agreement with Aldeyra Therapeutics, providing AbbVie the right to purchase a license for reproxalap in dry eye disease. The option can be exercised via written notification from AbbVie to Aldeyra within an exercise period contingent upon US FDA approval date for reproxalap, optional AbbVie payments to extend the option period, and 18 months from the effective date of the agreement at the latest.

The option agreement stipulated a US$1M non-refundable option fee and a US$5M option extension fee. Would AbbVie choose to exercise the option, Aldeyra would receive an upfront payment of US$100M less option fees plus additional regulatory and commercial milestones, in addition to a profit and loss-sharing approach for the United States versus royalties outside the United States (Aldeyra Therapeutics, 2023).

7.4 Straight Collaborations

Collaborations represent another strategic avenue that biopharma companies might pursue to augment their research and development pipeline and commercial activities. Specifically, a collaboration is an agreement between two or more organizations to work toward specific goals while remaining independent from each other.

Even though collaborations might be combined with other transactions like asset purchases, licensing, equity investments, or related options, we limit the discussion in this section to temporary licenses required for the collaboration with a field of use limited to the collaboration, as opposed to licenses aimed at uses outside of strictly defined collaboration activities. These other transactions (asset purchases, licensing, equity investments, or related options) have already been covered in previous sections and might conceptually simply be added to the collaborations covered under Section 7.4. Collaborations, as defined in this section, do not involve transfer or sale of intellectual property rights and assets other than temporarily to enable the collaboration.

There are various reasons why an organization might take part in a biopharma collaboration (Figure 7.22). A large pharma company might use collaborations to supplement its research and development activities (e.g., access to research platforms or software and Artificial Intelligence capabilities) without making significant upfront investments or financial commitments. Be it with a government agency or another company, a small

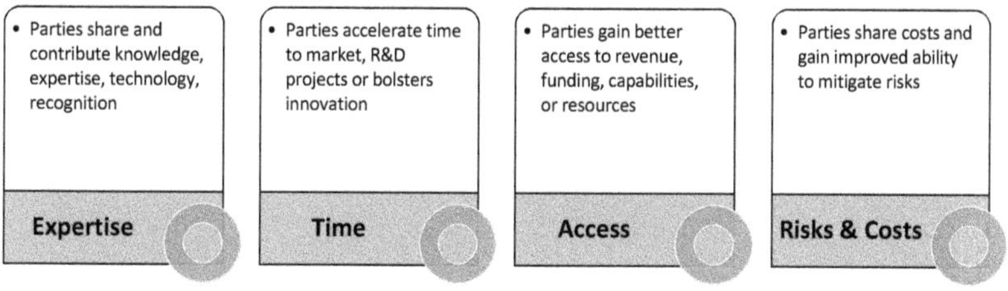

Figure 7.22 Conceptual benefits of biopharma collaborations.

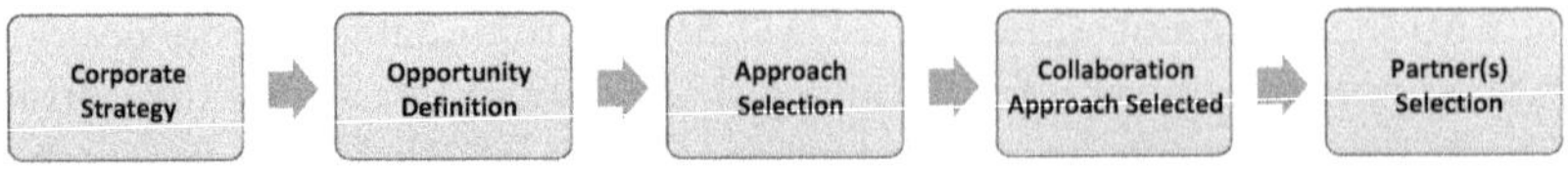

Figure 7.23 Strategy and collaborations.

biopharma firm might use collaborations as external signals of the company program's value or to secure key expertise that would be expensive to replicate internally. An academic institution might use collaborations as a vehicle to generate revenues from academic research or operational services.

Ultimately, any collaboration should align with the company's strategy (Figure 7.23) and be carefully evaluated based on the following factors:

- Clear drivers behind a collaboration model selection.
- Definition of realistic outcomes and timing.
- Objective measurement of value created and financial impact.
- Ability to manage risks given the collaboration construct.
- Negotiation and collaboration game plan.

A collaboration is normally encapsulated into a collaboration agreement that provides, e.g.:

- Collaboration objectives.
- Required licensing with geographical and field of use limitations.
- Contributions, roles, and responsibilities of each party.
- Governance and dispute resolution.
- Terms and duration.
- Risks, resources, and benefits sharing.
- Program definition:
    - Overall approach.
    - Regulatory.
    - Manufacturing.
    - Commercialization and distribution.
    - IP/knowledge creation with corresponding rights and licenses for each party versus joint; licensing improvements; IP assignment and IP transfers.
    - Technology.
    - Diligence/efforts responsibilities.
    - Program end and exit options.
- Funding (e.g., FTEs), revenue/payment structure, and amounts.
- Third-party licenses/sub-licensing.
- Exclusivity.

- Legal considerations.
  - Confidentiality.
  - Governing jurisdictions.
  - Binding versus non-binding aspects.
  - Press release and publication processes or rights.
  - Termination options (planned versus contingent).
  - Legal status for proceeding (e.g., withdrawal with or without liabilities).

In order to evaluate a collaboration and establish a suitable agreement, it might be helpful to use an analytical framework, like the "Partnership fit – Implementation – Outcome – Update" or "P.I.O.U." framework (Figure 7.24).

Case Example: Collaboration

In 2022, Pfizer, MorphoSys, and Incyte announced a Phase 1b/2 clinical trial collaboration to investigate a combination immunotherapy. Under the agreement (Pfizer, 2022):

- Pfizer sponsored and funded Phase 1b/2 study and provided the supplies of maplirpacept (TTI-622) and lenalidomide.
- MorphoSys and Incyte provided the supplies of Monjuvi (tafasitamab) for the study.

As open innovation becomes more prevalent, collaborations represent an important strategic option for biopharma companies as they can bring about a number of benefits, e.g.:

- De-risked opportunities.
- Access to R&D expertise or state-of-the-art equipment and facilities.
- Access to data or platforms.
- Faster time to market or higher translational impact.
- Improved publication ability and visibility.

There are many possible forms of biopharma collaborations (Figure 7.25). At one end of the spectrum there are collaborations simply aimed at gathering business intelligence: they might use a loose open structure, involving little risks to the company, retaining informal objectives, without management or oversight. At the other end of the spectrum, a collaboration might involve a long-term collaboration structure with pooled organizational capabilities, major strategic stakes for the organization, formalized objectives or targeted outcomes, and a collaboration management office to steer the relationship. Collaborations between these two ends of the spectrum may constitute a compromise between locking in a strategic direction and keeping exploratory options in play.

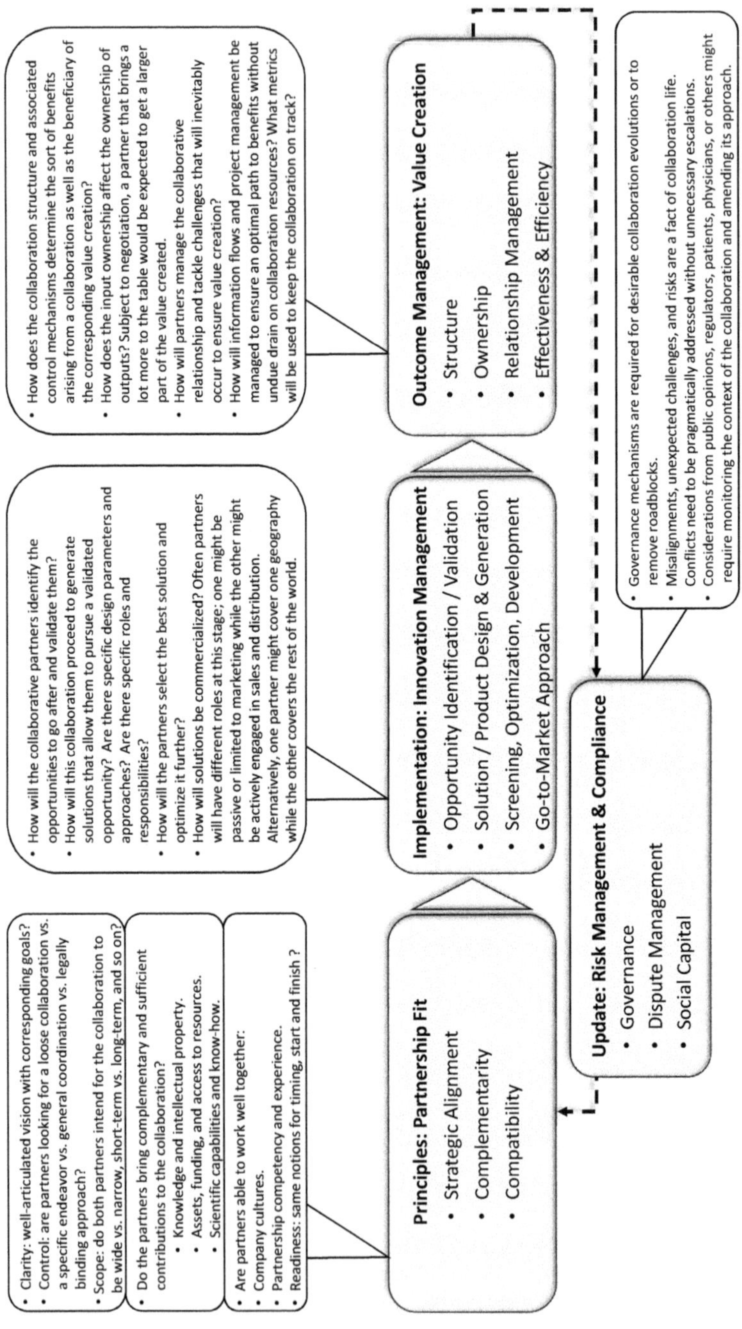

Figure 7.24 PIOU collaboration framework.

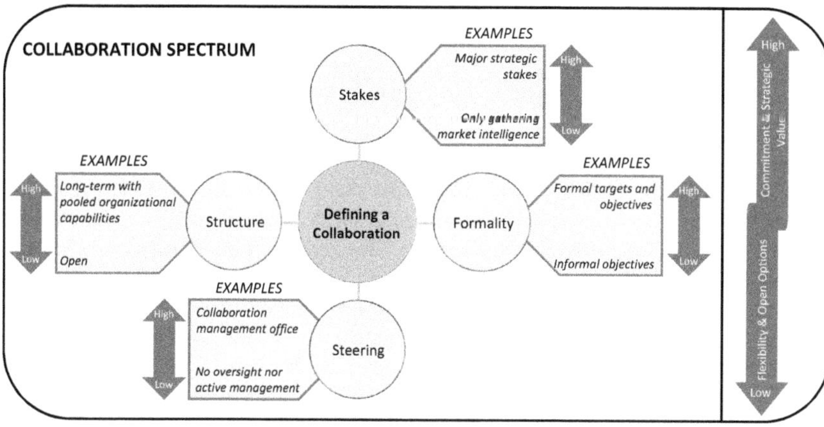

Figure 7.25 Collaboration spectrum.

References

2seventy bio. (2024, January 30). *2seventy bio Announces New Strategic Path Forward.* Retrieved 11/24/2024, from https://www.nasdaq.com/press-release/2seventy-bioannounces-new-strategic-path-forward-2024-01-30.

Aldeyra Therapeutics. (2023, November 1). *Form 8-K.* Retrieved 11/29/2024, from https://www.sec.gov/Archives/edgar/data/1341235/000119312523267697/d857697d8k.htm

Alvarez, Z., Curran, B., Salladin, A., Lovells, H. & Zhang, K. (2022, December 21). *JPM2023 Trendspotting: Evaluating CFIUS Risks in the Biotech Sector.* Retrieved 1/8/2024, from https://www.jdsupra.com/legalnews/jpm2023-trendspotting-evaluating-cfius-5687472/

American Bar Association. (2024). *2024 ABA Public Target Deal Points Study.* Retrieved 3/25/2024, from https://public.tableau.com/app/profile/aba.deal.points/viz/2024ABADealPointsStudy/Home1

AstraZeneca PLC. (2021, April 12). *Acquisition of Alexion Pharmaceuticals, Inc. by AstraZeneca PLC - Circular to Shareholders and Notice of General Meeting.* Retrieved 11/22/2024, from https://www.sec.gov/Archives/edgar/data/901832/000110465921049239/tm216588d8_425.htm

Avrobio. (2023, May 22). *AVROBIO Announces Agreement to Sell Cystinosis Gene Therapy Program for $87.5 Million.* Retrieved 11/28/2024, from https://www.businesswire.com/news/home/20230522005254/en/AVROBIO-Announces-Agreement-to-Sell-Cystinosis-Gene-Therapy-Program-for-87.5-Million

Baker McKenzie. (2022, December 2). *Global Private M&A Guide* 2021. Retrieved 1/8/2024, from https://www.bakermckenzie.com/-/media/files/insight/guides/2022/global-private-ma-guide-2021-limited-content-version-nov-2022.pdf

Berghauser Pont, L., Fleming, E., Moss, R., Robke, L., Smietana, K. & Wurzer, S. (2022, May 31). *McKinsey Insights - Innovation Sourcing in Biopharma: Four Practices to Maximize Success.* Retrieved 10/8/2023, from https://www.mckinsey.com/industries/life-sciences/our-insights/innovation-sourcing-in-biopharma-four-practices-to-maximize-success/

Capra, E., Fougner, C., Leclerc, O., Mäkitie, A., Suberski, A. & Suhendra, M. (2023, December). *What Early-Stage Investing Reveals About Biotech Innovation.* McKinsey & Company. Retrieved 3/4/2024, from https://www.mckinsey.com/~/media/mckinsey/industries/life%20sciences/our%20insights/what%20early%20stage%20investing%20reveals%20about%20biotech%20innovation/what-early-stage-investing-reveals-about-biotech-innovation.pdf

Emmerich, A. O., & Panovka, R. (2023, January 7). *Cross-Border M&A – 2023 Checklist for Successful Acquisitions in the U.S.* Harvard Law School Forum on Corporate Governance. Retrieved 1/8/2024, from https://corpgov.law.harvard.edu/2023/01/07/cross-border-ma-2023-checklist-for-successful-acquisitions-in-the-u-s/#:~:text=Cross%2Dborder%20deals%20were%2032, prior%20ten%20years%20(35%25).

Erasca. (2024, October 24). *Erasca Announces Strong Momentum for Naporafenib and RAS Targeting Franchise.* Retrieved 11/25/2024, from https://investors.erasca.com/news-releases/news-release-details/erasca-announces-strong-|momentum-naporafenib-and-ras-targeting

FDA. (2022, July 22). *Proposed Rule on Revising the National Drug Code Format.* Retrieved 11/24/2024, from https://www.fda.gov/drugs/drug-approvals-and-databases/proposed-rule-revising-national-drug-code-format

Ipsen. (2023, March 2). *Ipsen Completes Acquisition of Albireo, Expanding the Scope of Its Rare Disease Portfolio.* Retrieved 11/22/2024, from https://www.ipsen.com/press-releases/ipsen-completes-acquisition-of-albireo-expanding-the-scope-of-its-rare-disease-portfolio/

Jazz Pharmaceuticals. (2022, March 7). *Form 10-K for the Fiscal Year Ended* December 31, 2021. Retrieved 11/26/2024, from https://www.sec.gov/Archives/edgar/data/1232524/000123252422000012/jazz-20211231.htm

J.P. Morgan. (2023, December). *2023 Annual Biopharma Licensing and Venture Report.* Retrieved 4/7/2024, from https://www.jpmorgan.com/content/dam/jpmorgan/documents/cb/insights/outlook/jpmorgan-dec-2023-biopharma-licensing-and-venture-report.pdf

MeiraGTx. (2024, March 15). *Form 10-K for the Fiscal Year Ended* December 31, 2023. Retrieved 11/29/2024, from https://www.sec.gov/Archives/edgar/data/1735438/000155837024003309/mgtx-20231231x10k.htm#ITEM1 BUSINESS

Michaeli, D. T., Yagmur, H. B., Achmadeev, T., & Michaeli, T. (2022). Value drivers of development stage biopharma companies. *The European Journal of Health Economics, 23*(8), 1287–1296. https://doi.org/10.1007/s10198-021-01427-5

Mindset Pharma. (2023, September 19). *Notice of Meeting and Management Information Circular Relating to the Special Meeting of Shareholders of Mindset Pharma inc. to be held on* October 19, 2023. Edgar. Retrieved 11/22/2024, from https://sedar-filings-backup.thecse.com/00031304/2309221427314325.pdf

Novartis, & Erasca. (2022, December 9). *Exclusive License Agreement.* Edgar. Retrieved 11/25/2024, from https://www.sec.gov/Archives/edgar/data/1761918/000095017023009496/eras-ex10_20.htm

Ouimet, P. P. (2013). What motivates minority acquisitions? The trade-offs between a partial equity stake and complete integration. *The Review of Financial Studies, 26*(4), 1021–1047. https://www.jstor.org/stable/23355387

Pfizer. (2022, June 13). *Pfizer, MorphoSys and Incyte Enter into Clinical Trial Collaboration for Monjuvi® (tafasitamab-cxix) in Combination with TTI-622, a Fusion Protein Directed Against CD47.* Retrieved 11/29/2024, from https://www.pfizer.com/news/announcements/pfizer-morphosys-and-incyte-enter-clinical-trial-collaboration-monjuvir#:~:text=Pfizer%20Inc.%20%28NASDAQ%3APFE%29%2C%20MorphoSys%20U.S.%20Inc.%2C%20a%20fully,not%20eligible%20for%20autologous%20stem%20cell%20transplantation%20%28ASCT%29

Pfizer Inc., Bulldog (BVI) Ltd & Biohaven Pharmaceutical Holding Company Ltd. (2022, May 9). *Agreement and Plan of Merger.* Retrieved 11/22/2024, from https://www.sec.gov/Archives/edgar/data/1689813/000168981322000049/ex21agreementandplanofmerg.htm#i2a4d0d85dc7941df815984d55c4f90b7_44

Poseida. (2024, May 1). *Astellas and Poseida Therapeutics Enter into Research Collaboration and License Agreement to Develop Novel Allogeneic Cell Therapies in Oncology.* Retrieved 11/28/2024, from https://investors.poseida.com/news-releases/news-release-details/astellas-and-poseida-therapeutics-enter-research-collaboration

Ramos, A., Watson, K. & Quine, P. (2020, July 27). *Board Guidance: Getting to Business Judgment Rule Deference When You Have a Controlling Stockholder.* SheppardMullin. Retrieved 1/16/24, from https://www.corporatesecuritieslawblog.com/2020/07/business-judgment-rule-deference-mfw/#:~:text=%5B2%5D%20The%20business%20judgment%20rule,the%20best%20interests%20of%20the

Regeneron. (2024, April 25). *Regeneron and Mammoth Biosciences Collaborate to Pursue Next-Generation CRISPR-Based Gene Editing for Multiple Diseases.* Retrieved 11/25/2024, from https://investor.regeneron.com/news-releases/news-release-details/regeneron-and-mammoth-biosciences-collaborate-pursue-next

Sanofi. (2023, December 11). *Statement on FTC Challenge to Proposed License Agreement with Maze Therapeutics.* Retrieved 11/28/2024, from https://www.sanofi.com/en/media-room/press-releases/2023/2023-12-11-21-08-20-2794272

Sibbett, B., & Kim, H. (2022, January 21). *Cross-Border M&A: A Checklist of US Issues for Non-US Acquirers.* Retrieved 1/8/2024, from https://www.cliffordchance.com/content/dam/cliffordchance/PDFDocuments/2022-01-wolters-kluwer-blr-cross-border-m%26a-a-checklist-of-us-issues-for-non-us-acquirers.pdf

SQZ. (2024, January 23). *Schedule 14A.* Retrieved 11/27/2024, from https://www.sec.gov/Archives/edgar/data/1604477/000119312524013016/d813099ddefm14a.htm

Trutino Biosciences. (2022, June 15). *Boehringer Ingelheim Signs Option to Acquire Trutino Biosciences.* Retrieved 11/29/2024, from https://trutinobio.com/boehringer-ingelheim-signs-option-to-acquire-trutino-biosciences/

Wagner Partin, S., Flanagan, S. & Brown, H. (2023, May 19). *Anatomy of a CVR: A Primer on the Key Components and Trends of CVRs in Life Sciences Public M&A*

Deals. Sidley. Retrieved 12/18/2023, from https://www.sidley.com/-/media/publications/anatomy-of-a-cvr-a-primer-on-the-key-components-and-trends-of-cvrs-in-life-sciences-public-ma-deals.pdf?la=en&rev=849ca264e438474cb90d2c901a4b357e

Wang, N., Burr, A., Dechter, A. & Powers, C. (2022, October 17). *Why Pharma Needs to Shift to an 'Innovation Constellation' Investment Strategy*. ZS. Retrieved 6/2/2023, from https://www.zs.com/insights/why-pharma-needs-an-innovation-constellation-investment-strategy

Chapter 8

Contractual Considerations for Biopharma Deals

8.1 Agreement Models, Shared Aspects, and Specific Aspects

In this chapter, we discuss the contracts written for deals covered in Chapter 7 (e.g., company purchase, asset purchase, etc.). It is important to note that such agreements are commonly supplemented by other related agreements that may or may not be superseded by the main agreement, such as confidentiality or non-disclosure agreements, transition service agreements, registration, employment agreements, etc.

When it comes to contracts, it is important to understand each party's business and strategic objectives, and whether they correspond to standard industry approaches (which would require fewer specific aspects) or to more exceptional cases (that might require more deal-specific aspects), or perhaps to emerging standards that still represent substantive new terms (Figure 8.1). Examples of deal-specific objectives might include a particular

Figure 8.1 Major driver categories for contractual considerations.

DOI: 10.4324/9781003598046-8

geographic restriction or allowing the buyer to keep one product while subsequently spinning off the rest.

It is common for negotiations to include contract drafts, resulting in some of the aspects covered in this chapter occurring in early transaction process steps. Similarly to the due diligence process covered in Chapter 7, contractual reviews for a contemplated transaction will require functional reviews by various experts with the assistance of counsel and business development teams, to ensure that the contractual language aligns with both the deal intent and the functional requirements. In fact, it is common for written agreements to address sensitive points and challenges identified during the due diligence process.

Transaction agreements can be both lengthy (typically organized in various articles each constituted of various sections) and highly complex requiring the support of seasoned lawyers. There can also be subtle variances in contractual approaches depending on geography and jurisdiction. Failure to comply with one or more section(s) of a transaction agreement can effectively result in either stopping the transaction or in starting a litigation process. While business leaders might be tempted to focus mostly on "getting a deal done", such far-reaching consequences highlight the importance of carefully examining contractual implications.

We would be remiss not to mention that the biopharma industry's characteristics make contractual aspects more challenging than in other industries: technical aspects (e.g., mechanisms of actions, modalities, stages of development), intangibles, differentiated scientific characteristics, medical and patient considerations, and possibly the added complexity of several ownership interests due to previous licensing agreements. In addition, contractual language should pay specific attention to the allocation of the significant financial risks or rewards associated with the biotech and pharmaceutical industries.

8.2 Common Contractual Categories and Concepts

It is common to encounter similar wording and clauses, as well as a certain level of accepted standardization in biotech and pharma contracts, since such language and structure makes for streamlined reviews and discussions.

This section covers terminology and aspects (Figure 8.2) that tend to be common across transactions in the authors' experience (arguably based on transactions involving at least one US or European party).

Case Example: Illustrative Instances of Various Contract Types

The Securities and Exchange Commission (SEC) requires companies to file material contracts on EDGAR using "Exhibit 10" designation and

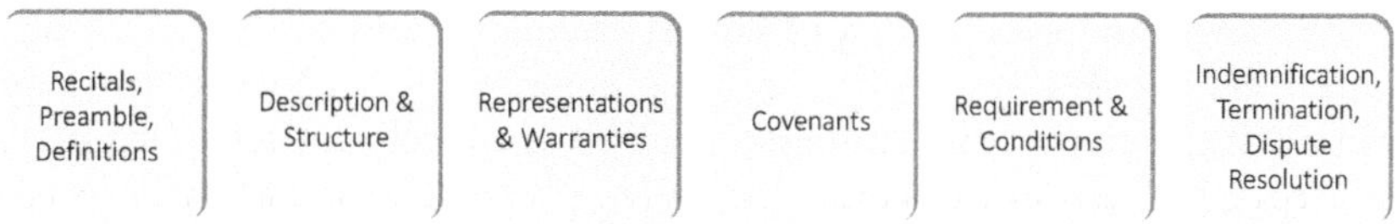

Figure 8.2 Common contractual categories for biopharma deals.

companies make disclosures on various contracts especially on forms 10-K, 10-Q, and 8-K, which may provide access to various relevant instances of contracts and precedents. Searches might be conducted on EDGAR at https://www.sec.gov/edgar/search/. Note that SIC codes can be used as part of the search: commonly used codes for pharma and biotech are 2833/2834 and 2836 respectively.

At the time of publication, using the referenced website and expanding the search options, one might locate the agreement and plan of merger between Pfizer and Biohaven, which required shareholder approval (see examples in Sections 7.2.1 and 7.3.1), by conducting the following search:

- Document word or phrase: "agreement" "Pfizer".
- Company name: Biohaven.
- Filing category: proxy materials.

The agreement will be included in the following filing result: DEFM14A (Proxy statement (business combination)) dated 2022-08-30.

8.2.1 *Recitals, Preamble, Definitions*

Recitals, preamble, and definitions are all aspects of an agreement intended to provide orientation, context, effective date, and definitions for the various terms and wording used in the agreement, in order to try and minimize potential disputes or misunderstandings at a later time. Definitions can have an important impact on the contract as their precision and specificity might affect terms throughout the contract in which they are used. It is critical to note that definitions may be found in various parts of the contract, even if there is a section entitled definitions that may or may not refer to additional definitions located elsewhere.

8.2.2 *Deal Description and Structure*

The deal description and structure provide essential information on what is acquired through the contemplated transaction, and the consideration to be provided in return (including method and timing of payment). Structuring a transaction involves numerous factors beyond identifying what is being purchased (stock, assets, rights, etc.) and determining the form of payment as well as the contracting entities. Such factors typically include third-party consents, process and timing, legal and tax aspects, and financial aspects. Note that for collaboration contracts, nothing might technically be purchased and the notion of purchase might need to be replaced by a broader notion of contribution exchanges.

8.2.3 *Reps and Warranties*

Representations, often shortened as "reps" in "reps and warranties", are statements by buyer or seller that concerns current or past situations or facts. Making untrue representations may result in damages or even void a contract, or open the door toward making claims in that direction.

Warranties are statements or assurances by buyer or seller that concerns current or future situations or conditions; correspondingly, not maintaining the conditions provided by warranties may result in a breach of warranties with various implications.

8.2.4 *Pre-closing and Post-closing Covenants*

Covenants provide assurances of certain performance (positive covenants) or non-performance obligations (negative covenants) by the buyer or seller. Either way, they typically belong to one of two categories: obligations before the transaction closes (by definition, such pre-closing covenants do not apply for simultaneous signing and closing), or obligations after the transaction closes. A clause by which the parties agree to maintain the confidentiality of the transaction prior to closing is a key element of the covenants section.

8.2.5 *Requirements and Conditions*

Closing requirements indicate what needs to happen before the respective parties are obligated to consummate the transaction and the conditions under which the execution of the closing will take place.

8.2.6 *Indemnification, Termination, and Dispute Resolution Clauses*

Such sections serve as a roadmap if things do not turn out as expected.

Indemnification clauses indicate remedies and what happens in case one party breaches the covenants or reps and warranties. Indemnification clauses serve as a mechanism to reallocate or share some of the risks resulting from the contemplated transaction.

Dispute resolution serves as guidance when the different parties do not see eye to eye whereas termination provides guidance as to how to proceed and what the consequences are of not closing the deal for deals where signing and closing are not simultaneous.

8.2.7 *Other Contractual Considerations*

Other considerations might commonly include assignability, publicity and communication around the deal, or post-merger integration.

8.3 Aspects Specific to One Contract Type

IMPORTANT NOTE:

This section uses the same terminology and elements covered in Section 8.2 but focuses specifically on aspects important to a specific type of contract (e.g., company sale versus licensing). The section discusses how a contract might reflect important deal aspects covered in Chapter 7 for that specific contract type, rather than reviewing their negotiation. The section is akin to a contract anatomy, highlighting where selected deal points might reside. Given the wide and diverse range of jurisdictions and practices, the current section is by necessity arbitrarily selective, illustrative, and intended to provide a general understanding rather than a comprehensive, systematic, or prescriptive analysis. It is important to recognize that individual contracts can differ significantly and might not adhere to standard industry practices or terminology. Consulting a competent experienced attorney authorized to practice in your jurisdiction to guide you through contractual negotiations and their implications is absolutely critical.

8.3.1 *Company Purchase Agreement*

As the company is transferred to a new owner, the company purchase agreement should critically incorporate aspects to ensure such transfer as well as provide confidence in enforcing the ongoing ability of the company to successfully navigate the transition and operate past that point in a regulatory compliant fashion. Corresponding salient points of a company purchase agreement to protect buyer and seller are highlighted below.

Recitals, Preamble, Definitions

To ensure transfer, recitals and preamble will typically state that the transaction has been approved by the respective governance (e.g., boards of directors) of the seller and the buyer, as clearly identified, as well as outline any further approval required.

Aspects critical to ongoing operations will be included in the definitions:

- Intellectual property: explicitly listing critical technology that will be included or excluded from the scope of the transaction.
- Material contracts, to be taken over or renegotiated by the buyer post closing, for which a list is typically provided in disclosures.
- Audited financial statements if these documents are required to be provided by the sell side (e.g., as evidence of financially sustainable operations).
- In many transactions, the acquisition price is adjusted to account for the acquired company's outstanding debts at the time of closing. Therefore, the buyer typically seeks to define "financial obligations" broadly to cover all potential liabilities owed by the company: financial institutions lending, obligations from various debt instruments, such as notes, bonds, factoring, derivatives contracts, letters of credit, financial guarantees, and capitalized lease obligations.

Description and Structure

As the transfer of company ownership can follow different routes as discussed in Chapter 7 (e.g., statutory merger, share purchase), the agreement needs to clearly indicate the specific transaction vehicle that will be used, the applicable legal framework (e.g., the General Corporation Law of the State of Delaware), the closing location and date, and the specific legal certificates (e.g., certificate of merger, amendment to certificate of incorporation) that will be filed to consummate the transaction.

As applicable, the future composition of the directors and officers of the acquired company may be described in this part of the agreement. It is common that the board of directors of the surviving entity is composed of the directors of the acquiring company, unless otherwise stated.

The agreement will explicitly describe the constitution and details of the consideration the company owners will receive to transfer their ownership interests, e.g., price per share in cash or in shares of the acquiring company. Where applicable, details will include contingent payments, e.g., public companies contingent value rights or private companies earnouts.

To avoid ulterior challenges to the transfer of property rights, contracting parties need to secure the accuracy of ownership rights inventory at closing. Specifically, using the most common case of a corporation, the buyer will need to limit the count to shares eligible for payment, while preventing any misses that might lead to indemnity claims post closing. Typical provisions are included in the agreement to show how various ownership interests will be converted, changed, or transferred; in this case, how stock options, restricted shares, or other equity awards will be converted into common stock, such as the following:

- All outstanding stock options will become fully vested and canceled at the closing date, in exchange for a price per share consideration (less applicable taxes to be withheld) if the exercise price of the stock options is lower than the purchase price per share.
- Similarly, restricted shares units will become fully vested at the closing date and receive a price consideration per share (less applicable taxes to be withheld). The purchase price for stock options (and restricted stock units) owned by employees will typically be paid through the payroll to each holder.

Again, in the case of a corporation, the agreement will usually require that any employee stock purchase plans be terminated, with no commencement of offering between signing and closing and without liability to the acquiring company post closing.

Reps and Warranties

The seller's representations and warranties should be structured to ensure a smooth ownership transfer while supporting the continued operation of the company, thereby protecting the buyer's interests (Figure 8.3). This includes confirming: the clarity and validity of the corporate structure (such as registration and capitalization), long-term value through effective governance, the absence of undisclosed liabilities, legitimate control of economic benefits (including asset ownership and regulatory compliance), and adherence to applicable laws and processes for the future.

Likewise, to protect seller's interests, contractual buyer's reps and warranties should attempt to ensure that the buyer is legitimate (organization, qualification, and legal entities with corporate power and authority), does not have dealings that would contravene the transaction (no conflict, all required consent, registration, declaration, or filings have been listed, no pending litigation proceeding, no broker other than those listed), has the means to consummate the transaction (funding, owner of buyer's entity used for transaction), addresses other required transaction aspects (e.g., tax), and can generally complete the transaction (processes).

Chapter 7 included relevant and illustrative discussions of company purchase agreement reps and warranties in the case of Pfizer's acquisition of Biohaven: see Section 7.2.1 for seller's reps and warranties and Section 7.3.1 for buyer's reps and warranties.

Pre-closing and Post-closing Covenants

Covenants also represent an important contractual component of a company purchase agreement to maintain ongoing company operations, preclude

Identification and validity of company and ownership interests to be transferred	Registration & capitalization	Company and subsidiaries duly qualified and in good standing in each jurisdiction in which they operate.
		Number of share per class and other authorized securities, issued and outstanding, as of signing, is precisely stated.
		Complete and accurate information provided regarding subsidiaries.
Company transferred in a way that preserves its long-term value	Governance	Board approved the transaction and shareholder vote will be solicited.
		Company is legally compliant with Exchange Act, Securities Act, Sarbanes-Oxley.
		Internal controls provide reasonable assurance regarding the reliability of the company's financial reporting. The company is not aware of any undisclosed instance of unlawful accounting or auditing matters.
No undisclosed responsibilities that might compromise ongoing company operations	Liabilities	From specific date to signing date, the businesses of the company and its subsidiaries have been conducted in all material respects in the ordinary course of business consistent with past practice, and no material adverse effect has been incurred.
		There are no undisclosed liabilities. No pending litigation proceedings. No claims or proceedings have been made nor started.
		The company is legally compliant with labor and employment matters. No labor disruptions are ongoing. Each material benefit plan has been disclosed and is legally compliant.
		Tax matters were provided accurately; there are no pending tax proceedings. The company is legally compliant with environmental laws and faces no pending environmental law proceeding. All material insurance policies have been set forth. The company has disclosed all relevant data privacy and information security practices, policies and information and is legally compliant in that respect.
Legitimate control over all aspects that contribute to the company's operations and economic benefits	Asset ownership and compliance	All franchises, grants, authorizations, licenses, permits, etc., are legally owned by the company and its subsidiaries.
		The list of material contracts provided is complete and correct. The company has provided an accurate list of the intellectual property it owns. The company has provided an accurate list of owned real property, leases, and subleases. The company has good and valid title to all of the tangible and intangible assets, properties, and rights.
		The company listed the largest customers by revenue and the largest Suppliers by cost and none of them has cancelled its relationship with the Company since specific date.
Company will be able to operate in regulatory compliant fashion	Regulatory compliance	The Company and its subsidiaries are legally compliant with anti-corruption laws, all Global Trade Control Laws, all FDA requirements, and with all Healthcare Laws.
Transfer of ownership can be achieved effectively	Process	Any takeover or anti-takeover statute have been rendered inapplicable to this transaction. No financial intermediary other than the financial advisor to the company is entitled to transaction fees. Based on the opinion delivered by the financial advisor, the consideration pursuant to the agreement is financially fair to the shareholders.

Figure 8.3 Illustrative seller's reps & warranties.

drastic changes that would represent a departure from such normal business operations, and enable a smooth and compliant ownership transfer.

Negative covenants would not permit the company being acquired to:

- Make significant changes to accounting policies.
- Amend organizational documents (e.g., certificate of incorporation, articles of association).
- Make any change to any shares of its capital stock except under certain permitted conditions.
- Create new subsidiaries, effect acquisitions, mergers, or reorganizations.
- Create or discontinue a line of business.
- Sell, lease, license, assign, pledge, or grant any liens on assets, property, or intellectual property.
- Make capital expenditures exceeding a defined plan or aggregate amount.
- Incur, assume, or guarantee new indebtedness or loans except under certain conditions.
- Authorize or pay dividends.
- Increase the compensation of directors, officers, employees, or consultants beyond ordinary course of business.
- Settle litigations exceeding a certain aggregate amount.
- Change any material tax election.

Positive covenants section might likewise commit the company being acquired to:

- Maintain cybersecurity, business continuity, and confidentiality.
- Ensure ongoing operations in ways consistent with past practice preserving company's organization, key employees, and third-party relationships. Note that the legal and operational implications of such a covenant are sometimes underappreciated but they can be significant since mandating ongoing business operations as if there were no agreement (e.g., maintaining competitive stance even against the other party, proceeding with recruiting activities, and other operational aspects that may not necessarily be consistent with the intended transaction).
- Provide reasonable access to information (e.g., financial, operating) and facilities to the buyer.

Lastly, covenants might need to include critical process and post-closing aspects, as applicable:

- Prohibiting both competitive third-party discussions and deal prevention mechanisms (e.g., new shareholder rights plan, poison pills).

- Key employee retention and benefit plan continuity.
- Delisting of company's stock post closing.
- Non-compete with subsequent partial divestiture.

Requirements and Conditions

For a company purchase agreement, closing requirements and conditions to closing should clearly highlight the necessary aspects to complete the transaction and effectively transfer ownership of the company, such as:

- Clauses requiring the sell side to obtain shareholders' approval.
- Clauses involving third parties: obtention of consent from specific authorities (e.g., antitrust agencies) or third parties.
- Clauses relating to confirmatory due diligence or pre-closing restructuring (e.g., formation of a spin-off company, conversion of LLC into corporation).

Indemnification, Termination, Dispute Resolution

With a company purchase, the emphasis is more on termination and indemnification rather than on dispute resolution, as the relation between buyer and seller terminates soon after closing compared with other types of agreements like licensing where ongoing relations remain post-closing.

Termination and indemnification approaches usually focus on ensuring that the transaction is not terminated unilaterally without valid reason and that when it is, appropriate indemnification is provided, as applicable.

With that in mind, typical clauses include:

- An option to terminate the agreement prior to completion by mutual written consent or if a competent jurisdiction prohibits the transaction.
- A material adverse effect clause allowing termination if significant negative events have occurred causing material changes to the acquired company.
- A clause indicating the termination of the agreement if all conditions have not been met by a specified date or end date. Automatic extension of the end date may also be specified for specific cases like delays caused by antitrust proceedings. In any case, an unsatisfied pre-closing condition is usually cause for termination (e.g., negative seller shareholder vote).
- An indemnification for termination clause under certain conditions to ensure that when a party unilaterally elects to stop the transaction, the other party receives a termination fee that can be substantial in order to discourage such termination without critical reason (e.g., breakup fee).
- Clauses setting boundaries around indemnification (e.g., survival period for reps and warranties, limits, deductible, cap, use of escrow funds, calculations).

Case Example: Company Purchase Agreement

The 2023 acquisition of Karuna Therapeutics by Bristol-Meyer Squibb (BMS) illustrates the full acquisition of the shares of a listed biotech company by way of a reverse merger. In the Agreement and Plan of Merger (Karuna Therapeutics & Bristol-Myers Squibb Company, 2023), recitals indicate that a wholly owned subsidiary of BMS will merge with Karuna, the latter being the surviving entity. Recitals also confirm that the transaction was authorized by the boards of directors on both sides.

The first article ("The Merger") provides the description and structure of the transaction with key information, such as:

- Scheme of the merger: Karuna becoming a wholly owned subsidiary of BMS, keeping all its rights and obligations.
- Consideration paid in cash at closing.
- Treatment of options and restricted stock units, to be automatically vested and canceled at closing, holders receiving a one-time cash payment via the company's payroll system.

In this agreement, reps and warranties made by Karuna encompass an extensive range of customary elements such as validity of corporate registration and capitalization, legal compliance (e.g., with SEC regulations), no undisclosed issues (e.g., tax liabilities), and ownership of assets. The company also indicates that the per share consideration is viewed as fair based on a financial adviser's opinion.

Reps and warranties by BMS confirm compliance with laws, and that no litigation or conflict would prevent them from executing the transaction. BMS also represents that it has been granted reasonable access to information by Karuna, has received authorization to execute the transaction, and has sufficient funds to fulfill its obligations.

The section "Conduct of Business Pending The Merger" details pre-closing covenants, with important limitations on Karuna: no corporate changes in the organization or capitalization, no disposal of assets, no new loans or dividends, no employee layoffs or capital expenditure more than certain thresholds. Karuna must also preserve its intellectual property (IP) protection and maintain its accounting, tax methods, and insurance policies. Additionally, specific procedures must be followed if Karuna receives an unsolicited higher offer.

Prior to closing, as stated in the contract, BMS and Karuna will cooperate in the preparation of the proxy statement to be filed with the SEC and Karuna will comply with regulatory requirements (e.g., stock exchange delisting). As contractual conditions for the merger, Karuna will organize a stockholders meeting to approve the transaction, and the companies will comply with the antitrust filing requirements.

Post-closing provisions cover aspects such as maintaining compensation and benefits for employees and providing indemnification and insurance to directors and officers.

Barring specified cases (e.g., mutual consent), if a party terminates the transaction, a termination payment shall be due to the other party.

8.3.2 *Asset Purchase Agreement*

The contractual points to document more specifically in an asset purchase agreement include first and foremost a detailed, explicit description of each acquired asset, tangible or intangible, as well as of each liability assumed by the buyer to precisely reflect what buyer and seller agreed to. This enumeration arguably constitutes the most complex part of asset purchase contractual agreements. Tax-related aspects are also crucial to contractually reflect since tax consequences usually represent a primary consideration for an asset purchase. Lastly, to ensure that the transferred assets can be used post closing, operational aspects will need to be carefully recorded: assignment of critical third-party contracts, schedule for transfer of assets and liabilities, and complementary documentation such as a transition service agreement. Likewise, the agreement will include specifications intended to preserve the value of the assets pre- and post-closing.

Recitals, Preamble, Definitions

To protect both buyer and seller, the definition section might be extensive and include definitions of:

- Each type of assets transferred (e.g., patent, inventory, land, facility, employees) accompanied by supporting detailed schedules or lists (e.g., list of patents, list of products) and extensive documentation appended.
- Important assets, tangible or intangible, that are not transferred and thus excluded from the transaction, for the avoidance of doubt.
- Obligations assumed by the buyer post closing.
- Obligations retained by the seller (which is normally the default option).
- Triggering event for contingent considerations or follow-up actions.

Description and Structure

As discussed, the description will be specific on the scope of assets (e.g., IP, tangible assets, employees, etc.) and liabilities transferred versus retained, down to their lowest component levels. As ongoing relationships might be required past closing (e.g., transition service agreement), it is recommended for the contract to state whether the parties intend to collaborate in the future (e.g., in specified scientific or commercial areas) and which activities or rights require to be maintained during a certain period post closing. A schedule is included that specifies the transfer dates, timing, procedures, and contingencies related to the transfer of assets and liabilities – such schedule can be used to validate the actual transfer.

The Structure section of an asset purchase agreement describes the financial terms, comprising a closing purchase price and, if applicable, contingent consideration (e.g., milestone payments). The agreement sets forth the form and conditions of payment (e.g., in cash by wire transfer) and, if applicable, each event triggering a contingent payment.

To allow an effective tax determination for both seller and buyer, the contract will include a purchase price allocation schedule describing how the purchase price is allocated among transferred assets (and liabilities, as applicable), by asset classes. This reference will be used by the seller to calculate its gain or loss from the transaction and by the buyer to determine its tax benefits basis.

Reps and Warranties

The reps and warranties reflected in the contract outline how risks and liabilities are allocated between buyer and seller, a fundamental notion for asset purchases. While the buyer's side uses the traditional focus that it can consummate the transaction, the seller's side provides more specific perspectives in support of the ownership and validity for the various assets transferred. The seller's reps and warranties might include:

- Seller's approval, as applicable (e.g., seller's board of directors approved the transaction).
- Asset ownership, e.g.:
  - The seller exclusively owns the IP.
  - No third party has sponsored the R&D or has any lien with the purchased assets.
  - No third party has any rights or claims regarding the purchased assets.
- Asset good standing and compliance, e.g.:
  - The seller is duly organized and qualified and in good standing.
  - The seller and its affiliates are legally compliant with taxes related to the transferred assets.

Pre-closing and Post-closing Covenants

Covenants for an asset purchase should ensure the integrity of transferred assets. Pre-closing covenants might include the following considerations:

- Between agreement date and closing date, the business related to the transferred assets will be conducted only in the ordinary course in accordance with past practice (e.g., normal inventory levels) and the assets considered for the transaction will not be disposed of, nor restricted by debt or other obligations.
- Seller shall deploy best efforts to assist buyer with asset transfer (e.g., assistance with employment efforts for employees buyer wants to retain, best efforts to keep intact the output capabilities or services provided by the assets, commercially reasonable efforts to close transaction).

Likewise, post-closing covenants might include, as applicable:

- Non-competition and non-solicitation by the seller for a restricted period of time to preserve the value of the transferred assets after closing.
- Discontinuation of use of IP by the seller after a certain time frame without buyer's consent (e.g., company re-branding).
- Tax payment responsibility of buyer for asset sales tax payment.
- Statement that the buyer will use commercially reasonable efforts to develop or commercialize the purchased products in case of payments to the seller contingent upon milestone achievements.
- Access to records by seller for a specific duration, especially for contingency payments.

Requirements and Conditions

Requirement and conditions in an asset sale will focus on transaction feasibility and on the ability to transfer all critical assets in a timely way that preserves their value. In addition to reps and warranties normally holding true and typical covenant compliance, important asset sale conditions precedent might typically include:

- Meeting regulatory obligations, such as antitrust clearance.
- Obtention of legal evidence at closing, such as a bill of sale (document attesting the transfer of assets and serving as record for the transaction in common law jurisdictions).
- Obtention of satisfactory tax, judgment, and other searches that transferred assets are free and clear of liens.
- Execution of ancillary agreements at closing (e.g., supply agreement).

Indemnification, Termination, Dispute Resolution

Although asset purchase deals typically involve buyer – seller relations of limited duration post closing, dispute resolution might be more important than for a company sale given the complexity of inclusions – exclusions for various assets and liabilities. While liabilities linked with transferred assets are typically the responsibility of the buyer post closing and the responsibility of the seller prior to closing, careful language contract is necessary, and might not always be sufficient, to avoid disputes. Dispute resolution contractual language for asset deals might include arbitration, and both general dispute resolution and expert determination approaches.

Given the different ownership of pre-closing and post-closing liabilities, dispute resolution might also cover assumption of defense against third-party actions and related support by the asset purchase transaction's buyer or seller.

Termination covers normal contractual termination options and events such as mutual consent, breach of provisions, or failure to close by "drop dead" date.

Indemnification clauses likewise cover:

- Reps and warranties expiration, survival, and treatment of shortcomings on either side.
- Remedies for buyer's failure to assume liabilities that should go with the acquired assets.
- Damages to one party caused by the other party and calculation of said damages.
- Remedies for terminations.
- Limitations on indemnification obligations.

Other Contractual Considerations

The use of ancillary agreements is common with an asset purchase to ensure that the buyer can take on and continue normal business operations for the transferred assets:

- Research collaboration agreement.
- Supply agreement.
- Pharmacovigilance or safety data exchange.
- Transition services agreement.

The asset purchase agreement will typically describe activities or rights maintained or granted for a transitional period after closing that are supported by such ancillary agreements. The agreement might indicate that a freedom-to-operate license is granted by the seller to the buyer, which might be necessary when transferred assets require IP retained by the seller.

Lastly the asset purchase agreement should specify transfers to the buyer (e.g., missing assets) and transfers back to the seller (e.g., assets erroneously transferred) post closing.

Case Example: Asset Purchase Agreement

In December 2022, Harrow Health and Novartis signed an asset purchase agreement for the acquisition by Harrow Health of the exclusive US commercial rights to five FDA-approved ophthalmic products from Novartis (Novartis & Harrow Health, 2022).

The recitals section of the agreement documents the transfer of specific assets and liabilities to Harrow, the licensing of related IP and technology by Novartis, as well as supply services as part of an ancillary transition service agreement.

The definitions section includes 77 definitions, providing an important lens with which to read and interpret the contractual document. For example, the applicable market (as listed under the "Territory" definition) covered exclusively for the transferred assets is defined as the United States. The full list of ancillary agreements is also provided under the "Ancillary Agreements" definition.

As part of the description and structure concepts, the "Sale and transfer of assets" article specifies both the nature of the "Transferred Assets" (product new drug applications, transferred IP, and transferred agreements) and a long list of "Excluded Assets" (e.g., assets and rights outside the US market, Novartis names and trademarks, pre-closing accounts receivable, employees, real property, any asset not identified as transferred). In particular, exclusions also include inventory that, as indicated, will be purchased separately (via the ancillary supply agreement).

The next article states liabilities assumed by Harrow versus excluded liabilities. Specifically, Harrow assumes post closing any liabilities arising from the transferred assets within the territory (United States). Excluded liabilities are also listed (e.g., liabilities related to the excluded assets, any legal proceedings, claims, or debt related to the pre-closing period, liabilities arising outside the Territory except for products purchased for Harrow).

The agreement specifies the licenses granted between the parties: in addition to IP rights granted to the purchaser in a license agreement, the purchaser provides also a grant-back license to the seller. The licenses are fully paid-up, royalty-free, and perpetual. The parties restrict their activities to their respective territories.

The "Payments" article provides the payments financial structure: upfront payment of US$130M and additional considerations contingent on commercial releases, not to exceed US$45M.

Conditions to closing include the concomitant closing of several ancillary agreements (license, supply, transition services agreements), as well as the delivery of documents and instruments of sale (e.g., bill of sale and assignment and assumption agreement). Several statements are annexed to the asset purchase agreement: list of domain names, trademarks, active pharmaceutical ingredients, NDAs, transferred agreements, and agreed-upon purchase price allocation (a critical element for asset purchases).

The reps and warranties made by Novartis are customary (e.g., compliance with laws, authority, valid ownership and protection of the assets, no litigation related to the transferred scope). Harrow provides certain reps and warranties such as its compliance with laws and authority to execute, no litigation preventing or delaying the transaction, and availability of funds.

Pre-closing covenants stipulate in particular that Novartis will maintain an ordinary course of business up to closing related to the transferred scope. On the buyer's side, Harrow will take all necessary actions to comply with antitrust regulations. The parties agree to negotiating a pharmacovigilance agreement post closing, and stipulated they would ensure payments received with respect to accounts receivable are directed to the right party.

Different potential causes of termination are listed: mutual written agreement, closing has not occurred 12 months post-signing, breach of reps and warranties by one party, or Novartis-initiated termination in the event of a change of control of Harrow. Lastly, indemnification clauses are subject to various limitations.

8.3.3 Licensing Agreement

With a licensing agreement, the main contractual focus necessarily revolves around permissions and restrictions in using the underlying property, in addition to performance obligations and related liabilities. As a licensing agreement creates a relationship between the licensor that retains property ownership and the licensee who obtains the right not to be prevented from using the property, contractual terms will also articulate the workings of said relationship, including the degree of collaboration and controls exerted, usually achieving a realistic contractual balance between desired specificity and necessary flexibility.

Recitals, Preamble, Definitions

In order to define the relationship between licensor and licensee, recitals and preamble will indicate the identity of the contracting parties and their motivation for the license.

Definitions will include several critical concepts such as:

- IP: naming explicitly critical technology or background IP included in or excluded from the scope of the transaction. Note that in the vast majority of situations, licensing will be for IP (e.g., patents) rather than for tangible property (although there can be exceptions such as the sharing of research materials or material repositories under a tangible property license or material transfer agreement); either way, the type of rights being licensed should be explicitly defined and captured in the contract. As applicable, definitions might distinguish which rights are licensed within each applicable type. Given the evolving nature of biopharma portfolios and R&D, definitions should also delineate whether the licensing contract applies to future IP (e.g., new molecule in a given portfolio, newer and improved AI-enabled discovery approach).

- Spectrum of IP covered by a definition for the avoidance of doubt (e.g., IP includes both registered and unregistered IP, copyrights include both economic and moral rights).
- Know-how: including know-how in the licensing agreement might have both operational (e.g., training, support, consultation by licensor) and financial (e.g., justification of royalties, possibly reduced, even after licensed patents have expired) implications.
- Affiliates: if the licensee is intended to include affiliates, it is critical to clarify which organizations are defined as affiliates or might be in case of mergers and acquisitions involving either licensor or licensee, as mergers and acquisitions may significantly alter the scope and desired applicability of the licensing contract (e.g., licensee is acquired by licensor's competitor, licensor acquires company with IP that would fall within the scope of the licensing contract).
- Commercially reasonable efforts will be defined as sustained efforts to be dedicated by a party with respect to a particular activity or predetermined plan.
- Financial concepts, such as each event triggering a milestone payment, the definition of net sales, profit and loss, expenses that are included in the cost-sharing basis, as applicable. Net sales is a particularly important concept to define given the vast list of possible deductions, such as rebates, discounts, allowances, sales taxes, customs duties, freight, shipment, and insurance costs.
- Specific concepts such as biosimilars.

Description and Structure

In order to contractually secure licensing benefits for both buyer and seller, the description and structure sections will in particular specify the rights granted, financial terms, buyer's and seller's responsibilities, and governance.

For rights granted, the agreement will clearly indicate the specific rights, family of rights, and type of rights being granted as well as specify their exclusivity (exclusive, non-exclusive, or co-exclusive rights), assignability, field of use, territory, and reciprocal aspects. Tailored approaches are possible and should be recorded accordingly within the contract, e.g.:

- Exclusive rights might be granted to develop and market a product (specific field of use and territory), whereas use of the corresponding technology is granted via non-exclusive rights.
- Contractual exclusion of previous exclusive licenses might be made using authority limitation (e.g., grant language "solely to the extent that Licensor has the authority to do so" might exclude from the licensing agreement a specific field of use or territory previously exclusively licensed to another party).
- With a co-development arrangement, the licensing contract typically specifies reciprocal grants of rights when collaborations or share of responsibilities are expected (e.g., research collaboration involving technologies of both parties, development of a combination product).
- When restricted to a specific program, the licensing contract might capture the corresponding approach by providing a list of activities (e.g., a development plan) attached to the contract.
- Platform and discovery stages typically represent the lion's share of licensing contracts in biopharma; however, for later stages, contractual language is likely to specify database rights and the use of data and information from pre-clinical and clinical studies, as applicable. Access to specific information and know-how is often critical to capture in the contractual language given the complex nature of R&D in the biopharma industry (e.g., the contract might stipulate that licensor would provide licensee with all information pertinent for specific regulatory filings). Likewise, manufacturing is normally covered, including sub-contracting of manufacturing through "have made" rights.
- When it is impractical to enumerate, list or otherwise categorize the various relevant IP, like for an AI or software technology license, parties might sometimes refer to "all rights" pertaining to the platform, AI product, or software in the licensing contractual language.
- With field of use restrictions (e.g., therapeutic applications of technology, disease target, or delivery mechanism), in addition to listing the field of use, the contract might indicate therapeutic areas or fields not covered by the license for the avoidance of doubt. From a licensor's perspective, the field-of-use language should be specific enough to allow separate licensing for separate fields of use.

For territories, commercial markets usually represent the main contractual consideration and the contract states the commercial markets covered by the license (e.g., worldwide or country-specific approach) and the ones that are explicitly out of the scope, as applicable. To facilitate contractual compliance with the license, territories or commercial markets clauses might be best aligned with the commercial organization of the licensee (e.g., EU5 might be more relevant for certain biopharma organizations than EU27).

The licensing contract will also state sublicensing rights the licensee might have under given conditions. Similarly, when allowed, it will specify whether the licensor receives a license back for derivative work or improvements made to a licensed technology. The contract may also specify if any IP discovered through the license will be co-owned or remain the distinct property of a single party.

Financial terms can be relatively complex and should be explicitly captured in the contract, as agreed after final negotiation, specifically the compensation mix and evolution for the licensing agreement between fixed payments (e.g., upfront payment), option fees, milestone payments, royalties, sublicensing income, equity compensation (e.g., licensee's common stock), cost reimbursements (e.g., regulatory expenses), and other financial adjustments (e.g., annual minimum payment). Irrespective of the many different possible scenarios, it is critical for the contractual language to precisely reflect the financial terms of the deal agreed to, as structured between the parties, e.g.:

- Royalty calculations are clearly specified: net sales calculation, flat rate or tiered royalties, territory differences, conditions for royalty adjustments, reporting and audit required, etc.
- Indication and tracking of triggering events for milestone payments, exhaustively recording explicit conditions for such milestone payment (e.g., fulfillment of certain licensor obligations like supply agreement to receive start of Phase 2 milestone payment) and indicating whether payment will be made once or several times for recurring events (e.g., quarterly sales performance threshold).
- List of activities eligible for cost sharing or reimbursement (e.g., development costs, commercial expenses).
- Payment process and terms (e.g., invoice by licensor, net 60).

Responsibilities and governance can span a broad range of scenarios, from a straight exclusive license where the licensor completely disengages from any further operational involvement to a close collaboration between licensor and licensee via co-development and co-commercialization. Either way, the agreement should outline the activities and responsibilities of each party (e.g., roles in research, development, technology transfer, manufacturing, regulatory, and commercial activities), including reporting and ancillary agreements by reference. The agreement also clarifies governance approaches and expectations, especially for more involved collaborations: joint committees (e.g., R&D, co-promotion, and manufacturing), conflict resolution, and oversight.

Reps and Warranties

Points of significant contractual importance for reps and warranties will typically revolve around the validity of the IP on the licensor's side (e.g., ownership, no actions, no infringement, no known infringers, no other licensees) and the ability to perform on the licensee's side (e.g., organization, authority, no conflict, capacity).

The licensor's part might include the following affirmations, as negotiated:

- Unless explicitly stated otherwise, the licensed patents are exclusively owned by the licensor, valid, and compliant with applicable laws.
- Patents are fully disclosed, with the complete schedule annexed to the contract.
- Patents are maintained and enforceable, and the licensor possesses valid written assignments from all identified inventors.
- There are no litigations or disputes that could limit the licensor's ability to execute the contract. The licensor has not infringed and has not breached any third-party rights. There are no litigations pending regarding the licensed rights.
- Disclaimer of implied warranties, exclusions, and exceptions to limit licensor's exposure.

The licensee's part might include the following statements, as negotiated:

- The licensee has full power and authority to execute the agreement and perform its obligations.
- The agreement does not present any conflict with other existing licensee's contract.
- The licensee has obtained all approvals and consents required for the execution of the agreement.
- The licensee has sufficient resources and capabilities to implement the activities under its responsibilities.

Pre-closing and Post-closing Covenants

Covenants will typically focus on the enablement of the licensing agreement. As the licensor depends on the licensee for licensing revenues, exclusive licenses are often contractually coupled with a duty to exploit (e.g., "commercially reasonable efforts" or "best efforts" clause). Alternatively, the agreement might state that each party will use commercially reasonable efforts in performing its obligations. Likewise, the licensee depends on the licensor to enforce the IP, and the contract should specify any enforcement obligations on the part of the licensor (since otherwise, the licensor might not have the obligation to pursue infringers).

Covenants might commonly include the following depending on previous negotiations:

- The licensor will not grant similar rights to other parties for the same field of use other than co-exclusivities already agreed upon.
- The licensor will maintain and enforce ownership and control on the IP during the term of the license, including extensions.
- The licensee may not assign licensing rights to third parties or delegate its duties without the licensor's prior written consent.

Requirements and Conditions

When used in a licensing contract, conditions precedent often capture in plain unambiguous language key contractual requirements before signing, such as execution of a supply agreement when materials are instrumental to implement the license. To reflect critical operational needs agreed upon between licensor and licensee, a condition precedent might also be used as condition for the agreement to become effective.

License agreements that do not raise to the threshold of antitrust filing and do not use specific conditions might on the other hand result in simultaneous closing and signing.

Indemnification, Termination, Dispute Resolution

The licensing contract will typically contain usual termination and indemnification clauses (e.g., breach of reps and warranties or covenants, gross negligence or willful misconduct, insolvency, bankruptcy). The agreement will also describe the indemnification procedure and insurance obligations. Limitations, caps, exceptions, and exclusions, as negotiated, are explicitly noted to contractually limit the exposure of licensee or licensor.

As applicable, the term of the licensing agreement may provide pre-defined conditions for termination or renewal (e.g., "term shall automatically renew for additional 1-year periods unless [...]").

Given the ongoing relationship between licensor and licensee, the effects of a termination are particularly important to record in the contract, e.g., survival of selected contractual terms (confidentiality, indemnification, warranties, limitations of liability, regulatory compliance, etc.), territory-level aspects (e.g., royalty payment changes), transitional license, transition assistance, return of materials, survival and assignment of sublicensees upon termination. On a related note, a sublicensee might want to negotiate a non-disturbance agreement at the time of sublicensing (i.e., securing contractual commitment from licensor to grant a direct license if the primary license is terminated).

Instances where termination is the sole remedy should also be noted (e.g., termination as sole remedy for failure to meet milestone).

Dispute resolution principles, organization, and process, as negotiated and agreed upon by the parties, are particularly important to document in the contract in the case of a licensing agreement given the complexity and relationship duality after closing. The contract might for example indicate that:

- Specialized committees will work to solve disputes related to specific topics (joint finance committee for cost and profit-sharing calculations).
- Matters not subject to a specialized committee will be referred to a governance committee or to the parties' executive officers.
- Parties agree to specific arbitration under predetermined rules for unresolved issues.
- A specific jurisdiction might be designated for certain types of issues (e.g., New York versus Delaware in the United States).

Other Contractual Considerations

In view of the dynamic nature of the biopharma industry, a license agreement may include various stipulations in the event of a change of control of one party:

- Notification of the other party.
- Restrictions on licensing rights (e.g., license becomes non-exclusive).
- Non-assignability without other party's prior written consent.
- Non-transferability without other party's prior written consent.

A potential licensee might want to evaluate a technology, platform, or molecule prior to entering into a licensing agreement, as part of their due diligence. The corresponding evaluation and licensing option agreement might serve as precursor to the ultimate licensing agreement, and guide some, or all, of the contractual terms.

Given the complex negotiation of biopharma licensing, contracts might feature a clause indicating that the agreement represents mutual efforts in order to avoid it being construed in favor of one party (in the case of an incomplete or ambiguous clause).

Case Example: Licensing Agreement

Novartis and Erasca signed an exclusive licensing agreement in December 2022 (Novartis Pharma AG & Erasca, 2022). As portrayed in the recitals section, the agreement is set for Erasca to license from Novartis the IP associated with naporafenib (LXH254) for development and commercialization.

As explained, Novartis has conducted clinical trials with naporafenib for the treatment of cancer.

Definitions are provided under Article 1 of the agreement. As usual, the section is relatively long (over 120 entries) and provides vital contractual information, e.g.:

- "Field" is defined as "any and all fields of use", which means that Erasca has no limitation on therapeutic areas where they might use naporafenib even if developed by Novartis for oncology.
- "Territory" is likewise defined in the broadest sense possible ("the entire world"), indicating that Erasca has no geographical limitation for the use of the license.
- "Development" specifies the inclusion of manufacturing, an important distinction for many aspects, including for the scope of the license.
- "Generic Product" specifies what is considered as generic, a notion used for the reduction of royalty rates.
- Various concepts affecting the object of the license such as "Licensed Compound", "Licensed Product", "Licensed Know-How", "Licensed Patents", and "Licensed Technology".

Articles 2 through 5 cover the description and structure of the agreement, stipulating noteworthy elements of the agreement negotiated between the parties, e.g.:

- Article 2 entitled "License Grant" specifies the exclusive, royalty-bearing, sublicensable, license to the "Licensed Compound" (i.e., naporafenib) and "Licensed Products" in the "Field" (i.e., any and all field of use) in the "Territory" (i.e., globally). In contrast, that same article also specifies "a non-exclusive, royalty-free, sublicensable [...], license under the Blocking Patents" (i.e., patents that might be necessary to make use of the exclusive patents such as compositions, methods of manufacture, or uses of naporafenib). Clarifications on licensing scope are also made in that same article (e.g., blocking patent license does not include corresponding Novartis proprietary compounds that may be included in a combination therapy).
- Article 3 entitled "Payments" indicates a US$20M nonrefundable upfront payment, a US$80M upfront equity issuance, regulatory and commercial milestones, and royalty payments from Erasca to Novartis. Numerous royalty determination clauses are included (e.g., rate reduction on a country-by-country basis in case of generic competition).
- Article 4 entitled "Patent Prosecution, Maintenance and Infringement" details IP rights and responsibilities, notably how joint versus sole inventions will be owned or deemed included in the license, as applicable.

- Article 5 entitled "Technology Transfer, Development and Commercialization" assigns sole responsibility to Erasca for the exploitation of the licensed products (as well as the corresponding costs). The article also documents several important expectations. In addition to reporting obligations, Erasca needs to develop and commercialize one licensed product in the conditions provided; Novartis needs to transfer the licensed know-how in the conditions provided. Both parties will negotiate post closing a Clinical Trial and Supply Agreement for trametinib, a product to be evaluated as combination therapy.

Next, Article 6 is entitled "Representations and warranties" and covers customary mutual representations related to organization, authority, and compliance. Additional Novartis representations and warranties concern the validity of the licensed IP (e.g., ownership and legal protection of know-how and patent rights, no litigation nor encumbrances). Licensed products are licensed "as is" with the agreement explicitly excluding representations, warranties, or conditions other than those documented in the agreement. Despite the title, that same article also includes covenants (e.g., general liability insurance to be maintained by Erasca).

The agreement, announced on the effective date, does not include conditions to closing.

There are four more articles to the contract. Article 7 lists the indemnification procedures and limitations. Confidentiality obligations and permitted disclosures or publications are described in Article 8. In Article 9, the agreement defines the term of the collaboration as tied to the "last-to-expire royalty term" and upon expiration, the licenses will become "fully paid-up, perpetual and irrevocable". The article lists potential causes of termination such as: breach of reps and warranties by one party, insolvency, termination at will by Erasca. Article 10 entitled "Miscellaneous" include a short dispute resolution section.

8.3.4 Minority Acquisition Agreement

An agreement for a minority equity purchase or minority acquisition agreement might more generally be referred to as an equity investment agreement, stock purchase agreement, share purchase agreement, or security subscription agreement. With minority acquisition agreements, important contractual aspects revolve around the definition of the equity purchased, the characteristics of that equity, the considerations used for the purchase, company's obligations, key terms and conditions, and aspects specific to the equity purchase rationale (e.g., linkage to collaboration agreement, board representation). Stock purchase agreements can be relatively straightforward using boilerplate language; at the other end of the spectrum, contracts might be heavily customized to reflect the specific financial and strategic objectives negotiated between buyer and seller.

Recitals, Preamble, Definitions

In addition to identifying the parties and the effective date, the agreement documents the legal framework under which the minority equity purchase will take place (e.g., "the Securities Act of 1933, as amended, and Rule 506 of Regulation D" or "in reliance upon the exemption from securities registration afforded by Section 4(a)(2) of the Securities Act of 1933, as amended").

When applicable, the agreement will also specify the context of the equity purchase (e.g., "concurrently with the execution of this Agreement, the Parties have executed and delivered a Collaboration and License Agreement" or "in partial consideration for the execution of a licensing agreement") as well as pre-existing agreements.

The agreement will also list the securities involved (e.g., common stock), the share price, the number of shares acquired, and the aggregate purchase price.

Definitions will include customary terms around holders, registration, expenses, transfers, related securities (e.g., warrant shares), various standards, and legal context or references. Definitions might also include deal-specific aspects such as:

- Strategic investor means any Person directly engaged in a related or complementary business to the business engaged in by the Company and/or any of the Subsidiaries.
- Financial Investor means an investor whose primary business is the investment of capital for financial gain.
- Long-stop date that defines a time limit or "drop dead" date beyond which the investor has no obligation to subscribe.

Description and Structure

At a minimum, the contract will state the source of the equity (e.g., issuance of shares), the types and mix of equity (e.g., common stock, restricted stock units, restricted stock awards, unit composed of preferred stock plus warrant), valuation (e.g., price per share, aggregate purchase price), payment information (including payment terms and conditions), as well as closing and delivery of said equity (e.g., seller's stock certificates in the name of the buyer, resolution approved by the board of the buyer, further assurances to ensure transfer of equity). With multiple buyers, a schedule will typically be attached to the contract, showing the number of shares acquired by each. If the transaction involves publicly traded companies, additional requirements should be reflected in the contractual language characterizing the necessary compliance with applicable stock exchange regulations and securities laws.

In addition, financial, strategic, and governance rights negotiated with the other party should be captured in the contract either directly or via reference to other contractual documents (e.g., side letter agreement, strategic rights agreement, and shareholders' agreement). Those rights will often reflect what motivated the minority acquisition in the first place.

The negotiated rights documented in the description and structure section might include, as applicable:

- Voting rights (e.g., rights greater than those inherent to purchased shares). Note that such clauses may have control implications, and thus accounting and legal ramifications.
- Veto rights (e.g., right to block the creation of new share classes or the disposal of specific assets of interest).
- Board seat (providing active governance participation) or board observer seat (providing access to board-level information without governance participation), subject to the maintenance of certain stock ownership threshold.
- Information rights related to, and participation in, specific committees providing privileged access to scientific information and an opportunity to provide expertise (e.g., scientific advisory board, clinical committee).
- Right of first refusal or right of first negotiation on any or on specific transactions (e.g., specific assets). Such rights may be recorded as notice rights or as full participation rights.
- Participation and liquidation preferences, according to the class of equity.
- Anti-dilution provisions, for which the method of calculation should be documented within the contract.
- In the case of preferred stock, convertible bonds and other applicable equity rights, conversion to common stock upon defined events.
- Redemption rights: to try and ensure an exit strategy on pre-defined terms, e.g., reclaim investment with appropriate return where allowed.

Reps and Warranties

Reps and warranties typically include buyer's and seller's authority to enter the agreement, aspects specific to the equity instruments, legal or financial materials, other information related to company obligations, and appropriate disclosure schedules.

The seller's reps and warranties will explicitly include, as applicable:

- Company's good standing, legal compliance, with power and authority to execute the transaction.

- Authorization and issuance of equity with corresponding rights, free and clear of liens or encumbrance.
- Agreement execution in compliance with all applicable statutes and regulations.
- No litigation that might challenge the transaction's validity.
- Company's structure (e.g., list of subsidiaries) confirmed as of closing date.
- Valid company's IP and assets in good standing.
- Financial statements prepared in accordance with applicable standards, appropriateness of internal controls maintained, and no undisclosed liabilities.
- Survival of reps and warranties after closing and upon termination.

If included, the buyer's reps and warranties might typically mention, as applicable:

- Not an intermediary – shares acquired for buyer's own account.
- Buyer's necessary qualification (e.g., accredited investor in the United States, residency).
- Acknowledgment that all requested information was received.
- Capacity and financial means to consummate the transaction.
- Understanding and ability to bear the risk of its investment.

Pre-closing and Post-closing Covenants

Beyond best efforts to close from both parties, pre-closing covenants will indicate the obligation by the company to conduct its activities in the ordinary course of business and to maintain unchanged corporate organization and governing documents between signing and closing. Barring written consent of the buyer, this usually precludes additional debt issuance, dividend payment, material changes beyond the scope of normal business operations, or changes in equity interests (including options and warrants) other than required by the transaction.

Post-closing covenants will cover contractual financial obligations after closing such as regulatory filings (e.g., Form 8-K), dividends, reclassification of equity instruments, triggering events on each party's side, rights, provision of information, and other financial considerations (e.g., cash instead of additional fractional shares). Post-closing covenants may also describe, generally or specifically, the use of transaction proceeds post-closing (e.g., not for debt payment or stock redemption).

Requirements and Conditions

Requirements will usually clarify the conditions under which the closing will take place, such as regulatory approvals, closing date, payment instructions and confirmation of book-entry issuance of the shares by a transfer agent. The agreement may require the company to deliver prior to closing a certificate attesting that the company is solvent

Contractual conditions to closing will include for each side the accuracy of material reps and warranties as of closing, the performance of all obligations and covenants, the delivery of the executed agreement along with the financial value (payment or equity) to be provided to the other side or evidence thereof. The buyer might provide irrevocable wire instructions as specified whereas the seller might provide irrevocable equity transfer instructions, prospectus, and executed lock-up agreement.

Other conditions to closing can include, as applicable, transaction approval by a board of directors and shareholders meeting or the preliminary execution of a collaboration or licensing agreement between the parties.

Indemnification, Termination, Dispute Resolution

Termination without penalty for breach of conditions or reps and warranties, or for failure to consummate the transaction before a "drop dead" date, is typically standard.

Barring fraud, misconduct, or misrepresentation, indemnification might be restricted to a specific period (e.g., 18 months post closing) and feature deductible and cap on indemnity.

Other Contractual Considerations

Other contractual specifications might include transfer restrictions (e.g., lock-up period during which buyer cannot dispose of purchased equity interests), voting right restrictions (e.g., standstill agreement), and reference to complementary agreements (e.g., shareholders' agreement).

Depending on the specific context, many different legal or boilerplate considerations might be added to the contract (e.g., jury trial waiver, severability, governing laws, confidentiality, no third-party beneficiaries, each party responsible for own fees and expenses, and restricted transactions like shorting the stock).

Case Example: Minority Acquisition

In August 4, 2023, Poseida Therapeutics and Astellas signed a securities purchase agreement under which Astellas US acquired a minority interest in Poseida for an aggregate share purchase price of US$25M at a price per share of US$3.00 (Poseida Therapeutics & Astellas US, 2023). The agreement closed three days later, on August 7, 2023.

The recitals section of the agreement indicates that the transaction is occurring under "Regulation D", making it an exempt private placement transaction (specifically under Rule 506 as illustrated within Figure 5.20); they also list the price per common share of US$3.00 and explicitly make reference to Schedule I that provides the schedule of purchasers, namely Astellas US LLC for 8,333,333 common shares at that price. For comparison, Poseida's previous SEC quarterly report listed a number of outstanding shares of 86,916,199 common shares as of August 4, 2023, pegging the private placement, as detailed in the contract, at approximately 8.8% of Poseida's outstanding stock.

Definitions are relatively limited with 11 entries and incorporated, together with the description and structure section, into Article 1, entitled "Purchase and Sale". These definitions introduce two critical documents attached as exhibits: a Strategic Rights Letter Agreement ("SRLA") in Exhibit D and a Registration Rights Agreement ("RRA") in Exhibit E – these agreements are available in Poseida's 2023 Form 10-K.

The description and structure section restates the US$3.00 price per share and the US$25M aggregate purchase price, making the same reference to Schedule I. Payment and other specifics are also provided (e.g., payment on closing date by wire transfer to Poseida's account, delivery within one day of closing to Astellas of book-entry statement showing them as registered holder of the shares as of closing).

The section also ensures contractually that the minority agreement is undertaken within a greater strategic context by including essential closing deliverables as part of the description in that "Purchase and Sale" section. Among others, the deliverables for both sides include the execution of the SLRA and the execution of the RRA.

In particular, the SRLA grants Astellas the right to attend, as non-voting observer, all meetings of the Board of Directors and of the Scientific Advisory Board (Poseida Therapeutics, 2023). With a US$25M upfront payment (separate from, and in addition to, the stock purchase) and an up-to-18-month term, the SRLA also provides for a change in control notice as well as for several terms favorable to Astellas in relation to a specific program of interest (referred to as "P-MUC1C-ALLO1" by Poseida), e.g.: transaction exclusivity period, right of first offer, right of first refusal, research collaboration (Poseida Therapeutics, 2023).

Likewise, the RRA provides further context to the minority acquisition agreement (e.g., confirmation that securities sold to Astellas will be registered on SEC Form S-3 no later than 250 days post closing, thus ensuring shares can be publicly traded).

The remainder of the securities purchase agreement contains five more articles:

- Poseida's representations and warranties in Article 2. These might be construed as customary (e.g., authority, capitalization, IP ownership and protection, internal accounting controls, no liabilities or obligations preventing the transaction). Note however that the capitalization provided as of July 31, 2023 can serve as reference for the level of ownership expected to result from the minority acquisition purchase.

- Astellas' representations, warranties, and covenants in Article 3 include aspects that qualify the private placement under Rule 506 mentioned above.
- Mutual covenants in Article 4 (including a 180-day lock-up period and an indemnification clause).
- Conditions to closing in Article 5 (e.g., closing deliverables discussed in the description, no Nasdaq objection, listing of new shares).
- Miscellaneous terms in Article 6 (e.g., each party is responsible for respective fees and expenses).

8.3.5 *Option Contract*

As "put options" represent uncommon business development approaches in the biopharma industry (see Section 7.2.5), we will focus on the "call options" or "options to purchase" discussed in Section 7.3.5. While the underlying assets behind an option contract may vary (e.g., company, a business or division, a technology, a platform, a compound, equipment, IP), molecule IP licensing options are arguably most common (especially in the context of a collaboration) and might be used in this section to illustrate certain contractual concepts. This said, it should remain clear that options are used for many other purposes beyond product IP licensing, e.g.: options to expand applications, co-development options, co-promotion options, options to manufacture, evaluation options, supply options, and asset acquisition options.

In all these cases, with an option contract, the main contractual aspects will include:

- The definition of the option.
- The definition of the underlying assets.
- Ongoing access to information, materials, and underlying assets to facilitate ongoing evaluations and an informed option exercise by the buyer.
- The payment structure.
- The waiting period and exercise period for the option.
- The rights of each party.
- All contractual considerations that would apply to a straight contract if the option were exercised.
- The option enforceability (an option has no value if the buyer is unable to exercise it) and termination conditions.

The fact that option contracts need to document the same aspects as a traditional non-option deal, in addition to the unique considerations related to its optional nature, demonstrates the contractual complexity of option contracts.

Recitals, Preamble, Definitions

In addition to the elements that correspond to the option, the contract needs to indicate the recitals, preamble, and definitions for a straight contract. For an asset acquisition option agreement, the contract would need to include all recitals, preamble, and definitions that would figure in the equivalent asset purchase agreement (see Section 8.3.2) if you take for granted that the option is exercised. Similarly, a licensing option agreement would need to include the same notions as a licensing agreement (see Section 8.3.3). Note that this will generally be the case for all the different aspects of the contract, be it definitions, description, reps and warranties, etc. We will not repeat that crucial consideration for other contractual aspects in the remainder of Section 8.3.5, but rather limit our comments to the option part for the sake of brevity.

Let us take a discovery-stage example ubiquitous within the biopharma industry: that of a research collaboration agreement with the option to license products at a later stage. Recitals might introduce the platform technology owned by a party and the objectives of the partners to collaborate on the identification and validation of new targets. The preamble might articulate how research achievements might open the door to further develop, manufacture, and commercialize the products under the option's license to be granted by the IP owner. In such a scenario, like for a licensing agreement, what might be licensed should be clearly articulated as well as field of use, collaborations, and so on.

Description and Structure

As the transaction resulting from the option exercise may not happen for several months or even several years, and as management, governance, and other constituencies may have changed on both sides, it is particularly important for the contract to precisely describe the assets to differentiate them from similar assets possibly acquired by the seller in the meantime. Similarly, that precise definition will help ensure that the rights of the buyer to exercise the option are not compromised by future seller's actions over that same time period.

To the extent that ongoing activities need to be performed by the parties between the closing of the option contract and the exercise of the option, such activities will also be described either directly or through reference to ancillary agreements.

The option contract should clearly indicate the option grant payment, the payment conditions expected along with the option conferred and the conditions of exercise of that option (e.g., notice), as well as important option characteristics such as the option period (e.g., within 6 months following the IND approval of a specific program). In addition, the contract that the option would give rise to, if exercised, is commonly annexed to the option contract to ensure the option can be exercised under the pre-specified conditions agreed upon (otherwise the parties might fail to agree on the terms of the agreement after the option is exercised). The contract in annex should clarify the transfer of rights and assets as applicable; it might also facilitate the required corporate and regulatory approvals.

Reps and Warranties

The seller's reps and warranties will typically include:

- Ownership and control of underlying assets for option contract (e.g., legal ownership and control over IP for licensing option).
- No prior agreement, assignment, obligation, or knowledge that would hinder validity of option contract and execution of contract following option exercise (e.g., no prior grant of rights to underlying assets).
- No litigation related to underlying assets.
- Compliance with laws, no infringement related to underlying assets, operations, and rights.
- Valid and binding contract following option exercise: contract annexed to the agreement shall constitute a complete, valid and binding agreement enforceable against seller in accordance with such terms.
- Accurate and complete description of underlying assets.
- Financial stability required to ensure viability of option contract over the option period.

The buyer's reps and warranties might typically mention, as applicable:

- Valid and binding contract following option exercise: contract annexed to the agreement shall constitute a complete, valid, and binding agreement enforceable against buyer in accordance with such terms.
- Not an intermediary – option contract established for buyer's operations in the context defined for the option contract.
- Acknowledgment that all requested information was received.
- Operational capacity and financial means to consummate the option contract.
- Understanding and ability to bear the risks of its investment.

Pre-Closing and Post-Closing Covenants

Covenants, both pre- and post-closing will express that no liens or obligations have been taken or will be taken by the company, that might conflict with the ability of the seller to consummate the transaction the option gives rise to (e.g., for IP related to the option, the seller will not grant any liens or security interests on the technology or grant rights to third parties that would conflict with the option rights until the option has expired).

Covenants will be included to try and ensure that the parties can undertake the transaction the option gives rise to, under the conditions negotiated, e.g.:

- A no-shop clause is almost always included to prevent challenges to the enforceability of the option.
- Post-closing covenants should likewise address adverse developments that might hinder the ability of the buyer to exercise the option (e.g., unless it is cause for termination, seller's bankruptcy filing might result in the rejection of option contract).
- Post-closing covenants might also attempt to address and manage the tax implications resulting from the financial structure of the deal the option permits so as to maintain the interests of the various parties.

Requirements and Conditions

Both the seller and the buyer need to fulfill similar requirements to traditional agreements, covering board approval and antitrust filings as applicable.

On the seller's side, to ensure ongoing enforceability of the option contract, any corporate approval (e.g., board, shareholders) needs to be legally positioned in ways that do not permit later challenges to the contract the option gives way to (e.g., execution of shareholder support agreement precluding them from accepting other offers).

Indemnification, Termination, Dispute Resolution

Indemnification clause often includes indemnification by seller for claims made against buyer in relation to underlying assets. Similar buyer indemnification clause is also included. Both of these typically cover aspects specific to the option deal. In addition, the contract will cover the management of legal proceedings to address third-party claims.

As already mentioned for post-closing covenants, the indemnification clause should address adverse developments that might prevent the buyer from exercising the option (e.g., if not addressed by the termination clause, seller's bankruptcy filing).

The option contract typically specifies termination under specific conditions, with or without indemnification, e.g.:

- Expiration of the option period.
- Material breach.
- Bankruptcy or insolvency filing.

Dispute resolution needs to be documented in particular throughout the option's exercise period and specify an appropriate process and forum (e.g., referral of the dispute to joint discussion committee, escalation to senior officers of both buyer and seller, and referral for final arbitration thereafter)

Other Contractual Considerations

An option agreement might sometimes be incorporated into a larger agreement (e.g., collaboration and option agreement, sponsored research agreement); in such a case, the same contractual option considerations would apply in addition to considerations specific to that larger contract.

Case Example: Option Contract

In December 2022, Ono Pharmaceutical Co., Ltd and Equillium, Inc. (Nasdaq: EQ) entered into an exclusive option and asset purchase agreement (Ono Pharmaceutical & Equillium, 2022), in which Equillium wishes to grant Ono the option to purchase certain rights and obligations related to itolizumab, a clinical-stage first-in-class anti-CD6 monoclonal antibody in exchange for upfront payment and development costs reimbursement, as captured in the contract's recitals. Indeed, when the contract was signed, Itolizumab was in Phase 3 for acute graft-versus-host disease ("aGVHD") and in Phase 1b for lupus nephritis ("LN"). Recitals also indicate the simultaneous signing of a development agreement between the parties.

The extensive definitions section contains close to 200 entries, including precisions on "Program Patents" (details annexed to the agreement), "Development Costs" incurred by Equillium (subject to reimbursement by Ono), programs excepted from the transaction ("Excluded Programs"), and option period (commencing from payment of the upfront until the end of "Data Package Review Period" or upon termination). The "Ancillary Agreements" definition provides the list of ancillary agreements. Definitions also clarify when the option can be exercised ("Option Period"): commencing on the date of full upfront payment (minus applicable deductions) and ending on the earliest of the agreement termination or the end of the "Data Package Review Period", which is more specifically defined later in the contract as a function of the delivery date of specific documentation to Ono by Equillium (in Article 8, entitled "Program Activities").

The description and structure section covers the options (grant, upfront payment, exercise, disclosures, and effect of not exercising them) under Article 2 entitled "Purchase Option", then, under Article 3 entitled "Purchase and Sale", the scope and financial terms of the transaction. Specifically, the description and structure section stipulates the following:

- Irrevocability and exclusivity of option granted to Ono by Equillium in Article 2.

- One-time upfront payment by Ono to Equillium of JPY ¥3.5 billion (i.e., approximately US$26 million) in Article 2.
- Ono's sole discretion in exercising the option during the Option Period (Article 2). Upon option exercise, Ono must notify which party will be responsible for the remaining development activities.
- In Article 3, the list of "Purchased Assets" (e.g., transferred IP, regulatory materials, acquired contracts, inventory, books, and records), "Excluded Assets", "Assumed Liabilities", and "Excluded Liabilities", similarly to a straight asset purchase agreement.
- Considerations for asset purchase upon option exercise, defining the closing date: payment of Closing Payment by Ono to Equillium (Closing Payment figures among the many definitions provided in the contract, representing JPY ¥5 billion plus applicable milestone payments).

Conditions to closing are captured in the agreement under Article 10. They include satisfying reps and warranties, fulfilling covenants, and executing contracts (e.g., executed Bill of Sale and Assignment and Assumption Agreement) in addition to regulatory/antitrust clearance and release of encumbrances.

Representations and warranties are captured in Articles 4 through 6. Reps and warranties made by Equillium (Article 4) are customary regarding the company, ownership and quality of the assets (e.g., compliance with laws, authority, valid ownership and legal protection of the assets, no litigation related to the transferred scope, no warning letter from regulatory authorities). Article 5 includes a variety of limitations on Equillium's reps and warranties and is followed by customary buyer's reps and warranties from Ono (e.g., compliance with laws and authority to execute, no litigation preventing or delaying the transaction, and availability of funds) in Article 6.

Covenants are provided in Article 7. Pre-closing covenants include Equillium's commitment to pursue its activities in an ordinary course of business up to closing to preserve intact the transferred scope (e.g., not issue new encumbrance, amend core contracts, compromise material rights related to the assets) and to afford Ono reasonable access to information regarding the assets' business.

As specified in that same Article 7, the parties agree to collaborate on the transfer of regulatory materials to Ono. After the date of the option exercise, the parties will cooperate to comply with the antitrust regulations and the parties will share a final purchase price allocation.

The agreement states in Article 8 ("Program Activities") that Equillium is responsible for conducting all R&D on the product pre-closing (according to a Development Plan annexed to the agreement), all documented development costs being reimbursed by Ono.

The indemnification clauses, listed under Article 11, are subject to procedures and limitations. The agreement includes different potential causes of termination, such as termination by Ono in its sole discretion, mutual written agreement, option has not been exercised before a long-stop date, breach of reps and warranties by one party.

Case Example: Collaboration and Option to a License Agreement

Nurix Therapeutics, Inc. and Seagen Inc. signed a multi-year collaboration and license agreement in September 2023 (Nurix Therapeutics & Seagen, 2023) to advance a new class of cancer therapeutics. As provided for by the recitals, the agreement establishes an exclusive option to obtain an exclusive license to develop and commercialize certain Nurix compounds optimized to bind and cause the degradation of specific targets (designated in the contract as "Collaboration Degrader Targets" that are part of homologue sets designated as "Collaboration Degrader Target Sets"). The long list of definitions, with close to 300 entries, includes these collaboration degrader targets and target sets, providing further context for this critical aspect of the option agreement.

The contract devotes several articles to the definition of these targets within the planned collaboration, e.g.:

- Establishment and evolution of targets in Article 2: initial list, additions, removals, etc.
- Designation of target sets as available for the collaboration, in Article 3 entitled "gatekeeping".
- Joint research approach in Article 4.
- Development by Seagen with Nurix support in Article 6.
- Management of regulatory matters by Seagen with Nurix support in Article 7.
- Seagen sole manufacturing rights in Article 8.
- Seagen commercialization responsibility with Nurix opt-in option in Article 9.

Specifics around the option are provided through Article 5 entitled "degrader license option" (e.g., exclusivity, option exercise, option period extension) and Article 13 entitled "financial terms".

Lastly, without getting into specifics, the contract covers many additional aspects in the broader collaboration context as well as traditional contractual agreement clauses.

8.3.6 *Collaboration Contract*

As discussed in Section 7.4, there are many possible collaborations models, with different levels of formalization. The scope, magnitude, and complexity of the contractual agreement will typically reflect the significance and depth of the collaboration model and the importance of the commitments made.

Given the very wide spectrum of collaboration models, the primary contractual considerations will generally focus on defining the collaboration (e.g., parties, term, aspirations), identifying its major objectives and intended outcomes (e.g., purpose and scope), clarifying its operational and financial principles (e.g., respective roles, responsibilities, obligations, compliance, systems and processes, reporting, contributions, and benefits), and providing appropriate contractual safeguards to protect the parties' interests over the collaboration time frame and beyond (e.g., IP, confidentiality, non-disclosure, non-solicitation, governance, oversight, risk management and insurance, indemnity, termination, and dispute resolution).

As a general rule of thumb, the importance of the safeguards is driven by risk factors whereas the sophistication of the operational and financial principles is driven by investment considerations (Figure 8.4).

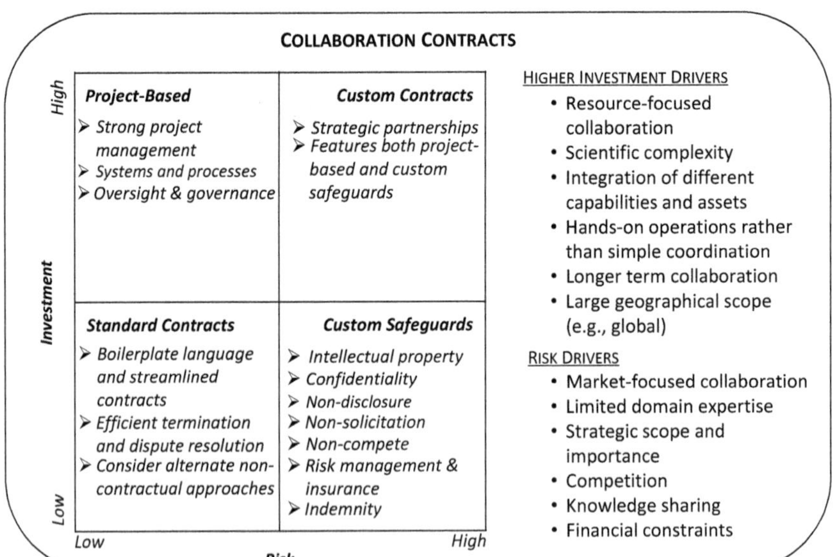

Figure 8.4 Collaboration contract framework.

Recitals, Preamble, Definitions

Recitals and preamble describe briefly the parties, the time frame, the aspirations, the general scope, and overall purpose of the collaboration. The definitions section characterizes aspects of the activities that will be shared or pooled (e.g., joint clinical data, joint invention) and important financial concepts (e.g., FTE cost, allowable expenses, development budget), particularly if the collaboration includes cost sharing.

Description and Structure

As applicable for collaborations featuring significant interface between buyer and seller ("project-based" contracts and "custom contracts" in Figure 8.4), the contract describes the roles and responsibilities of each party, cooperation and interdependencies, and how the resources will be contributed. The timing and documentation of deliverables are usually specified. The contract may also reference ancillary agreements possibly annexed to the contract (e.g., manufacturing and supply agreement). In addition, the contract will typically capture organizational requirements (e.g., a joint development committee for a clinical trial collaboration) and reporting procedures (e.g., adverse events reports).

Particularly for collaborations involving higher levels of risk, the contract may specify certain aspects of ownership, e.g.:

- Each party retains respective ownership of pre-existing IP.
- Specific licenses may be granted (non-exclusive and fully paid-up, if appropriate) only for the term of the collaboration, as applicable.
- Specific technologies, applications, and fields of use may be explicitly excluded from the collaboration.
- Specific assignment of IP discovered through the collaboration (e.g., co-ownership).
- A specific party may retain ownership of regulatory materials and approvals.

Usually for high-investment collaborations, the contract will detail how financial aspects will be managed. For example, financial provisions may stipulate that some activities may be exclusively borne by a party, shared, or charged on a fee basis to the other party (e.g., clean room reservation fee).

The contract will typically describe the budgeting, forecasting, reporting, invoicing and reimbursement procedures, and the methodology for calculating shared revenues and expenses, as applicable.

Reps and Warranties

The collaborators' representations will typically cover the following aspects:

- Good standing, legal capacity, with power and authority to execute the transaction.
- Ownership, control, or license for IP used in the collaboration.
- Ownership, control, and right to tangible assets and resources used in the collaboration.
- Capacity to fulfill the obligations described in the collaboration agreement.
- Enforceable, legal, valid, and binding nature of the collaboration agreement.

The collaborators' warranties will typically include the following:

- Confidentiality.
- Compliance with applicable laws and regulations.

Pre-closing and Post-closing Covenants

Pre-closing covenants typically include:

- Confidentiality.
- Restrictions on taking actions that would result in material conflict for the collaborator's participating in the collaboration.
- Normal business performance to maintain assets and capabilities required for the collaboration.
- Notification for material events relevant to the collaboration.

Post-closing Covenants Often Include

- Best commercial efforts to perform agreed-upon activities.
- Collaboration preservation (e.g., no undertaking of activities that would prevent an effective collaboration) and exclusivity.
- Confidentiality.
- Non-compete and non-solicitation.
- Legal proceeding and ongoing regulatory compliance.
- Notice of development that would materially affect the collaboration.
- Reporting.

In addition, the parties may specify limitations regarding materials, processes, or information used during the collaboration. They may grant each other the right to conduct legal compliance audits of the other party's activities, books, and records.

Requirements and Conditions

Customary conditions to closing include no material change to the collaborators, any required approval and regulatory clearance, reps and warranties, as well as pre-closing covenants. Requirements and conditions to closing might also include aspects related to specific high-risk factors for the collaboration (e.g., maintenance of certain levels of insurance, availability of specific domain expertise, and specific market situation).

Indemnification, Termination, Dispute Resolution

For low- to medium-risk collaborations, indemnification is often contractually limited to cases of negligence or willful misconduct, violation of applicable law, or breach of contract. Higher-risk collaboration contracts might specify further indemnification language: insurance levels for parties to be able to meet indemnification caps.

Provisions may allow a party to terminate the collaboration for convenience with appropriate notice (and indemnity for collaborations involving significant investments), or upon specific events (e.g., patent dispute, bankruptcy), or in case of compliance breach by the other party.

Dispute resolution mechanisms are often documented for significant investments or high-risk collaborations.

Other Contractual Considerations

The contract may preclude assignment of the collaboration contract without prior written consent from the other party. It may also state that in the event of a change of control, the successors shall be bound by the same obligations.

Case Example: Collaboration Agreement (Combined with Licensing Agreement and Equity Investment)

Arvinas and Pfizer established a worldwide collaboration agreement in 2021 to co-develop and co-commercialize Arvinas' products (Arvinas & Pfizer, 2021). As provided by the short recitals section, entitled "background", the collaboration focuses on "pharmaceutical products containing an oral estrogen receptor targeting protein degrader for the treatment of certain cancers".

Article 1 of the collaboration agreement provides an extensive list of definitions numbered from 1 to 227. These definitions include Arvinas' IP, field and indications covered by the collaboration, FTE costs, net profit or losses, shared program activities, shared territory, compounds requiring a license are defined, as well as ancillary agreements (Pharmacovigilance, Supply, Quality, Transition, and Stock Purchase agreements).

The description and structure section is also extensive, including eight articles, numbered 2–9:

- The governance (Article 2) is detailed via the organization of seven committees to oversee all collaboration areas, with procedures for decision-making and dispute resolution. The agreement stipulates that alliance managers will be appointed by the parties.
- Collaborative activities are described in Articles 3–6: development, regulatory matters, commercialization (including medical affairs), manufacture, and supply. These articles specify allocation of responsibilities, activity planning, and cost sharing for all activities, as applicable. Critical project management aspects for development activities are clearly spelled out, e.g.: a joint development plan, including clinical trials and nonclinical studies and regulatory plans, joint budget, cost reporting, and rules regarding potential cost overruns. The commercial approach is likewise documented in the contract, e.g.: lead party per territory for regulatory matters (e.g., Arvinas in the United States), joint commercialization plan, joint commercial budget, profit and losses reporting for shared territory, guidance for collaboration on business aspects such as detailing, sales force hiring, composition and training, advertising, promotion, and medical activities. Similarly, the manufacturing and supply section describes key aspects such as the clinical supply, technology transfer, and commercial supply responsibilities, also referring to ancillary agreements (e.g., supply agreement).
- Article 7 documents the respective grants of licenses (co-exclusive or non-exclusive, as applicable) necessary to perform their activities within the scope of the collaboration.
- Article 8 focuses on the financial terms of the agreement, including an equity investment by Pfizer and a product licensing to Pfizer that are both integrated within this collaboration agreement. This article specifies a US$650M upfront payment (plus milestone payments) to Arvinas by Pfizer and the US$350M equity investment in Arvinas by Pfizer supported by a separate stock purchase agreement. Article 8 also specifies the 50/50 joint development cost sharing and describes how net profits (or losses) are reported and financially shared.
- Last but not least, Article 9 provides rules for IP ownership.

Reps and warranties, as well as covenants, all captured under Article 10, appear relatively customary and brief compared with the overall contract length. Pfizer makes no other representations than mutual reps and warranties that cover the compliance with laws and authority. Arvinas' reps and warranties include ownership and legal protection of the technology, no litigation or encumbrances, good accounting controls. Covenants cover the term of the collaboration, during which both parties commit to maintaining compliance and ethics programs, system of internal accounting controls, and adequate policies and procedures. The contract also includes a "no-shop" clause: both parties will not enter into agreements with third parties that would conflict with their obligations.

Article 11 lists the indemnification procedures and limitations while dispute resolutions are described in Article 14 mainly outlining arbitration rules. In Article 13, the agreement defines the term of the collaboration (i.e., until products are no longer commercialized or developed) and includes different potential causes of termination such as: breach of reps and warranties by one party, insolvency, termination by Pfizer for convenience, or mutual written agreement.

References

Arvinas, & Pfizer. (2021, July 21). *Collaboration Agreement by and Among Arvinas, Inc., Arvinas Operations, Inc., Arvinas Estrogen Receptor, Inc. and Pfizer Inc.* Retrieved 12/21/2024, from https://www.sec.gov/Archives/edgar/data/1655759/000119312521221390/d160222dex101.htm

Karuna Therapeutics, I., & Bristol-Myers Squibb Company. (2023, December 22). *Agreement and Plan of Merger.* Edgar. Retrieved 12/15/2024, from https://www.sec.gov/Archives/edgar/data/1771917/000119312523302210/d630414dex21.htm

Novartis, & Harrow Health. (2022, December 13). *Asset Purchase Agreement.* Retrieved 12/17/2024, from https://www.sec.gov/Archives/edgar/data/1360214/000149315222035372/ex10-1.htm

Novartis Pharma AG, & Erasca, I. (2022, December 9). *Exclusive License Agreement.* Retrieved 12/23/2024, from https://www.sec.gov/Archives/edgar/data/1761918/000095017023009496/eras-ex10_20.htm

Nurix Therapeutics, & Seagen. (2023, September 6). *Collaboration and License Agreement by and between Nurix Therapeutics, Inc. and Seagen Inc.* Retrieved 12/21/2024, from https://www.sec.gov/Archives/edgar/data/1549595/000154959524000025/nrix-20231130ex1025seagen.htm

Ono Pharmaceutical, & Equillium. (2022, December 5). *Asset Purchase Agreement.* Retrieved 12/20/2024, from https://www.sec.gov/Archives/edgar/data/1746466/000095017023009492/eq-ex10_31.htm

Poseida Therapeutics, I. (2023, August 4). *Strategic Rights Letter Agreement.* Retrieved 12/25/2024, from https://www.sec.gov/Archives/edgar/data/1661460/000119312523204578/d480632dex103.htm

Poseida Therapeutics, I., & Astellas US, L. (2023, August 4). *Securities Purchase Agreement.* Retrieved 12/24/2024, from https://www.sec.gov/Archives/edgar/data/1661460/000119312523204578/d480632dex101.htm

Chapter 9

Essential Regulatory Notions

Both global regulatory affairs competency and global regulatory strategy are essential for biopharma companies, across their entire company lifecycle from startup to maturity. By understanding the required regulatory hurdles to move products forward and by enhancing regulatory communications, companies maximize their likelihood of regulatory approval, streamline their research and development process, improve their market access and time to market, making therapies available to patients faster, and generally build their credibility with investors as well as with health authorities.

This highlights the central role played by the global regulatory affairs function as a "strategic partner in development from conception all the way to registration and beyond" as coined by a regulatory affairs senior executive working for a top ten biopharma company. Indeed, once the early principles of a biopharma research and development program are in place (such as the target product profile and the clinical development plan), the global regulatory affairs team contributes to development decision-making, evaluating strategic choices that should increase market access, building acceptance of the submission approach in light of recent regulatory evolutions, and accelerating approval rather than simply submitting regulatory dossiers.

9.1 Global Regulatory Strategy

A global regulatory strategy can be defined as a proactive and efficient course of action (e.g., activities, submissions), in light of specific program objectives and market conditions (e.g., competition, patients, unmet medical needs, regulatory changes, and pricing), to ensure that the Investigational Medicinal Product (IMP) meets effectively all regulatory hurdles from discovery through development, market approval, and post approval in applicable jurisdictions.

Early-stage biopharma companies might take a more limited definition of regulatory strategy, focusing instead on reaching only a specific development point that represents an appropriate exit point for their investors such

DOI: 10.4324/9781003598046-9

as securing excellent Phase 1 results or reaching a favorable proof of concept after completion of Phase 2 study.

In all cases, a regulatory strategy will need to account for many factors, e.g., relative ability to set prices versus related constraints (such as regulated pricing, use of price references, or need to negotiate with central country payer), targeted patient populations, geographies representing higher profitability/prices after applicable reductions and discounts, regulatory review requirements and timing, company commercial capabilities, marketing and distribution collaborations, manufacturing and supply chain considerations.

The document that encapsulates a company's global regulatory strategy is commonly referred to as a "global regulatory plan". The global regulatory plan will typically include a robust understanding of the applicable regulatory environment (regulatory landscape: applicable guidance and policy, applicable regulatory intelligence and information from competitive/related products), an optimized regulatory pathway (available programs or opportunities for development/review acceleration, available programs or opportunities for expanded access), optimized discovery, preclinical and clinical approaches, including lifecycle planning (pediatric development, device/diagnostic development, pharmacovigilance, etc.), regulatory submission plan and documentation approach (e.g., common technical document), communication plan with regulatory agencies (advisory, proposed communication, communication outcomes, program implications), overall risk management (benefit – risk assessments) and mitigation pre- and post-approval (regulatory, safety, technical).

Case Example: Impact of Global Regulatory Strategy

Ultimately, the global regulatory strategy impacts in-country drug availability and launch timing in applicable geographies. Global regulatory strategies tend to prioritize the United States and correspondingly reflect FDA regulations: the vast majority (85%) of new drugs launched from 2018 to 2022 were launched in the United States first or during the same quarter they were introduced in another country, with over half of the total launching in the United States first (U.S. Department of Health & Human Services, 2024).

This said, other countries may hold a prominent place in a global regulatory strategy as a quarter of the drugs evaluated were found not to be available in the United States (26%) versus 17% of drugs available only in the United States (U.S. Department of Health & Human Services, 2024). From an economic perspective, however, most important drugs tend to have more global regulatory strategies since 57% of drugs available both in the United States and other countries accounted for at least 90% of both US new drug spending and new drug spending in other OECD countries.

Japan and Germany were the two OECD countries that showed the smallest drug availability lag compared with the United States; they were also the most common first (or concurrent) launch country outside of the United States with Japan and Germany representing 19% and 8% of new drugs respectively. The average lag between the US launch and major OECD market launch was one year (U.S. Department of Health & Human Services, 2024), which reflects the typical staggered country approach commonly used in regulatory strategies.

9.2 General Regulatory Approaches

Regulatory Landscape

Various health authorities throughout the world ensure that biopharmaceutical products are safe, effective, and of appropriate manufacturing quality for patients. In addition to providing guidelines biopharma companies must comply with, they review and approve new medicines, monitor company compliance with regulations and update regulations, in particular to respond to technological evolutions and to industry trends. They provide clinical research oversight and ensure that clinical trials within their jurisdictions comply with applicable laws in addition to reflecting appropriate local and international standards (e.g., good clinical practices, protection of clinical trial participants through informed consent and safety monitoring, suitable data management approaches aimed at integrity, privacy, and accuracy). In addition, they ensure that approved medicines are manufactured, stored, and distributed in ways that ensure ongoing quality; they also ensure that medicine advertising and promotion are not misleading, do not extend to areas outside of their approval label, but stay within the limits of their regulatory framework. These health authorities include:

- World Health Organization (WHO).
  The WHO leads efforts to improve health globally. With participation from 194 countries, the WHO primary programs from a budgetary perspective focus on universal health coverage, health emergencies, emergency operations, and appeals, as well as WHO operational function and operational improvements. Among many other contributions, the WHO helps set global standards for clinical trial design and conduct, advocating in particular for research capabilities in low- and middle-income countries. The WHO has an International Clinical Trials Registry Platform and provides critical guidance such as the International Classification of Diseases (ICD), the International Classification of Health Interventions, or the list of regulatory authorities that comply with its requirements.

- International Conference on Harmonization of Technical Requirements for Registration of Pharmaceuticals for Human Use (ICH).
  The ICH aims, through worldwide harmonization, to ensure that safe, effective, and high-quality medicines are efficiently developed and registered. ICH is of utmost importance to biopharma companies, and plays a critical role in clinical development by providing a standardized framework across jurisdictions to facilitate regulatory collaborations and conduct clinical trials. This results in standardized good clinical practices (GCP), reduced duplication of trials and regulatory dossier data, optimized review processes, stronger global study design and data guidance, ultimately benefiting patients. The ICH publishes guidelines and terminology across multiple disciplines, such as medical terminology, nonclinical safety studies, electronic standards for the transfer of regulatory information, and drug interaction studies. ICH provides multiple technical standards such as the common technical document (CTD) organizing information about an IMP's quality, safety, and efficacy (e.g., out of the five CTD modules, the first one is region-specific while all the others are common across regions). ICH guidelines cover many practical regulatory aspects such as clinical study reports (ICH E3), ethnic factors in the acceptation of foreign clinical data to permit clinical data collected in one region to be used in another one (ICH E5), GCP (ICH E6), studies in geriatric populations (ICH E7), general considerations for clinical studies (ICH E8), and choice of control groups (ICH E10) just to name a few.
- U.S. Food & Drug Administration (FDA).
  The prominent importance of the US market in the biopharma industry makes its health authority, namely the FDA, a prime consideration. The mission of the FDA is to protect and advance public health by assuring the safety, efficacy, and security of human and veterinary drugs, biological products, medical devices, food, tobacco, cosmetics, and radiation-emitting devices. The FDA plays a pivotal role for the biopharma industry, significantly impacting research, development, and submissions (e.g., overseeing design, conduct, and reporting of clinical trials, ensuring participant welfare and safety, setting numerous standards, inspecting relevant biopharma industry clinical and manufacturing facilities or laboratories, in and outside of the United States). Studies regulated by the FDA must be registered electronically with ClinicalTrials.gov (either by the sponsor or the principal investigator). The FDA also maintains numerous guidance documents for the biopharma industry and is available for consultation in defined situations (see Figure 9.2). Note that ethics committees (discussed later in the chapter: ethics committees protect human participants' rights in biomedical research) are usually called institutional review boards (IRBs) in the United States.

- European Medicines Agency (EMA).
  With a role similar to that of the FDA for the European Economic Area (EEA), the EMA, oversees this other large and prominent biopharma industry market. Specifically, as a European Union agency, the EMA evaluates and monitors medicines to ensure public health and animal health. With a centralized procedure to evaluate and authorize medicines, the EMA provides a single-application marketing authorization pathway for the EEA. Specifically, the EMA's Committee for Medicinal Products for Human Use (CHMP) reviews the application and, if favorable, sends a recommendation to the European Commission (EC) to approve the medicine. Once granted, the EC central marketing authorization is valid in the entire European Union, Iceland, Norway, and Liechtenstein. The EMA centralized procedure is not the only pathway for Europe: a decentralized procedure might be used in certain cases to secure approval with the respective national competent authorities in several EU countries. Alternatively, for medicines already approved in one EU country, a mutual recognition procedure might be used to extend that approval to other countries. However, the centralized procedure is mandatory for many innovative medicines (e.g., new active substances to treat cancer, diabetes, neurodegenerative diseases, and viral diseases) and the lion's share of new innovative medicines uses that centralized procedure. All initial clinical trial applications in EEA must be submitted through the Clinical Trial Information System, a system that includes all ongoing clinical trials in EEA after January 30, 2025 (see euclinicaltrials.eu).
- National Medical Products Administration (NMPA).
  Together with the National Health Commission (NHC), the NMPA oversees clinical research in China. The NMPA is responsible for both clinical trial applications and marketing authorization applications, also granting permission to conduct clinical trials in China. In contrast, the NHC formulates health policies and systems. The NMPA uses three drug categories (Chinese medicines, chemical medicines, and biological products) and different classes depending on whether the drug is new and whether it has been marketed in China versus other geographies. Examples of NMPA-specific aspects include the requirement for drug registration application to be submitted by a Chinese legal entity. Similarly, the application process typically includes different types of meetings in addition to specific materials and data. Also, the NMPA might require data in local populations or bridging studies for approval. And the NHC adds many requirements for the collection, storage, and management of biological specimen in the context of China's human genetic resources the NHC is responsible for.
- Therapeutic Goods Administration (TGA).
  Part of the Australian Department of Health and Aged Care, the TGA is the national regulatory authority in Australia responsible for clinical

trial approvals, oversight as well as inspections. It also regulates supply, import/export, manufacturing, registration, and promotion of all therapeutic goods (which include prescription drugs and vaccines). TGA provides two regulatory schemes to be selected by the sponsor, depending on the level of regulatory involvement expected: Clinical Trial Notification (CTN) versus Clinical Trial Approval (CTA) which involves data review for the drug. Clinical trials need to be registered on a publicly accessible register such as the Australian and New Zealand Clinical Trials Registry before a first patient can be recruited.

- Health Canada (HC).
  One of five federal health agencies within Canada's Ministry of Health, HC is the national regulatory authority in Canada responsible for clinical trial approvals, oversight as well as inspections. In addition to Canada being an official ICH member, HC aims to provide regulatory flexibility in support of industry innovation and product development. Note that Ethics Committees are usually called Research Ethics Boards in Canada. Clinical trial application and regulatory submissions, in French or English, need to be made to the appropriate HC directorate (pharmaceutical drug versus biologics).
- Medicines and Healthcare products Regulatory Agency (MHRA).
  As a result of Brexit (the United Kingdom's effective withdrawal from the European Union in 2020), the United Kingdom is no longer regulated by the EMA, despite interim recognition of certain regulatory processes during a transition period as well as differences in approaches specific to Northern Ireland. Part of the UK Department of Health and Social Care, the MHRA is the national regulatory authority in the United Kingdom responsible for clinical trial approvals, oversight as well as inspections. The sponsor (or legal representative) needs to be in the United Kingdom or in the EEA. Another public body worth mentioning in connection with the MHRA is the National Institute for Health and Care Excellence (NICE) whose remit is, however, officially England as opposed to the MHRA that also covers Wales, Scotland, and Northern Ireland. Like other large payer organizations throughout the world, NICE evaluates drugs, specifically their clinical and cost-effectiveness, after they have been approved by the MHRA for the United Kingdom. NICE's evaluation and subsequent funding decision has significant impact as it determines the availability of the new drug to patients in the UK universal healthcare, referred to as the National Health System.
- Pharmaceuticals and Medical Devices Agency (PMDA).
  The PMDA is Japan's national agency for the regulation of drugs and medical devices, including over-the-counter and generic drugs. The PDMA follows review procedures leading to review reports submitted to the Minister of Health, Labor, and Welfare, who has authority to approve

new drugs. Phase 3 data typically needs to include Japanese patients, whereas Phase 1 and 2 might not. The PMDA issues foreign manufacturer accreditation, and as FDA and EMA, performs good practice assessments regarding laboratory, clinical, post-marketing surveillance, manufacturing, quality management aspects, performs facilities inspections, including outside of Japan and provide foreign manufacturer accreditations. It is important to note that the Japan marketing authorization needs to be held by a Japanese entity with a pharmaceutical business license, leaving foreign biopharma companies with the option of having a local subsidiary versus a distributor for Japan that would hold the authorization.

- Ministry of Food and Drug Safety (MFDS).
  Formerly known as the Korea Food & Drug Administration, or KFDA, the MFDS is South Korea's main regulatory agency for drugs, medical devices, food, and cosmetics. Korea is a full ICH member. The MFDS has a number of local requirements such as a local South Korean presence for clinical trials in the country, or specific import license with the Korea Pharmaceutical Traders Association to import IMPs. Also, South Korea might require data in local populations or bridging studies for approval.
- Agência Nacional de Vigilância Sanitária (ANVISA).
  An independent administrative agency linked to the Ministry of Health, ANVISA is the national regulatory authority in Brazil responsible for regulating, controlling, and supervising products and services involving public health risks, which includes drugs for human use.
- Central Drugs Standard Control Organization (CDSCO).
  Headed by the Drugs Controller General of India (DCGI), CDSCO is the national regulatory authority in India responsible for clinical trial approvals, oversight as well as inspections. Note that India might require local clinical trials for approval although that requirement might be waived in some cases for drugs approved in regions like the United States, the European Union, Japan, and the United Kingdom.
- Turkish Medicines and Medical Devices Agency (TİTCK).
  TİTCK is the national regulatory authority in Türkiye responsible for clinical trial approvals, oversight, and inspections. The TITCK is a member of ICH.
- Swissmedic (SMC).
  SMC is the national regulatory authority in Switzerland responsible for clinical trial approvals, oversight as well as inspections. Information on studies conducted in Switzerland is available on the Swiss National Clinical Trials Portal.

On a related note, the top 10 countries for Phase 1–3 clinical trials from 2021 to 2023, ranked by significance, were: the United States, China,

Australia, Spain, Canada, Germany, the United Kingdom, Japan, South Korea, and France (IQVIA Institute, 2024).

On the surface, clinical development plans might look very similar across various jurisdictions (Figure 9.1). However, despite harmonization efforts, international cooperations, and numerous international efforts at convergence, differences between jurisdictions remain, requiring careful planning on the part of biopharma companies, especially when it comes to expensive large multi-country multicenter Phase 3 studies. The conduct of such global clinical trials might need to accommodate regulatory differences such as different clinical trial application languages, whether or not the required review by the Ethics Committee (or IRB) can be concurrent with the regulatory agency review, whether or not the clinical trial needs to be registered, what legal age to use for adulthood in the context of informed consent and other aspects for studies with younger participants, whether or not clinical data needs to include country participation, what entries need to figure on the IMP label, or simply whether biological specimen might be exported out of the country to a central lab. In addition to international standards like ICH, each health authority likely has their own regulations, interpretations, and definitions for regulatory dossiers, ethics committees, clinical trial submission and reporting processes, study sponsorship, insurance and compensation of participants, access to treatment after study conclusion, informed consent process, definition, and management of IMPs, data management and protection, definition, and requirements for biological specimen.

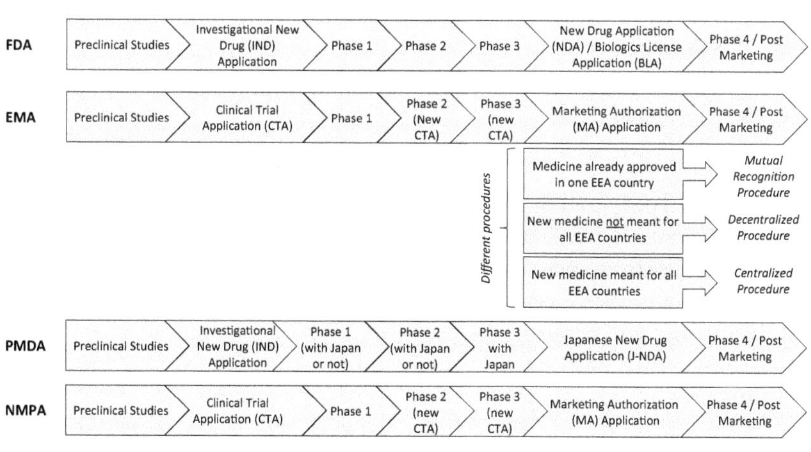

Figure 9.1 Simplified clinical development view for United States, Europe, Japan, and China.

Typical Regulatory Pathways

While regulatory constraints and guidance typically have much less influence on earlier stages of the drug lifecycle, these early stages may have important downstream implications on aspects important to regulatory agencies such as safety and manufacturing quality (Figure 9.2).

Indeed, before an IMP undergoes human trials, it will have gone through numerous evolutions over the years (Figure 9.2). The earlier steps for target identification and validation, exploratory research, and preclinical studies are designed to steer a program in directions favorable to regulatory approval by guiding the selection of products with relevant characteristics.

The research initially focuses on uncovering promising targets that relate to certain diseases or indications by using various tools such as biorepositories, real world evidence, bioinformatics research tools, animal models, molecular pathways, and cell lines, allowing researchers to generate and test various target hypotheses, iteratively evaluating the corresponding disease pathophysiology. Such iterative work allows researchers to identify targets (e.g., a certain protein, gene, or RNA) relevant to a specific disease. In order to validate the target identified, they will assess various aspects, e.g., relevant and druggable target with clear linkage to targeted disease, that should not give rise to major safety concerns based on existing literature review (e.g., no significant risk of intolerable side effects mentioned), representing a sound strategy (e.g., unmet needs, unsatisfactory standard of care, relatively unencumbered intellectual property area in terms of freedom to operate). Note that these aspects play a central role in regulators' evaluations of a product benefits/risk profile, making them important for regulatory consideration.

A validated target marks the beginning of the search for molecules that will affect the target in question, which is the goal of the subsequent exploratory research – finding a suitable preclinical candidate. As applicable, the validated target will also mark the beginning of target pharmacology studies to understand potential drug – target interactions and the start of biomarker developments to provide predictive or response mechanisms related to the target and disease (upon qualification, biomarkers can provide surrogate endpoints – a measure considered to predict clinical benefits, or companion diagnostics and measure disease progression depending on their predictive or responsive nature). Well-validated targets with existing biomarkers can thus present advantages for development, although they usually come with more encumbered drug intellectual property landscapes. Lastly, predictive and response biomarkers are not the only types used in a regulatory context – other biomarker uses might include safety, susceptibility, and prognosis.

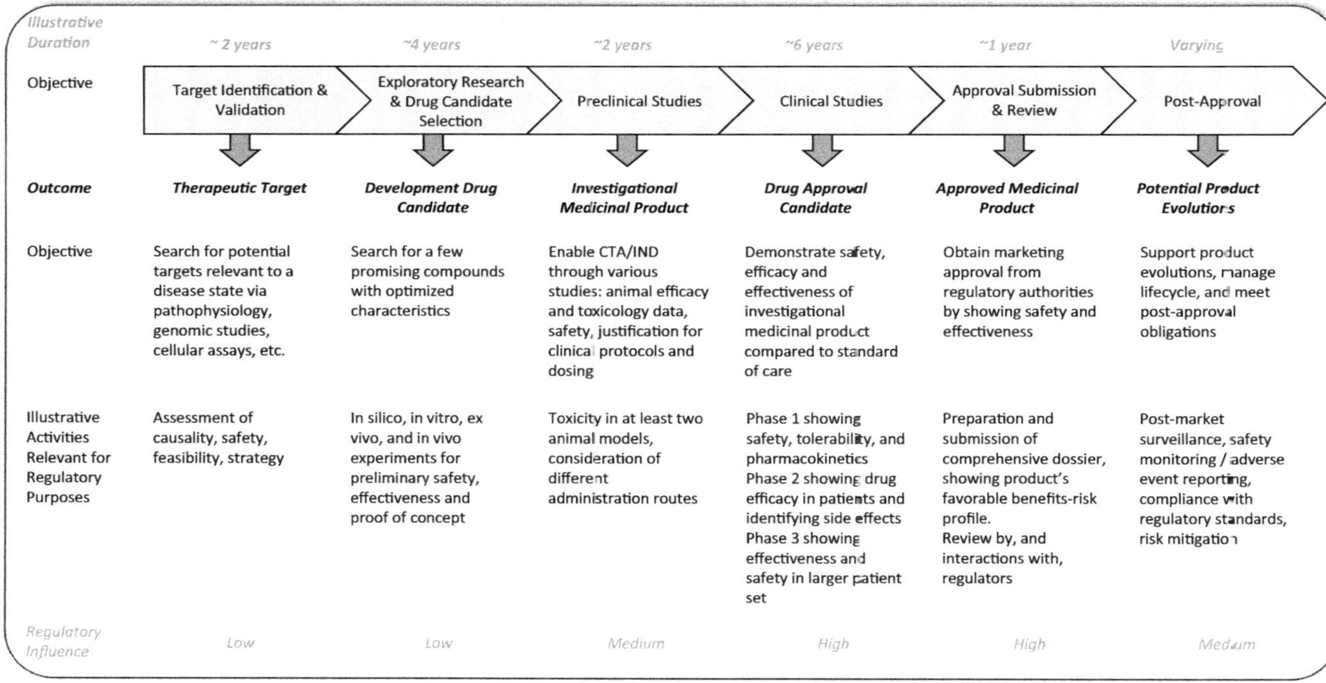

Figure 9.2 Increasing regulatory-relevant information across the R&D lifecycle.

The exploratory research process to select development drug candidate (encompassing various assays, libraries, characterizations, platforms, Artificial Intelligence and other technologies as well as in silico, in vitro, ex vivo, and in vivo studies) varies significantly between pharmaceutical compounds and biologics, or even between different modalities. Regardless of the actual process used, significant emphasis is increasingly put on translational science through safety profiles, early manufacturing considerations, and predicted effectiveness. At this development drug candidate stage, key compound characteristics have been optimized, such as target selectivity, potency, safety profile, and manufacturability.

Next comes the preclinical stage, a stage at which the program strategy comes in full force with the early establishment of the Target Product Profile (TPP) and the typical addition of a Regulatory Affairs team member as part of the regular program cross-functional team. The TPP is a brief document that outlines the desired characteristics and features of the drug product, e.g., ideal case versus minimum acceptable, typically in two separate columns. Although TPPs can vary significantly from product to product, characteristics and features commonly include primary indication, target patient population/market size, competition, differentiation, treatment duration, delivery mode, dosage form, regimen, efficacy/bioavailability/duration of action, drug target, endpoints, risks/contraindications/side effects, and modality/mechanism of action (MOA), Chemistry, Manufacturing, and Control (CMC) profile, patent, special regulatory designation (e.g., breakthrough therapy, orphan drug). Having such a document facilitates regulatory strategy considerations and can guide numerous program decisions, including regulatory communications, clinical study design, and manufacturing. It is important to note that the TPP is not a static document reviewed once but rather represents a constant progress checkpoint that also evolves as the program advances.

Preclinical studies establish the basis for the submission of the Investigational New Drug (IND) Application, or CTA, required before starting clinical trials in humans depending on the jurisdiction. Using the TPP, the tentative clinical development plan, and the CTA or IND requirements for the country (or countries) in which the Phase 1 study is expected to take place (including information needed for pre-IND or pre-CTA meeting with regulatory authorities), the Regulatory Affairs team member will work backward with the rest of the team to identify preclinical stage requirements. Preclinical activities necessary to enable the CTA/IND regulatory path forward typically include:

- Manufacturing for the drug substance or active pharmaceutical ingredient.
- Formulation and dosage design.

- Development and validation of analytical and bioanalytical methods, to characterize and quantify chemical properties for the drug as well as to measure its concentration in biological samples.
- Metabolic and pharmacokinetic studies, also referred to as ADME studies.
- Good Laboratory Practice (GLP), toxicology, and safety studies.
- Good Manufacturing Practice (GMP) and drug product documentation for clinical trial use.

CMC represents particularly important considerations from a regulatory perspective to ensure that a drug is made under controlled conditions and will meet requirements of identity, purity, potency/strength of API, stability (given the temperature, humidity, light, and storage conditions), initially for at least the duration of the studies. CMC aspects will of course change as the biopharma company evolves their manufacturing approach toward optimized production, scalability, and formulation. On a related note, information on placebo will likewise be required, as applicable. Note that some jurisdictions, like China, may place a more significant emphasis on CMC.

After the preclinical stage, obtaining an IND or CTA to start trials in humans requires substantial data and information. On a related note, there is a significant regulatory difference between an IND and a CTA in the geographies that use one versus the other: the IND authorizes the use of the investigational drug whereas the CTA authorizes the clinical trial: each interventional study typically needs a CTA whereas multiple studies can be run under an IND. As a result, a CTA typically requires less info and is faster to prepare; substantial protocol amendments require CTA approval and new protocols require a new CTA, whereas such changes and additions are covered by an IND. Indeed, for the IND, it may be desirable to have a pre-IND meeting with the FDA to present the project and request preliminary guidance and points in the development since the IND remains until marketing approval. The regulatory dossier for the CTA will typically include the clinical protocol (document outlining the steps involved in conducting the clinical trial in addition to its design, objectives, and methods), the informed consent (process through which participants indicate their willingness to participate in the clinical trial after being informed of all relevant aspects), the investigator brochure (comprehensive document that provides all relevant information, clinical and nonclinical, for investigators to make informed decisions and understand the study rationale, risk and benefits, and to effectively manage participants for the study), the IMP dossier with corresponding CMC data, as well as various other forms and information such as insurance. Arguably most importantly, the dossier will explain the principles used to determine a safe starting dose in humans for the drug, e.g., determination of the NOAEL (no observed adverse effect level) in the most appropriate animal species from the preclinical stage, derivation of HED (human equivalent dose), and application of an appropriate safety factor to the HED plus other safety considerations to establish the MRSD (maximum recommended starting dose).

In the European Union, to request a CTA for trials involving the European Union, sponsors submit a single online application on the CTIS platform. This platform is used by the national EU/EAA regulators to review, authorize, and supervise clinical trials, allowing collaborative oversight for multi-country studies. Feedback on the CTA can take four months with the centralized procedure whereas IND feedback from the FDA is faster (30 days).

In addition to the CTA/IND approval, regulatory authorities require biopharma sponsors to secure review and approval by an Ethics Committee called the IRB in the United States. While terminology and regulations vary (e.g., concurrent EC and CTA approval authorized versus EC approval needed prior to CTA approval, use of central EC/IRB for all clinical sites in the country, different EC composition requirements), an EC or IRB is a group formally designated to review, approve, and monitor biomedical research involving human participation to ensure the protection and welfare of participants. EC approval for every protocol is required prior to study initiation.

Depending on the jurisdiction, other processes, forms, or authorizations might be required prior to study initiation. In the United States, the sponsor must obtain a signed statement from the investigator, on FDA Form 1572, to document the investigator's agreement to provide information and comply with regulations. In Australia, research authorization must be secured from the institution in which the research is conducted after review and site-specific assessment. China requires specific processes and organizations at clinical sites (e.g., establishment of a clinical study administration committee).

During clinical studies, sponsors are expected to maintain their CTA or IND through various activities. Specifically, they typically need to meet particular requirements for protocol amendments, safety reporting, as well as interim and annual progress reporting, in addition to various other requirements (e.g., data and records management, personal data protection, risk and quality management, end-of-study notification, new investigator notification) depending on the jurisdiction. In the European Union, the Clinical Trials Regulation (CTR) requires that a sponsor monitors adherence to the protocol, requests authorization for protocol amendments (clinical trial or site modifications), and conducts safety surveillance. Serious adverse events must be reported within 24 hours (unless indicated otherwise in protocol) and unexpected events that affect the benefit – risk balance of the clinical trial (e.g., genotoxicity findings for the IMP) must be reported within 15 days.

As discussed, before drugs can be submitted for approval to be used for the general public in a given health authority's jurisdiction, they must undergo a systematic series of clinical trials in humans, each corresponding to what is referred to as a phase. Regardless of the phase and the health authority under which they are conducted, clinical trials require a systematic and scientific approach and follow regulatory guidelines in terms of EC oversight, ethics, adherence to study protocol, reporting, and data management. Each clinical trial phase has a consistent designation across the various regulatory authorities (e.g., Phase 1 sometimes divided between 1A for single dose and 1B for multiple doses, Phase 2 sometimes divided between smaller Phase 2A and larger Phase 2B, Phase 3 sometimes divided between 3A and 3B for pre- and post-approval, Phase 4) and attempts to address specific facets that will be necessary to understand for the drug to be approved, building on research and results to date. Collectively, as carefully designed and controlled studies that investigate safety, efficacy, and benefits of medical treatments, clinical trials aim to show whether the drug can be used in specific patient populations with appropriate safety and effectiveness, at an acceptable level of uncertainty. Phases 1–3 are typically required before a drug can be approved for marketing, with some notable exceptions discussed below. Clinical trials are typically conducted according to GCP standards such as the ICH E6 guideline that provides a unified GCP standard for the European Union, Japan, and the United States and takes into account Australia, Canada, Nordic countries, and the WHO.

Phase 1 clinical trials mark the first human testing stage and are typically conducted with a small number of healthy volunteers (e.g., 20–80 participants, depending on the study statistical analysis plan), although testing in patients is also possible (e.g., in oncology). Phase 1 trials primarily assess safety, tolerability, pharmacokinetics, and pharmacodynamics. A Phase 1 trial tests the safety, side effects, best dose, and timing of the investigational treatment. The dose is normally increased progressively to establish the highest dose without unacceptable side effects (referred to as MTD or maximum tolerated dose). The trial may also test the best administration route and how the treatment affects the body.

In addition to reporting requirements according to GCP requirements, a Phase 1 trial might be followed by an end-of-Phase-1 meeting with regulatory authorities, depending on the program, company's regulatory approach, and regulatory framework. In the United States, end-of-Phase-1 meeting with the FDA are usually meant for investigational products under accelerated approval for serious or life-threatening illnesses. Interactions with the EMA can be requested by a sponsor at any stage of a product's development (for scientific advice or protocol assistance).

If the IMP is deemed safe at the end of Phase 1, it will successfully enter Phase 2, which typically occurs for two products out of three. With Phase 2, clinical trials shift away from the exclusive safety Phase 1 focus, to determine if the IMP provides sufficient evidence of efficacy as well as to further evaluate safety and refine the TPP. Phase 2 studies commonly include several hundred patients with the condition targeted by the drug, primarily investigate the efficacy of IMP, and determine the relationship between dose and response. Phase 2 may be split into Phase 2A for evidence of efficacy (proof of concept), side-effects identification, and safety, and Phase 2B for dose range and frequency finding, and mode of delivery determination. The larger number of participants in a Phase 2 study allows for more accurate efficacy and safety evaluations.

When successful, a Phase 2 trial is often followed by an end-of-Phase-2 meeting with regulatory authorities, depending on the program, company's regulatory approach, and regulatory framework. Such meeting represents a crucial milestone to determine the regulatory pathway forward; typically, one in three drugs will move to Phase 3.

Phase 3 studies are larger trials (from several hundred to several thousand participants with the condition targeted by the drug) intended to evaluate the efficacy of the IMP in large populations and monitor adverse reactions. At this stage, regulators expect the manufacturing process to be fully validated in order to show that the process can consistently produce the IMP at the quality level necessary and at commercial scale. Indeed, as explained in ICH Q8 guidelines, significant differences between pivotal trial manufacturing process and the process intended for commercial production should be discussed in the quality section of the submission CTD.

After Phase 3 results and prior to submitting a marketing application, the sponsor will request meetings with regulators to ensure that the trials provide a relevant basis in view of the marketing application and labeling.

As drug development might not always be economically viable and takes a long time for patients to be able to access new therapies, regulatory authorities throughout the world have put in place mechanisms that can facilitate development and enable or accelerate patient access to treatment, especially in the case of serious and life-threatening diseases and unmet medical needs (see Sections 9.3–9.5 for further information). Such expedited or privileged pathways might take the form of:

- Increased guidance from, and priority interactions with, regulatory authorities.
- Shortened approval timelines enabled by higher allocation of resources on the regulatory authority's side.
- Earlier authorization based on more limited sets of data (e.g., surrogate endpoints) followed by confirmatory post-market studies.

Upon completion of clinical trials, after applicable pre-submission meeting, the sponsor files their application for market approval. The actual designation of this application varies from region to region, e.g., new drug submission (NDS) in Canada, new drug application (NDA) or biological license application (BLA) in the United States, marketing authorization application (MAA) in the European Union, or Japanese New Drug Application (JNDA) in Japan. Thankfully transmitted electronically, such a regulatory dossier would otherwise represent a hundred thousand pages of printed documentation and weigh as much as a gorilla. While ICH's common technical document (CTD) is the predominantly agreed-upon structure to submit a marketing authorization regulatory dossier for a new pharmaceutical drug or biologic, the review process and time may differ significantly between regulatory authorities. Different questions might arise at different times and in different venues for different regulatory agencies, with the potential to affect approval outcomes or timing. Certain regulatory agencies might make more pronounced use of meetings, while others make more pronounced use of written communications. Particular agencies like the FDA might have more data-driven approaches to their evaluation, using sponsor data sets to conduct their own analyses; in comparison, other agencies like the EMA might rather depend on sponsor analyses. Agencies might also conduct facility inspections. In any case, the CTD is structured in five modules:

- The first module is region-specific and contains administrative and prescribing information.
- Module 2, harmonized across regions, covers summary information on the next three modules, namely, quality, nonclinical, and clinical study reports.
- Module 3, harmonized across regions, is also designated as the quality module and covers CMC information.
- Module 4, harmonized across regions, includes nonclinical study reports.
- Module 5, harmonized across regions, includes clinical study reports.

At the outset of the regulatory review, the regulatory agency, depending on its authority, will issue either its decision (e.g., approval versus response letter) or its recommendation and assessment report to the regulatory authority that would ultimately issue a marketing authorization. In all cases, an approval will document the specific indications and usage approved by the regulatory authority along with other key information, such as contraindications, warnings, adverse reactions, drug interactions, use in specific populations, and clinical trials.

Once the drug is approved, regulatory imperatives are far from over. First, approvals for different markets tend to be staggered as discussed earlier in the chapter, so that regulatory approval is really a series of events rather than a singular one. In addition, there are many ongoing regulatory challenges for the biopharma sponsor company to tackle:

- Implementing, submitting, and obtaining approval for changes (e.g., new active substance supply, shelf-life change as a result of more extensive manufacturing experience).
- Maintenance of various registrations (e.g., establishment engaged in manufacturing, labeling, and distribution) with regulatory authorities.
- Annual reporting, pharmacovigilance, and reporting of adverse events.
- Ongoing conduct of drug programs required by regulatory authorities, such as risk evaluation and mitigation strategy (REMS) programs in the case of the FDA, or risk management plans (RMP) in the case of the EMA.
- Conduct of required post-approval studies such as Phase 4 clinical trials to evaluate a drug's side effects and effectiveness over the long term in a large population (these studies may involve thousands of participants) to observe medication in real-life conditions. Such studies might also support label expansion or point to new potential indications.
- Ensuring ongoing market supply to avoid being listed on official regulator's drug shortage list, which might temporarily compromise the biopharma company's exclusivity.

Other post-approval regulatory activities might be more strategic in nature, such as label updates, extension of marketing authorization, or a new dual branding strategy. In a similar vein, to optimize drug market exclusivity and mitigate the forthcoming impact of generic entry in commercial markets, pharma companies may pursue patent extension strategies. Such regulatory approaches may involve pediatric research to benefit from the extension of patent exclusivity, application for patent extension, or supplementary protection certificates. Some regulatory designations may already allow sponsors to benefit from patent extensions (e.g., orphan drugs designation, qualified infectious disease product designation by the FDA).

As their patents cliff approaches, using appropriate regulatory approaches, having considered remaining exclusivity in various markets, sponsors may resort to introducing their own generic version, transferring the marketing authorization to another company, or requesting a market withdrawal.

Case Example: Challenges of Drug Shortage

Tirzepatide, a dual GIP/GLP-1 receptor agonist compound, approved by the FDA in 2022 for Type 2 diabetes and in 2023 for chronic weight management is commercialized by Eli Lilly under the brand names Mounjaro and Zepbound, respectively.

Tirzepatide was added on December 15, 2022 to the FDA drug shortage list due to supply limitations and high patient demand (Shaw, 2024).

Under Sections 503A and 503B of the Federal Food, Drug, and Cosmetic Act respectively, such listing allowed compounding pharmacies and outsourcing facilities to make and distribute versions of the drug under the narrow exceptions and policy obligations provided by the regulations.

Having received evidence from Eli Lilly that supply was meeting or exceeding demand (based on finished product inventory, semi-finished units, and planned production), the FDA removed tirzepatide from the drug shortage list on December 19, 2024, and granted a transitional period for compounders to stop distributing or dispensing tirzepatide injections. The FDA continues to monitor tirzepatide supply and demand to determine if a shortage occurs again (Shaw, 2024).

Common Regulatory Assessment Considerations

In preparing an application for use in clinical trials or marketing approval, sponsors have to anticipate the "reading grid" used by regulatory agencies to assess if a drug product is ready for use in humans. The assessment by agencies is based on typical criteria such as:

- Would the drug product be used/commercialized under reasonable safety conditions?
  Approval for use in humans will be favorably considered when drug products present familiar characteristics such as an already known biological target (i.e., addressed by comparable products in the same class), a simple mode of administration (e.g., reusable pen injector), or low-level dosing. Unfavorable characteristics would be uncertain occurrences of adverse events, evidence of high toxicity in the same class, and high-level dosing.
- Has the information gathered been grounded on robust and scientifically driven data?
  The agencies will want to understand the relevance of quantitative methods and their statistical significance to determine efficacy or safety. They will scrutinize parameters such as sample size, diversity of participants and inclusion/exclusion rules, and relevance of endpoints in study design.
- Is the benefit – risk balance considered favorable?
  The regulatory review process will come to a conclusion as to whether the estimated benefits of the drug product outweigh the safety risks. This review process uses a holistic approach over the entire product's lifecycle. We will review later in this chapter the importance of benefit – risk considerations.

Considering uncertainties, the agencies may approve a product under conditions (e.g., monitoring post approval like REMS), or change over time their regulatory requirements. For sponsors, such evolution may generate uncertain regulatory paths and unclear transferability of results to other countries.

Health Authority Meetings

Meetings with regulatory agencies present particular interest for drugs with novel MOA for which no precedent regulatory pathway is available, or for new treatments in areas known for a high attrition rate of clinical trials. In more usual cases, meetings with regulators will be the opportunity for sponsors to obtain clarification on regulatory requirements or to provide specific demonstration. For biological or nonbiological products, several types of formal meetings with the FDA can be requested by a sponsor, as shown in Figure 9.3.

Formal meetings with different health authorities might be required or highly recommended under different circumstances. For example, processes for meeting the EMA are different from those used with the FDA. At any stage of a product's development, interactions with the EMA via the IRIS platform can be requested for scientific advice or protocol assistance. The EMA offers opportunities for clarification meetings, including the pre-MAA submission meeting, held via teleconference. Support and guidance are provided by the CHMP. In Japan, PMDA has established options for regulatory

Examples of FDA Regulatory Meetings
Under the Prescription Drug User Fee Act (PDUFA)

"Type A" Meeting – Discussion of stalled development and important safety issues

- Sponsor appeals
- Discussion of clinical holds
- Post-action meeting after receipt of FDA regulatory action (other than approval)

"Type B" or "Type B (EOP)" Meeting – Development milestone discussion

- Pre-investigational new drug application (pre-IND) meetings
- Pre-emergency use authorization meetings
- Pre-new drug application (pre-NDA) / pre-biologics license application (pre-BLA) meetings
- Meetings regarding risk evaluation and mitigation strategies (REMS) or post marketing requirements
- End-of-phase 1 meeting
- End-of-phase 2 meeting

"Type C" Meeting – Consultation meeting

- Early consultation on the use of a biomarker as a new surrogate endpoint

"Type D" Meeting – Discussion on critical narrow issues to move program forward

- General question about an innovative development approach

INTERACT Meeting – Discussion of novel product / development program with unique early development challenges

- IND requirements

Source: FDA Draft Guidance for Industry (September 2023) – Formal Meetings Between the FDA and Sponsors or Applicants of PDUFA Products Guidance for Industry

Figure 9.3 Examples of regulatory meetings with the FDA.

science consultations aimed at universities, research institutions, and venture companies with promising early-stage research or technology. In China, similarly to the FDA, the NMPA provides opportunities for predefined categories of meetings around clinical trials: category I for major technical or safety issues, category 2 before Phase 1, after Phase 2, before submission, and to review risks and controls, category 3 for other major development situations.

The Importance of Benefit – Risk Considerations

For clinical trials and drug approvals, the concept of safety is always considered in the context of the benefit – risk profile of the drug, causing benefit – risk considerations to be a crucial part of development reviews and drug approvals. While the concept of comparing risks versus benefits is intuitive, regulatory evaluations typically require more systematic approaches, making consistent, transparent, and predictable approaches, models, and evaluations desirable where possible. With the increasing patient centricity used in biopharma product development, benefit – risk approaches are likewise evolving to take patient perspectives into account. In addition, discussion of benefit – risk is characteristically ubiquitous in biopharma company meetings with regulatory authorities. Last but not least, the various regulatory agencies will expect confirmatory clinical trials to provide an adequate basis for regulators to assess the benefit – risk relationship in order to support a marketing approval decision, as highlighted in ICH E8 guidelines.

Regarding safety in human trials, an important consideration is whether the therapeutic target is already known and addressed by comparable products in the same class. On the other hand, high or unknown dosing, previous failures in the same class for toxicity reasons would constitute major risk factors. The agencies will assess the importance of the target product profile (efficacy vs comparators; breakthrough vs. convenience) in the context of the epidemiology (e.g., prevalence) data and prevailing unmet needs.

The FDA benefit – risk framework features four dimensions to evaluate a new drug: analysis of the condition, current treatment options, benefits of the new product, as well as risks and risk management options. For each dimension, the reviewers will note evidence and remaining uncertainties to then derive specific conclusions and document the underlying reasons for such conclusions (FDA, 2023).

The benefit – risk assessment typically becomes more robust with the lifecycle of the product. At the IND/CTA stage, the assessment will focus on preclinical data, Phase 1 protocol, manufacturing quality, and safety monitoring. At a later stage, clinical trial information such as side-effects and adverse events data can enrich the initial assessments, as well as guide labeling and risk management approaches that might accompany an approval. Post approval, surveillance programs, risk management plans, safety reporting, and post-approval commitments required by regulatory authorities will further enrich the benefit – risk profile of the drug and trigger regulatory actions (e.g., label update, market withdrawal) when unfavorable.

Illustrative Regulatory Affairs' Partnership Approach

In developing a global regulatory strategy, the regulatory affairs team works closely with clinical operations and other biopharma development team members – their joint approach might include the following steps (based on discussion with a regulatory affairs executive):

- Nonclinical and toxicity studies showing safety and MOA prior to filing an IND and starting Phase 1 first-in-human studies. The regulatory strategy will hinge on those nonclinical and toxicity studies, as IND-enabling studies, to plan for Phase 1 where regulatory affairs work with the clinical operations team on a clinical development program before targeting a clinical center that can recruit the patients or healthy volunteers required by the Phase 1 study protocol. In particular, regulatory affairs will work to validate that the inclusion and exclusion criteria (criteria that delineate what participants might or might not be recruited for the study) featured in the Phase 1 study protocol can be acceptable to the IRB or Ethics Committee-based on previous studies in addition to feasibility considerations considering the country in which Phase 1 will be conducted.
- One key regulatory affairs question in terms of safety is to consider if preclinical studies are adequate to enable the program to move forward with Phase 1. Precedence is also an important regulatory consideration. If another company had a major issue on a similar study, regulatory affairs would work with the overall team to identify additional studies that might be required by health authorities in light of such precedent and benefit – risk considerations specific to the disease area (e.g., what might be acceptable with a life-threatening disease in oncology might not be for mild atopic dermatitis).
- After Phase 1, entering proof of concept in Phase 2, the regulatory affairs and clinical teams start looking further into the target product profile, working with more hands-on data and perhaps a less ideal picture; they might be working with a subpopulation, and generally change and adjust the proposals to the health authorities.
- After favorable safety data and a Phase 2 that confirms benefits and risks, the regulatory affairs team will lead an end-of-Phase-2 meeting with the regulatory authorities, which is really critical. As the Phase 3 confirmatory study that follows is the most expensive study, the team needs to ensure they are planning the right number of patients for specific countries and that they are not missing anything. This end-of-Phase-2 meeting is also the meeting in which they start discussing the targeted label, which makes a significant difference at the commercial stage.
- Then comes Phase 3 and submission.

Note that for diseases with combined Phase 2/3 such as rare diseases, a favorable end of Phase 2, or proof of concept as it is called, would be a major milestone.

Commercial considerations can also influence a regulatory strategy. For a crowded indication like Alzheimer's, where several different programs pursue the same indication, in a large biopharma company, the regulatory affairs team might rely on input from the commercial team as well as from the Clinical team and Key Opinion Leaders (i.e., respected experts with influence over other physicians or researchers) to understand what would make a significant difference on the market and work back from that to drive the regulatory strategy, asking "what do we need to get there?" There might be safety aspects, dosage (one pill versus two pills), different modes of action, different risks and benefits, different remaining patent exclusivity periods even between two drug candidates within a single company. The description and drug profile are what will make a difference. This said, the countries targeted and regulatory authorities are likely to be similar between two programs for the same indication. This is usually driven by factors that would be the same across both programs like disease prevalence, market, and pricing. Market access and product manufacturing costs and pricing might, however, influence the list of targeted countries.

Lastly FDA and EMA are often considered as key priorities for large biopharma companies with the financial capacity to address them.

Case Example: Program Regulatory Pathway

Mavacamten, an oral small-molecule cardiac myosin inhibitor acquired by BMS in 2020, was approved by the FDA in April 2022, by Health Canada in October 2022, and by the EMA in June 2023, to treat obstructive hypertrophic cardiomyopathy (oHCM) and diseases of diastolic dysfunction. At that time, no treatment was available for the underlying abnormal heart function causing oHCM (EMA, 2024). The program regulatory pathway from IND to first approval took over 7 years with numerous regulatory interactions and designations enabling faster time to market – see Figure 9.4 and Keam (2022). Mavacamten US patents are expected to expire in 2034, not including extensions due to patent restoration or regulatory exclusivities (MyoKardia, 2020).

In addition to deciding that mavacamten's benefits outweighed the risks, regulatory agencies required a number of safety measures, e.g.:

- The need to measure and monitor safety risks influenced the design of the studies during the whole development plan. The Phase 1 program included two single-ascending dose (SAD) trials and one multiple ascending dose (MAD) trial. The PIONEER Phase 2 study was followed by an open-label extension study. The EXPLORER Phase 3 study was associated with an independent data monitoring committee to monitor

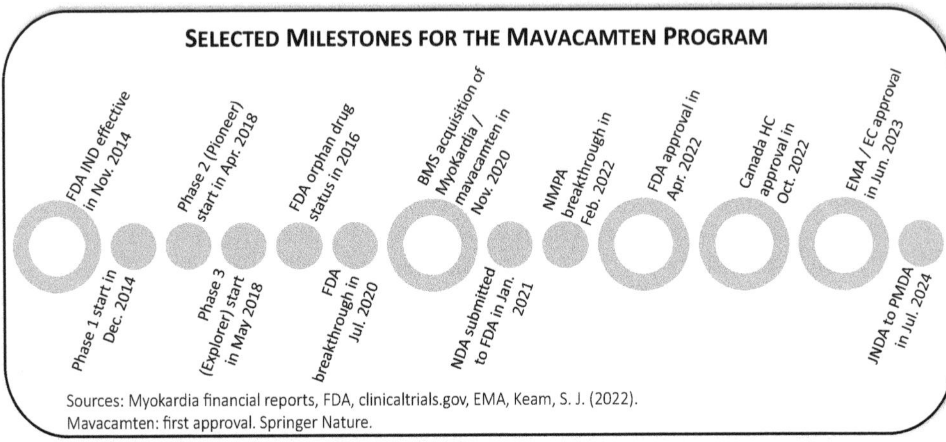

Figure 9.4 Selected mavacamten regulatory milestones.

safety and completed by a long-term extension study to assess long-term safety (MyoKardia, 2020).

- In the United States, the labeling for mavacamten contains a boxed warning regarding heart failure and mavacamten is available only through a monitored program under a risk evaluation and mitigation strategy (Keam, 2022).
- In Europe, patients are provided with a patient card containing important safety information. An alert card contains information on the risks of drug interactions and healthcare professionals are provided with a checklist regarding risks management in addition to information provided in the package leaflet (EMA, 2024).

Once a drug like mavacamten is approved, it constitutes a regulatory precedent, and the next drug candidate would be evaluated with different risk – benefit considerations than the first drug, characterized by remaining unmet medical needs, possibility for safer drugs, or similar benefit – risk performance expectations. See for instance Sebastian et al. (2023) who discuss the benefits of aficamten versus mavacamten.

"Moving Parts": The Impact of Artificial Intelligence (AI)

AI will have a growing impact on the way of conducting regulatory affairs in biopharmaceutical companies, as it helps to automate and optimize areas such as data collection, administrative tasks and quality control, compliance with regulations, dossiers preparation and submission, and assist decision-making.

As explained by a top ten biopharma regulatory affairs executive, AI brings about more effective administrative and competitive intelligence solutions, e.g.:

- Generating clinical study reports.
- Drafting regulatory dossier sections such as CTD Modules 2 and 3.
- Searching for databases for questions asked by Health Authorities.
- Assessing probabilities of success.

Another relevant field of application for AI is what is commonly referred to as model-informed drug development (MIDD). MIDD is a process where key program decisions are supported by AI or other mathematical models that predict likelihood of success for key drug or clinical trial characteristics. MIDD might be based on AI, disease models, systems biology, clinical trial simulations, or other approaches and applications might include dosing optimization, toxicity prediction, patient selection, or study design. AI can be instrumental in augmenting the strategic partner contributions made by regulatory affairs. In the United States, the goals set for PDUFA VII (seventh installment of the Prescription Drug User Fee Act) include modernizing regulatory evidence generation and drug development tools, with a specific mention for the intent to advance consistency and predictability around the use of modeling and simulations. AI analyses currently used in regulatory submissions might include outcome predictions, covariate selection, confounding adjustments, pharmacometrics, or anomaly detection.

Case Example: AI-Based Patient Selection Used in Regulatory Submission

In November 2022, anakinra (KINERET®), an interleukin-1 receptor antagonist approved by the FDA for rheumatoid arthritis and other indications, was granted an emergency-use authorization to treat COVID-19 in hospitalized adults requiring supplemental oxygen who are at risk of progressing to severe respiratory failure (FDA, 2022).

Phase 3 clinical trial SAVE-MORE, registered on ClinicalTrials.gov under NCT04680949 and conducted in Greece and Italy from December 2020 to June 2021 was considered as the primary source of evidence of effectiveness of anakinra in the treatment of COVID-19.

In this study, biomarker soluble urokinase plasminogen activator receptor (suPAR) was the recognized inclusion criterion (suPAR $\geq$ 6 ng/ml) to identify patients with risk for severe respiratory failure.

As the suPAR tests are not available for use in the United States, alternative criteria were developed by the sponsor and the FDA. The sponsor developed a scoring rule based on different combinations of baseline variables that may be predictive for suPAR $\geq$ 6 ng/ml. As an improvement of the sponsor's method, the FDA review team developed a dual AI-based approach:

- A machine-learning classification model allowed to determine an alternative patient identification criterion to predict the risk for SRF with comparable effectiveness as suPAR.
- A neural network-based model confirmed the alternative criterion as a valid inflammation- and immune-related biomarker (Ibid).

Other Innovative Evolutions

From ongoing and faster global regulatory evolutions to new trial approaches, such as decentralized trials, to more radical changes like digital health and patient centricity, biopharma companies need to adapt their regulatory strategy and processes while maintaining a high level of compliance with regulations. Multiple areas are being explored in the field, such as:

- Regulatory affairs could implement new ways to collect patient data that may not involve actual prospective randomized clinical trials.
- Digital biomarkers via wearable or implantable devices capture patients' real-time health data and could help to operate clinical trials remotely. Data collected via digital health technologies still face challenges such as ambiguities in differentiating actual biomarker data with clinical outcomes assessment and in defining meaningful and acceptable "digital endpoints".
- Real world evidence (RWE) will likely be used for proof of safety, but this is further in the future and its wide acceptance could pose challenges. The EMA established in 2024 a coordination center named DARWIN EU, providing RWE from real world healthcare databases across the European Union.
- To simplify regulatory interactions with health authorities, cloud-based documents may allow for continuous communication with authorities instead of submission approach featuring automated composition that still needs to be reviewed.

Other Important General Regulatory Notions

Listed in alphabetic order below are selected regulatory notions important to consider in the context of the biopharma industry, although not otherwise mentioned in this brief regulatory overview chapter.

- Form 483 and equivalent observations.
  Upon inspections, regulatory agencies will characteristically issue a written summary of their inspection observations. In the case of the FDA,

Form 483 observations are issued post-inspection providing a written list of objectional conditions. While not a list of objectionable findings, the EMA provides an inspection report for each site inspected, as well as an Integrated Inspection Report that summarizes all critical findings at all inspected sites. In Japan, the PMDA similarly issues a notice for deficiencies observed during GMP inspections to the responsible person; for significant findings that might benefit others, the PMDA also issues "ORANGE" notices to the industry (without the identity of the offender) documenting the situation and findings to facilitate voluntary industry improvements.

- GDP.
  GDP are better spelled out as they might refer either to good distribution practices or to good documentation practices.
  Good distribution practices are a set of guidelines to ensure the quality and integrity of medicinal products is maintained throughout the supply chain. Good documentation practices are a set of standards for managing documentation and ensure quality and integrity of data to support regulatory compliance.
- GLP.
  Good laboratory practices (GLP) are a set of guidelines established by regulatory authorities, aimed at ensuring the quality of nonclinical laboratory studies.
- GMP.
  Good manufacturing practices (GMP) are a set of guidelines established by regulatory authorities (e.g., ICH Q7 GMP guidance for active pharmaceutical ingredients), aimed at ensuring that medicinal products are consistently produced with the expected quality, purity, and safety. GMP compliance is expected to secure and maintain trial and marketing approvals.
- GxP.
  GxP is a shorthand often used in the industry to refer to the collective applicable practices such as GCP, GDP, GLP, and GMP. A lowercase c before any of these, more commonly used for GMP (e.g., cGMP), designates the current version of the practices.
- PDUFA and regulatory agency fees.
  Various regulatory agencies, such as those listed in the regulatory landscape of Section 9.1, collect fees from biopharma companies in connection with their clinical trial or drug approval process and might provide certain exemptions or fee reductions under certain conditions (e.g., small business, orphan drugs). In the United States, the Prescription Drug User Fee Act (PDUFA), a law that must be reauthorized every five years, allows the FDA to collect fees from drug manufacturers to provide for timely review of NDAs and BLAs.

- Phase 0 clinical trials.
  Phase 0 trials, also named exploratory clinical trials by the ICH guidance M3(R2), are streamlined studies to gain preliminary knowledge of the physiological and pharmacological drug – target effects in humans. Such trials in patients or healthy volunteers, designed to limit human exposure (e.g., with microdosing), do not have therapeutic intent and do not measure clinical tolerability. They might be used in oncology to evaluate whether a compound modulates its target in a tumor under subtherapeutic doses.
- Warning letters.
  Warning letters represent a formal notification to a company by the regulatory authority for significant regulatory violations. These letters are typically more severe than observations, provide the opportunity for corrections or regulatory interactions, and require timely action on the part of the company. FDA warning letters are published on the FDA website and typically require a written response within 15 working days. Similarly, the EMA publishes non-compliance reports with good standard practices (e.g., GMP).

9.3 Expedited Programs Overview

The typical biopharma company's approach to expedited programs is relatively straightforward: the regulatory affairs team will try to use expedited options to accelerate every drug program at every opportunity they have. They might accept to conduct more studies if they can accelerate the drug's approval (e.g., post-marketing studies, additional study even if not directly impacting approval, long-term study). As a senior regulatory executive put it, "we go after all of them" but "we know which [expedited programs] are likely versus not".

There are four programs designated as expedited by the FDA: fast track designation (see Section 9.3.1), breakthrough therapy designation (see Section 9.3.1), accelerated approval (see Section 9.3.2), and priority review designation (see Section 9.3.3).

Possibly the most valuable of these accelerated programs is the breakthrough designation in that it uses the company's data to grant that designation.

Accelerated approval is desirable as well since it allows approval based on surrogate endpoints (i.e., a measure considered to predict clinical benefits) and provides a streamlined path to market, contingent on confirmatory trial. If the confirmatory trial demonstrates clinical benefits, the agency will grant full approval, otherwise the product could be withdrawn from the market.

Lastly, programs like priority review are attractive but difficult to predict prior to submission. In the United States, by granting priority review designation, the FDA will prioritize attention and resources and commit to review an NDA with four months less than for a standard application.

The following subsections, providing further information on selected expedited programs, are by no means exhaustive (e.g., the South Korea GIFT program, similar to the FDA Breakthrough program, is not included).

9.3.1 Fast Track, PRIME, and Breakthrough Therapy

Fast track is a US designation. A biopharma sponsor may request, under the designation of "fast track product", the facilitation of development and expedited review of drugs intended for the treatment of serious or life-threatening diseases or conditions, demonstrating the potential to address unmet medical needs. Determination is to be made by the FDA within 60 calendar days of fast track request for such products as well as for products designated as a qualified infectious disease product (21 US Code § 356). With a fast track designation, the FDA will take actions that help expedite the development and review of the application for approval of such a product. In practice, the FDA will have more frequent meetings with the sponsor involving senior staff and provide support regarding study design and biomarkers. Fast track products may qualify for accelerated approval or priority review.

PRIME is an EMA designation, similar to fast track, for drugs demonstrating the potential to significantly address unmet needs. PRIME products receive enhanced EMA support and accelerated review (e.g., typically six months faster than other new biopharma products). Application can be made after preliminary clinical evidence and proof of concept, although academia and small- and medium-sized companies may apply earlier after proof of principle to gain earlier EMA support. The timeline from start of procedure to PRIME determination is 40 days.

Breakthrough therapy is a US designation. A biopharma sponsor may request, under the designation of "breakthrough therapy", the expedited development and review of drugs intended for the treatment of serious or life-threatening diseases or conditions, demonstrating preliminary clinical evidence of substantial improvement over existing therapies on clinically significant endpoints. Determination is to be made by the FDA within 60 calendar days of breakthrough request (21 US Code § 356). Drugs receiving breakthrough therapy designation will receive all the benefits received with a fast track designation plus intensive guidance on an efficient drug development program and FDA's commitment through senior managers' involvement. Latest, the request should be made before the end-of-Phase-2 meeting.

9.3.2 *Accelerated Approval and Conditional Marketing Authorization*

Accelerated approval is a US designation. The FDA may approve, under the designation of "accelerated approval", an application for approval of a product for a serious or life-threatening disease, demonstrating the effect on an appropriate surrogate endpoint or clinical endpoint (21 US Code § 356). The accelerated approval may be conditional to appropriate post-approval confirmatory studies, with FDA's ability to grant full approval status or withdraw the product under various conditions (e.g., sponsor's failure to conduct post-approval studies or unverified benefits).

For products addressing unmet medical needs and demonstrating a favorable benefit – risk ratio, sponsors may request from the EMA a Conditional Marketing Authorization (CMA), based on less comprehensive data than for the MAA, 6–7 months prior to MAA submission. This process may also be used for public health emergencies like a pandemic. After the CMA request, the EMA assesses the benefits of early availability versus the risks associated with incomplete data to make a determination. When granted (under conditions the sponsor must fulfill), the CMA is valid for one year, renewable annually.

PMDA in Japan has also implemented a Conditional Early Approval System allowing fast track approval of drugs targeting serious diseases. Drugs are approved on the condition that post-marketing surveillance confirms the product's safety and effectiveness. Four criteria are required: seriousness of indication, high clinical utility, conducting confirmatory studies would require long duration due to small subject population, and clinical trials performed pre-submission have shown promising efficacy and safety. A notable difference with FDA and EMA is that PMDA requires post-marketing observational studies (and not confirmatory studies) to confirm efficacy and safety.

A number of other regulatory agencies have also set up conditional approvals. TGA may provide provisional approval for drugs with promising treatment for serious or life-threatening conditions, making the drug available in Australia while sponsor finishes clinical trials. Likewise, Canada may accommodate a "notice of compliance with conditions", which is a conditional approval based on limited evidence (e.g.: Phase 2 trials or trials with only surrogate markers), thereby providing patients with earlier access to therapies for serious, life-threatening or severely debilitating diseases.

9.3.3 *Priority Review, Priority Review Vouchers, and Accelerated Assessment*

In the United States, although the sponsor may request it, the FDA decides on priority review for every NDA or BLA submitted. If granted, the priority review designation reflects the FDA's aim to review the application faster (in six months rather than ten). Priority review is typically granted to drug applications that would represent significant improvements over current treatment standards for serious diseases.

On a related note, FDA priority review vouchers (PRV) might be used for any FDA approval application to get the same benefits as a priority review. Those PRV may be obtained upon successful FDA drug or biologic approval for rare pediatric disease indications as an incentive to develop such programs. When granted, the sponsor may redeem the voucher to obtain a priority review on a different product or sell the voucher to another sponsor.

Case Example: Priority Review Voucher

Day One was granted a PRV following the FDA approval of tovorafenib in April 2024. The company sold this PRV for US$108 million in May 2024 to an undisclosed buyer (Day One Biopharmaceuticals, 2024).

Under the EMA centralized procedure, sponsors may request an accelerated assessment program in the case of medicines of major interest to public health such as therapeutic innovations. When granted, accelerated assessment provides for evaluations in 150 rather than 210 days.

In Japan, sponsors may apply for the sakigake designation established to promote R&D in Japan and for innovative therapies (e.g., new MOA) targeting serious and life-threatening diseases and offering significant potential to improve patient outcomes. When granted, the designation provides sponsors with priority PMDA discussions, priority review of MAA, as well as support for clinical trials and post-marketing surveillance.

In Canada, HC may grant upon request a priority review to eligible applications, with a review shortened from 300 to 180 days. Eligible drugs target serious or life-threatening illnesses with no existing treatment or drugs showing significant benefit – risk improvement.

9.3.4 Authorization under Exceptional Circumstances

Under exceptional circumstances (e.g., rare conditions) when comprehensive efficacy and safety data cannot be obtained under normal conditions, the EMA may grant a Marketing Authorization Under Exceptional Circumstances. The sponsor will have to provide information on the safe and effective use of the product and implement specific safety monitoring and reporting procedures.

9.3.5 Other Expedited Programs

Other expedited programs have been introduced by regulatory agencies to accelerate patient access to innovative medicines. The EMA implemented an Adaptive Pathways pilot program to allow for early and progressive access to products in areas of high medical needs. This approach follows iterative development steps supported by regulatory processes such as EMA scientific advice, compassionate use, patient registries, and conditional approval path (for life-threatening conditions). The approach enables staged approvals starting with restricted patient populations that can then be expanded.

The global COVID pandemic has also illustrated the need for emergency approvals across regions, which most regulatory agencies have addressed in one way or another. In Japan, the PMDA offers two emergency approval routes: a "special approval for emergency" for products approved in other regions and an "emergency approval" for confirmed safety and estimated efficacy.

9.4 Orphan Drugs

Orphan drugs regulations set by health authorities are meant to help address the challenges associated with drug development for life-threatening or debilitating rare diseases: low or very low prevalence, lacking financial viability (insufficient financial returns without regulatory incentives given the limited number of patients), and serious medical needs (e.g., no treatment or inferior treatments for life-threatening conditions).

Orphan Drug Designation Programs' benefits may include research grants, tax credits for clinical research, and protocol assistance for the development of drugs for rare diseases and disorders. The program also provides marketing exclusivity for approved orphan drug products.

There are several relevant orphan drug regulations, as illustrated in Figure 9.5.

9.5 Expanded Access and Compassionate Use Programs

As clinical developments take many years before new innovative treatment options are commercially available, and clinical trial participation opportunities are limited (e.g., patients might not meet a study's inclusion/exclusion criteria), expanded access or compassionate use programs have been established by various regulatory agencies to provide early access to promising drugs under development for patients with serious or life-threatening diseases for which no comparable therapeutic options are available.

In the United States, expanded access, regulated under 21 CFR Part 312 Subpart I, is a regulatory pathway allowing patients to have access to an IMP under specific circumstances:

- Serious or life-threatening conditions for which no comparable therapeutic options are available.
- Consensus on IMP use between the licensed physician, the IRB, and the pharmaceutical company (typically its medical group).

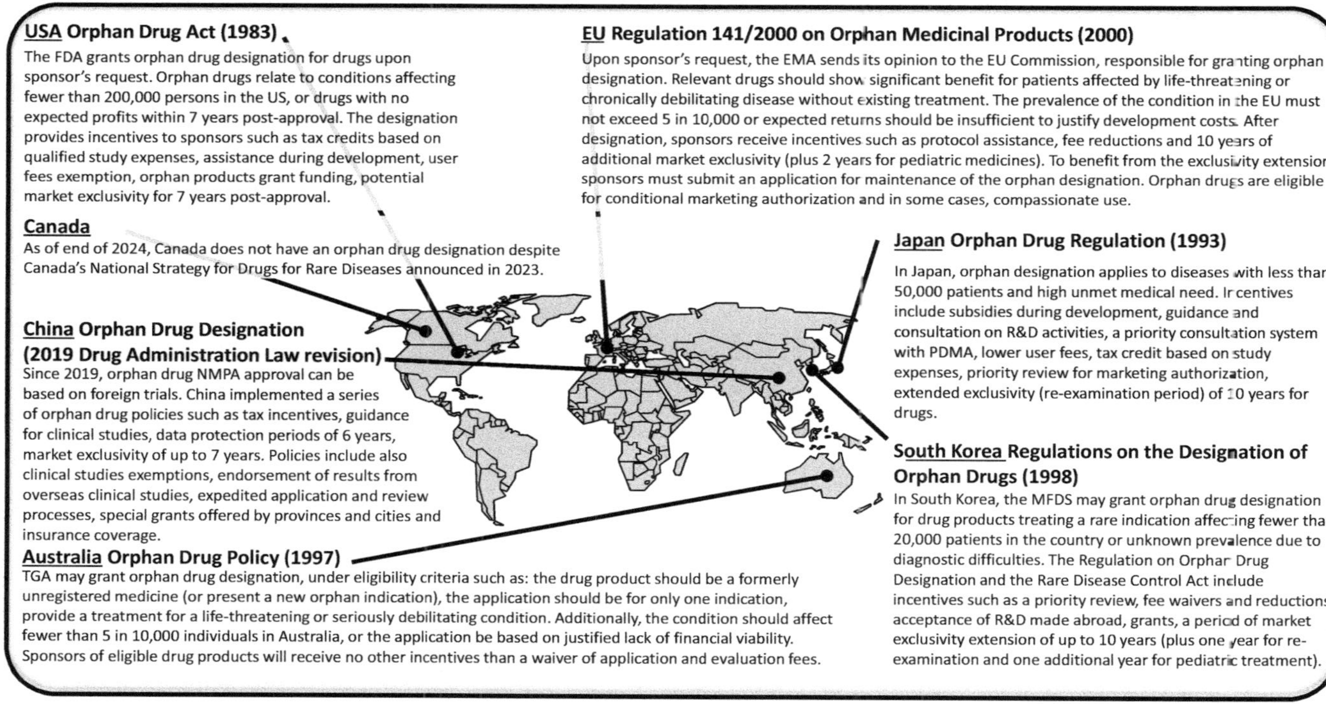

Figure 9.5 Selected orphan drug regulations.

The licensed physician will manage the request with FDA and IRB as well as patient care and reporting. Considering the risks posed by a product still in development, IRB will review the expanded access plan including the patient's informed consent and the FDA will decide on the authorization.

In the European Union, compassionate use programs are implemented by each Member State under the EU regulations (Article 83 of EC Regulation 726/2004). Similarly to the United States, the IMP undergoing clinical trials or marketing authorization can only be used for patients with a serious or life-threatening disease, with no authorized available treatment.

In Japan, expanded access clinical trials likewise allow exceptional access to IMPs for patients with life-threatening diseases without existing effective treatment. Canada has implemented the Special Access Program with comparable eligibility criteria.

Oncology has historically been a prominent therapeutic area for expanded access. At Pfizer, oncology represented three fourth of the requests over a total number of expanded access requests in excess of 2,000 across approximately 70 countries in 2022 (Pfizer, 2023).

In the United States, the Right to Try Act offers a pathway for patients with life-threatening diseases and for whom a physician has certified that all treatment options have been tried and the patient cannot be part of clinical trials. The Right to Try allows patients (upon written informed consent) and their physician to interact directly with a pharmaceutical company to access a drug under clinical study. The FDA does not approve requests and is not involved in this process.

9.6 Prescription Drug to Over-the-Counter Switch, Generics, and Biosimilars

The switch from prescription-only (Rx) to over-the-counter (OTC) marketing status must typically follow strictly regulated procedures. Regulatory agencies will require new preclinical tests, clinical trials, and medical assessments to demonstrate that self-medication by consumers is safe, proper, and effective. Post-marketing safety surveillance data might be required to monitor inherent safety and safety related to consumer usage. In the United States, for example, to initiate a full Rx-to-OTC switch, a sponsor must submit an Efficacy Supplement to an approved NDA or a 505(b)(2) application. An Efficacy Supplement is a supplement to an approved NDA proposing to modify a product labeling. The Efficacy Supplement or new NDA must include data from new clinical trials showing efficacy and safety in a nonprescription setting. In Europe, an application for a change of classification of a centrally authorized medicinal product may be made via the centralized procedure or in each country. According to the Directive 2001/83/EC, a change of classification may benefit from one year of protection.

Sponsors who want to obtain approval for a generic version of an innovative drug product going off patent must follow specific regulatory procedures. In the United States, a sponsor of a generic drug product must submit an Abbreviated New Drug Application (also named the 505(j) ANDA pathway). The FDA requires that sponsors demonstrate scientifically that the generic drug is bioequivalent (i.e., provides the same in vivo performance) as the innovator drug. This demonstration can be done via comparative bioavailability studies that will measure the rate of absorption of active ingredients into a patient's bloodstream, or the rate of absorption of active ingredients and level of availability at the biological site of action (for drug products not absorbed in the bloodstream). Bioequivalence studies will allow to demonstrate if a generic drug product is bioequivalent to a reference drug product.

These studies allow to avoid lengthy and costly duplication of clinical trials. In the United States, the FDA may grant a 180-day exclusivity to the first company submitting an ANDA and challenging a listed patent. The applicant may then be the sole marketer of a generic product for 180 days.

9.7 Regulatory Strategy for Early-Stage Companies

For an early-stage biopharma company with a limited drug pipeline, successfully achieving the initial regulatory checkpoints (e.g., IND acceptance, approval of initial CTA, end-of-Phase-1 meeting) will represent major milestone objectives. And, as discussed at the beginning of Section 9.1, early-stage companies might focus their regulatory strategy up to the point of an appropriate exit point for investors such as reaching a favorable proof of concept after completion of Phase 2 study.

To enable a successful transition from discovery to preclinical and into the clinical development stages, the early-stage regulatory plan will have to align with the Target Product Profile and the Development Plan for the product or asset.

The regulatory affairs team will evaluate the program's objectives, parameters (e.g., targeted patient populations, technology or MOA, label, expected timeline, product competitive landscape) and identify required regulatory activities as well as major risks to address for regulatory submissions. They will consider precedents created by similar products and past risk-mitigation plans.

Licensing agreements, a common financing avenue for early-stage companies, have major regulatory strategy implications, given the allocation of responsibilities between the licensor and the licensee, and the negotiation of milestone payment terms based on regulatory events.

When using a limited regulatory approach (up to an investor exit point), the early-stage company is likely to limit or defer regulatory meetings for which they might not have sufficient internal resources. Indeed, 62% of emerging biopharma companies outsource their regulatory activities (IQVIA, 2024). The company might also select a jurisdiction providing more convenient access (e.g., local country), stronger regulatory support, more limited demands, or more leeway given their specific situation. With one molecule or program without other options to fall back on, a company might use a simplified, yet more aggressive, regulatory strategy that selects one more manageable geographical area (e.g., Australia), build a corresponding rationale along with mitigation plans for other regulatory agencies.

Overall, for an early-stage company, the most important aspects of a regulatory strategy include a specific identification of the target markets, patients and indications, a practical understanding of regulatory constraints and timelines, a clear regulatory pathway at least up to their exit strategy, and a robust quality management to ensure compliance with the applicable relevant regulations.

The successful execution of the regulatory strategy will be contingent upon proactive actions from the leadership team to secure appropriate financing (see Chapter 5) and plan for an appropriate exit deal (see Chapter 7).

References

Day One Biopharmaceuticals. (2024, May 30). *Day One Announces Sale of Priority Review Voucher for $108 Million.* Retrieved 1/3/2025, from https://ir.dayonebio.com/news-releases/news-release-details/day-one-announces-sale-priority-review-voucher-108-million

EMA. (2024, May 9). *Camzyos - Mavacamten.* Retrieved 1/4/2025, from https://www.ema.europa.eu/en/medicines/human/EPAR/camzyos

FDA. (2022, November 29). *Emergency Use Authorization (EUA) for Kineret (Anakinra).* Retrieved 1/6/2025, from https://www.fda.gov/media/163546/download

FDA. (2023, October). *Benefit-Risk Assessment for New Drug and Biological Products - Guidance for Industry.* Retrieved 1/2/2025, from https://www.fda.gov/media/152544/download

IQVIA. (2024, April 10). *Streamlining Compliance: The Power of Outsourcing in Pharmacovigilance and Regulatory Affairs.* Retrieved 1/7/2025, from https://www.iqvia.com/blogs/2024/04/streamlining-compliance-the-power-of-outsourcing-in-pharmacovigilance-and-regulatory-affairs

IQVIA Institute. (2024, July 10). *Rethinking Clinical Trial Country Prioritization - Enabling Agility through Global Diversification.* Retrieved 12/26/2024, from https://www.iqvia.com/insights/the-iqvia-institute/reports-and-publications/reports/rethinking-clinical-trial-country-prioritization

Keam, S. J. (2022). Mavacamten: First approval. *Drugs, 82*(10), 1127–1135. https://doi.org/10.1007/s40265-022-01739-7

MyoKardia. (2020, February 27). *Form 10-K For the Fiscal Year Ended* December 31, 2019. Retrieved 1/4/2025, from https://www.sec.gov/Archives/edgar/data/1552451/000156459020007418/myok-10k_20191231.htm

Pfizer. (2023, April). *Position on Expanded Access to Investigational Drugs*. Retrieved 1/4/2025, from https://cdn.pfizer.com/pfizercom/Policy-paper-Expanded-Access-to-Investigational-Drugs-FINAL-2023.pdf

Sebastian, S. A., Padda, I., Lehr, E. J., & Johal, G. (2023). Aficamten: A breakthrough therapy for symptomatic obstructive hypertrophic cardiomyopathy. *American Journal of Cardiovascular Drugs: Drugs, Devices, and Other Interventions, 23*(5), 519–532. https://doi.org/10.1007/s40256-023-00599-0

Shaw, G. (2024, December 20). *FDA Declares End to Tirzepatide Shortage*. Retrieved 1/6/2025, from https://www.pharmacypracticenews.com/Online-First/Article/12-24/FDA-Declares-End-to-Tirzepatide-Shortage/75792

U.S. Department of Health & Human Services. (2024, February). *Comparing New Prescription Drug Availability and Launch Timing in the United States and Other OECD Countries*. Retrieved 12/30/2024, from https://aspe.hhs.gov/sites/default/files/documents/430a3e61c234f06270b04414e797ad3a/new-drug-availability-launch-timing.pdf

Index

For Product Safety Concerns and Information please contact our EU
representative GPSR@taylorandfrancis.com
Taylor & Francis Verlag GmbH, Kaufingerstraße 24, 80331 München, Germany

www.ingramcontent.com/pod-product-compliance
Ingram Content Group UK Ltd.
Pitfield, Milton Keynes, MK11 3LW, UK
UKHW022346190926
475702UK00015B/2138

* 9 7 8 1 0 3 2 9 7 6 2 1 1 *